Crown and Calumet

Colonel Guy Johnson, painted by Benjamin West in 1776. See p. iv. (National Gallery of Art, Washington; Andrew W. Mellon Collection)

Crown and Calumet

BRITISH-INDIAN RELATIONS, 1783-1815

By Colin G. Calloway

UNIVERSITY OF OKLAHOMA PRESS : NORMAN AND LONDON

Library of Congress Cataloging-in-Publication Data

Calloway, Colin G. (Colin Gordon), 1953–
    Crown and calumet.

    Bibliography: p. 305.
    Includes index.
        1. Indians of North America—Canada—Government relations.   2. Indians
of North America—Government relations—1789–1869.   3. Indians of North
America—Public opinion.   4. Public opinion—Great Britain.   5. Indians of
North America—Commerce.   I. Title.
    E92.C18   1986   323.1'197'071   86–16151
    ISBN 0–8061–2033–9 (alk. paper)

Frontispiece painting: As superintendent of Indian affairs, Colonel Guy Johnson
(c. 1740–88) accompanied Joseph Brant on his first visit to England, where Johnson posed for the expatriate American artist Benjamin West. Johnson's clothing
in the painting was typical British Indian Department attire. The Indians in the
background reflect the importance of his office. To Americans, however, their
ominous presence at Johnson's shoulder symbolized the threatening nature of
British-Indian relations.

The paper in this book meets the guidelines for permanence and dura-
bility of the Committee on Production Guidelines for Book Longevity of
the Council on Library Resources, Inc.

To my parents and Marcia

Contents

Illustrations

MAPS

Preface

RELATIONS between the British and the American Indians were of vital importance and exerted tremendous influence in the development of the North American frontier. The policies adopted by Britain toward the Indians in the colonial and revolutionary periods have received considerable attention, and some valuable studies have been done of postrevolutionary British Indian policy (of which the best are those by Reginald Horsman, listed here in the Bibliography). On the whole, however, British-Indian relations in the critical years between 1783 and 1815 have not attracted the consideration that they merit. This study seeks to enhance our understanding of those relations, not by compiling a chronological narrative but by examining what Britons and Indians thought of each other and considering the factors that governed those attitudes. I will also show that British-Indian connections were not merely a side issue in Anglo-American affairs but constituted an important and extensive relationship in their own right.

By 1783 contact and experience had altered many tribal societies and had modified British perceptions of those societies. Preconceived notions about "noble savages" and "brute savages" persisted in appraisals of American Indian cultures, and British views betrayed heavy ethnocentric bias. In the thirty years or so following the end of the

American Revolution, however, racial stereotypes and inherited notions of cultural superiority seem to have played a secondary role in the formation of attitudes and relationships between Britons and Indians. In the critical era between the Peace of Paris and the Peace of Ghent, the main concerns were military and commercial. The British judged the Indians according to how well they performed as allies in war and how effectively they functioned as partners and customers in the fur trade. Although the Indians appear to have based their judgments of Britons on much the same criteria, they went to war for their own purposes and had their own motives and methods for engaging in trade.

The great diversity of Native American societies, and the radical changes occurring within those societies, made it impractical for Indians or whites to adhere to any single attitude toward one another. The views and opinions about the Indians that Britons expressed as a result of contact were not usually unthinking racial generalizations; rather, they were based on military, political, economic, and religious, as well as ethnocentric, considerations. Opinions varied according to the character, the experience, the state of mind, the political affiliation, and the immediate circumstances of the individual who voiced them. One generalization can be made with confidence, however. The Indians were not mute and passive innocents who tamely accepted their British "fathers'" assumptions of superiority. They were accomplished politicians, formidable warriors, and canny traders who held their own civilizations in high esteem and saw little in the subjects of George III to make them change their minds.

I have used the terms *Indian* and *white* as convenient alternatives to *Native American* and *Euro-American*. Being of Anglo-Scottish parentage myself, I am acutely aware of the distinction between English and British. I have applied the term British widely but not carelessly. In considering British attitudes, I sometimes include non-Britons who worked in the British interest, notably French-Canadian employees of the North West Company. I recognize the limitations of the term tribe, but I retain it as a term of convenience suggesting a group of people bound together, however loosely and briefly, by ties of kinship, custom, leadership, or subsistence. Loaded terms such as "savage," "civilization," and "degeneration" occur repeatedly in the records. In some cases, quotation marks are employed to give special emphasis but to use quotation marks whenever such terms appear would be distracting. The reader should appreciate that these terms are intended to convey the bias of the sources, not the judgments of the author.

I am indebted to many individuals and institutions for the help they afforded at various stages in the research and writing of this study. The bulk of the research was presented as a Ph.D. dissertation at the University of Leeds, England, in 1978. For a number of years, teaching commitments in England and then moving to the United States and making the transition to high school teaching allowed only intermittent attention to the task of transforming the dissertation into a book. In North America, I have added useful research at the libraries of Dartmouth College, Indiana University, the Newberry Library in Chicago, and the Public Archives of Canada in Ottawa, and have benefited from conversations and interchange with scholars working in Indian history. Nevertheless, the book remains the product of work carried out in libraries and record offices throughout Great Britain. I owe thanks to the staffs of the British Museum, the Public Records Office, the National Library of Scotland, the Scottish Record Office, the Library of the Royal Commonwealth Society, the Leeds University Library, the Leeds Central Reference Library and Archives Department, and the archives of the United Society for the Propagation of the Gospel, in London. The Newberry Library provided financial help in obtaining and reproducing illustrations.

My supervisor at Leeds University, the late Dr. John A. Woods, gave freely of his time and advice and set an example for meticulous scholarship. Peter Marshall of Manchester University offered helpful criticism in his capacity as external examiner. Michael Green of Dartmouth College provided frank and valuable comments on the unrevised manuscript, and Bernard Sheehan of Indiana University gave guidance on structure.

The book was written in England, revised in Vermont, and prepared for final publication in Chicago. It is dedicated to my parents and my wife. Their support has been constant and their contributions insufficiently acknowledged during the years in which this book struggled to the surface.

To all of the above, I am extremely grateful. For what is written in the pages that follow, I alone am responsible.

Chicago, Illinois   COLIN G. CALLOWAY

Crown and Calumet

Introduction: 1783

FRANCIS PARKMAN, the nineteenth century's most prolific historian of conflict between Indians and Europeans, maintained that "Spanish civilization crushed the Indian; English civilization scorned and neglected him; French civilization embraced and cherished him."[1] In the one hundred years and more since Parkman wrote, his portrayals of Indians have been severely criticized and his generalizations soundly challenged. Nevertheless, a stereotypical image persists of the Englishman on the North American frontier as an arrogant red-coated officer who treated the Indians with contempt and considered it beneath his dignity to sit around a smoky council fire with people whom he regarded as uncouth savages.

In fact, far from scorning and neglecting the Indians, the British cultivated and observed them. In the thirty years or so following the end of the American Revolution, the normal British interest in Indians was reinforced by two overriding concerns: the need to maintain their friendship as actual or potential allies in war and the need to retain their custom and cooperation in the fur trade. Few Britons had any doubt that Indians were savages, noble or otherwise, and that certainty colored their interpretations of Indian society and behavior. In the conditions that obtained in North America in the critical period between 1783 and

3

1815, however, inherited racial preconceptions proved to be less important than military and commercial considerations in determining British attitudes toward Indians and Indian attitudes toward Britons.

The notion that British-Indian relations revolved around Englishmen cooped up in isolated posts in northeastern North America contrasts with the reality of the British presence in North America. Military and commercial endeavors brought people from throughout the British Isles into contact with Indians across the continent. Scots dominated the higher echelons of the North West Company, and Orkneymen provided manpower for the Hudson's Bay Company. Prominent members of the British Indian Department were of Scots or Irish descent, and British regiments recruited from Scottish glens and Welsh valleys as well as from the towns and villages of England. Moreover, military posts were often also the foci for a number of political, social, and economic activities that brought together British redcoats, French-Canadian traders, Indians from far and near, mixed-bloods, and their wives and children in fluid and heterogeneous communities.

Different Indian tribes, and different groups within those tribes, pursued independent courses of action that changed according to their particular needs, just as British interests could be expected to shift in response to changes of ministry or of circumstance. British-Indian relations, therefore, hardly constituted an alliance. People are not necessarily allies simply because they trade together and pursue certain common interests. Nevertheless, in the years from 1783 to 1815, the British entered into or continued relationships of formal cooperation with a considerable number of Indian groups, and these formal relationships were sufficiently consistent in their concern with certain objectives of mutual interest that they may conveniently be termed alliances.

Alliances, even if they exist for limited military and economic purposes, imply certain obligations on the part of the participants. Britons and Indians sometimes differed in their understanding of what these obligations were, and both complained that their "allies" were not meeting their obligations. The complaints of the British that Indians were unreliable and mercenary stemmed mainly from their own failure to understand Indians and from their tendency to misconstrue the nature of the relationship entered into. Indians also misinterpreted the implications of relationships as understood by the British. Some British relations with the Indians were punctuated by actions about which there could be little confusion, however. British abandonment of the Indians in 1783, to a lesser extent in 1794, and again in 1814, constituted betrayal even in British terms and represented a breach of the alliance as they understood it.

In 1783 news reached North America that the British and American negotiators in Paris had agreed upon provisional terms of peace, bringing an end to the war of the Revolution. By the Peace of Paris, ratified that year, Great Britain recognized the independence of its thirteen former colonies and acknowledged the sovereignty of the United States north to the Great Lakes, south to the Floridas, and west to the Mississippi River. The peace settlement made no mention of the Indian peoples who inhabited this territory, even though many of the tribes had fought in the war as allies of the British. Nevertheless, the treaty caused relations between Britain and the Indians to move into a new phase. Britons and Indians alike now had to contend with the United States, and after 1783, British-Indian relations existed against the backdrop of a delicate international situation. Indian tribes who had grown accustomed to dealing with King George and his red-coated representatives found that, in many cases, their territory had been transferred to the United States and that the Americans claimed their lands by right of conquest. This new situation prompted the British and the Indians to reassess their relationship and influenced events on the frontier for the next thirty years.

The Peace of Paris caused many Indians to view with

suspicion and distrust the British, who they felt had neglected and betrayed them. The treaty also increased the
threat to Indian lands and cultures which had driven the
Indians to the British in the first place. In the following
decades, Britons and Indians found themselves bound by
a common fear of American expansion and a joint determination to protect the fur-bearing wilderness from the
land-hungry settlers of the young Republic. British policy
on the American frontier in the aftermath of the Revolution in many cases represented a belated attempt to make
amends for abandoning the Indians and jeopardizing the
fur trade in 1783. Relations with the Indians centered on
mending and preserving intact connections that the Peace
of Paris had threatened to shatter.[2]

During the revolutionary war Britain's Indian allies had
increased the potential for victory on the frontier. Indian
war parties wrought extensive destruction in the west and
tied down resources and manpower that the rebels badly
needed elsewhere. Some tribes suffered dreadfully as a result of their participation in the war. In 1776, Cherokee
warriors launched damaging raids on outlying settlements
in Georgia, the Carolinas, and Virginia only to have their
own villages put to the torch that same year. Dragging Canoe and his band of Chickamauga diehards held out beyond the end of the war, but Cherokee power was broken
forever and, in 1782, the tribe was obliged to buy peace
from the Americans by ceding portions of their shrinking
territory. The Iroquois League of the Six Nations, which
had once held sway over the northeast, fell apart during
the Revolution. The Oneida tribe and half of the Tus-
caroras sided with the rebels, while the other member
tribes—the Senecas, the Cayugas, the Onondagas, and the
Mohawks—remained loyal to the Crown. The bloody battle
of Oriskany in August 1777 marked the beginning of civil
war for the Iroquois, and the League's council fire at Onondaga was ceremonially extinguished that same year, leaving each tribe free to pursue its own course of action. In
1778, Iroquois warriors and Tory rangers ravaged the

Mohawk and Susquehanna frontiers, but the Americans retaliated the following year with a devastating expedition into the heart of the Iroquois country. Major General John Sullivan's army destroyed crops and villages and caused such suffering that the Iroquois were driven to the British at Niagara for sustenance. Shawnee warriors, barely recovered from Lord Dunmore's War in 1774, wreaked havoc among frontier settlements in Kentucky, but their raids triggered destructive counterstrokes that burned Shawnee villages and killed women and children in 1780 and again in 1782.

Nevertheless, long after Lord Cornwallis had surrendered in the east, Indian warriors carried on the fight in the west. While Joseph Brant's Iroquois terrorized the Mohawk valley, Shawnee, Delaware, and Miami war parties raided across the Ohio River and into Kentucky. The last year of the war saw the Indians achieve some of their greatest victories. In June 1782 a force of five hundred Delaware, Wyandot, and Mingo tribesmen scattered Colonel William Crawford's militia at Sandusky, capturing and torturing the unfortunate Crawford. Two months later an Indian force directed by British agents William Caldwell, Alexander McKee, and Simon Girty routed Daniel Boone's Kentuckians at Blue Licks.

The Indians expected that their sacrifices and achievements would earn them lasting gratitude and protection from George III. Instead, just when it seemed that the war in the west was being won, news came that Britain had had enough; it was abandoning the fight and, it seemed, had betrayed its Indian allies.

A major cause of Britain's neglect of the Indians was that the ministry that concluded the Peace of Paris was not the same one that had conducted the war. News of the surrender of Lord Cornwallis's army at Yorktown brought down Lord North's wartime government in March 1782. A period of ministerial instability ensued that lasted until William Pitt the younger came to power in 1784. During the critical months when the terms of the preliminary and definitive treaty were being worked out, a weak ministry was in power, headed first by Lord Rockingham and, after his death, by the Earl of Shelburne. Parliament condemned further offensive fighting in America, and Shelburne was determined to terminate hostilities. In the subsequent negotiations Britain made important concessions to the Americans, including recognition of the Mississippi River as the western boundary of the new Republic. The question of sovereignty over the west did not strike Shelburne as crucial, since he hoped for a restoration of Anglo-American harmony and envisaged joint British participation in the commercial development of the Mississippi valley. Ministers who had denounced the government from the opposition benches in Parliament for employing "bloodthirsty savages" had few qualms about abandoning those Indians once they were in power. In the long debates in Parliament over the terms of the peace treaty, only two members voiced any concern over the Indians' treatment. The Earl of Shelburne reacted to charges that the government had treated the Indians shamefully by declaring that "the Indian nations were not abandoned to their enemies; they were remitted to the care of neighbours, whose interest it was as much as ours to cultivate friendship with them, and who were certainly the best qualified for softening and humanizing their hearts."[3] If he was sincere, Shelburne showed a total misconception of the character and objectives of American frontier expansion.

Indians who had begun to think that they were winning suddenly found that they were being treated as if they were a vanquished people. After the Peace of Paris, the United States claimed the Indians' lands by right of conquest and proceeded to "give peace" to the tribes in a series of separate treaties, granting them, in effect, portions of their own lands. In American eyes, the Indians could have no complaints about the loss of their lands; justice demanded that they should make some atonement for the atrocities they were supposed to have committed during the war. Indeed, the United States believed it was being generous in not demanding that the tribes remove to Canada. Euro-Americans adopted a double standard as to the sovereign status of Indian groups. No European state acknowledged the sovereignty of Indian tribes in its dealings with other European states. Europeans regarded North America as a vacant land that could be claimed by right of discovery or settlement and which could be conquered and transferred by one nation to another. Treaties with Indian tribes did not alter these claims or rights. The United States expected and claimed the interior of North America on the basis of charter rights and as successors to the rights of the British Crown.[4]

The Indians, however, saw themselves as free peoples, not as defeated subjects of George III. They had suffered no defeat to merit the loss of their lands, nor had they given their consent to the Peace of Paris. The tribes considered their territorial boundaries to have been set by various prerevolutionary treaties to which they had agreed, not by the Peace of Paris which had ignored them. In particular, the northern and western tribes adhered to the Treaty of Fort Stanwix of 1768, which had fixed the Ohio River as the boundary between Indian land and white settlement. They expected that line to be respected. As Governor Frederick Haldimand warned Lord North in November 1783: "These People my Lord, have, as enlightened Ideas of the nature & Obligations of Treaties as the most Civilized Nations have, and know that no infringement of the Treaty in 1768 . . . Can be binding upon them without their Express Concurrence & Consent."[5] As far as the Indians were concerned, the king had no right to cede their lands to anyone, and much of the tension in postwar British-Indian relations stemmed from Britain's conflicting commitments to the Indians and the United States. Eventually, the Americans came to accept that all that was ceded in 1783 was the right of preemption to Indian lands, but the Indians consistently refused to recognize any such agreement as binding upon them. For example, in 1793, the Western Indians declared: "If the

white people as you say, made a treaty that none of them
but the King should purchase of us, and that he has given
that right to the U. States, it is an affair which concerns you
& him, & not us. We have never parted with such a power."[6]

From the first, the British knew that the Indians would
interpret their actions as a betrayal. Lord Townshend instructed Frederick Haldimand to assess what effect the
peace terms were likely to have on the tribes and to act accordingly. When Haldimand read the preliminary articles,
he saw clearly the effect they would produce and tried to
keep them secret in the hope that the definitive treaty
would contain some provision for the Indians. Word of the
terms seeped out, and when the Six Nations heard the
rumors, they sent Joseph Brant and John the Mohawk to
Quebec to learn the truth from Haldimand himself, much
to the governor's embarrassment.[7]

In the Indian country British officers and agents bore
the brunt of the Indians' outrage. The Indians were "thunder struck" at the peace settlement which fell so far short
of what they had been led to expect, and they were alarmed
at the prospect of being left alone to face the vengeance of
the Americans while the British withdrew across the sea to
safety. As the Six Nations informed Colonel John Butler in
July 1783, "In endeavouring to assist you, it seems we have
wrought our own ruin." The British assured their disgruntled allies that all that had been ceded was the right of
preemption to the Indian lands, but there seemed to be
more truth in the American claim that the king, instead of
providing for his red children, had neglected them "like
Bastards."[8]

The Iroquois warriors who were congregated at Niagara
demanded to know the truth. From what they had heard
of the peace settlement, they regarded it as an act of treachery and a breach of faith on the part of the redcoats. They
told the post commander, Allan Maclean, that they never
could believe that King George would hand over to the
Americans what he had no right to give: "That if it was
really true that the English had basely betrayed them by

pretending to give up their Country to the Americans without their Consent, or Consulting them, it was an Act of Cruelty and injustice that Christians only were capable of doing, that Indians were incapable of acting so; to friends and Allies, but that they did believe we had sold and betrayed them." In the circumstances, Maclean thought it advisable to have Joseph Brant detained where he was in Canada, since the Mohawk was well aware of the miserable situation in which Britain had left his people and might cause trouble. In July 1783, Sir John Johnson journeyed to Niagara to try and calm the Indians' fears. Johnson met with 1,685 Iroquois in a series of councils, but he could do no more than make vague promises that Britain had no more intention of ceding the Indians' lands than, he believed, the Americans had of seizing them. Six months later the Mohawks still believed they were being kept in the dark about the peace terms. They told Daniel Claus that the king's Indian allies still held the war ax in readiness, but that their minds were troubled: "[B]esides we are ashamed to Death for we don't consider ourselves conquered and our Warriors Spirits are still strong & firm, wherefore we would be glad to know the Certainty of the Matter now."[9]

The situation in the south was equally tense. The Treaty of Augusta, drawn up in 1768 between Georgia and the Creek Indians, and the treaties of Hard Labor (1768) and Lochaber (1770) between Virginia and the Cherokees had established boundaries to settlement similar to that created in the north by the Treaty of Fort Stanwix.[10] The Peace of Paris ignored these treaties, and in addition, Britain ceded Florida to Spain without reference to the Indians. As in the north, the Indians at first could not believe that the king had betrayed them and given away lands that were not his to give. Creek and Cherokee warriors had fought and bled in the king's cause; it was inconceivable to them that he would abandon his allies in their hour of need. Some were so incredulous that they simply dismissed reports of the peace settlement as a "Virginia lie."[11] The British authorities took measures to guard against possible reprisals by withdrawing officers and traders from the Indian country, but they took no steps to protect the Indians against the Americans. Many Indians expressed their determination to evacuate along with their British allies, but their requests for shipping to the Bahamas or some other part of the king's dominions were discouraged.[12]

The mixed-blood Creek chief, Alexander McGillivray, speaking for the Creeks, the Cherokees, and the Chickasaws, objected strongly that the Indians were not party to the Peace of Paris and that they had never given the king any power to hand over their lands, unless they could be deemed to have done so by fighting and dying in the royal cause. The British betrayal was doubly perfidious to the Indians because they felt that the war had been England's struggle in the first place. They had answered the British calls for help and had endured nine years of hard fighting, only to find that their allies had made peace for themselves and given up the Indians' lands to be divided between the Americans and the Spaniards. McGillivray did his best to keep his people in the dark about the betrayal, but Little Turkey of the Cherokees saw clearly what had happened: "The peacemakers and our Enemies have talked away our Lands at a Rum Drinking—."[13]

The British commander in chief, Sir Guy Carleton, denied that there had been any breach of faith; any promises to the Indians never to give up East Florida had been made without authorization and, in any case, the peace was not made from choice but was dictated by necessity. Nevertheless, the Indians remembered the Peace of Paris as an act of desertion. William Augustus Bowles, a Maryland Loyalist who had fought for the Crown with the Creeks, shared and remembered their bitterness: "The British Soldier, when he left the shore of America on the proclamation of peace, had peace indeed, and returned to a Country where Peace could be enjoyed; But to the Creek and Cherokee Indians was left, to drain to the dregs the bitter cup of War, unassisted & alone."[14]

Governor Haldimand feared that Indian resentment might flare into open warfare against either the British or the Americans. The best way to avoid a bloodbath, Haldimand believed, was to hold the frontier posts in the northwest. These posts stretched from Lake Champlain to Michilimackinac, controlling the Indian country and the waterways along the United States–Canada border. Under the terms of the peace settlement they were supposed to be delivered to the United States "with all convenient speed." Officials and merchants in Canada warned that if Britain relinquished the posts it would incite an Indian rebellion and lose control of the fur trade. The government in London cited continued American persecution of Loyalists and failure to comply with the debt provisions of the treaty as justification for holding onto the posts.[15]

As British prestige among the tribes crumbled, the fur trade played an invaluable role in retaining Indian allegiance to the Crown. Britain continued to dominate the North American fur trade at the end of the American Revolution. British traders, peddling goods of a price and quality which the Americans could not match, operated with impunity in United States territory and enjoyed a virtual monopoly in the Upper Mississippi valley, while the formation of the North West Company strengthened British influence with bands beyond the Great Lakes. In the south the Spanish authorities permitted the British firm of Panton, Leslie and Company to continue its monopoly of Indian trade, and the firm's main competition in the southern Indian trade came not from Spaniards or Americans but from other Loyalist merchants based in the Bahamas. British fur companies funneled the products of the Industrial Revolution into native North America at a rate no one could match. Nevertheless, British merchants feared that their business would be safe only so long as the Indians retained their lands, and for years to come fur traders regarded the 1783 treaty as a grave mistake.[16]

Governor Haldimand considered Indian friendship to be vital, not only to preservation of the fur trade but also to the very security of Canada. In the aftermath of the war Haldimand made great efforts to recover the Indians' confidence. The British government made a formal grant of lands to Joseph Brant and the Mohawks as a reward for their services and as compensation for the loss of their homelands in the United States. The grant, on the Grand River in Ontario, provided the Mohawks with a refuge from American expansion, but was also to prove a source of contention between Brant and both the British government and Iroquois critics who accused him of profiteering.[17]

Most tribes, however, were left to make their own response to the new situation and the American threat. Some bands decided to come to terms with the new master. Others preferred to escape American dominion by adopting the old pattern of westward retreat. Such migrations caused chain reactions and reverberations even on the Great Plains, adding to the upheaval occasioned by the native tribes' acquisition of horses, their competition for European goods and guns, and the devastation of a recent smallpox epidemic.[18] The majority of the tribes, however, correctly identified American policy as one of divide and rule and responded accordingly. Late in the summer of 1783 delegates from thirty-five tribes met at Sandusky in the Wyandot country, where Joseph Brant harangued them on the need to organize a defensive alliance. Ten years earlier, when British officials had not foreseen the outbreak of revolution, the task of the Indian Department had been to break up a potential Indian confederacy. Now the British encouraged the development of an Indian confederacy which, in the years that followed, came to include the Six Nations; the Seven Nations of Canada; the Wyandots, Miamis, Shawnees, and Delawares of northern Ohio and Indiana; the Ottawas, Chippewas, and Potawatomis of the Great Lakes region; the Piankeshaws and Kickapoos; and, as occasional participants, the Sauks and Foxes, Creeks, and Cherokees.[19] The confederacy disavowed all treaties made subsequent to the Treaty of Fort Stanwix in 1768 as lacking the unanimous consent of the now united tribes.

General Sir Frederick Haldimand, painted by Mabel B. Messer after Lemuel Francis Abbott (1760–1803). A former Swiss mercenary, Haldimand (1718–91) rose to prominence in the British service. As governor of Quebec he presided over British-Indian relations in the final years of the American Revolution and during the critical period following the Peace of Paris. (Public Archives Canada, Ottawa; C-3221)

The Shawnees, Delawares, and Cherokees still bitterly resented the Iroquois, who had sold out their claims to the
left bank of the Ohio River in 1768, and the confederacy
was plagued by internal strains and external pressures.
Nevertheless, the warriors closed ranks to defend the Ohio
as the limit to white settlement and succeeded in checking
American expansion for the best part of a decade, badly
defeating General Josiah Harmar in 1790 and routing
Arthur St. Clair in 1791. Indian military power made a
mockery of American claims to their territory by right of
conquest, and by 1793 the United States looked ready to
negotiate and settle on a compromise boundary line. Brant
and the Six Nations now counseled moderation, but the
western tribes refused to give up any more land. The following year, General Anthony Wayne inflicted a telling defeat on the intransigent tribes at the Battle of Fallen Timbers and followed up his victory by dictating peace terms
to the dispirited Indians who assembled at the Treaty of
Greenville in 1795.

The official British stance during the Indian wars that
erupted in the 1780s and 1790s was one of neutrality. The
Indians made repeated requests for military aid, and
Joseph Brant even traveled to England to plead the Indians' case, but the government gave only evasive replies.
Britain was prepared to advise and supply the tribes, but it
would not risk rekindling the Anglo-American conflict by
giving open assistance.[20] The situation was aggravated because Britain wanted peace between the Indians and the
United States, but insisted that security of the Indians'
lands should be the prerequisite of such a peace. In this
way Britain sought to safeguard its own interests and to
make belated amends for its neglect of the Indians in
1783. Indeed, the British hoped that a neutral Indian state
might be constructed as a barrier between their own territory and that of the United States. These hopes reached
a peak when the western Indians routed St. Clair in 1791,
persisted as long as the tribes remained united, and re-

emerged during the peace negotiations that ended the War of 1812.[21]

The Peace of Paris demonstrated Britain's attitude toward its Indian allies and indicated the pattern of British Indian policy for the next thirty years. Relations were to be maintained in good order so that Britain could enjoy the profits from an undisturbed monopoly of the fur trade and call upon Indian auxiliaries in the event of a renewed war with the United States. The Indians were, however, expendable and were to be abandoned if and when the international situation demanded. For the Indians the Peace was the first in a trilogy of betrayals at the hands of the British. Many tribes felt they had been betrayed by the French withdrawal in 1763. Now, in 1783, the British neglected them in the peace settlement and left them to the mercy of the Americans. In 1794, after having encouraged the warriors with promises of support, the British failed to help them in their hour of need and once again left the tribes to come to their own terms with the United States while Britain negotiated Jay's Treaty and handed over the frontier posts in 1796. In the War of 1812 many Indians responded to British appeals for aid and fought bravely against the United States only to see history repeat itself when the British sacrificed them on the negotiation table at Ghent in 1814.

The tribes became increasingly suspicious of the British and disenchanted with the alliance. Nevertheless, the Indians realistically appraised their predicament and recognized that good relations with Britain constituted their best hope of postponing dispossession and destruction at the hands of the Americans. Unfortunately for the Indians, British aid and interference served only to delay the establishment of the American dominion prematurely recognized in the peace settlement of 1783. From 1783 to 1815, Britons and Indians maintained close relations, but the strength of the relationship was testimony to the threat posed by American expansionism and the benefits to be derived from the fur trade, rather than to any friendship and mutual respect between the British and the Indians.

Most of the participants in British-Indian contact situations left no written records of their impressions. To achieve an understanding of what went on, we have to rely on the writings of the minority of Europeans who put pen to paper on the subject, on the letters of a handful of literate tribal leaders, and on Indian orations imperfectly translated and recorded by observers.

Nevertheless, such limited sources speak volumes about British-Indian relations and convey some idea of Indian attitudes which have too often been dismissed as nonexistent, unobtainable, or, worse still, insignificant. Those soldiers, traders, and travelers who expressed their thoughts in writing may not have been typical of their fellows, but they nevertheless produced a considerable body of literature containing much information (and some misinformation) about the Indians with whom they came into contact. From this emerges a fairly comprehensive picture of British attitudes toward the Indians.

Expressions of Indian points of view are far more rare. A suspicion that oral history is nonhistory has long blinded historians to the value of American Indian traditions handed down by word of mouth. Moreover, as evidenced by surviving winter counts and calendars of the Plains Indians, Indian societies did not necessarily concern themselves with recording the things that Europeans deemed important. Recorded Indian history has generally been Euro-American history with some reference to Indians where they fitted into it. Yet, although there is a dearth of Indian sources, Indians did express opinions that were recorded in writing. At the end of the war of the Revolution, for example, the Six Nations realized the disadvantages they had been under in having no means of broadcasting their point of view, while the Americans had been able to print whatever lies they wished about the Indians in their newspapers. When the Iroquois recognized the problem, their complaints were recorded.[22] European observers frequently interpreted and noted down speeches delivered in council by Indian orators. Moreover, post commanders, Indian agents, traders, missionaries, and travelers, who went into the Indian country largely to keep an eye on the native inhabitants, often acted as pens for Indians' thoughts. They reported what they believed to be the Indians' opinions, paraphrased their talks, and recounted conversations held with them. In some cases, they wrote with real understanding and sympathy for the people with whom they lived in prolonged close contact.

In this way white men were usually the spokesmen for the Indians. In addition, there were in this period a very few literate Indians who could commit their thoughts to paper. The Mohawk chieftain Thayendanegea, usually known as Joseph Brant, had attended Moor's Charity School in Lebanon, Connecticut, under the guidance of the Reverend Eleazor Wheelock. He could speak and write both Mohawk and English, and his great value as an interpreter helped secure him an important position in the British northern Indian Department. In the south the mixed-blood Creek chief Alexander McGillivray had had a formal education at a boarding school in Charleston, South Carolina, before securing a commission as assistant commissary in the British Indian Service during the Revolution. McGillivray's rival for leadership of the Creek confederacy was a former British army officer, William Augustus Bowles; Brant's successor was a literate Scot-Cherokee, John Norton, who had been adopted into the Mohawk tribe. Joseph Brant and John Norton both worked on translations of the Gospels into Mohawk and on books dealing with Indian history, while the Sauk war chief Black Hawk in later life dictated an autobiography which, "despite the intrusive hands of interpreter and editor, is basically a tale told by an Indian from an Indian point of view."[23] These men may not all have been full bloods, but they were all articulate champions of the people among whom they lived.

The questionable reliability of the available sources presents an additional problem. Some works are of dubious authenticity.[24] Expressed opinions varied in value and truth, according to who was speaking, about whom, for what reasons, and under what circumstances. That fur traders were usually experienced and knowledgeable about Indians did not mean that their appraisals were necessarily accurate or unbiased. As will be seen, traders were too often motivated by economic considerations for the comments to be accepted without question. Similar reservations apply to soldiers, agents, missionaries, travelers, and philanthropists. They all observed Indians for their own particular reasons, and they made their judgments according to how well the natives fitted in with their notions of what constituted a "good Indian." Indians were not as lazy as traders complained they were, nor as cowardly as they sometimes appeared to soldiers, nor as irreligious as missionaries described them. A person's expressed opinions often reveal greater insights into his or her situation, state of mind, character, and prejudices than they do about the object supposedly under discussion. The monotony, danger, and hardship of life in the wilderness could engender a depressive mood and intolerance in normally objective and fair-minded individuals. Loneliness and depression were the unavoidable lot of many an Indian agent and fur trader. Life in the Indian country offered the best opportunities for observing the inhabitants, but it hardly provided conditions conducive to unbiased and thoughtful comment on peoples who often represented an additional threat or posed additional difficulties in an already unpleasant environment.

The scarcity of Indian sources should not lead one to assume that those statements that were recorded are sufficiently reliable to be accepted at face value. For example, after the War of 1812 some Indians, the Sioux chief Little Crow among them, continued to visit the British on Drummond Island to request supplies and to express their undying loyalty to the Crown and their hatred of the Americans. Later, when the Sioux had taken stock of the situation and came to terms with the United States, Little Crow's recollection of the Drummond Island council of 1816 changed considerably. Now, apparently, the Sioux had gone there simply to express their contempt for the British and to kick away the presents which their erstwhile allies attempted to shower upon them, declaring, "After we have fought for you, endured many hardships, lost some of our people, and awakened the vengeance of our powerful neighbours, you make a peace for yourselves, leaving us to obtain such terms as we can. You no longer need our services; you offer us these goods to pay us for having deserted us. But no we will not take them; we hold them and yourselves in equal contempt."[25]

This "revised" version may be a fairly accurate expression of the Indians' feelings toward allies who had sold them out, but the episode reveals more about the Sioux chief's abilities as a politician, altering his pronouncements to suit the current situation, than it does about tribal attitudes. Similarly, at a council held in April 1815, when Indians were requesting from the British reward for their services, relief from their suffering, and compensation for their losses in the recent war, the Onondaga speaker declared: "At the commencement of the troubles, We who live at the Grand River . . . did not hesitate to take up the Tomahawk."[26] In fact, as will be seen, at the outbreak of war in 1812 the Grand River Iroquois had been so reluctant to take up the tomahawk that the British authorities seriously suspected their loyalty. Indians, like Europeans, did not necessarily possess an unwavering regard for truth, not the clearest of memories, when it went against their interests to do so.

Information offered by Indians was often thought to be unreliable. Indians often tended to tell the questioner what he wanted to hear—although whites, of course, sometimes heard only what they wanted to hear—and many Indians apparently liked to indulge in storytelling to test the credulity of whites who went among them.[27] Indian statements about other Indians cannot necessarily be accepted as true, especially when the informant was talking to a trader about more distant tribes. Slanders of other tribes as bloodthirsty, treacherous, and thieving were designed to discourage traders from going among those tribes and thus were economically motivated. They do not generally convey an accurate impression of the people in question, nor even of the informant's true feelings toward them. Fur trader David Thompson was fortunate to find an Indian informant, Saukampee, a Cree living among the Piegans, who seems to have been both informative and reliable.[28]

Recognition of the prejudices, interests, and characters that limit the reliability of both Indian and white commentators does not preclude accumulation of sufficient information to establish what were generally accepted attitudes. Biased and subjective comments have value, revealing as much about the commentator as about the persons under discussion. Each individual was a part of the total contact process, but with his or her own peculiar character, opinions, and prejudices, and meriting observation for that reason.

Contact modified all participants. The British had to fit into the Indian world just as the Indians had to adapt to the presence of alien newcomers. Similarly, maintenance of the relationship depended on both parties, with Indians exerting just as much influence as Britons. The military alliance was not simply a case of Britain using Indians to fight its battles, even though the British may have wanted such an arrangement. Rather, Indians clearly recognized the desperate nature of their situation and sought to alleviate it by allying with the redcoats. Neither party wholly trusted the other, but each was driven by necessity to maintain and renew an alliance that was grounded in the common fear of American expansion and reinforced by common interests that demanded preservation of the fur trade from the encroachments of settlement. The British fur trade was rarely an operation in which gullible Indian customers were swindled out of their hard-won pelts in transactions of which they had no experience or understanding. More often the trade was an arrangement of mutual exploitation for mutual advantage, entered into by Indians who frequently occupied favorable positions as middlemen in existing native trade networks. Experienced in the intricacies of bartering, they drove hard bargains and, especially in this period of intensive competition among British and Canadian fur companies, they exploited their positions to the full. Again, in appraisals of Indian and European culture, there was not complete conviction, among Indians *or* whites, that "civilization" was preferable to "primitive" life. George III's subjects may have been convinced that their civilization was superior to all others, but there is little or no evidence to indicate that Indians shared that view, and much to show that they preferred by far their own ways of living. The line that supposedly divided "savagery" and "civilization" was indistinct and recognized as such by both Indians and white men. British conduct at moments of crisis further convinced many Indians that Britain was an ally meriting but little respect, and that due only to its power and resources rather than to any virtue and worth.

Part One

BRITONS AND INDIANS IN A
CHANGING WORLD

1

Contact and Change Across a Continent

THE OLD NORTHWEST constituted the primary area of British-Indian affairs in the years following the American Revolution. Here, in a roughly triangular territory bordered by the Ohio River, the Great Lakes, and the Mississippi, British agents operated among the Indian tribes, offering the warriors advice and promising them assistance in their struggle against American expansionism. Here occurred councils, conflicts, and treaties that determined the outcome of that struggle and affected the nature of relations between Great Britain and the United States, as well as between King George and the Indian tribes. Yet by the late eighteenth and early nineteenth centuries British-Indian relations had stretched far beyond the Old Northwest. By then contacts had occurred across virtually the whole continent of North America. The objectives, circumstances, and outcomes of the encounters varied, but common to every meeting of Briton and Indian was the inescapable fact that the world in which they moved was undergoing radical and irreversible change.

As the Industrial Revolution gathered momentum, Britain experienced social and economic transformations that were to change forever the face of the English countryside and literally shake the world. In many ways, contemporaneous changes in American Indian societies were no less dramatic. The European invasion of America sent a series of shock waves reverberating across the continent. By 1783 many Indian societies had experienced the full impact of European contact, with invariably disastrous results. Other native peoples were feeling only the first repercussions of an invasion that had begun nearly three centuries before. The majority of Indian peoples with whom the British had dealings in this period were experiencing a painful process of readjustment as they struggled to survive in a world rendered deadly and chaotic by European contact.

Competition for land between Indians and Europeans, and the vicious conflicts fought along the moving frontier, constituted but one element in a process of destruction and acculturation that had begun when the first European set foot in the New World. The European fur trade proved to be the downfall of native North America. Nothing caused greater upheaval in the New World than the invasion of Old World diseases. From the time of first contact, epidemics of smallpox, plague, measles, influenza, typhus, and cholera spread like wildfire among the Indian populations, who had no immunity to the new diseases. Repeated epidemics wrought social and demographic disruption. They scythed Indian populations to a fraction of their former strength, tore holes in the social fabric, induced migration and resettlement, and produced spiritual and psychological upheaval. Lethal pathogens fanned out far ahead of the European invaders who introduced them, and Indian civilizations crumbled under the onslaught of recurrent pandemics. Observers who estimated Indian populations at the time of contact often were counting only the remnants of once-populous tribes in the wake of biological cataclysms. Recent upward revisions of precontact native populations give a better indication of the size and vitality of Indian societies on the eve of their destruction by the killer epidemics, which frequently carried off 90 percent of the population.[1]

The survivors found themselves in a world of violent turmoil. Indians readily incorporated European goods into their technologies, but traditional craft skills were sometimes eliminated as a result. European firearms revolutionized tribal warfare, increasing intertribal conflicts in range and deadliness as warriors competed for guns as the key to survival and adapted their tactics in response to the new weapons. Commerce replaced subsistence as the basic economic endeavor of many communities as Indian hunters bartered pelts for trade goods. Time-honored patterns of seasonal movement and settlement were disrupted or abandoned, with corresponding dislocations of social and ceremonial cycles. The symbiotic and sacred relationships that Indians sought to preserve with their ecosystem were extremely fragile and easily upset by the hammerblows of European wars, trade, and disease. Depletion of game resources to meet the demands of the fur trade produced famine. Reports of Indian starvation and dependence upon Europeans for handouts signified economic dislocation rather than inefficient traditional methods or inadequate sources of subsistence. Indeed, it has been argued that Indian subsistence economies were remarkably efficient and left the Indians so much leisure time that European observers assumed them to be lazy.[2] The attacks of European missionaries who demanded social and cultural revolution, and the ravages of alcoholism, wrought further despiritualization of the Indians' lives.

Into this world of chaos and uncertainty ventured British traders, travelers, soldiers, and agents, adding by their very presence to the existing forces of disruption. Demands of commerce and empire carried King George's subjects from the Atlantic to the Pacific, from the Arctic Ocean to the Gulf of Mexico, bringing them into contact with a diverse array of customs, languages, political and social structures, ceremonial practices, religious beliefs, world views, subsistence patterns, physical appearances, and reactions to external influences. Even where it was possible to draw distinctions between Indian peoples on the basis of environment, local customs and politics confused the picture. Moreover, each society that the British encountered was itself undergoing a process of fundamental and sometimes traumatic change.

Indians frequently became acquainted with British goods long before they met any British people, and English trade goods permeated the continent from the Arctic to the southern plains, from Florida to the northwestern Pacific Coast. The Hudson's Bay Company had been operating in Canada since 1670 and, for almost a century, had enjoyed a lucrative business by attracting Indian middlemen to its posts around the bay. However, after the fall of New France in 1763, Canadian peddlers began to push westward in an effort to bypass the middlemen and reach the fur-trading bands themselves. The Hudson's Bay Company either had to follow suit or see its trade diverted to more adventurous rivals. In the early 1770s the company dispatched Samuel Hearne northward to the Arctic and Matthew Cocking westward as far as the Blackfoot country. As early as 1772, Englishmen were reported trading with the Yscani, Tuacani, and Taovaya Indians in the Red River region of Texas.[3] There was virtually no limit to the spread of British influence through trade. By its very nature the fur trade had to continue expanding into virgin territory as other areas became exhausted, and it thus provided the motive, the means, and the medium for explorations such as those undertaken by Alexander Mackenzie, Simon Fraser, David Thompson, and even George Vancouver. These explorers carried British trade and the Union Jack to distant tribes. They also carried with them the seeds of destruction.

Some British observers recognized that the tribal societies with whom they came into contact were in various stages of cataclysmic change. They lamented the decline of formerly proud and free warriors to a state of drunkenness and depravity. But, in most cases, they simply assumed that what they saw was typical of Indian character and aboriginal society. When fur traders encountered hard-dealing Indian middlemen, they attributed it to the greed and cunning which they felt was inherent in the Indians' character; few admitted that the Indians were successfully adapting to a world revolutionized by European merchants and their values. Observers who saw Indian war parties come and go and Indian societies geared for war assumed that the Indian was warlike by nature; few observed that the Indian warrior fought because he had to if his people were to survive in a world made unusually hostile by European invaders and European firearms.

The Indian tribes who inhabited the area roughly south of the Great Lakes, west of the Atlantic Coast, and east of the Mississippi featured prominently in the wars for empire waged by European powers in the North American wilderness. Long-standing feuds between Iroquoians and Algonquians intensified into economically motivated intertribal warfare under the pressures of the European fur trade in the seventeenth century. Enmity continued during the colonial wars as Iroquois and Algonquian tribes assumed the role of native auxiliaries for the English and French respectively. King Philip's War (1675–76) drove many New England tribes northward to seek refuge in French Canada; in later years those same refugee warriors returned to raid familiar areas, often in the company of French expeditions against the New England settlements. As the Anglo-French conflict dragged on, so the involvement of the Indians continued. King William's War (1689–97), Queen Anne's War (1701–13), King George's War (1744–48), and the French and Indian War (1754–63) saw Indian warriors participating in conflicts the roots of which lay thousands of miles away, but the outcome of which the Indians correctly identified as having vital bearing upon their future. The British takeover from the French in 1763 sparked a brief but bloody war known as Pontiac's Revolt in which, in an impressive display of united action, Ottawa, Chippewa, Delaware, Shawnee, Seneca, Potawatomi, Miami, Kickapoo, Wyandot, and Wea warriors overran every British fort in the west except Detroit and Fort Pitt, before meeting defeat at the hands of Colonel Henry Bouquet. A royal proclamation in October 1763 reserved the country west of the Appalachian Mountains as hunting grounds for the Indians but failed to put a stop to the encroachments of white settlers on Indian lands. The "dark and bloody ground" of Kentucky became the scene of bitter skirmishing, which climaxed with Lord Dunmore's War in 1774 and the defeat of the Shawnees at Point Pleasant in present-day West Virginia.

By the time the revolutionary war ended in 1783, the Six Nations and many other tribes had endured almost a hundred years of wars generated by European land hunger and competition for empire. Their participation in warfare was to continue for the next thirty years, as Indian warriors, with and without British assistance, fought to hold back American settlement. Additional conflicts, of varying size and severity, with other tribes made the eighteenth century an era of almost endemic warfare for the Indian groups east of the Mississippi, though the situation was not of the Indians' making. In the new world created by European contact, Indian societies survived by existing on a war footing. This placed an intolerable strain on the tribes' cultural, economic, social, and political foundations. The peoples of the "warrior societies" with which the British dealt were, by the late eighteenth and early nineteenth centuries, taxed to breaking point by generations of warfare. Caught up in the maelstrom of change, tribes like the Shawnees, the Senecas, the Miamis, and the Mohawks could only buy time by successful adjustment to new conditions. Already greatly weakened by the time of the Revolution, they were broken and powerless by 1815.

In the south, from the Atlantic to the Mississippi, from Tennessee to the Gulf of Mexico, lived populous tribes like the Cherokees, the Creeks, the Chickasaws, and the Choctaws. Settled in farming towns and organized into powerful confederacies, they had attained cultures so resilient that they were able to survive disastrous defeats; they adapted to European contact so successfully that the invaders came to refer to them as the "Civilized Tribes." But these societies lived under tremendous strains, and mounting external pressures aggravated internal divisions. This period saw the separation of the Seminoles from the Creek confederacy. Alexander McGillivray endeavored to centralize Creek government and unite the nation in the face of adversity, but he was unable to reconcile rivalries that escalated and finally erupted in the Creek civil war of 1813–14. Like their northern counterparts, the southern tribes were living on borrowed time, until American expansionism dictated that they be driven from what remained of their homelands and force-marched west of the Mississippi.

The lands to which the southeastern tribes migrated lay on the periphery of the Great Plains, which supported a world of tremendous activity as the native inhabitants reacted to and assimilated external influences. There was a confusion of movement, change, disruption, and adaptation as various groups evolved the horse cultures that were to earn them the designation Plains Indians. The plains accommodated not only the equestrian tribes, so familiar in distorted and stereotyped fashion to twentieth-century cinema audiences, but also farming peoples who lived in semipermanent villages. In fact, by the late eighteenth century, two distinct subcultures had emerged on the Great Plains.

On the eastern fringes of the plains lived farming tribes like the Mandans, the Hidatsas, the Arikaras, the Omahas, and the Pawnees, who cultivated extensive crops and sheltered in fortified earth-lodge villages. These peoples had a long history of adaptation to their environment and to external influences. For example, by the time European explorers reached the Mandan villages on the Upper Missouri River in the mid-eighteenth century, Mandan culture was "the result of five hundred years of adaptive response to the Missouri River ecology, fusion with other earth lodge cultures of the Eastern Plains, contact with prehorse nomads and internal adjustments to the new settlement pattern." Increasing pressures had obliged the Mandans to abandon living in numerous scattered hamlets and to congregate in nine large villages within about twenty miles of one another along the banks of the Missouri. This concentration of villages and greater population density required more elaborate means of societal integration and social control.[4] The stockaded villages of the farming peoples afforded their inhabitants a measure of protection against raiders from the west, but became veritable death traps when European diseases scourged the plains in the late eighteenth and early nineteenth centuries. The ravages of smallpox, combined with the attacks of Sioux and Assiniboine enemies, had reduced the Mandans to only two villages by the time Lewis and Clark visited that tribe. The neighboring Arikaras, who once peopled as many as thirty-two villages, were huddled into two or three by the 1790s.[5] British traders who arrived in the Upper Missouri villages at the end of the eighteenth century came into contact with people living in an altered condition and dealt with tribes who were a shadow of their former selves.

Farther west on the plains, hunting tribes like the Teton Sioux, the Crows, the Cheyennes, the Arapahos, the Blackfeet, the Kiowas, and the Comanches practiced little or no agriculture. They lived in autonomous bands and dwelt in easily transportable skin tipis. Where the more sedentary inhabitants of the plains had cultures that stretched back hundreds of years, the life-style of the equestrian Indians developed rapidly, flourished briefly, and was to prove relatively short-lived. These tribes were comparatively recent arrivals on the Great Plains and, in the late eighteenth century, were jostling for position on the rich buffalo grounds. The increased range and mobility each tribe achieved when it acquired horses served only to intensify this competition. Scarcely had the tribes assimilated the horse into their cultures than European goods and, more significantly, guns began to penetrate their world. As had happened in earlier centuries among the tribes in the east, these things wrought dramatic changes in tribal culture, social organization, economy, commerce, warfare, and locations. From the late eighteenth century to the mid-nineteenth century, the peoples of the plains enjoyed an era of unprecedented power and prosperity. They acquired benefits from acquisition of horses and European goods, but had not yet felt the full impact of white contact and coercion. The still-vast herds of buffalo allowed these Indians to remain temporarily independent of white traders and their goods. White men might venture onto the plains and penetrate a tribal society, but this was still very much an Indian world in which the Plains warriors called the tune.[6]

Writers of tribal monographs often assume that the western Indians' history began with their meeting with the American explorers Meriwether Lewis and William Clark in the early nineteenth century, or at least that that meeting marked the beginning of a new era for the tribes concerned. The Lewis and Clark Expedition was enormously important, but not as significant from the Indian point of view as many writers have implied. That Lewis and Clark were the first white men to provide extensive information on many tribes does not necessarily mean that they were the first to have any contact with those tribes. The tendency to regard the Lewis and Clark journals as the beginning of recorded history west of the Mississippi has led many writers to neglect earlier records of French, Spanish, and British explorers and traders. Farther north the Scottish-born explorer Alexander Mackenzie had completed the first continental crossing north of Mexico a dozen years before Lewis and Clark ventured west. The Lewis and Clark Expedition was important because it brought Americans into contact with the western Indians, but those Americans ventured into an Indian world already radically altered by the European presence and influences.

The Indians of the plains were, for the most part, accomplished horsemen by the late eighteenth century. Their arrival at that stage was of comparatively recent date, however. The Cheyennes had just completed their transition from a semisedentary horticultural economy to an equestrian hunting economy. The Crows had split from their Hidatsa kinsmen on the Missouri River to move west toward the rich territory of the Yellowstone. The Teton and Yankton Sioux had begun their expansion into the central plains, but the culture of their Santee relatives remained essentially Woodland until as late as 1800. The horse brought many changes which, if not always revolutionary, at least accelerated and sometimes altered the direction of developments already under way. Horses and guns together created a chaotic situation in which, as in the east, warfare came to dominate tribal life and sap the strength of native societies.

The flow of horses onto the plains from the southwest and the diffusion of guns from the northeast meant that the location of a particular tribal group to a great extent determined its survival potential. A tribe in an unstrategic geographic position could not hope to compete with neighbors who had access to both horses and guns. Thus, while European diseases wrought demographic havoc, Indian groups shifted location and competed for access to European guns. Possession of guns enabled a tribe to expand at the expense of unarmed neighbors until they too acquired firearms and the tide was stemmed or reversed. The Crees expanded west, thereby coming into conflict with the Blackfeet, and the Blackfeet, who previously had suffered from the Snakes' prior possession of horses, exploited their new-found firepower to extend their territories at the expense of the Snakes, the Flatheads, the Kootenais, and the Crows.[7] In the mid-eighteenth century the Snake Indians, mounted on horses obtained from their Comanche cousins to the south, had been perhaps the most powerful tribe on the northern plains. But the new aggression on the part of the Blackfeet, coinciding with an Arapaho movement west and a Crow movement south, effectively drove the Snakes from the northern plains. Although there may have been groups of Snake Indians on the plains as late as 1790, they were gone after 1805.[8]

The Snakes were soon replaced by the newly arrived

Sioux as the dominant power on the plains, although the Blackfeet continued to harass and control the north until their confederacy suffered crippling losses in the smallpox epidemic of 1837.[9] The Sioux, with the newly armed Chippewas to the east of them and rich buffalo grounds to their south and west, drifted out of their Minnesota homeland across the Missouri and onto the plains. The Teton Sioux were assured of supplies of guns and ammunition from their Yankton and Sisseton kinsmen east of the Missouri River, and they ruthlessly exploited their advantage at the expense of tribes weakened by European diseases. In the mid-eighteenth century, the westward drift of the Tetons had halted before the fortified villages of the Mandans, Hidatsas, Arikaras, and Omahas. Following the outbreak of smallpox, however, the Sioux terrorized the village peoples. The Tetons reduced the balance of power on the Missouri to a shambles, and, as they advanced west, they took lands from the Arikaras, the Mandans, the Hidatsas, the Assiniboines, the Omahas, the Iowas, and the Poncas. The majority of the Tetons were still on the banks of the Missouri when Lewis and Clark ascended the river, but the Oglalas, spearheading the Tetons' advance on to the plains, had reached the Black Hills about 1775. Once they had established themselves on the plains, the Tetons proceeded to push the Crows north and the Kiowas south. By the early nineteenth century, the Sioux were emerging as the dominant force west of the Missouri, and they were to continue their program of expansion until they clashed with the United States in its drive west in midcentury.[10]

British traders who penetrated the Great plains in this period entered a world in flux; but the changes occurring in western tribal societies were by no means confined to the plains. The Kootenai, the Flathead, the Nez Percé, the Cayuse, and the Spokane tribes inhabited the plateau region to the north and west, beyond the Rockies, but by the end of the eighteenth century they had adopted much of the lifestyles of the horse and buffalo Indians of the plains. Farther west, Pacific Coast peoples like the Nootkas, the

Tlingits, the Kwakiutls, the Chinooks, and the Tsimshians came into increasing contact with maritime traders on their shores. As on the northern plains, so the extension of European trade into the Athabasca and Mackenzie Basin regions far to the north led to shifts in the balance of intertribal power, strengthening the Beaver Indians at the expense of the Sekanis and Chipewyans.[11]

Historians have traditionally and persistently neglected the amount of intercommunication between nonwestern peoples. In fact, Indian tribes enjoyed wide-ranging and frequent contacts with other peoples and other areas for military, social, economic, and ceremonial purposes, and Indian villages commonly included captives, refugees, visitors, and spouses from other tribes. The European fur trade increased intertribal intercourse but did not create it. A network of Indian trails covered the continent. The age-old Warrior's Path, with its many branches, ran from Cherokee country in North Carolina, north and west through the Cumberland Gap, and on to the Ohio River. The Iroquois war trail ran south through western Pennsylvania, and there were countless lesser trails.[12] In the first decade of the nineteenth century the Shawnee war chief Tecumseh traveled the country from the Great Lakes to the Florida Seminoles' area in his efforts to unite scattered tribes into a powerful confederacy opposed to American expansion. Piecemeal movements and migration were a recurrent experience for tribes like the Shawnees and the Delawares. Indeed, the linguistic map of native North America was confused and complicated by many and wide-ranging migrations that gave Indian tribal distribution a mosaic character and, in some cases, scattered members of a single language family across the continent. For example, the Algonquian-speaking Cheyennes and Blackfeet migrated west with the result that, by the nineteenth century, they had more in common with Siouan neighbors on the Great Plains than with linguistically related tribes farther east. On the plains, intertribal contacts facilitated the spread of horses north and the diffusion of European goods, while some bands covered immense distances in pursuit of buffalo herds, to trade, and to fight. Indians from far away journeyed to the great Spanish trading center at Santa Fe to obtain horses, and in 1787 a Piegan war party raided as far south as the Spanish settlements. In 1801 a band of "Tattoed Indians" (Arapahos or possibly related Atsinas) arrived at the Hudson's Bay Company post on the Saskatchewan after a journey of forty-five days; and Mandan, Blood, and Blackfeet Indians traveled more than a thousand miles to York factory and back, a round trip of more than three months.[13]

Between 1779 and 1783 the rapid spread of smallpox dramatically demonstrated the extent of intertribal movement and communication. The disease broke out in the Spanish settlements in the southwest and was then transmitted from tribe to tribe across the Rocky Mountains, over the plains, on to the Upper Missouri drainage, and into the Canadian forests. According to trader David Thompson, the Indians suffered about a 60 percent mortality rate in those areas where the smallpox raged in 1781–82. The hard-hit Blackfeet turned to the adoption of women and children from enemy tribes as a means of offsetting their losses. The epidemic carried far north into the barren lands where Cree, Chipewyan, Beaver, Yellowknife, Sekani, and Naskapi bands struggled to wrest an existence from the vast boreal forest south of the Arctic tundra. These peoples rarely gathered in groups any larger than the extended family band, since any greater assemblage placed undue strains on the delicate relationships of exploitation that they had developed with their ecosystem. Even so, the disease spread with devastating effects: the Chipewyans, formerly the largest Athapaskan-speaking group in the central subarctic, lost about 90 percent of their population in 1781. Some tribes survived and recovered. The Assiniboines increased in number between 1763 and 1821, despite epidemics in 1781 and 1819. On the whole, however, the four-year-long smallpox epidemic was a disaster for native North America.[14]

Clearly, the Indian worlds with which the British came into contact in the late eighteenth century were not isolated, uniform, or static. Each tribal society was subject to modification by interaction with other Indian cultures as well as with Europeans. In addition, Europeans generally were bewildered by the loose political structures that they encountered. The British endeavored to conduct orderly relations with a variety of Indian groups whose political organizations were often as fluid as they appeared unfathomable to officials accustomed to hierarchy and regularity. The British consistently looked for authoritative individuals or bodies with whom they could make binding agreements, but the diversity, the factionalism, the fragmentation, and the individualism within Indian societies precluded the possibility of such orderly relations. In the 1790s and again in 1814, John Ferdinand Smyth Stuart, a refugee Loyalist, wrote to the British government, advocating the establishment of an "Apalachian Indian Empire." Under British auspices, the various tribes would unite in one giant confederacy with a capital, a constitution, and "civilized" organs of government.[15] Such a proposal displayed a fundamental misconception of the dynamics of native society and politics.

In reality, the British were fortunate if they could negotiate with duly authorized representatives of even the individual tribes. Joseph Brant presumed to speak for the confederated tribes after the Revolution, the Mohawks considered themselves the leading voice of the Six Nations, and the Six Nations in turn claimed an outdated hegemony over other tribes to the west. More often, however, separate tribes, and even the individuals within them, held themselves to be sovereign and independent, subject to no authority higher than their own will and restrained only by custom and the force of public opinion. Many tribes practiced a kind of voluntary communism so that no member of the group should starve or feast alone, but otherwise individual autonomy was jealously guarded. Indian trader and interpreter John Long explained with frustration that, "the Iroquois laugh when you talk to them of obedience to kings, for they cannot reconcile the idea of submission with the dignity of man. Each individual is a sovereign in his own mind, and as he conceives he derives his freedom from the Great Spirit alone, he cannot be induced to acknowledge any other power." Traders among the Teton Sioux found that those warriors held no chief in higher esteem than the next man and that "chaque homme etoit chef de sa cabanne."[16]

An Indian chief was not the leader of his people in the sense that a subject of George III could easily appreciate or understand. Usually an Indian chief lacked institutionalized power; his influence stemmed from his personal abilities as warrior, orator, and gift-giver and from his standing and connections. His role was to advise and request rather than to dictate because decisions rested upon the will of the people, perhaps expressed in tribal council. A leader could impose his will by reason of his prestige, by persuasion, by threatening and cajoling, but Indian societies rarely possessed the machinery for regular implementation of such policy decisions as were made. Indian captive John Tanner described a joint expedition launched by Cree, Chippewa, and Assiniboine warriors against their common Sioux enemies, which proved abortive because "of the whole fourteen hundred, not one . . . would acknowledge any authority superior to his own will. . . . It is true that ordinarily they yield a certain deference, and a degree of obedience to the chief each may have undertaken to follow, but this obedience, in most cases, continues no longer than the will of the chief corresponds entirely with the inclination of those he leads."[17]

Europeans persistently overestimated the authority of Indian chiefs. The British interpreted the Creek word *miko* as "king," but the miko was little more than the head of a tribal council and spokesman for his people. He could take no significant action without the advice of the council and could be replaced if the tribe held him responsible for a decline in its fortunes.[18] Joseph Brant was possibly the most influential Indian of his day, but he was not a chief in any of the officially recognized Iroquioan senses of the term. He was not of sufficiently distinguished birth to be a sachem or civil chief; he was not an official war chief, and, though he achieved sufficient prestige to be counted a "pine tree chief," that office carried no voting power. Brant's position of leadership in the Six Nations rested solely on his achievements as warrior, politician, and diplomat, enhanced by his connections with the British. Indeed, for a long time during Brant's rise from relative obscurity among the Mohawks, whites regarded him as far more important than did his own people.[19]

Indian societies frequently distinguished between military and civil functions, with one chief or set of chiefs for peacetime affairs, another for war. The village or peace chiefs were experienced tribal counselors who mediated minor disputes, offered guidance on everyday matters, and represented their people in negotiations with friendly tribes. War chiefs tended to be younger men who had gained a reputation as successful warriors and who led their people only in time of war. The almost chronic warfare of the period led British observers to assume that the office of war chief was more important than that of the village chiefs, but in fact both categories exercised a limited authority. Often-heard pleas by Indian chiefs that they could not control their young men and bind them to treaties were not lame excuses so much as explanations of the normal state of affairs in the highly individualistic Indian societies. White men, of course, tended to interpret such a situation as evidence that Indian treaties, though concluded with great solemnity, were nothing more than the words of children, "no sooner uttered than forgotten."[20]

Official British instructions stipulated the need to cultivate the friendship and confidence of the most important chiefs, but it was not always possible to identify who those chiefs were.[21] Consequently, the British sometimes resorted to the practice of "creating" chiefs in order to facilitate negotiations and stabilize relations. They bestowed commissions and medals as a means of investing chosen chiefs with additional prestige and influence, transferring some of the visible symbols of authority which, the British believed, so impressed the Indians. Unfortunately, such meddling in the complex world of Indian politics tended to confuse matters further. British influence, exerted in time of war or in expectation of war, promoted the authority of war chiefs, creating imbalance in the system and emphasizing the militaristic elements of Indian societies. During the revolutionary war, the government favored Joseph Brant but had to tread carefully lest it alienate other Iroquois leaders more deserving of attention. Likewise, when the Shawnee chief Blue Jacket received a commission in the 1790s, other chiefs complained that they had a better claim to it.[22] The history of Indian-white relations offers many instances where Indian peoples repudiated treaties and land cessions made by so-called chiefs whom they regarded as compliant tools of the white man.

In addition, Indian societies frequently split into war and peace factions, or pro-British and pro-American parties, or into groups advocating varying degrees of nativism and assimilation. As a result, those chiefs who did possess significant influence often found that they had a rival in the struggle for leadership. During the Revolution the pro-British Delaware chief, Captain Pipe of the Wolf clan, had to contend with a pro-American rival, White Eyes of the Turtle clan. In the post-war years Red Jacket, the traditionalist Seneca, consistently opposed the Mohawk Joseph Brant as spokesman for the Iroquois. Black Hawk, leader of the pro-British band of Sauks, met a rival in Keokuk, who supported the United States. The Shawnee chief Black Hoof had fought against the Americans in the 1780s and 1790s, but opposed Tecumseh and the Shawnee Prophet in the early 1800s.

Many Indian nations were in fact loose and fluid confederacies with which it was impractical to deal as a body. The Six Nations of the Iroquois dominated the northeast and the imaginations of European empire builders and enjoyed a reputation as the most advanced native polity north of Mexico. But member tribes retained considerable autonomy even before they went their separate ways during the Revolution. The Seven Nations of Canada were in fact composite communities settled in villages along the Saint Lawrence, rather than distinct tribes. The huge Chippewa, or Ojibwa, Nation was composed of many bands scattered across a vast territory around Lake Superior and the northern edge of Lake Huron. In the north they were closely connected with the Crees, while in the south the Chippewas, Ottawas, and Potawatomis formed a loose confederacy, the Three Fires. The Shawnees traditionally comprised five major divisions: the Chillicothes, Maykujays, Thawakilas, Piquas, and Kispokogis. Farther west British traders and agents encountered eastern bands of the Sioux, who were a nation divided into three major groups, seven tribes, and a number of bands and subbands, stretching from the Mississippi to the Great Plains. The Mdewakantons, Wahpetons, Wahpekutes, and Sissetons constituted the Santee or Dakota branch; the Yankton (Nakota) division included the Yanktons and Yanktonais; and the largest and most westerly group, the Tetons or Lakotas, was composed of the Oglala, Sans Arc, Brule, Hunkpapa, Minneconjou, Blackfoot, and Two Kettle bands. The Blackfeet who figured prominently in the accounts of British fur traders were a confederacy of Algonquian tribes on the northern plains occupying territory from the North Saskatchewan River almost to the Upper Missouri and from the Rocky Mountains into Saskatchewan. Composed of the Siksikas (or Northern Blackfeet), the Bloods, and the Piegans, and with the Atsinas and Sarsis in close alliance, the Blackfeet were the strongest military power on the northern plains, despite suffering appalling losses in the 1781 smallpox epidemic. The three main tribes generally united against their common enemies but seem to have remained mutually independent. In the southeast, the Creek confederacy formed the largest division of the Muskhogean family and occupied some fifty towns in which a half dozen distinct languages were spoken. They were never united as a "nation" and individual towns frequently

split over issues of peace and war. Other smaller confederacies and tribes were similarly fluid and flexible in organization. Bound by ties of kinship, language, and custom,
they usually managed to present a united front to their
enemies, but unity of policy on a consistent basis was rare.
Multitribal confederacies were subject to immense internal strains, schisms, and disagreements. Indians tended to
think in terms of family, clan, band, and perhaps tribe,
rather than in terms of confederation or race. The Tribe
seems to have been largely a concept created by Europeans
in an effort to regularize their dealings with Indian societies, and was often of limited importance even as an ethnic unit.[23] The small band was more often the effective
unit of social, political, and economic life. During the
winter months the exigencies of a hunting economy forced
many tribes to divide into groups large enough for security but small enough to subsist, and Indian communities
changed in composition and character with the rhythm
of the seasons. What organs of political control did exist—
for example, the Plains Indian police and soldier societies—were largely confined to operation during the summer months. The episodic character of tribes facilitated
movement between bands, to the further confusion of
Europeans.

In British eyes, fluid and flexible political structures,
which served well the needs of the societies that had developed them, implied disorder and lack of discipline. Some
interpreted what they saw as an indication that Indians
lacked political acumen and could be treated as gullible
savages. Experience proved that any such assumptions
were not only ill-founded but also extremely dangerous.
In 1763 the Ottawa war chief Pontiac had demonstrated
that a leader of ability could weld scattered and uncon-
nected tribes into a powerful and devastating coalition.
Headed by the Miamis, the Shawnees, and the Delawares,
the western confederacy continued to develop and, in the
decade after the Revolution, combined with the Six Nations and other tribes to present the United States with

the most formidable array of Indian power mustered in united opposition. In the same years, the leadership and reforms of Alexander McGillivray gave the Creek confederacy its greatest centralization, and the Creeks constituted the most important factor in the Anglo-American–Spanish contest for empire in the southeast.[24]

In the decade before the War of 1812, Tecumseh transformed a religious revival initiated by his brother the Prophet into a movement of Indian nationalism, with a doctrine of joint tribal ownership of all Indian lands in common that represented a direct challenge to the American policy of divide and rule. By 1812 warriors from some thirty tribes, stretching from Canada to the Gulf of Mexico, fought under Tecumseh. The Shawnee war chief is the only figure of the period—Indian or white—for whom all sources are unanimous in expressing admiration. Even William Henry Harrison, Tecumseh's constant adversary and eventual conqueror, bestowed grudging praise, describing the Shawnee as "one of those uncommon geniuses who spring up occasionally to produce revolutions, and overturn the established order of things."[25]

A galaxy of Indian leaders that included McGillivray, Tecumseh, Red Jacket, Cornplanter, and Little Turtle represented the formidable array of military and political talent with which white men had to contend in the postrevolutionary decade. Yet no individual had more extensive relations with the British, or caused them more problems, than Joseph Brant. Brant had risen to power during the revolutionary war and his influential connections stretched from Indian council fire to the British royal family. British Indian agents and officers recognized that Brant was a man of education, intelligence, and ambition and, as such, represented a source of potential trouble to the British. Brant visited England after the Revolution to solicit help for his people, who were in dire straits after the war, and to discover how much help the Indians could expect in the event of renewed war with the United States. The visit caused the government considerable embarrass-

Joseph Brant, by George Romney. Several artists painted the cele-
brated Mohawk. This portrait was done in the spring of 1776 when
Brant was in London. (National Gallery of Canada, Ottawa; 8005)

ment and did little to placate the Mohawk. On his return Brant "did not hesitate in all Companies to reprobate the weakness and folly of our ministers, damning Ld S [illegible: Sydney?] for a stupid Blockhead: and versed in all the Grievances and Language of Opposition."[26] Brant was a valuable ally to the Crown but he was not a compliant tool. As he showed during the controversy over the Grand River lands, he was quite capable of giving the government problems.

The Grand River lands were granted to the Six Nations, and to Brant's Mohawks in particular, as an asylum and in reward for their services and compensation for the loss of their homelands within the United States. Governor Haldimand secured by purchase from the Missisauga Indians in May 1784 a tract of lands in southern Ontario from which the Iroquois were granted an area "Six Miles deep from each Side of the River beginning at Lake Erie, and extending in that Proportion to the Head of the said River, which them & their Posterity are to enjoy for ever."[27] The Mohawks began to arrive in late 1784 and early 1785. Brant took the line that the grant created an estate in fee simple and recognized the Indians as competent to arrange their own affairs. The British authorities, however, later denied Brant's interpretation of the grant. British policy with regard to Indian lands was to view the Indians as possessing a right of prior occupancy but not of sovereignty, and stipulated that cession of Indian lands could be made only to the Crown. Indian spokesmen frequently proclaimed that land could be occupied only, not owned, and that it was the right to use lands rather than actual ownership that was transferable. But when the government tried to establish that the Indians had rights only to the *use* of the Grand River lands, Brant maintained that those lands were the exclusive property of the Six Nations, to be managed as they (or he) saw fit. The issue came to a head when the Mohawk sought to lease and sell some of the lands to white settlers. The government found itself in an awkward position and dared not risk alienating Brant; the Grand

River grant had been intended to serve not only as a refuge for the Indians but also as a protective buffer for British settlements at the western end of Lake Ontario. With the Mohawks disaffected, those lands could equally well constitute a threat to Upper Canada's defenseless western flank. In 1797 rumors of a projected French and Spanish invasion of Upper Canada circulated through the colony, and Brant, dissatisfied with the apparent inconsistency of British policy, began to assume an increasingly menacing posture. Some suspected that the Mohawk himself was responsible for spreading many of the rumors of impending invasion. Under the pressure, the authorities in Upper Canada felt obliged to confirm the sale of some 381, 480 acres. The crisis passed but the question of the Grand River lands did not end there. First Brant and then his successor John Norton carried the controversy well into the nineteenth century.[28] The government enjoyed easier relations with Captain John Deseronto's band of Mohawks who selected land on the north shore of Lake Ontario at the Bay of Quinte. The Tyendinaga Mohawks, as they came to be known, pursued a course of action independent of their kinsmen on the Grand River, quietly minding and managing their own affairs.[29]

What the British perceived as the fragmentation and disunity of Indian societies did not necessarily signify that Indians were unable to match the British in legal, landed, or political disputes. Brant was an exceptional individual and the Grand River crisis an unusual event, but it served to remind the British that Indians were capable of effective demonstrations of political acumen. In most cases, British-Indian relations in this period occurred in the Indians' world where they held many advantages and called many of the shots. The British had to operate in unfamiliar territory and deal with peoples who seemed an unknown quantity. Officials who looked for orderly negotiations followed by mutually binding agreements struggled to function in the complex world of Indian politics and council fire diplomacy where each tribe had its own set of international relations. The British had to try and adapt their political practices to suit the situation in native North America where, instead of dealing with a centralized government or royal representatives, they faced a bewildering turmoil of separate but often intertwining dealings with confederacies, tribes, bands, factions, war chiefs, peace chiefs, influential warriors, orators, and prophets, at a time when dramatic changes were exerting a radical impact on relations between the Indians and the Crown.

2

The Indian Department and the Indian Agent

INTERCOURSE between the British government and the American Indians normally took place at the end of a chain of command and report that stretched from the cabinet and Colonial Office in London to the governor and lieutenant governor in Canada, and then down through the British Indian Department or the army to the individuals operating in the Indian country. The effectiveness of this chain in conveying orders and information was hampered by distance and delay. This meant that ministers in England, even when not preoccupied with events in Europe, had only a faint grasp of what was happening in the North American backcountry and could issue only very general directives. The British government had to make the best of a difficult situation and use the machinery and individuals at its disposal to try to achieve a degree of order and regularity in its dealings with the Indians. The Indian Department provided the machinery; the individual agents acted as the government's on-the-spot representatives. In the years between the end of the Revolution and the end of the War of 1812, the government in England relied heavily on both for the conduct of official Indian relations and the implementation of official policies toward the tribes. This dependence was the source of some additional problems since the government had only limited control over its distant representatives.

Initially formed in 1755 during the final and decisive French and Indian war, the Indian Department became the keystone of British policy in the North American interior. The defeat of France brought many more tribes within the department's orbit and changed the circumstances in which it operated. The department was soon directing its efforts among the tribes to the defeat of a new enemy. Working closely with the British army in North America, the Indian Department rallied local tribes to the cause of preserving British jurisdiction and political institutions over much of North America from the threat of American republicanism. From the Indian point of view, the department offered organization and assistance in the struggle to preserve native lands and cultures from the threat of American expansionism. The Indian Department provided invaluable service, coordinating British policy and Indian activity, during the revolutionary war, the struggle for the Ohio valley, and the War of 1812.[1]

The Indian Department was subject to both civil and military control. There was, however, no clear division of authority. Partly, this was due to the fact that, while the department itself was under the direction of civil authorities, its funds came out of the military budget. In addition, it was because army post commanders were men of standing and importance in Indian relations. Official policy demanded that they be present at all Indian conferences and handouts as representatives of the king, but that they refrain from interfering in the affairs of the Indian Department.[2]

The department itself still enjoyed considerable prestige from the reputation of the late Sir William Johnson, superintendent of Indian affairs in the Northern Department from 1755 to 1774. Johnson had come to the Mohawk valley in 1738, had established himself as a trader and landowner, and was soon the most influential white man in the Iroquois country. It was thought important that the head of the Indian Department should be a member of the Johnson clan. Thus, upon Sir William's death in 1774, his nephew and son-in-law, Colonel Guy Johnson, had taken over the running of the department, only to be removed on charges of embezzlement in 1782. He was succeeded by Sir William's son, Sir John Johnson, who took charge under the new title of superintendent general of Indian affairs and inspector general of the Indian Department, with rank and income suitable to the position, which he held until 1828.[3] Sir John's name and office carried weight. In the summer of 1783, Johnson met with the warriors and sachems of the Six Nations, who were assembled at Niagara in a series of councils. Great efforts had been made to get him there in the hope that he might quiet the fears of the Indians, who were justifiably apprehensive over the news of the peace settlement. Johnson could offer little comfort to the Indians; the British clearly hoped that the influence of the Johnson name would ease the situation.[4]

The Indian Department could not afford to rely on one man to solve its problems, however. In 1794 the office of superintendent general was created to assist Sir John Johnson because he was so frequently absent. Colonel Alexander McKee first held the new post until his death in 1799; then from 1800 to 1826, Colonel William Claus, nephew of Sir John Johnson and grandson of Sir William, occupied the position. In addition, the department maintained resident deputies at major posts in the Indian country. John Butler and then William Claus served at Niagara, McKee and Matthew Elliott at Detroit.

Considerable intermingling occurred at the grass-roots level between department employees and Indians. Close connections were officially encouraged so that, for example, interpreters might become more proficient in their work.[5] Equally important was the need to build up influential connections among and within the tribes by taking Indian wives. Individual marriages by British subjects living in Indian bands helped to establish important ties of kinship and reciprocity, which formed a basis for good relations between the tribes and the Crown. Traders and agents who took Indian wives entered into the fabric of na-

Sir John Johnson, from an engraving by F. Bartolozzi for Col. A. S. DePeyster's *Miscellanies* (Dumfries, 1813). The son of Sir William Johnson, John Johnson (1742–1830) took over the running of the British Indian Department in 1782. (Public Archives Canada, Ottawa; C-2847)

tive societies and became pivotal figures in relations between their British countrymen and their Indian kinfolk. The government, mindful of the example and success of Sir William Johnson, recognized intermarriage as a key to maintaining good relations with the Indians and saw to it that representatives of influence and prestige lived among powerful and pivotal tribes.[6]

Before and during the Revolution, the Johnson dynasty helped secure the allegiance of the Six Nations to the Crown. Although the confederacy split during the Revolution, the Iroquois and others apparently still clung to the notion that they held the balance of power on the continent, and their influence over other tribes was still extensive, if fading, after 1783.[7] Under the leadership of Cornplanter and Red Jacket in the United States, and of Brant and John Norton in Canada, the Iroquois continued to dominate the New York State–Grand River region and occupied a prominent position in the Indian affairs of both the American and British governments until at least the War of 1812, by which time their power was but a shadow of its former strength.

As the course of events and the center of Indian affairs shifted westward, the influence of the Shawnees grew while that of the Iroquois waned. Although never a numerous people, the Shawnees emerged as one of the foremost tribes in the Indian confederacy that fought to secure the Ohio River as a boundary to American expansion in the 1780s and 1790s. The Battle of Fallen Timbers and the subsequent Treaty of Greenville were major setbacks, but the Shawnees reasserted their position as leaders of the opposition to the United States in the first decade of the nineteenth century. The Shawnee Prophet headed a powerful nativist religious movement at the same time his brother Tecumseh formed a related and renewed Indian confederacy. In Alexander McKee and Matthew Elliott the British Indian Department had two agents married into and influential among the Shawnees operating at the hub of Indian affairs. It was vital to have the right man in the right place at the right time. Matthew Elliott had been removed from office on charges of corruption, but he was recalled in the critical year of 1808 when it was felt urgently necessary to renew and strengthen British connections with the Indians in preparation for a likely war with the United States. Elliott replaced Thomas, the inebriate mixed-blood son of the late Alexander McKee, as deputy superintendent of the western tribes at Amherstburg, to exert his influence among the pivotally located Shawnees.[8]

Farther west, the Sioux controlled the Upper Mississippi and Missouri rivers and dominated the neighboring tribes. Not surprisingly, the British government took steps to secure the attachment of this powerful nation, vesting considerable authority in the influential Scottish fur trader Robert Dickson, who was brother-in-law of a Yanktonais Sioux chief, Red Thunder.[9] Different tribes came to the fore at different times as leading forces in the Indian world, whether by virtue of numbers, resolution, geographical location, or influence, and the British conducted their relations accordingly.

The Indian Department was not an exclusively English or even white organ of government. People of mixed ancestry served as interpreters, and both Joseph Brant and John Norton were on the department's books. Agents like the notorious Simon Girty seemed to some to be more Indian than white. A painting done around 1780 of Sir John Caldwell, lieutenant colonel of the Eighth Foot, in the dress of an Indian chief, illustrates the mixture of native and European culture that frequently developed with contact in the Indian country and which was, indeed, a characteristic of the Indian Department. Caldwell appears wearing Indian headdress, decoration, breechcloth, scarlet leggings, and moccasins. Indian jewelry hangs from his nose and ears, and he holds a pipe-tomahawk and a belt of wampum. On the other hand, the short sword at his side, the gorget around his neck, and the cloak over his shoulders are British.[10]

Sir John Caldwell, lieutenant colonel of the Eighth Foot (King's Regiment), in the dress of an Indian chief, as he appeared at a war council in 1780. The artist is unknown. Several of the articles worn by Caldwell are in Canada's National Museum of Man, Ottawa. The pipe is eastern Sioux, the garters are Chippewa, and the pouch, knife, and sheath are from the eastern Great Lakes. Caldwell was given a Chippewa name, acquired some knowledge of Indian language, and returned to England with a collection of Indian artifacts. (Courtesy Merseyside County Museums, Liverpool)

American observers saw the nature of the Indian Department and of British contact with the Indians at the grass-roots level as the source of English influence. United States Indian agent Thomas Forsyth wondered why, when English and Americans shared common language, customs, and means, the United States should have comparatively so little influence over the Indians. The reason was, he thought, that the American system was wrong.

The British Government have brought their method of treating Indians to a perfect system; they have [a] well regulated Indian department with a store of goods and a blacksmith at every post for their use. No person is eligible for the place of agent, unless he can speak some one of the languages. It would be supposed that an agent thus appointed is acquainted with the manners and customs as also with the different chiefs and Head Men of the different Nations of Indians.

A British Indian Agent will not think it derogatory to his rank to smoke and converse with Indian chiefs, by which means he cannot be imposed upon by designing interpreters, as sometimes happens with us. It is my decided opinion that our Government ought to establish a district department for Indian affairs in this country.[11]

Here, as elsewhere in North America, the British built on French foundations. The French enjoyed a reputation for amicable relations with Indians and the British sought to emulate their success. In many ways, British Indian policy after 1763 was a continuation of French policy. Until 1759 the French had urged their Indian allies to confederate and form a buffer between New France and the English; after 1783 the British urged tribes to confederate and form a buffer between Canada and the Americans. The British government continued the French practice of regulating trade with the Indians and attempting to protect their lands from encroachment. In the fur trade, British companies continued to draw on French experience and employed French-Canadians in the northwest. The belief that the French possessed a unique facility for harmonious relations with Indians was expressed by Francis

Parkman in the nineteenth century and was for a long time accepted without question. Indians themselves may have looked back with nostalgia and viewed the years of French domination as a halcyon period before the British and the Americans took over, but there seems little evidence to suggest that French-Canadian traders got along with Indians any better than did their Scots or English counterparts in this period. The French certainly had had their share of Indian troubles, notably with the Iroquois and Fox tribes. Nevertheless, the British Indian Department was also keen to make use of French expertise and connections, and it employed French residents as officers in the west, such as Charles Langlade at Green Bay and Charles Gautier at Prairie du Chien.[12]

The Indian Department saw itself as the sole link between the Indians and the British government. Joseph Brant and John Norton each encountered considerable opposition and aroused distrust when they resolved to go to England in disregard of the Indian Department.[13] The department's purpose was to maintain amicable relations with the Indians as actual or potential allies, assuring them of the king's paternal regard and operating in the manner best calculated to ensure their loyalty. The Indian Department, ideally at least, fed the Indian when he was hungry, clothed him when he was naked, gave him medical help in times of sickness and, if that failed, saw to it that he got a decent burial. The Indians came to expect good treatment at the British posts, and forts at Niagara, Amherstburg, and Michilimackinac served as major emporia for the supply of the tribes. It is perhaps indicative of the role of the department, and reveals the agents' concept of their work, that when the department acquired a new boat in 1793, one suggestion was to call it the "Indian Feeder." More tactfully, Matthew Elliott hoped it would be given the name "Shawanoe."[14]

The Indian Department maintained that experience showed that the Indians had to be treated like children and be governed by a mixture of firmness and indulgence, kindness and deceit.[15] A firm hand was considered essential to the successful management of Indians. The department did not adhere to the doctrine that Indians understood nothing but force, but it was widely believed that Indians would misinterpret the absence of force and mistake kindness or clemency as a sign of weakness. Surrounded by feuding Sioux, Chippewas, and Ottawas, Robert Dickson warned against "mistaken lenity" in dealing with Indians and recommended making a severe example as the best way to render the Indians more manageable and less of a threat to traders like himself.[16] Popular opinion advocated swift and sure punishment of Indian transgressors on the grounds that any delay might be interpreted as fear among a people "whose Law is Retaliation, . . . while a well timed legal Severity will secure their future good Behaviour."[17]

British justice might be swift, but it was rarely blind in dealing with the Indians. The British recognized that their actions reverberated throughout the Indian world and that they must maintain a reputation for enforcing their word and their law; but they also knew that they must be flexible when circumstances demanded. When Joseph Brant requested that the murderer of a drunken Delaware be hanged at Niagara so that the Indians could see justice to be done, Haldimand complied and the guilty white man was executed on the site where the crime was committed.[18] In contrast, an Onondaga warrior who murdered a drunken white man was excused the extreme penalty and handed over to his own chiefs because of his influential connections and the fear that his execution might cause further bloodshed and alienate many of the Iroquois.[19] The authorities could be pliable when entanglement in tribal politics and a loss of British influence might result from rigid implementation of British justice.

The other side of the coin to firmness was indulgence, and this aspect of Indian "management" caused the government the most trouble, especially on the question of presents and supplies. The giving of presents was a time-

honored custom in Indian society, surrounded by ceremonial and symbolic observances and indicative of friendship, sympathy, and goodwill. Gifts were essential to the
successful conduct of Indian diplomacy and were presented to reinforce a speaker's words and impress listeners
with his sincerity. A Seneca chief made this point with
sledgehammer subtlety when, at a council held at Detroit
in November 1782, he told Colonel Arent De Peyster:
"give us necessaries in abundance . . . otherwise we shall
imagine you do not speak from the Heart." The chief also
indicated that his own authority to direct his warriors according to British instructions depended upon his having
British goods to distribute.[20]

The distribution of large quantities of gifts had played a
vital part in the Anglo-French contest for Indian allegiance
in mid-century. Consequently, when the outbreak of the
Revolution ushered in a generation of hostility and tension
with the United States, Britain looked to supplies of presents as a proven means of securing Indian friendship. One
American newspaper carried a report in 1792 that the British were providing Indians with presents "like Stacks of
hay." The range of goods supplied was enormous. A sample
inventory listed the following items: blankets, buckles,
armbands, earrings, belts, fishhooks, awls, spears, mirrors,
knives, razors, scissors, combs, thimbles, jew's harps, rifles,
pistols, powder, shot, flints, lead, beads, needles, toma-
hawks, pipes, tobacco, laced hats, flags, plumes, medals,
coats, bridles, kettles, lace, ribbon and, of course, rum.
The British Indian Department demanded that the goods
given to the Indians be of the highest standard, and Indians easily recognized the difference between, for example, the solid medals given by the British and the American medals that were hollow. English muskets were also in
a class apart and held in esteem by Indians, who rejected
European substitutes during the War of 1812.[21]

The British regarded the presents distributed to the Indians as a down payment for their future services and a
guarantee of continued support. Indians, however, consid-

ered presents as rewards for past services, as their source of supply in time of war, and as an indication of British power and commitment. British reliance upon presents to secure Indian friendship placed them in an awkward and embarrassing situation when goods were not available. Difficulties arising from shortages in the king's stores could be eased by purchasing goods from private traders in the area, and the Indians knew it.[22] The Indians received regular handouts, usually annually in peacetime, but the British supplemented these with additional gifts, especially to influential chiefs, as was thought to be merited or necessary. Some thought this practice got out of hand. Brigadier General Allan Maclean complained that "the People at the head of Indian Department Seem to Vie with Each other who Shall Expend Most Rum, and the great Chiefs are Striving who Shall Drink most Rum."[23]

The distribution of presents required vigilance and attention. In British eyes, Indians seemed to be indifferent to problems of transport and expense and to be concerned only with getting as much as they could. Indian expectations, they felt, frequently became unreasonable. The Indians seemed to possess a full repertoire of ruses and deceptions designed to secure the maximum amount of goods from their British suppliers. Late in the Revolution, the British realized that many of their forest allies wanted to prolong the conflict, with as little fighting as possible but with frequent supplies; and Indians were known to raise false alarms of enemy invasions in order to keep the flow of provisions coming. Indian warriors knew that if they left their guns and ammunition at home when they set out on an expedition, the British would have to rearm them in the field, and Indian women were said to send their men virtually naked to the British posts, knowing that they would be equipped anew. Indians even brought in old scalps in an effort to secure the bounties offered for fresh ones during the revolutionary war, and they used various ploys to obtain liquor.[24]

Not surprisingly, the Indian Department was regarded

as a source of enormous expense to the government. The department and the army faced the dilemma of trying to retain Indian loyalty at the same time as they had to economize in accordance with repeated instructions. The papers of Sir Frederick Haldimand, governor of Quebec from 1778 to 1786, abound with orders and efforts to reduce expenses, especially during the transition from war to peace, both by weeding out peculation and reducing Indian supplies. Nevertheless, the Indian Department remained open to abuse and corruption, with the Indians often shouldering the blame for the dishonesty of officials. Joseph Brant was not the only one to take umbrage that the Indians should be considered such an enormous expense when so many of the supplies intended for them never reached them.[25] It was never an easy matter to cut back on Indian presents; retrenchment after the Seven Years' War had been a major factor in bringing about Pontiac's Revolt in 1763. The quality and quantity of their manufactured goods gave the British an edge over their rivals in the competition for Indian allegiance; thus, within the Indian Department, a bountiful supply of presents gave the men responsible for their distribution corresponding power and prestige among the recipients. The role of gift-giver became a jealously guarded privilege, one that caused considerable controversy in the cases of John Norton and Robert Dickson. Norton was able to win to his interest Indians of another officer's region because, as one Indian explained: "As to the Snipe (Captain Norton) having got some of our young men to join him, I only say, He speaks loud, and has Strong Milk, and Big Breasts, which yield plentifully."[26]

Tribal rivalries, political ambitions, and personality clashes created factions within the Indian Department as men like John Norton and William Claus vied for positions of power and influence. The Department attracted persistent criticism, but in the face of Indian, departmental, individual, and national interests, little was achieved in the way of effective retrenchment and reform. As long as Britain continued to woo the tribes, it had to accept that gift giving and the problems and expense that it created was essential to the successful conduct of Indian relations.

In the chain of command and communication between London and the Indian country, the Indian Department was the link between the British authorities in Canada and the Indians. A fundamental problem raised by geographical and hierarchical considerations was the difficulty of adapting policies formulated in London or Quebec to the conditions existing in the Indian country where those policies had to be implemented. In the intricate world of tribal politics there could be no hard and fast rules or standard answers, and the British sometimes had to revise policy in order to avoid trouble. Since the situation could change rapidly and new problems arise from international, interracial, and inter- or intratribal developments, the critical work devolved upon the Indian agent present at the time. The agent was the ears, the voice, and the eyes in the Indian country of a government which, for reasons of time and distance, was effectively deaf, mute, and blind. He was a dual representative of the government and the Indians, a source of information and a means of executing policy, the last vital link between government and Indian. Broad governmental policies could, in the last resort, depend upon the agent for their success and even their implementation. His character and integrity, his prestige among the Indians, his ability to strike the correct balance between firmness and indulgence, between assertions of British power and pleas for help, his ability to assess the Indians' disposition and sincerity, and his honesty and fairness in distributing gifts from the king's stores, became factors of enormous importance when British policy came to depend upon individual relations at the grass-roots level. In recognition of the importance of the agent's position, the government issued periodic instructions as guidelines to conduct, stressing the need for patience and forbearance, persuasion, civility, solemnity, caution, regularity, and generosity (but with economy), in dealings with the Indians.[27] The agent also had to use his initiative and provide ad hoc answers to unexpected developments, even if that only meant evading the issue until orders arrived. The Indian agent, and often the commanding officer at a post too, had to be a frontier diplomat. He was expected to ensure a successful outcome to, and therefore be an expert participant in, the painstaking and time-consuming business of Indian diplomacy, with its ceremony, harangues, gift exchanges, and frustrations. He had to be acquainted with the subtleties and intricacies of Indian councils and to match Indian speakers who, far from being limited to monosyllabic utterances, were often first-rate orators and actors, expertly playing on the sensibilities of their audiences. Moreover, the agent had to be a man of infinite patience. Indians carried their extreme democratic practices over into their dealings with other tribes and powers, conducting all important business in formal and open council where all had a right to speak before any decision was reached. British representatives, at the foot of an orderly hierarchy, found such negotiations frustrating, tedious, repetitious, and often nonproductive. With the British supplying food and provisions for as long as the Indians were assembled, the latter saw little reason to hasten proceedings to a close. Indian councils could, and frequently did, drag on for days and even weeks. Brigadier General Allan Maclean reckoned from his experience that such councils served only to create expense and should be avoided whenever possible. He advocated sending officers out to the different nations, rather than having the chiefs of each nation meet at the British posts, because the chiefs were always accompanied by a full retinue of followers and hangers-on who made the visit costly and troublesome. Lieutenant John Enys said of an Indian council that took place at Niagara in July 1787 that it was "as unentertaining a thing as can well be to any but the Indians who generally get presents and Liquor enough to make them all drunk."[28]

British Indian diplomacy depended upon assembling delegates from distant tribes at key locations. The great multitribal council held at Sandusky in the late summer of 1783 took some ten days simply to assemble, from dispatch of the runners to the arrival of the last of the tribes.[29] Council proceedings eventually got under way, perhaps with a procession to the meeting place, followed by the formal smoking of the calumet, expressions of gratitude offered to the Great Spirit for the opportunity to meet, fraternal greetings, and the ceremony of condolence in which wampum was presented to symbolically wipe the eyes and ears and to clear the throats of those attending so that the council might proceed without impediment. After the preliminaries came recapitulations of previous meetings, with reference to wampum belts as the Indian records of proceedings, and the actual business of the council, conducted in lengthy talks. The business was punctuated by mutual assurances of good faith, by consultations and adjournments, and by the presentation and acceptance of wampum belts to emphasize the truth and importance of what was said and to serve as symbols of binding agreement. Finally, the British gave the Indians liquor—having withheld it to the last to ensure sobriety and as a disincentive to delay—and encouraged them to return to their camps.[30]

This elaborate ceremony of forest diplomacy and council fire rhetoric could prove extremely frustrating to British officers and agents who were eager to conclude business that might have a crucial bearing on international relations. The government recognized the importance of meeting the Indians on their own terms, however, and official policy demanded that, "All Public Meetings should be conducted with the greatest decorum and formality, those present assuming an Air of Seriousness and Gravity, which command Respect with, and is very pleasing to Indians."[31] The government believed that such occasions served as an opportunity to exert British influence and further British interests among the tribes. British speeches were delivered in a tone of friendship and firmness, stressing both the strength and generosity of the king and the need for the Indians to remain loyal and fulfill their commitments.[32] Europeans generally adopted the Indians' style of speech when in council with them. Indians employed kinship terminology in council, depending upon the relative standing and seniority of the party, Indian or white, with whom they were dealing. Thus, the Shawnees addressed the Wyandots as their elder brothers. The British readily adopted similar terms of address as indicating the Indians' relationship to the representatives of the king. Governor Frederick Haldimand, for example, was portrayed to the Indians as the father who could bestow protection or withdraw it if his Indian children did not behave as they ought.[33]

Operating in an Indian world, the British employed existing methods of communication with the scattered tribes. Indian runners carrying wampum belts or other tokens represented the quickest and surest means of reaching bands far from such centers of Anglo-Indian relations as Niagara, Detroit, and the Miami towns.[34] The system of wilderness communications did not always function to the advantage of the British, however. They were unable to control the diffusion of news through the Indian world, and information leaks, false reports, and rumors irritated and angered the authorities. "Indian news" became a synonym for suspect information. Officials tried continually to curb the spread of rumors and to discourage the Indians from listening to "bad birds." Agents and officers in the Indian country had instructions to tell the Indians only what they knew to be facts.[35] In times of international or intertribal tension careless talk could produce catastrophic results and the agent was expected to exercise control over what the Indians heard.

British involvement in tribal society also necessitated a degree of entanglement in Indian politics. The successful agent had to tread carefully lest he arouse jealousies either by usurping authority himself or by favoring unduly one chief or faction. The situation was never very stable, and agents had the unenviable task of trying to maintain amicable relations with chiefs who often seemed as fickle as they were skilled practitioners of council fire politics. Nor could the British afford to become embroiled in the turmoil of intertribal hostilities and feuds; alliance with one tribe must not earn Britain the enmity of that tribe's enemies. The agent had to navigate the turbulent and treacherous waters of inter and intratribal animosity. His own judgment and abilities, backed by the reputation and resources of the Crown, constituted his safeguards against disaster. Small wonder that one agent complained wearily of "the old Subject of the intrigues and cabals of the Six Nations."[36]

The Indian agent could command tremendous influence over the tribes in his region, but on the whole the agent's lot did not seem particularly enviable. Even a deputy superintendent general of Indian affairs, William Claus, complained that he enjoyed no privacy because the Indians regarded his home as an open house whenever their business brought them to Niagara.[37] George Ironside, a clerk and storekeeper in the Indian Department at Detroit, who held an M.A. from King's College, Aberdeen, and had an Indian wife, felt himself similarly plagued in 1795. He wrote to his superior, Alexander McKee: "I could really wish you were here as [the Indians] are such jealous stupid wretches that I am at a loss how to deal with them. They say they have a great many other complaints to make, what they are God knows." Ironside's troubles were compounded by the arrival of George White Eyes, a pro-American Delaware employed by Anthony Wayne, who was working mischief as fast as he could.[38]

Officers, agents, and traders farther west had to endure monotony, loneliness, privations, and frequent near-starvation. Duncan Graham, an officer in the Indian Department, found himself at Prairie du Chien in March 1815, with the neighboring Indians starving as a result of the British government's failure to supply them with ammunition at the proper time. He committed his discomfort to paper: "It is easier for you to judge than for me to describe our situation here. We are nearly on the eve of seeing upwards of two thousand Indians, and not a pipe of tobacco, nor a shot of powder to give them. As for eating it is out of the question. I wish to ask you as a friend, whether you would wish to be a doorkeeper in hell, or be concerned in the Indian Department on such footing." Conditions were made even worse by the development of party spirit and factions between the men of the garrison and the Indian Department, and Graham reckoned that three months of winter and worry had made trader-agent Robert Dickson look ten years older.

Here we are, posted since last Fall, without news from any quarter, and destitute of provisions, sociability, harmony or good understanding. Not even a glass of grog, nor a pipe of tobacco, to pass away the time, and if a brief period don't bring a change for the better, I much dread the United Irishmen's wish will befall this place, which God forbid it should—a bad Winter, a worse Spring, a bloody Summer, and no king. Owing to scarcity of provisions here, a gloom appears on every countenance; and if ever I take an idea to resign, I mean to recommend Mr. Hurtibis to supply my place, as I think him the properest person in the time of famine, as he has no teeth.[39]

Graham's may have been an extreme case, but it does show the despondency that could affect those isolated in the Indian country. Lieutenant Colonel William McKay, the captor of Prairie du Chien from the Americans in 1814, complained that "a man having to do with Indians in my present situation is more tormented than if in the infernal regions." Even Robert Dickson, a fur trader with considerable experience of life in the wilderness and dealings with Indians, had had enough in the winter of early 1814. His normally difficult position was aggravated by war, Indian waverings, lack of supplies, and the threat of starvation. Dickson ended one letter: "I want to get rid of the people, Indians, & c. Adieu." In another, he wrote that he was surrounded by starving Indians and confessed, "I am heartily tired of this kind of Life—anything for a Change."[40]

Moreover, just as the attitudes of the Indians toward Britain were influenced by the agent who worked among them, so too their relations with that agent were affected by the conduct of Britain in its dealings with the Indians. The plight of the agent who had to explain changes of governmental policy and apparent British perfidy to Indians who now regarded him as at best powerless to implement his promises, at worst a liar, could be extremely embarrassing.

The Indian agent or officer in the Indian country did, however, possess a power to influence policy far out of proportion to his official position. Not only did the agent translate official policy into language and terms the Indians could understand, but given the British government's preoccupation with revolutionary and Napoleonic France, he became increasingly responsible for the implementation of that policy insofar as it concerned the Indians. The government in London depended on the governor in Quebec; he in turn relied on the lieutenant governor, who relied on the superintendent general of Indian affairs and the agents resident among the Indians. It needed only a slight shift of emphasis at each level of command for official policy as formulated in London to assume a different character by the time it was being translated to the Indians around a wilderness council fire.

Here lay the roots of the difference between official and effective British policy, since the outlook of the men responsible for that policy varied according to their location. Ministers in London viewed British North America as part of a worldwide empire and in the light of international considerations. To them the Indians were of regional and distant importance. The authorities in Quebec were concerned for the future and safety of the colony, and the Indians loomed larger in their thinking. For agents in the Indian country, however, local and native problems took immediate precedence. The government had to rely on the men in contact with the Indians, but to do so ran the risk of deviation from official policy. The actions of isolated individuals in response to local developments could well be inconsistent with the instructions they received. Even the lieutenant governor of Upper Canada could be so out of touch with the government in London as to be pursuing, in effect, policies contradictory to orders from across the Atlantic. In the summer of 1794, John Graves Simcoe was convinced that John Jay's peace mission to England would be fruitless and that war with the United States was inevitable. Governor Lord Dorchester, Lieutenant Governor Simcoe, and Alexander McKee each assumed this to be the case and said as much to the Indians. Meanwhile, however, instructions were on their way from Whitehall ordering that a contrary course of action be taken. The situation is perhaps best illustrated by Simcoe's statement on 15 November 1794 to the commanding officer at Detroit, that, in his opinion, the western posts, which Britain had held contrary to the treaty since 1783, were as far from being given up to the United States as they had even been. Three days later, Jay's Treaty was signed, and Simcoe was ordered to prepare the Indians for the surrender of those same posts.[41] With cabinet and lieutenant governor so out of touch, there was little likelihood of Indian agents conforming rigidly to the wishes of a government several months and various intermediaries away.

Of course, the individual agent could often defer action and evade embarrassing questions by pointing out to the Indians that he was "only a small Finger of the hand of your Father at Quebec" and could do nothing without orders.[42] Sometimes, however, the Indian agent had to act on his own initiative, and it was then unfortunate that he could not always be trusted to act without bias. British agents who worked, married, and spent most of their lives among the Indians developed a degree of sympathy for them. That sympathy, however, could jeopardize the success of such delicate policies as those pursued before the War of 1812, when Britain was preparing the Indians for war, but at the same time restraining them from taking up the hatchet until the right time. As Major General Isaac Brock realized, Matthew Elliott, who was in charge of the Indian Department at Amherstburg in 1811, was a good man and highly respected by the Indians, but he had, from living so much among them, inevitably imbibed their feelings and prejudices. So, "although I entertain great respect for the personal character of Mr. Elliott, yet I should be unwilling to place entire dependence, in an affair of such manifest importance, upon a judgement biassed [sic] and prejudiced, as his is known to be in everything that regards the Indians. To act with due prudence, he participates in and feels too keenly the grievous wrongs they have suffered."[43]

Perhaps Alexander McKee, who like Elliott had married into and lived among the Shawnees, offers the best example of an agent "adapting" British policy to suit Indian interest, as he saw them, in relations with the United States. In the summer of 1793, Simcoe complained to McKee that some Shawnee emissaries to the Creeks and Cherokees had assured the southern Indians that Britain intended to aid the tribes in their war against the States. The Shawnees had no authorization to make such promises, but Simcoe probably addressed the complaint to the right man, since the Shawnees, unless it was pure fabrication on their part, had obviously been led to expect British help by somebody. McKee may well have induced the Indians to mistake his wishful thinking for a statement of official policy.[44] McKee seems also to have exerted his considerable influence in deciding the Shawnee-led western tribes to hold out for the Ohio boundary in their proposed meeting with the American commissioners, to be held at Sandusky in 1793. Joseph Brant had hoped the Indian confederacy would accept a compromise boundary, and he blamed McKee for the intransigence of the Shawnee faction, saying that the agent had held private midnight meetings, from which he, Brant, was excluded, with the key chiefs of the western tribes.[45] Indeed, after the resultant breakdown in negotiations and the split in the Indian confederacy, McKee wrote to Simcoe, in effect defending him-

self in advance against the accusations which he expected
would be leveled at him:

> However conscious I may be of having used no improper
> influence in the Councils of the Confederacy, so as to prevent
> the attainment of peace, which I again assure your Excellency,
> would have afforded me a most sensible gratification; I never-
> theless expect from the malevolent, disappointed & all ill dis-
> posed, to be blamed for the Opinions which the Indians have
> adopted for their Resolution which put an end to the Negotia-
> tion. I shall not, however, lament on account of their Animad-
> versions while I continue to be honoured with your Excellency's
> Approbation of my conduct.[46]

Why McKee should have expected criticism if he had done
nothing to merit it is open to question, but presumably he
lost no sleep; a month later Simcoe recommended him
for an increase in salary. Indeed, in his report to Lord
Dorchester, the lieutenant governor pictured the western
tribes as persisting in their demand for the Ohio boundary
despite McKee's efforts, and laid the blame for the split in
the confederacy at the feet of Joseph Brant rather than the
deputy superintendent of Indian affairs.[47]

The American commissioners clearly believed that the
British agents were calling the tune in the negotiations. On
August 1, Simon Girty translated the speech of a Wyandot
chief, telling the commissioners they might as well return
to Washington. As the council was breaking up, Matthew
Elliott went to the Shawnee chief, Kakaipalathy, and told
him that the last part of the speech was wrong. The Shawnee returned to the council and said the speech was wrong.
Girty said he had interpreted what the Wyandot chief had
said. A hurried consultation followed, and then Girty
asked the commissioners to remain where they were until
the Indians had time to consult their head warriors.[48]
Though Simcoe exonerated McKee from charges of ex-
ceeding his authority by promising British support as a
boost to the western Indians' intransigence, he could not
totally discount the possibility of British interference in the

Indians' councils. Writing to the Duke of Portland, he said: "At the same time your Grace must be convinced that the different *Traders* from interest, would make use of that language which would best conciliate the favour of the Indians; and that the *British Officers,* not immediately entrusted with particular duties in respect to those People, could not be at all times prevented from expressing in strong terms, that Compassion, which in this Province, is universally felt for those unhappy Nations."[49]

Obviously, if McKee did exceed his authority and did hold secret meetings with various Indians, he left no written record of his machinations, and Brant was not the most reliable and unbiased of commentators. Nevertheless, it does not seem that McKee acted merely as a disinterested observer, and one reason for the unpopularity of the Indian Department in Upper Canada was the widespread belief that the Indian-American hostilities "have been fomented and supported by Persons in the Department, not on public, but personal motives; and beyond the Orders or intentions of Government."[50]

Their own sympathies aside, agents had a difficult task in implementing policies that often seemed contradictory, especially to the Indians to whom those policies had to be explained (or from whom they had to be concealed). Thus in 1811 the British government wanted the Indians to be made ready for war and to be made to understand that Britain expected their help if and when an Anglo-American conflict broke out. At the same time, the Indians had to be restrained from committing any acts that might bring about that war. The Indian agent thus faced a virtually impossible task since to supply the Indians with arms and ammunition in anticipation of war constituted a virtual invitation to begin hostilities, which belied British verbal restraint. In short, wrote Lieutenant Governor Francis Gore to William Claus, "it will be expected from the Department under your Superintendence that His Majesty's Government, as far as may be, should preserve its faith with the United States of America, and its relations with the

John Graves Simcoe (1752–1806). As lieutenant governor of Upper Canada, Simcoe faced a difficult situation when Indian expectations of British assistance against the Americans threatened to embroil his colony in international conflict. (Public Archives of Canada, Ottawa; C-13182)

Indian Nations unimpaired, by the most liberal construction of neutrality towards the former, and benevolence to the latter."[51] In the light of strained Anglo-American relations and the conditions on the frontier in 1811, it was easier for the government to expect such a happy situation than for the Indian agent to effect it.

In sum, distance and the need to delegate responsibility placed the Indian agents in the forefront of Anglo-Indian, and even Indian-American, relations. However, those agents, by their background, sympathies, and location, were not the people most likely to implement British policies without favor or modification, nor without upsetting an already delicately balanced international situation. Americans were all aware of the dichotomy between the avowals of the government in London and the conduct of its agents in the Indian country. Looking back over "a bitter experience of thirty years," John Quincy Adams proclaimed in 1818 that "all the Indian Wars in which we had been involved, had been kindled by the pestilential breath of British Agents and Traders, in whose intrigues and machinations the British Government had loudly and invariably disclaimed having had any participation."[52]

In actuality, the British Indian Department was able to maintain good relations with the Indian tribes as potential allies, but was unable to prevent the drift to war which necessitated employment of those allies. When that war broke out in 1812, the department reverted to the role it had fulfilled during the Revolution—supplying and directing the Crown's Indian allies against the Americans.

Part Two

THE MEETING OF CULTURES

3

British Views of Indian Life

IN THE YEARS BETWEEN 1783 and 1815, a considerable number of British subjects came into contact with North American Indians in their native environment. Indian agents, fur traders, soldiers, travelers, and missionaries entered the Indian world, and though few went there for the purpose of observing Indian cultures, many left written accounts of the peoples and ways of life they encountered. These records are often of limited value as accurate observations of Indian life and cultures, but they constitute invaluable documentation of British perceptions of themselves, of the Indians they encountered, and of the process of cultural interaction. British views of Indian society inevitably were bound up with evaluations of their own civilization; British observers judged and described Indians according to their own beliefs, values, and institutions.

Euro-Americans employed mirror images of themselves to describe Indians, and many opinions and attitudes rested on preconceptions about "savagery" and "civilization."[1] By "civilization" Britons usually meant a settled way of life, an agricultural subsistence, an identifiable social and political order, a Christian (preferably Protestant) religion, "proper" modes of sexual and social behavior, facility in the English language, a degree of literacy, possession of material comforts, and abandonment of native dress and

79

hairstyles. British descriptions of Indian societies tended, therefore, to be couched in negative terms and to point out what the Indians "lacked" in laws, discipline, religion, and "progress." The points on which the British felt themselves superior, however, had little meaning for native societies who inhabited a different world and who viewed that world in terms incomprehensible to most of George III's subjects.

In the decades following the American Revolution, British men and women of different backgrounds and prejudices, with varying degrees of awareness, sensitivity, and tolerance, encountered native peoples possessing widely divergent customs and characteristics. Consequently, different opinions were voiced on the same tribe, and whatever one observer said about Indians from his experience of one group was subject to qualification by reference to other groups who displayed dissimilar traits. Robert Berkhofer regards the tendency to generalize from one tribe's society and culture to all Indians as a persistent feature of white interpretations of Indians, and traveler John Ferdinand Dalziel Smyth recognized that "seeing one nation will enable a person to form a very just and exact opinion of all the rest."[2] Nevertheless, many commentators in this period recognized diversity in the tribal societies, and some noted that there was often as much difference between one tribe and another as there was between nations elsewhere in the world.[3]

Travelers and explorers frequently confused different tribes and locations and sometimes mistook separate bands and villages of the same tribe as distinct tribes in themselves, with the result that information about tribal locations and populations was often grossly inaccurate.[4] By 1811 the interior tribes of North America had been so frequently described by a host of travelers that, according to John Pinkerton's *Modern Geography,* little needed to be said about them. Many of that work's comments, notably on totemism and cannibalism among Northwest Coast In-

dians, suggest that much of the vast amount of information available about Indians was erroneous.[5]

Even experienced observers made mistakes. Fur trader
Daniel Harmon, venturing to speak about Indians with
whom he was not personally acquainted, said that the
Flatheads practiced head deformation; in fact, the Flatheads acquired their misnomer from coastal neighbors
who did practice ornamental head deformation and therefore regarded an undeformed head as flat.[6] Likewise, David
Thompson had either his Indians or his notions of mo-
rality confused when he wrote that the Fall Indians demanded "the strictest chastity" of their women. Thompson
confused the Fall Indians, otherwise known as the Atsinas
or Gros Ventres of the plains, with the Hidatsas or Gros
Ventres of the Missouri, calling both tribes Fall Indians
and thinking them separated bands of the same people. In
fact they were unrelated; the Hidatsas were a Siouan
group, while the Atsinas belonged to the Algonquian family. Alexander Henry traded among the Atsinas and, unlike Thompson, correctly distinguished them from the
Missouri tribe. Henry found them to be anything but
chaste; he regarded them as without shame or modesty
and complained that they proved troublesome in offering
their wives and daughters as articles of temporary barter.[7]

When the "experts" erred and disagreed, it was not surprising that reading Englishmen and women occasionally
received conflicting and misleading reports on American
Indians. The *Quarterly Review,* like Harmon, believed er-
roneously that it was the Flatheads who deformed their
heads. In 1808 the London *Times,* basing its judgment on
American sources, declared that the Arikara Indians appeared to be "the most barbarous and uncivilized race on
the whole Continent, as they have no customs that at all resemble those of human beings." They apparently went
naked with no sense of shame or decency, were mostly covered with vermin, ate raw meat out of the same dishes as
their dogs, smeared fat on their bodies, and never cut their

nails. Seven years later, the *Quarterly Review,* on the basis of
Lewis and Clark's published travels, described these same
Indians as "a fine tribe in stature and person, and with
many good qualities," who were abstemious and disgusted
by the excesses of white traders.[8]

Although much of the information available is thus of
little or dubious value, a survey of the sources does convey
an overall impression of British perceptions of Indian life.
Even travelers' lies can be informative because biased opinions and distorted truths are as valuable as coldly reported
facts in discerning attitudes of one culture toward another.

What emerges from a study of British appraisals of
tribal life is that Britons viewed the Indian world with a
mixture of attraction and revulsion. British reactions to
Indians varied from "noble redman" to "dirty savage."
Tribal societies struck many Britons as having lives of extremes and unfathomable paradoxes. Charles Mackenzie,
a trader with the North West Company, declared:

> I believe that whoever has studied the Indians and the nature
> of their passions must have been struck with their versatility.
> Their whole life is a life of extremes. No being can bear with
> more fortitude a wound inflicted at war, but should they cut
> their feet accidentally with an axe, should they fall sick, they are
> quite the reverse. They are indolent, capricious, contemptuous,
> revengeful and domineering to the extreme, and yet their pas-
> sions do not seem to disturb the quiet of their mind, which al-
> most always appears regular and calm.

Captain Thomas Anderson expressed similar sentiments
about the Winnebago Indians of Rock River with whom he
spent the winter of 1802–03. Anderson found them "the
most filthy, most obstinate, and the bravest people of any
Indian tribe I have met with."[9] Nor was the character of a
given tribe uniformly the same as that of the individuals
composing it. As David Thompson said of the Piegans:
"The character of these people appear[s] to be brave, steady
and deliberate, but on becoming acquainted with them
there is no want of individual character, and almost every
character in civilized society can be traced among them,

from the gravity of a judge to a merry jester, and from open hearted generosity to the avaricious miser."[10]

Indian ways of life held a certain amount of attraction for many whites and a great deal of attraction for a few. The degree of vice or virtue accorded to Indians often tended to increase and diminish according to the closeness of the contact, but the Indian way of life exerted its attraction irrespective of distance. Life on the frontier ensured no immunity from the desire to live like and with the Indians; nor was living in London any guarantee that one would fall victim to the urge. Dr. Samuel Johnson, who dominated intellectual life in eighteenth-century England, had little admiration for people whom he regarded as savages, and he certainly had no desire to partake of their existence.[11] On the other hand, the impulse to "go native" was not confined to any one particular class; common frontiersmen, women and children, traders, and at least one gentleman of fortune, education, and refinement, all fell under the spell.[12] Attraction to the Indian way of life, then, depended largely upon the circumstances and how receptive the individual was to its lure. De Crèvecoeur, the "American Farmer," contemplated returning to nature, but feared to do so lest his younger children be caught by its charm and prefer their new carefree existence to civilized life. He reckoned that there must be something singularly captivating and more congenial to man's natural dispositions in Indian life than could be found in civilization.[13]

The stories of some whites taken captive by Indians gave British readers further evidence that the Indian way of life exerted a magnetic influence. Indians took captives often for the specific purpose of adopting them into the tribe to offset losses suffered in war, and from the moment of capture, they made sustained efforts to purge the prisoners of their "whiteness" and to educate them in Indian ways. The process was remarkably effective, especially among young captives, and many whites remained with their captors. Captives who were liberated often expressed real grief at being separated from their Indian friends and relatives and anguish at the prospect of returning to their former homes. Even those who returned to white society willingly sometimes retained a lingering affection for the Indians with whom they had lived in captivity. Others, especially women who had been abducted into Indian camps, felt ostracized from the white world. While many whites chose to live among the Indians, few Indians seemed willing to renounce their supposedly savage life for the blessing of civilization.[14] That the history of the American frontier furnished many examples of people who rejected their own Euro-American society to live with the Indians enhanced the notion that Indian life had much to offer.[15]

The captivity narrative enjoyed enormous popularity as a literary genre, but it would be going too far to attribute this popularity to the appeal of the Indian way of life. In many cases, published narratives of capture and escape from Indians were simply blood-and-thunder stories in which sensationalism, horror, and adventure predominated at the expense of any serious insight into Indian culture or any accurate record of experience. Moreover, while the authors of some valuable and authentic narratives might declare their preference for the Indian way of life, such professions should be taken lightly since the authors obviously had returned to white society and chosen to stay there.[16]

Recognition of admirable qualities in the Indian way of life did not necessarily instill the urge to share that existence. Charles Mackenzie spent six pleasant days with the Cheyennes in 1806, but he expressed no desire to make his stay permanent.[17] On the other hand, resistance to the appeal of living the free and easy life of "the virtuous though uncultivated Indian" did not necessarily imply blindness to the qualities possessed by the Indians or obtaining in their society. During the War of 1812, George Gleig participated in a British embassy to the Choctaws. When confronted with the assembled Indians he felt compelled, "*almost in spite of myself,* to regard these half-naked wretches with veneration.[18] Alexander Ross, looking back over many years' experience in the Indian trade, wrote:

However strongly we may abhor heathenism, and deprecate the savage character in its natural state as compared to civilized humanity, yet we ought not in our zeal for the one or abhorrence of the other to suppress the truth; and the truth, therefore, compels us to admit that there are many traits of virtue to be met with in the Indian character. They are brave, generous, and often charitable; and to their credit be it said that there is less crime in an Indian camp of 500 souls than there is in a civilized village of but half that number. Let the lawyer or moralist point out the cause.[19]

In similar vein, David Thompson maintained that though the Indian must suffer in comparison with educated and Christian people from Europe, he was nevertheless fully equal to those of his own "class" there. From his observations on the Crees, Thompson declared that: "Those acts that pass between man and man for generous charity and kind compassion in civilized society, are no more than what is everyday practised by these Savages; as acts of common duty."[21] Many Britons who knew them well took pains to point out that, contrary to popular belief, the Indians possessed virtues. As Indian agent George Woodbine wrote to Lieutenant Colonel Edward Nicholls: "The Indian Character has been much mistaken and has been most unjustly stegmatized [sic] as bloody and ferocious, you have been long enough among them to observe many most amiable traits in them, which only want the fostering hand of instruction and the light of Christianity to mature."[21] In fact, what Europeans considered to be the Indians' virtues were often more likely to disappear than to mature under the influence of European civilization.

Indian hospitality was almost proverbial. No matter how poor the tribe, a visitor was assured of food and shelter, and some whites suffered considerable embarrassment because their Indian hosts' ideas of sharing included wives and daughters.[22] The Indians' natural politeness earned favorable comment, as did instances of native honesty.[23] Equally admirable for some was the fact that Indian societies were governed by custom and kinship rather than by laws, kings, and governments; for others, most impressive was the way in which many tribes successfully preserved individual freedom within social systems that ensured that the weak and poor were provided for.[24] Northern bands might abandon the old and infirm to the elements in times of dire necessity, but the Indians' care for the less fortunate, plus their universally acknowledged fondness for and kindness toward their children, prompted Andrew Graham to recollect that: "Nature has implanted into the rudest savages some principles of humanity and association and parental affection, perhaps in a stronger degree than civilized nations are endowed with."[25]

In addition to these virtues, British observers recognized qualities of dignity and nobility in Indians. A number of Indian speakers frequently impressed listeners with their considerable oratorical powers, and Governor Simcoe's lady likened them to the orators of ancient Greece and Rome.[26] The Indians' supposed stoicism perhaps did most to earn them a reputation for dignity. British commentators commonly pointed out that Indian impassiveness and apathy were affected rather than real and liable to dissolve under the influence of drink, but they viewed with respect the Indian warrior's ability to stifle displays of fear, pain, sorrow, or joy as the situation demanded.[27]

Good qualities that were attributed to the Indians were widely regarded as stemming from the environment, the product of harsh necessity rather than a sign of inherent Indian virtue. In the same way, Indians were considered most talented in the performance of peculiarly "Indian" activities. George Heriot maintained that Indians esteemed no qualities except ability in hunting and war and fortitude and perseverance in suffering and hardship. Others commented on Indian woodmanship, agility, and powers of endurance. Isaac Weld cited the example of a young Wyandot brave who ran 80 miles in one day, apparently without fatigue. Explorer Alexander Mackenzie had thought his Canadians the most expert canoe handlers in the world, but they themselves had to admit that they were inferior in this skill to the Indians of the Bella Coola River.[28]

Some observers said that the only obstacle to the Indians' complete happiness was their propensity for revenge.[29] Some favorable commentators, however, pointed to what they saw as the limitations in Indian culture. John Lambert confessed himself impressed with the intelligence of one Indian chief, but regretted "that such an excellent genius should be sunk in the petty chieftain of a horde of wild savages." Hugh Gray could not say whether the Indian possessed mental powers equal to those of Europeans because, he said, allowance had to be made for the fact that Indian environment and society called for the display of only certain kinds of talents.[30] When Britons acknowledged instances of Indian virtue and the attractiveness of Indian life, they frequently qualified their observations, as when Francis Baily attributed his favorable impression of Cherokee life to the gratitude he felt toward Indians who had fed him and his hungry companions.[31]

British travelers and commentators regularly pointed out what they considered to be the virtuous aspects of Indian life, but firsthand observation did little to enhance the notion that the Indian was a "noble savage." Hugh Gray saw hundreds of Indians on his travels, but he felt that they were such a miserable, disgusting, filthy, vermin-ridden, stupid-looking weaklings that their extinction would be no great loss to humanity.[32] John Lambert's experience of Indians was limited likewise to the acculturated peoples of Lower Canada, and he found nothing in the "half-civilized, half-savage wretches" who wandered the streets half-naked and clutching a bottle of rum to resemble "the Indian warrior, whose high-minded pride and spirit have been so much extolled."[33] Tribes farther removed from contact with white society did not always fare much better. Writing from his experience on the Missouri, French-Canadian trader Pierre-Antoine Tabeau reported:

"If the Ricara, if the Sioux, is the man of nature so much praised by poets, every poetic license has been taken in painting him; for their picture makes a beautiful contrast to that which I have before me. All that one can say is that, if these barbarians leave no doubt that they are human, intelligent beings, it is only because they have the form, the face, and the faculty of speech of human beings." Tabeau emphasized his point by listing the "barbarians'" vices at some length.[34] Travelers frequently derived a poor impression of Indians in general from their first meeting with a particular group, and many would have agreed with the statement of one traveler who came across none of the high qualities attributed to Indians: "If I carried with me any respect for savage life, it is obvious that I brought none away."[35]

British observers frequently indulged in speculation as to the origins of the American Indians, and as to whether they were of Jewish, Asian, or even Welsh descent. James Adair, who had had almost forty years' experience as agent and trader among the southern Indians, and among the Chickasaws in particular, devoted the first half of his *History of the American Indians,* published in 1775, to proving that the Indians were the descendants of the lost tribes of Israel. Others, like Quaker missionary Ann Mifflin, saw evidence of the Indians' Asiatic origins. The theory that the Indians were of Welsh descent also received considerable credit during this period. The Mandan in particular were reckoned to be the descendants of a twelfth-century Welsh prince named Madoc, and several attempts were made to locate the "Welsh Indians."[36]

Usually, however, the physical appearance of the Indians first attracted the Europeans' attention. Descriptions of Indians varied enormously, of course, as did, for example, opinions as to whether the Indians were beardless by choice or by nature and whether their complexions were dusky genetically or simply as a result of exposure to the elements.[37] As a rule, British observers judged according to European ideas of beauty and found Indian women to be far less attractive than Indian men. Britons were surprised to find that Indian braves took greater pains over their appearance than did Indian women. Fur trader Alexander Henry's description of the Siksikas, or Northern Blackfeet, accorded with white reactions to many of the Plains tribes: "The young men appear proud and haughty, and are particular to keep their garments and robes clean. The women are a filthy set." Irishman Ross Cox expressed a similar sentiment with regard to the Indians of the Columbia River; he found the men "horribly disgusting," but, "Then the women,—Oh ye gods!"[38] Lady Liston, wife of British diplomat Robert Liston, was impressed by the handsome young men she saw on her journey through the remnants of the Catawba Nation in 1797, but not by the females, who seemed very ugly to her. George Gleig thought Choctaw women "as much the reverse of beautiful as it is easy to conceive," and described them as timid and servile drudges whose figures were ruined by hard labor and whose faces were disfigured by ornaments.[39] The harsh life of Indian women exerted a telling effect on their beauty and they seemed to European observers to age prematurely. Time and again, Britons described Indian women as dirty, repulsive, and lacking any sense of decency. Fur traders and trappers who spent long months in the wilderness commonly desired Indian women, but David Thompson's party, nearing the end of their journey to the Pacific Coast in 1811, refused the offer of Indian women; the latter were "so devoid of temptation that not one pretended to understand them."[40]

Occasionally, a trader or traveler would acknowledge that they might find Indian women attractive if they had fair skins and wore flattering dresses instead of having dusky complexions and wrapping themselves in dirty blankets. Even the *Quarterly Review* realized that the practice of head deformation (which, the magazine suggested, tended to increase the Indians' "natural stupidity") showed that "their ideas of beauty do not much accord with those of the old world."[41] To judge by the relations of European fur traders with Indian women, inherited notions of beauty did not prove to be an unsurmountable barrier, and Robert Hunter, Jr., a young London merchant, certainly found Indian girls attractive. Many of his observations, as he traveled the length of North America, concerned the opposite sex. Even Alexander Henry, who was usually vocal in his denunciations of Indian women as repulsive and indecent, seemed to be covering his eyes yet peeping through his fingers at the sight of some women bathing: "The disgusting creatures were perfectly composed, and seemed not to notice me. Although they stood naked in different postures, yet so close did they keep their thighs together that nothing could be seen."[42]

Europeans often maintained that the sexual practices of Indian women were as disgusting as their physical appearance, and they frequently commented that chastity was rarely considered a virtue, much less an essential, in Indian womanhood. Many Britons displayed a considerable interest in Indian marriage customs and sexual practices. Few, however, went so far as did Alexander Henry in his discussion of "unnatural lusts" among the Crows and the Hidatsas.[43] Almost the whole range of variations in marriage customs found throughout the world existed in North America,[44] but the one that aroused the most comment was the practice of polygamy, or, to be more exact, polygyny. British observers considered Indians to be sexually lax, although many tribes inflicted severe punishments for adultery, and tribal custom frequently demanded restraint and respect between particular members of the sexes. Polygyny was not a means of satisfying carnal desires, it was a product of necessity and served to take care of the surplus of women created by losses in war. Alexander Ross, judging by his European and Christian moral standards, thought polygamy the greatest source of evil among an otherwise happy people. But, judged by the circumstances of Indian life, the taking of several wives was a necessary good rather than an unnatural evil.[45]

Marriages in Indian society tended to be economic arrangements that created and strengthened social bonds between families and clans. A warrior-hunter needed women to tend to his catch and his home, just as women needed a man to provide food and protection. And all individuals needed kinship ties to give them a position in society. Consequently, many tribes practised the sororate and levirate, whereby a widow or widower would marry the brother or sister of the deceased spouse in order to take care of them or be taken care of, and to maintain the kinship tie. British observers looked with disdain on Indian marriage practices, but marriages in Georgian England were often social and economic arrangements, and kinship ties and family connections were of prime importance among the upper ranks of English society, as well as among the Scottish clans who dominated the Canadian fur trade.

Similar economic reasoning partly explained the male-female division of labor that attracted a great deal of attention and adverse comment from white observers. The drudgery, hard labor, and maltreatment Indian women endured was invariably contrasted with the idleness of the men, who, when not away fighting or hunting, seemed to sit around smoking. Lady Liston naturally felt the injustice of the comparison more acutely than did most male observers. She came across a party of Indians returning home from Niagara, burdened with their annual supply of presents from the British. The women staggered along, weighed down by goods and children, but "The lordly Husband is loaded only with his *Gun* on his shoulder, and the *Rum* for which he has possibly exchanged half his Blankets,—in his head." According to John Bradbury, Sioux women were so badly treated that they often destroyed their female offspring to save them from such misfortune and sometimes committed suicide.[46] There was ample evidence to support the view that Indians did regard and treat their women as inferior. British males ignored other female roles and assumed that all women could hope to do was to bear sons who would one day become warriors. The problems and demands facing Indian societies, and the expectations of the individuals within those societies were, however, very different from those of modern western society and of most of eighteenth-century British society. Englishmen conceived of agriculture as something done by the males; the sight of Indian women cultivating crops convinced them that Indian men were idle. The women attended to the continuous and laborious tasks and left the men free to concentrate on the strenuous, but less constant, activities of fighting and hunting. Travelers who denounced Indian men for their indolence usually saw them only in their idle moments at home, not when they were away at war or hunting. A man who accused Indian warriors of laziness had obviously not run endless miles from sunup to sunset with an Indian war party.

The exigencies of the environment dictated the Indian way of life and provided some explanation for apparently unfeeling and inhumane conduct. Nowhere was this more true than in the abandonment of the old and infirm by northern Indians, notably the Chipewyans. This practice, which provided the inspiration for William Wordsworth's "The Complaint of a Forsaken Indian Woman" (1798), was a necessary response to a harsh environment wherein the safety of the traveling band as a whole could not be jeopardized by the weakness of a few. Even among the Chippewas farther south, treatment of the old was apparently dictated by the reasoning that once a person was of no use he was as dead to his society, and the band was no longer bound to support him.[47] Such harsh realities tempered any lingering notions that observers might entertain about Indians living happily in a state of nature. To many commentators, Indian life seemed prone to tragedy and suffering.

In their comments on the Indians' appearance, conduct, customs, and practices, British observers inevitably judged Indian society by their own standards. Some, like David Thompson, Andrew Graham, and Alexander Ross, made a conscious effort to view Indian culture and society objectively and to recognize that man was a product of his environment,[48] but there was nevertheless considerable misunderstanding and misinterpretation of Indian life. Nowhere was this more evident than in observations of Indian religion. Time and again, in both British and American sources, Indian religious beliefs were dismissed with a statement to the effect that the Indians had some vague notion of a supreme being and a future state, an idea close to the convenient but oversimplified formula of "Great Spirit" and "Happy Hunting Ground."[49] There were a number of reasons for whites' failure to appreciate the complexities of Indian religion. Missionaries went among the tribes to eradicate what they regarded as primitive superstition, not to study it. Even when whites did show an interest and ask questions, the translations and interpretations, difficult at the best of times, proved inadequate to the task of conveying beliefs that had meaning only to the Indians, of which the inquirer had little or no concept. Whites found it particularly difficult to understand the Indians' belief in a universal power that pervaded all aspects of their life, especially as such beliefs existed as feelings rather than formalized creeds. In addition, Indians were notoriously reticent about their religious beliefs. This often led whites to dismiss native ideas as "vague" or "confused." Fur trader Peter Grant, for one, realized that reluctance or inability to give information on religious beliefs did not necessarily indicate the absence of such beliefs: "No people are more tenacious in their religious opinions, and less communicative on religious subjects than the *Sauteux*. To question them on such a subject is not only frivolous, in their opinion, but impertinent; some will laugh and pretend ignorance on the subject, others will relate, with a most serious air, a long series of absurdities which they had by tradition from their ancestors."[50]

Native religions laid down no catalog of tenets that Europeans could identify. British observers drew distinctions between "magic," "supernaturalism," and "religion," but for Indians mythology was not distinct from religion, nor religion from daily life. Religion permeated the Indians' day-to-day life in the sense that they endeavored to avoid

alienating any of the sacred forces that governed their uncertain world. In a hostile environment, Indians tended to
seek supernatural aid for good fortune in this world, rather
than for the promise of eternal happiness in the next. Indian life revolved around the attempt to propitiate forces
beyond man's understanding or control by the practice
of taboos, the observation of omens, and the search for
power in dreams and visions. Indians did not appear to
worship a god in the Christian sense of the term; they
prayed for help to a personification of the mysterious
forces controlling their world—the Algonquian *manito,*
the Iroquoian *orenda,* the Siouan *wakanda.* Indeed, the
Nascapees of Labrador apparently believed in the existence of good and evil spirits but prayed only to the evil
one because the good spirit sought only to do them good
and would do so without being asked.[51] The concept of the
Great Spirit as a benevolent father owed much to the influence of Christian teaching, which also affected nativist
movements such as those led by the Shawnee Prophet,
Tenskwatawa, and the Seneca Handsome Lake. Europeans
saw little but superstition in Indian religions; they looked
down on people who imputed natural occurrences to the
supernatural and saw no irony in their own belief that God
governed their lives and fortunes.[52] Britons in general adhered to the notion that Indian religions were little more
than primitive imitations of the Christian theology, only
shrouded in ignorance and fearful superstition. Removal
of this shroud would open the way for instruction in the
one true religion. The notion grew from the European
Christian mind rather than from Indian reality.

   A natural corollary to the idea of the "superstitious savage" was contempt for the "filthy savage." Georgian Britain was not known for its health and cleanliness, and the
new towns that sprang up during the Industrial Revolution faced unprecedented and appalling problems of sani-
tation. Nevertheless, Britons were repulsed by what they
saw as the overwhelming dirtiness and unsanitariness of
Indian life. Descriptions of Indian habitations generally

dwelt on the nastiness and filth, just as descriptions of the Indians themselves were often as much about dirt as about humans. Wrote trader James McKenzie: "In common with the rest of the ancient inhabitants of this continent, the Nascapees are in all their habits of body filthy and nasty in the extreme. Their garments swarm with vermin, which they eat as fast as they can catch." [53]

Long acquaintance with the Indian way of life did not necessarily produce immunity to nausea at its less pleasant aspects. Alexander Henry, experienced in avoiding dunghills in Indian villages from the Missouri to the Columbia, still could not suppress his disgust at having to drink the same water the Indians drank quite happily. The water, Henry reckoned, "consisted of equal parts of horse dung, urine, and stagnant water," being drawn from a pool where horses had been drinking, and that was in the comparative cleanliness of a Cheyenne camp. Similarly, even the experienced nostrils of trader Duncan McGillivray found offensive the smell emanating from the buffalo pound near a Piegan camp, "which would have proved fatal to more delicate organs." [54] Indian eating practices drew frequent derogatory comment, especially when some Indians preferred raw and putrefying meat to that freshly cooked. Perhaps traveler John Lambert showed the most restraint with his understatement: "They are not very nice in their cooking." Britons pictured the Indian as a strong-stomached individual who would and did eat anything he could lay his hands on, be it live, raw, cooked, or decaying, but it should be remembered that Indian agriculture was often highly productive and that from the discovery of the New World, Europe acquired such a cornucopia of foodstuffs (notably potatoes, tomatoes, Indian corn, and beans) from the Indians as to effect "a dietary revolution unparalleled in history," and provide the basis for the modern diet. [55]

All in all, Indian life, like the Indian himself, was recognized as possessing some virtues, but it seems to have fared best when viewed from a distance. The unspoiled life of the child of nature was an attractive ideal for many Britons in the late eighteenth and early nineteenth centuries; some even found the reality of native existence attractive. Few, however, found Indian life sufficiently magnetic to adopt it as a permanent alternative to the civilization to which they were accustomed. The widely debated notion that Indians enjoyed unparalleled freedom and liberty in their natural state was attractive to many subjects of George III. After all, Englishmen prided themselves on possessing a unique constitution that provided and protected liberties undreamed of in most of Europe. Accustomed to the sovereignty of Parliament and the rule of law, however, Britons rarely perceived any order or structure in the freedom enjoyed by members of tribal societies, and many observers saw only disorder and anarchy, which in their eyes was no freedom at all.

The best of wills, intentions, and interest could falter before realities. Irishman Isaac Weld had intended to spend a considerable amount of time among the Indians in order to study them in their purest state, but his samplings induced him to renounce his intention and gave him no desire "to cultivate a more intimate acquaintance with them." Weld acquired a most favorable opinion of the Indians themselves, but the filth and wretchedness of their dwellings, the repulsiveness of their foods, and their general failure to adhere to European standards of cleanliness, proved too much for him. On reflection, he summarized the general feelings of Britons who came into close contact with native society: "few persons, who had ever tasted of the pleasures and comforts of civilized life, would feel any inclination to reside amongst [the Indians], on becoming acquainted with their manner of living."[56]

British observers of Indian life based their assessments solely upon their own experience and understanding. Indians were thus judged by alien standards. British commentators rarely succeeded in conveying any of the complexity of tribal culture, showed little understanding of societies living in unstable symbiosis with their environment, and sometimes created an image of the Indian that had no counterpart in reality. Nevertheless, firsthand experience allowed soldiers, traders, travelers, and missionaries to see many sides of Indian life. Some found what they saw attractive; most did not. Some saw virtue and nobility in the Indian; most were appalled by what they regarded as filth and brutality. The majority recognized these as the extremes of Indian life and, if they made ethnocentric generalizations, they at least generally avoided praising all Indians as "noble savages" or dismissing them all as "dirty savages." Most Britons who encountered Indians in the period following the Revolution had, in fact, little interest in how Indians lived, unless that lifestyle affected their military or commercial performance. The Indians' usefulness as allies and as partners in the fur trade far outweighed their cultural and social attributes in determining the attitudes of George III's subjects.

4

Indian Views of the British

ON A JOURNEY to Niagara Falls in 1799, British diplomat Robert Liston and his party met two canoes of Indians and were obliged to encamp just across a stream from them. The prospect of passing a night in the wilderness within a few yards of a band of "half naked Savages" proved too much for Lady Liston, and she prevailed upon her husband to move camp "both for health & safety." Next morning, however, when she was able to observe the Indians more calmly, Lady Liston got the impression that they had been "at *least*" as afraid of her and her companions as she had been of them.[1] As always, contact was a two-way process that placed both Briton and Indian in a new situation and obliged each to assess and react to the other.

Indians rarely committed their impressions to paper, but their opinions did find expression in the records of the time, both directly and indirectly. White observers often recorded verbatim speeches delivered in council by Indian orators and chiefs; other whites reported what they believed to be the Indians' opinions on the basis of experience, sympathy, and conversation. Indian comments recorded in this way bore the mark of European interpretation, and often what purported to be a record of the Indian point of view more accurately represented what European writers thought the Indians were thinking.

Europeans also frequently resorted to the technique of employing the Indian, either as a mouthpiece or as a standard of comparison, as a vehicle for comment upon their own society. The practice was less than reliable for the production of authentic Indian comment and usually revealed far more about European than about Indian attitudes. In the late eighteenth and early nineteenth centuries, however, Romanticism flourished in Britain and the idea of the noble savage—"any free and wild being who draws directly from nature virtues which raise doubts as to the value of civilization"—was still very much in vogue.[2] Throughout the reign of George III, Britons made implicit and explicit criticisms of their own society through their comments on an Indian world that appeared relatively uncorrupted and free from the artificial restraints imposed by civilization. Comments like that made by John F. D. Smyth were not uncommon: "They enjoy the sweets of liberty and freedom in the truest sense, and certainly are not guilty of the many iniquitous and scandalous vices that disgrace Christianity and Europeans." According to Isaac Weld, although the English in Canada could not banish from their minds the idea that the Indian was inferior, many reckoned their own society would be much improved if they behaved but half as well toward one another as the Indians did toward them.[3]

Indian society served as a mirror in which the traits of one's own world were reflected, often with startling clarity. The fashionable whims, vanities, and corruptions of contemporary England were favorite targets for unfavorable comment. Thus, Lieutenant Governor Simcoe's wife observed that the idle, drunken, dirty Missisaugua Indians sauntered up and down town all day "with the apparent Nonchalence [sic], want of occupation & indifference that seems to possess Bond street Beaux"; Lady Liston (attending an Indian dance which caused her considerable discomfort) noted that "their *Balls suits* were pretty much like those of the present *fashion*, . . . nearly naked." Andrew Graham complained that Indian women, "like their sisters

on the other side of the Atlantic," made too much use of
paint; and Alexander Ross pointed out that Chinook head
flattening was but a native custom as was an English lady's
compressing of her waist. Other writers generalized from
specific similarities. David Thompson, referring to an Indian woman who had become so "common" as to be despised, who had turned "prophetess" for a livelihood and
had found fools enough to support her, reflected, "there is
scarce a character in civilized society that has not something like it among these rude people." Others, like Francis
Baily, pressed comparisons home, not being content to let
"savage" merits pass without reference to the respective
"civilized" demerits: "You may perhaps be surprised to
hear of politeness in the wilds of America. To be sure it is
not such as you meet with in a court or ballroom; but it
is dictated by a much better spirit. *There* it is a cloak to
hatred, malice, envy, and every evil propensity; *here* it is
the effect of a hospitable and benign disposition: it is the
effusion of a beneficient mind, breaking out in acts of
kindness."[4]

Indians who exposed the follies of "civilization" in true
Brobdignagian fashion were more often the creations of
white imaginations than real forest sages. Nevertheless, an
Indian visitor to English society was a convenient instrument for satire and scathing comment on that society. In
the late eighteenth and early nineteenth centuries, Indian
visits and delegations to Britain were not rare but were still
a curiosity. Iroquois, Creek, and Cherokee Indians had all
been to England in the first half of the eighteenth century.
In 1775, Joseph Brant had crossed the Atlantic with Colonel Guy Johnson and Captain Tice of the Indian Department. He had become friendly with James Boswell, who
wrote an account of him for the *London Magazine,* and with
the Earl of Warwick; and he had his portrait painted by
George Romney. Ten years and a revolution later, the Mohawk was back. Again Brant received a flattering reception, and he was no miser when it came to spending the
government's money in London. Charles James Fox pre-

sented him with a silver snuff box and he was loaded with presents for the principal Six Nations warriors. He met playwright-politican Richard Sheridan, Edmund Burke, George III, and Queen Charlotte. The Mohawk even accompanied the Prince of Wales on some of his excursions through the night life of eighteenth-century London. The Creeks and the Cherokees sent a delegation in 1790–91, and their interests were promoted in the periodic visits to the capital by William Augustus Bowles. Bowles was the son of a London immigrant to America. A former Maryland Loyalist turned adventurer, he masqueraded as a Creek chief, was a success in London society and attracted considerable publicity. Brant's successor, John Norton, was also a frequent visitor to both England and Scotland. He kept in touch with William Wilberforce and the Clapham Sect in the work of "improvement" among the Mohawks, although the Canadian authorities regarded him as another imposter playing on the susceptibilities of important people in England and lining his own pockets. Creek and Seminole leaders continued to arrive even after the War of 1812; a party of Senecas toured the country in 1818; and in 1821, John Brant, son of Joseph, visited England.[5]

Indian visitors to Britain, as to Quebec and Montreal, were treated to displays of the finest achievements of British culture, industry, and military power. They were also no doubt mystified and shocked by a society with such well-developed and relatively rigid divisions between rich and poor, aristocrat and commoner, by the severity of English laws and the institutions for their enforcement, by the discipline imposed upon children and the restraints on individual freedom, by crowded living conditions and filthy streets, and by a multiplicity of strange customs and practices.

The press in particular made full use of the Indians' apparent naïveté for satirical or critical comment on those and other aspects of English life. John Norton, however, seems to have felt quite at home in English society and was quick to answer aspersions cast on his authenticity, and

baiting about living among "savages," with his own observations upon the "savages" found in English society.[6]
Whether such anecdotes were a true reflection of the Indians' opinions or whether they were embellished by the
fertile imaginations of reporters and editors is difficult to
say. It seems to have been the case, however, that the Indians who were removed to England or to the eastern
United States, often for the very purpose of overawing and
impressing them, remained, or at least managed to convey
the impression of remaining, singularly unimpressed and
preferred their native woods and wigwams to the fine
buildings of British or American cities. Much of their impassiveness was, of course, a facade affected for the benefit
or frustration of whites, who expected the Indians to stand
wide-eyed and open-mouthed before the glories of civilization.[7] However, there was much in that civilization that was
singularly unimpressive. As British observers in North
America saw Indian societies in process of change, so Indian visitors to Britain saw a country in the throes of social
and economic upheaval. Indians who were allowed to see
beyond a small area of London—and a few even traveled
through the industrial heart of the country—caught at
least a glimpse of the squalid living conditions, inhumane
working conditions, regional poverty, and glaring ineq-
uities that lay behind the facade of Georgian elegance and
which constituted life for many of George III's subjects.

Indians generally do not appear to have possessed any
great veneration for either white men or their civilization.
Rather, they regarded the whites' way of life and their
claims to superiority with disdain and the white men themselves as inferior. Initial contacts might see the Indians
viewing European newcomers with awe, but the impression
soon wore off, as fur traders, with their repertoire of poses
and techniques for maintaining Indian respect, knew only
too well. Europeans were at a disadvantage from the beginning of contact because they could hardly match the Indian
in the Indian world. As trader Peter Grant explained about
the Sauteux, or Chippewas: "Though they acknowledge the

superiority of our arts and manufactures, and their own
incapacity to imitate us, yet, as a people, they think us far
inferior to themselves. They pity our want of skill in hunting and our incapacity of travelling through their immense
forests without guides or food. . . . The highest compli-
ment which they bestow on a white man is that he is in
every respect like one of themselves, but no man can aspire
to that honor who has not a tolerable knowledge of their
language and customs."[8] To such Indians, British intrud-
ers bore a strange appearance, wore impractical and un-
comfortable clothing, spoke in unintelligible dialects, and
indulged in incomprehensible and even antisocial behavior.

Haughty warriors regarded other Indians, as well as
non-Indians, as inferior, and many tribes were reported to
think themselves the finest people on earth. The Piegans
were said to think themselves superior, braver, and more
virtuous than even their northern allies and relatives, the
Bloods and the Blackfeet.[9] So-called "wild" Indians had
little but contempt for tribes who had succumbed to acculturation or for black slaves who had lost their liberty.
What Euro-Americans admired as worthwhile industry
seemed no more than drudgery and slavery to an "indolent" and independent Indian.[10] Whites condemned the
Indians for their idleness and failure to exploit the land
to the full, but the Indians were appalled by the back-
breaking, dawn-to-dusk labor by which whites struggled
to master the environment and to accumulate more property than they could use. An Iroquois spokesman in 1806
referred with casual disdain to "the superfluous wants
of Europeans." The Indians generally had more respect
for a good warrior and hunter who retained his native
habits than for a "chief" who curried favor with white
men, adopted white manners, and acquired wealth that he
kept for himself. Joseph Brant may have made himself as
many enemies among his own people as he did friends
among the British.[11] Yorkshireman Robert Sutcliff, traveling through North America in the early years of the nineteenth century, thought it not unlikely that the feelings of

pity and compassion he felt toward an Indian family might
be reciprocated by those "children of the forest, towards
those who may consider themselves as raised far above
them in education and civilized life." Former Indian captive John Hunter agreed: "The white people commiserate
the Indians, on account of their thousand misfortunes and
sufferings, and congratulate themselves on the superior
privileges and blessings they enjoy. The Indians reverse
the position, and thank the Great Spirit for not having
made them white, and subjected them to the drudgery of
civilized life." [12]

White men seem to have found it particularly vexing
that not only did Indians think themselves superior, but
also they made certain that others knew they thought so.
British traders among the Chippewas were left in no doubt
as to their standing in that tribe's estimation. [13] When the
Indians at Malden were told that Isaac Weld and his companions had crossed the Atlantic especially to see them,
they formed a favorable opinion of the travelers: "they ap-
prove highly of the undertaking, and say that we have employed our time to a good purpose. No people on earth
have a higher opinion of their own consequence; indeed,
they esteem themselves superior to every other race of
men." [14] A group of southern Indian chiefs went aboard the
British fleet prior to the expedition against New Orleans
and caused considerable amusement by their haughty conduct and ludicrous appearance. One apparently inquired
if the king of England was as great a man as himself. [15]

Nor did the Indians find much in British people, British
culture, or British arguments to induce them to alter their
opinions. The Indians' attachment to their own ways of life
seemed to withstand every allurement to change. [16] Certain
elements from the Europeans' world, notably manufactured goods and liquor, might be keenly sought, but that
world as a whole held no attraction for Indians. It was
widely agreed that the people with whom the Indians
came into contact on the frontier were not usually of the
kind likely to impress them with a favorable idea of the civi-

lization the whites had left behind, but there is little evidence to suggest that Indians had any higher opinion of whites in general than they did of the particular class who impinged on their world. John Tanner, an American who spent some thirty years as an Indian captive and who seemed completely Indianized when Daniel Harmon saw him in 1801, recalled seeing some Scots laborers, employees of the Hudson's Bay Company, who "were much more rough and brutal in their manner than any people I had before seen. Even when they had plenty, they ate like starved dogs, and never failed to quarrel over their meat." John Hunter remembered that the prejudices he had acquired from the Indians gave him no very favorable impression of white people. Actual contact did nothing to improve this impression, while the greed and dishonesty of traders only strengthened it.[17] As Joseph Brant realized, this attitude of contempt for and distrust of white men naturally made Indians reluctant to accept what whites regarded as the blessings of their civilization. Attempts to convert and educate Indians fell short of success, either because, like Joseph Brant, Jr., Indian boys preferred the freedom of their native woods to the restraints of a schoolroom, or because "the Indian nations soon saw how little better the English themselves were for being Christians, and they soon left off sending their children to their schools for education." John Norton devoted much of his time to educating and Christianizing the Mohawks, but he too recognized that the Indians derived a poor impression of Christianity, "judging of it, not by the security of its tenets, of which they are ignorant, but by the practice of many of its professors, of which they have had experience."[18]

British observers and commentators sometimes found themselves the object of observation and comment. A young London merchant, Robert Hunter, Jr., traveling in Canada in the 1780s, "observed one fellow laughing and making his remarks upon everybody and everything that passed. I make no doubt but that he thought our manners and customs as curious as we think his." A party of Osage warriors, whom Sir Augustus John Foster saw during their visit to Washington in the winter of 1805–1806, were well-mannered and anxious not to offend and conducted themselves with decorum throughout. Even so, one of them found it noticeably difficult to suppress a smile at the goings-on he observed in church.[19] British writers might denounce Indian treatment of their women and their apparent lack of any moral standards, but Indians found European attitudes toward the opposite sex bewildering. Kansa Indians asked French traveler Perrin du Lac if the people in his country were as great slaves to their women as the white traders in the Indian country seemed to be. The Chipewyans apparently could not understand why men should ever want to fight and spill blood over women, who, after all, were good for little else but work and as beasts of burden.[20]

Moreover, Indians showed an irritating reluctance to regard Europeans as omniscient or to accept their beliefs as absolute truths. David Thompson recalled his interest in seeing a vast herd of reindeer rushing along in their spring migration in 1792. The Indians asked him, as a man of supposedly higher knowledge, to tell them the cause of the herd's regular march: "I replied, 'Instinct.' What do you mean by that word. Its meaning is 'the free and voluntary actions of an animal for its self preservation.' Oh oh, then you think this herd of Deer rushed forward over deep swamps, in which some perished, the others ran over them; down steep banks to break their necks; swam across large Rivers, where the strong drowned the weak; went a long way through woods where they had nothing to eat, merely to take care of themselves. You white people, you look like wise men, and talk like fools." Reluctantly, Thompson had to give up his doctrine of instinct and accept the Indians' interpretation that the reindeer were controlled by their Manito, who directed the herd's movements. Similarly, in September 1811, Daniel Harmon attempted to dispel Indian alarm at the eclipse of the sun by explaining the real cause of it. The Indians thought his explanation reasonable but were surprised that he should know about such things. Four years later, himself striving to lead a more Christian life, Harmon endeavored to explain to some Indians about God. Again, the Indians thought his arguments were reasonable and admitted that what he said might be true, but wondered how he came to know so much about it.[21] Trader James McKenzie acknowledged that it was difficult to teach the Indians new ways and to convince them that Christian notions of religion were preferable to their own, especially as "however absurd these may appear to us, it is certain ours seem no less to them."[22] The Indians' religion sufficed for their own needs and they were understandably reluctant to accept that of an alien culture.

The Seneca orator Red Jacket voiced what were perhaps the most articulate arguments against the white man's insistence that others accept his as the only way of life. Unlike the progressive Six Nations leaders, Brant and Cornplanter, Red Jacket was a staunch conservative and defender of Indian culture against white influences. Replying to Christian offers to bring their religion to his people, the Seneca demanded how the white people knew that they were right and the Indians lost. Indians, he said, did not have "the book," and so only knew what the white people told them; but how could they ever know what to believe, having been deceived so often by white men? Moreover, if there was but one religion and one way to worship the Great Spirit, why did white people differ so much among themselves about it? Since the Great Spirit had made all men, but had obviously made them different, was it not possible that he had given Indians and whites different religions, according to their understanding? The Indians, Red Jacket concluded, did not want to destroy the Christians' religion or to take it from them; they only asked to be left alone to enjoy their own.[23] On the other hand, despite Red Jacket's plea for tolerance, Indians themselves could be similarly intolerant, as trader Duncan Cameron discovered when frustrated by the adherence of Chippewa Indians to their own religions beliefs: "To disapprove their ideas, or argue with them on the absurdity of any of their tenets is only proving yourself a fool, for if you had any sense, you would allow them to be the first people on earth both in wisdom and knowledge."[24]

On the whole, Indian societies demonstrated a remarkable ability to embrace technologies and beliefs from outside their experience without losing their own integrity. Protestant missionaries demanded total capitulation, however. Some Indians accepted the missionary message and became converts. Most rejected missionary efforts and held the missionaries arms' length and seem, like Red Jacket, to have parried Christian arguments for conversion with a theory of cultural dualism.[25] Christians saw the Indian as facing a simple choice between heathenism and the one true religion, between eternal damnation and salvation. For the Indian, however, the meeting of Christian and traditional beliefs presented a complex variety of decisions and resulted in syncretism more often than conversion or outright rejection. The complexity of Indian responses was reflected in revitalization movements like that of the Delaware Prophet in the mid-eighteenth century and of Handsome Lake and the Shawnee Prophet in the early nineteenth century. These movements permitted selective acculturation but on the whole called for a return to ancestral customs and a renunciation of the evils derived from contact with white men.

Indians responded in a variety of ways to the new situations forced upon them, selecting, adapting, and rejecting different aspects of European culture, even as they clung tenaciously to their time-honored ways. They incorporated European goods into their technologies, admitted Euro-Americans into their societies, and integrated some European notions into their view of the world. Most Indians, however, steadfastly refused to regard white civilizations as superior to their own. They rejected many of the so-called "blessings of civilization" and consistently maintained the equal worth or superiority of their own cultures. They were just as liable as Europeans to regard themselves as the highest form of human existence, and many regarded Britons and their values with a mixture of bewilderment and contempt. Nevertheless, whereas Europeans could choose simply to ignore the Indians and their world, the Indians could not avoid the advance of settlement, which compelled response and demanded assimilation or migration as the only alternatives to extinction. In this situation the Indians found that they had a potential ally in the British, whose political, military, and fur-trading interests prompted them to make common cause with the tribes in an effort to halt American expansion before it engulfed the Indians' hunting grounds. In return the Indians expected the British to provide trade and military assistance.

5
"Savagery" and "Civilization"

CULTURES DO NOT MEET; people do. The meeting of British
and Indian civilizations in North America was a mingling
of various peoples, rather than a confrontation of two cultures. English, Scots, Welsh, and Irish each had their own
traditions, cultures, historical experiences, dialects, and rivalries. When English met Scots or Irish a degree of cultural interchange occurred just as surely as when Mohawks
met Chippewas or Shawnees. The posts and villages that
became the centers of British-Indian relations were often
busy frontier communities where delegates from distant
tribes mingled with neighboring Indians, where French-
Canadian traders operated alongside British redcoats,
and where Indian agents and mixed-bloods functioned as
cultural intermediaries. The meeting of cultures on the
British-Indian frontier was a multi-cultural exchange between a variety of social groups on both sides of the
British-Indian equation.

British observers and many Indian spokesmen, however, saw British-Indian relations in simpler terms. Their
eyes focused on three kinds of boundaries in the years following the end of the American Revolution. Indians and
British soldiers fought to defend, or to alter in Britain's
favor, the international boundaries that divided British,
American, and Spanish possessions in North America. In-

dians and British traders likewise endeavored to maintain
or to push back the boundary between settlement and Indian lands that had been fixed by treaty or, more often, by
the limit of American expansion. Indians and Britons alike
also imagined the existence of a third kind of boundary
that separated their cultures. The British referred to this
as the line dividing "civilization" and "savagery." Their belief in this dividing line induced Britons to interpret any
mingling of people and cultural traits as either degeneration or progress from one world to the other. Even
when their cultures remained separate, Indians and Britons alike expressed considerable doubt as to just how far
their respective cultures merited description as "savage" or
"civilized."

When Britons and Indians met, they recognized that
each responded to and exerted a degree of influence upon
the other, so that what each party saw was an individual or
a society already changed or changing as a result of the en-
counter. British-Indian relations were part of a wider process of contact and conflict between the European and
Amerindian worlds and were subject to the demands of
that process. Tribal societies reeled under the hammerblows of disease, alcoholism, and increased warfare. They
faced dispossession of their lands and depletion of game
resources. They saw the despiritualization of tribal life, the
decline of tribal religion, the questioning of traditional values, the loss of traditional skills, the corruptions of individual integrity, and the destruction of collective hope. Consequently, when British observers wrote about Indians, they
paid more attention to what the Indians seemed to have
lost than to what they preserved. By the late eighteenth
century few Britons saw "the unchanging Indian"; rather,
they witnessed the effects, upon Indian and Briton alike,
of the collision of Indian and European civilizations.

The belief that "civilization" and "Indianness" were in-
herently incompatible, and the failure of Europeans to
understand the nature of tribal society, meant that there
was little possibility of peaceful coexistence and that the

image of the Indian as "savage" was used to rationalize conquest and conversion.[1] Despite the limited success of attempts to convert Indians to European ways and beliefs, the more powerful and aggressive cultures of Euro-America devoted themselves to eradication of the Indian ways of life and the substitution of white civilization. The interaction of cultures and the power of the environment in North America, however, finally rendered vague any distinctions between civilization and savagery. One English traveler indicated the extent of the confusion when he described the Caughnawaga Indians of Lower Canada as simply "civilized savages."[2] The British commonly argued that American settlers and frontiersmen behaved more like savages than did the Indians; reports of frontiersmen murdering Indians, with an indifference born of a mentality that regarded such atrocities as no crime, appear repeatedly in both British and American sources.[3] At least one English farmer maintained that he preferred the Indians to the ignorant, uncouth, unruly squatters whom he met on the American frontier; traveler John Mair reckoned that the inhabitants of the South Carolina backcountry were "more savage than the Indians"; Lord Dorchester, governor of Quebec, anticipated historian Frederick Jackson Turner in his belief that Americans moving to the frontier adopted many of the characteristics inherent in the wilderness environment, and many observers described backcountry settlers as "white savages" who lived in squalid conditions and adopted Indian ways.[4]

Those with experience in Indian societies could see that despite what they regarded as brutal, treacherous, immoral, and disgusting behavior on the part of the natives, man's state depended on his situation and environment rather than the color of his skin. Fur traders seem to have held Canadian voyageurs in no higher esteem than they did their Indian customers, and the "Indian savage"–"civilized white" situation sometimes seemed completely reversed in the wilderness. Fur trader Daniel Harmon spent much of his time in the Indian country longing for friends and society, but he found little solace on 1 January 1811 because the North West Company's employees passed New Year's Day in their customary way—drinking and fighting. The following year, however, Harmon was able to dine with a group of Sekani and Carrier chiefs who behaved in a manner that he deemed proper and decent; after eating, the Indians drank a little rum and then sat around smoking and conversing rationally about the differences in customs between Indian and white people.[5]

The meeting of British and Indian cultures did not occur exclusively in the Indian country. Remnants of Indian tribes remained long after the frontier had passed them by on its way west, and some individuals managed to transcend the limits of environment and culture. In the decades following the American Revolution, Alexander McGillivray and William Augustus Bowles in the south, and Joseph Brant and John Norton in the north, demonstrated the frailty and flexibility of ethnic barriers and indicated that the gap between Indian and white was not the impassable gulf imagined by Francis Parkman. Brant, Bowles, and Norton each traveled to England and became celebrities in Georgian society. Joseph Brant seems to have taken his adoption of European trappings to an extreme, running his Grand River estates like a baronial landlord, dressing his black servants in livery, and serving guests dinner from the best English china, crystal, and silver. His son John received an English education, and British Lieutenant Francis Hall, who saw the young Mohawk in 1816, described him as a "fine young man, of gentleman-like appearance, who used the English language correctly and agreeably, dressing in the English fashion, excepting only the moccasins of his Indian habit."[6]

John Norton, whose Indian name was Teyoninhokerawen, seemed to be equally at home in either society. The son of a Cherokee father (or, at least, of a man living among the Cherokees) and a Scottish mother, Norton was a Mohawk by adoption. A frequent visitor to Britain, he lived in one culture but wrote for the other, being a man of

considerable education. Thomas Scott wrote enthusiasti-
cally from Canada to his brother, Sir Walter, describing
the Mohawk as "a man who makes you almost wish to be an
Indian chief." Norton, he said, spoke about a dozen Indian
languages in addition to English, French, German, and
Spanish. Widely read in all modern literature, he had apparently read Scott's *Lady of the Lake* with delight and had
even translated that work, together with the Scriptures,
into Mohawk. In addition, he had a history of the Five Nations and a journal of his own travels awaiting publication
in London, although the book does not appear to have
been published in his lifetime. (Indeed, because Norton
was afraid that the *Edinburgh Review* would be hard on his
book, Thomas Scott had promised to ask his brother to
have it reviewed in the *Quarterly*.) Norton became the personal friend of such influential men as William Wilberforce, Walter Scott, and the Duke of Northumberland. He
dedicated his book to the Duke of Northumberland in
gratitude for the latter's friendship to himself and the
Mohawk people. Norton's abilities were highly thought of,
and George Canning interested himself in the chief's affairs when Norton was in England in 1804–1805 engaged
in translating the Gospel of Saint John into Mohawk under
the auspices of Wilberforce and the Clapham Sect. The
British and Foreign Bible Society encouraged his work,
and its secretary, the Reverend John Owen, became Norton's friend and supporter. On Christmas Eve, 1804, Norton gave a speech before the Bath and West of England
Agricultural Society after they had elected him an honor-
ary member. In subsequent months he was introduced to
"the ancient and respectable University of Cambridge."
Brant too seems to have started writing a history of the Indians, but Norton succeeded him as the person best able to
translate the Gospels into Mohawk. John Norton of literary
aspirations and Christian zeal, and Teyoninhokerawen of
the war dance and the longhouse, were one and the same.[7]

Not all individuals who transcended the limits of their
particular culture were favorably regarded, however. Rene-

ohn Brant (Ahyouwaighs), the son of Joseph Brant. John Brant received
n English education and fought for the Crown in the War of 1812. (Chi-
ago Historical Society)

gades who fought with the Indians and "squaw men" who lived with the Indians often were viewed with hatred and suspicion. Renegades earned universal loathing as cruel traitors to their own kind, but they also demonstrated the flexibility of the barrier that supposedly divided white and Indian. A man who abandoned his own society was regarded with distrust and disgust and was believed to combine the characteristics of a white outlaw and an Indian savage. The Girty brothers, Simon, James, and George, offered notorious examples of white men who had turned renegade and become Indianized to an alarming degree. Captured as youths during the French and Indian War, the Girtys had been distributed among the tribes. Simon was adopted by the Senecas, James lived with the Shawnees, and George with the Delawares. Liberated in 1759, they earned a living in subsequent years as traders and interpreters on the Pennsylvania frontier. Simon served the British in the period of Dunmore's War and earned a reputation for ability among British and Indians alike. During the Revolution, disappointed at his treatment by the patriots, he went over to the British at Detroit. Alexander McKee and Matthew Elliott also saw that loyalty to the Crown best served their interests and sympathies, and joined Girty in his flight to Detroit, where Governor Henry Hamilton put them to work in the British Indian Department. James and George Girty followed suit, although an elder brother, Thomas, remained in Pennsylvania. In the border warfare of the Revolution and the wars for the Old Northwest that followed, Simon Girty and his brothers fought alongside the Indians, served as interpreters in their councils, and moved with ease between British frontier society and Indian villages. Americans regarded the Girtys as traitors who had abandoned both their country and their own kind to join the Indian savages and their British paymasters.

The offspring of white men and Indian women also attracted considerable contempt. Patrick Campbell argued that cross-breeding was as advantageous among humans

John Norton (c. 1760–1831?), painted by Thomas Phillips. A Scot with Cherokee ancestry, Norton went to live among the Mohawks, became the adopted nephew of Joseph Brant, and succeeded him as a leader of the Grand River Iroquois. (Courtesy His Grace the Duke of Northumberland)

as in other animals, a contention supported by the general agreement that mixed-blood children, especially the daughters, were uncommonly handsome. Nevertheless, Campbell described the sons of Sir William Johnson and Molly Brant as having a reputation for being "somewhat wild," and the general belief was that mixed-bloods inherited the worst rather than the best characteristics of both parents. In 1815 the Earl of Selkirk, responding to William McGillivray's allegations and denouncing the depredations committed by the North West Company in its struggle against his colony of emigrant Scottish Highlanders, pointed out that "these outrages were not committed by any of the Indian Natives, but by Canadians, mixed with the bastard sons of others, who have thrown off the restraints of regular society, & cohabiting with Indian Squaws have formed a combination of the vices of civilized and Savage life." Alexander Henry maintained that "mongrels" or "half-breeds" who chose to live with the Indians were evil in themselves and exerted a bad influence on the full-blood Indians.[8]

Indians do not appear to have been so concerned about racial purity. A significant number of mixed-bloods—Alexander McGillivray, Cornplanter, John Norton, William Weatherford, Menawa, McIntosh, Osceola—rose to positions of leadership in Indian society. McGillivray was the son of a Creek woman and a wealthy Scottish planter-trader. Besides holding a British commission and having important trade connections with Panton, Leslie and Company, he was a member of the influential Wind clan. Like Brant, he was ideally suited to playing a transactional role between his Indian people and his British friends. This period saw the twilight of full-blood leadership among the Chickasaws and other southern nations, as the mixed-blood factions exercised considerable influence over the management of tribal affairs. In addition, some white men gained acceptance and prominence in the Indian world, notably William Augustus Bowles, Simon Girty, and frontier scout William Wells. William Bowles represented him-

William Augustus Bowles (1763–1805), painted by Thomas
Hardy, an English portrait painter who flourished at the end of
the eighteenth century. Self-styled "Director-General of the
Creek Nation," Bowles was involved in various intrigues in the
Floridas and worked to establish a southern Indian state under
British protection. He died in a Spanish dungeon in Morro
Castle, Havana, in 1805. (Courtesy Florida State Archives; from
a negative owned by Dr. J. Leitch Wright)

self as a Creek chief to the British government and as
an agent of the British government to the Creeks, and
bolstered his position by marrying the daughter of chief
William Perryman. Simon Girty was the only white man
the western Indians would admit to their crucial councils
at the Glaize in 1792.[9]

To many whites the mixed-bloods personified the mutually corrupting process of degeneration that seemed to occur whenever alien civilizations intermingled. The belief
seems to have been universal that Indians who came into
contact with the white world retained their native vices but
lost any virtues they had possessed formerly, replacing
them with new vices adopted from civilization. Alcoholism
was the most glaring example of the process. In the summer of 1787, Lieutenant John Enys of the Twenty-ninth
Regiment of Foot came across the Seneca chief Sayenqueraghta at a council held at Niagara Falls. Sayenqueraghta
was "the only Crowned head in America," having inherited a crown that Queen Anne had sent to his ancestors as
"kings" of the Seneca Nation, and he had fought courageously at the bloody Battle of Oriskany ten years before.
Now, however, he presented a very different image. Enys
described him as "a sensible old man and has been a very
good Warrior in his day but like all the rest is very much
adicted [sic] to his Liquor, for no sooner was the council
over than his Majesty was dead drunk rolling in an Out-
house amongst Indians, Squaws, Pigs, Dogs, &c. &c."[10]

In the same way that British agents and traders adopted
some of the native dress when living in the Indian country,
an Indian's contact with Europeans was reflected in his outward apparel. The Indians whom John Lambert came
across in Lower Canada presented a particularly sorry
sight, barely covered in tattered European clothes. Likewise, those Creek and Choctaw chiefs who went aboard the
English fleet in 1814 wearing a mixture of native and European dress struck observers as ludicrously symbolic of
cultural decay, not unlike the famous painting done by
George Catlin in 1832 of an Assiniboine Indian en route to

Washington in buckskins and feathers and returning later with coat and tails, top hat, high-heeled boots, and whiskey bottle. An Indian's clothing, together with the length and style of his hair, gave a pretty accurate indication of the extent of his acculturation.[11]

The theory that man progressed by stages from savage to civil life did not fare well in the test of experience. Civilization, it was believed, ruined the Indian, who pined away for want of his accustomed freedom. Alexander Ross expressed the fur trader's view: "The Indian in his natural state is happy; with the trader he is happy; but the moment he begins to walk in the path of the white men his happiness is at an end. Like a wild animal in a cage, his luster is gone."[12] Britons frequently drew comparisons between what they perceived as the virtues of uncorrupted Indian life and the degeneracy of those exposed to the influence of white society. Many Britons held the Mohawks in special regard, but those tribes who were most distant were often held in highest esteem. The British identified something of a scale of Indian virtue, which had its low point among the acculturated peoples in the east, improved with progression west to the plains and mountains, and then descended to a new low on the Pacific Coast where the tribes were in contact with maritime traders. Alexander Henry rarely gave Indians a favorable report, but the Flatheads constituted an exception: "Their morals have not yet been sufficiently debauched and corrupted by an intercourse with people who call themselves Christians, but whose licentious and lecherous manners are far worse than those of the savages."[13] Britons in general looked with the greatest admiration upon those Indians who managed to avoid or resist the corrupting influences of civilization. John Lambert explained: "Those who give themselves up to drunkenness and debauchery, which unfortunately form a great majority, exhibit a depravity of mind, and stupid sensibility bordering upon a state of brutality. The few who resist the temptation of those odious vices, and preserve their constitutional and mental facilities unimpaired, display such superior talents and virtues, and astonish by such strength of invincible reasoning and argument, that one is almost tempted to doubt the superiority of civilized society over a state of nature." Some believed that Indians became degenerate when they became civilized; others thought that degeneracy stemmed from a *lack* of civilization. Different observers held different views as to what constituted savagery or degeneracy. An inconsistent John Lambert criticized the Indians of Lower Canada as degenerate because they roamed the woods in search of a precarious subsistence instead of pursuing agriculture, commerce, and the arts; in other words, because they adhered to their "state of nature" and resisted the temptations of "civilization."[14]

Contact modified Britons and Indians alike. British observers generally thought that the process exerted an adverse effect on both cultures. The influence of the frontier in shaping character was recognized long before Turner promulgated his thesis of American development. Common opinion held that, whereas Indians might prefer their own ways of life and resist assimilation into the white man's world, civilized man reverted easily to a state of nature. Fur traders and explorers donned Indian dress and adopted Indian practices as more convenient and appropriate to existence in the Indian world, yet pointed frequently to the degeneracy of whites who slipped into "savage ways." Alexander Ross maintained that, "An Indian, accustomed to squat on the ground, and double himself up in the lodge, is long, long indeed before he can reconcile himself to sit in a chair; but the white man is at once at home in the Indian lodge, and becomes as easy and contented sitting, squatting, or lying amongst dirt and filth, dogs and fleas, as if in his armchair at home—showing how much more easy and natural it is for civilized man to degenerate than for the savage to elevate himself to the habits of civilized men."[15]

Some Indians demonstrated growing acumen in landed and financial matters. Some, like the Creeks and the Cherokees before the disastrous Creek War of 1813–14, began to make what impressed white commentators as a successful transition from war and hunting to agriculture and commerce. Others accepted the benefits European medicine offered, especially the smallpox vaccine.[16] To the British, such things were signs of progress on the part of the Indians. The British government, however, made little attempt to aid such progress or to ensure that the Indians received the blessings rather than the evils of "civilization." Dominated by economic and military considerations, the British concentrated upon winning the Indians' loyalty by satisfying their immediate wants and devoted slight attention to safeguarding their future welfare. The United States government, unable to compete with the British supply of goods and eager to be perceived as acting with justice and humanity toward America's original inhabitants, sought to pursue a longer-term policy of assimilation. Americans, Englishmen, and Indians all realized that Britain lagged behind.[17] The British government was really interested in the Indians' welfare only insofar as it affected their attitude toward Britain or their conduct in war or trade. Programs for improving the Indians' lot or helping them to deal with a changing world were left to philanthropic or missionary efforts.

Some thought that the establishment of Christianity among the Indians would be the best first step in bringing them around to living a "civilized" existence.[18] The Society for the Propagation of the Gospel had begun its missionary work among the Mohawks in 1704, and the British and Foreign Bible Society promoted Christianity among the Grand River Mohawks a century later. The more common belief, however, was that Indians must become civilized—at least to the extent of leading sedentary, agricultural lives—before they could appreciate or accept the truths of Christianity. This was due in part to the white man's insistence that the Indian convert accept his way of life in its entirety, but there was also more than a suspicion that the Indian lacked the mental powers and training to grasp the simple tenets of the Christian faith. The Indian, therefore, had to be educated in "civilized" ways in general before he could be taught Christianity to any real purpose. Quaker missionary Ann Mifflin regarded the Oneidas whom she saw in 1802 "as the fallow ground, which hath need to be ploughed for receiving the seed of the kingdom."[19] Sir Augustus John Foster, British minister plenipotentiary to the United States in 1811–1812, argued that civilization must be introduced to the Indians by means of a steady and gradual program: "It is beginning at the wrong end to take full grown men from the woods and push them forward into the broad blaze of civilization. It it like presenting the sun to one recovered from blindness. But the young might be schooled and the old persuaded to allow of it, and by degrees cultivation of roots at least or the care of cattle as in the Creeks' country might be introduced among them."[20]

Agriculture constituted the first step on the road toward civilization and Christianity, in the eyes of the British. The Indian was no stranger to agriculture. New World pioneers had occupied lands which, in many cases, had been cleared and cultivated by the previous Indian inhabitants. European and American soldiers brought back tales of extensive orchards and crops seen during their campaigns against Indian villages. Nevertheless, the image persisted of the Indian as an improvident wanderer who made no good use of the land's bounties, and this doomed him in the eyes of Britons who regarded the land as a resource to be exploited to the full. Yet there was hope that the transformation of nomadic hunters into settled farmers would instill industrious habits, a sense of private property, and other characteristics esteemed as virtues by Englishmen.[21] Conversion to Christianity thus demanded not simply a change in religious beliefs and practices but also a complete transformation of Indian life and culture, to be initiated by a social and economic revolution which, in many cases, would reduce warrior-hunters to performing what they considered to be women's work.

The Indians, however, rejected the Euro-American assumptions of cultural superiority, and missionary efforts met with limited success. Those Indians who accepted Christianity often faced discrimination from whites and from unconverted Indians alike. Missionaries, in fact, faced a dilemma: in order to Christianize Indians they had to "civilize" them, but to do so all too often exposed the Indians to the corrupting influences of that civilization. (Hence, the Moravian practice of settling their neophytes in separate villages.) When the work of inculcating Christian principles began, the missionaries had to contend with problems resulting from Indian contacts with white society as well as traditional Indian beliefs and practices. John Stuart, of the Society for the Propagation of the Gospel, found that the Mohawks among whom he was working had acquired bad habits from British soldiers during the revolutionary war; many others found drink the greatest obstacle to the Indians' religious "improvement."[22]

The major obstacle to programs of conversion and acculturation lay in the Indians' adherence to traditional ways and beliefs. The Mohawks seemed to be something of an exception to the rule and represented the missionaries' main hope for success. Even here the "march of progress" was hindered by lack of clergy and schoolteachers, by Indian reluctance or negligence in sending their children to school, by alcoholism, by the tendency to relapse into old habits, and by "the unconquerable Love of Savage Life." The Society for Propagating Christian Knowledge had seriously to consider whether it could afford to spend any of its limited funds on Indian missions and education when the outcome was so often in doubt and the results so often disappointing.[23] In 1809, Lord Castlereagh made inquiries as to the progress made by the Indians of Canada in agriculture, the arts, and religion, but he received no very encouraging replies from Lieutenant Governor Francis Gore. Gore reported but two or three instances of agricultural improvement among the Five Nations, none in the arts. Christianity and literacy were to be found in only two villages of the Five Nations, in each of which the government had built them a church several years before. Moreover, Gore reported, the introduction of Christianity and education did not seem to have improved the Indians' conduct. The missionaries, he felt, could have little influence over so large a body of Indians as inhabited Upper Canada. Nor did it appear that those with missionaries were any better than those without. Fur trader Duncan McGillivray thought that Indian converts, especially those living near the settlements, were in a far worse condition than those unacquainted with either civilization or its religion. John Norton, on the other hand, after paying a visit to Cornplanter's Senecas, thought that those who had received instruction in Christianity had made greater progress than any others.[24]

The success of missionary efforts was difficult to assess. Unlike Christianity, native religions tended to be neither dogmatic nor exclusive. Indians frequently managed to assimilate Christian doctrines with their traditional beliefs, or even to incorporate them into religious movements, as did the Seneca prophet Handsome Lake. Moreover, the Indian custom of listening with politeness and patience to a speaker, especially a stranger, instead of interrupting to disagree or ask questions, led to misunderstanding. Wrote former Indian captive John Hunter: "It is this trait in the Indian character which many of the missionaries mistake for a *serious* impression made on their minds; and which has led to many exaggerated accounts of their conversion to Christianity."[25] Much of Indian conversion seems to have been superficial and ephemeral. John Norton saw his adopted people making progress in temperance, industry, and agriculture, "But religion does not flourish as might be wished—there is too much catching at the Shadow and neglecting the Substance."[26] This seemed to be particularly true in the case of Indian conversions to Roman Catholicism. Anglicans, Quakers, and the rest attributed the appeal of Roman Catholicism to its pomp and ceremony, not to tenets, without understanding that Indians often adopted Christian symbols and attached their own mean-

ings to them. Lady Liston watched the Indians at the Lake
of the Two Mountains go through the motions at morning
mass as ignorant of the truths of the religion as they were
of the language in which they heard it.[27]

John Norton reckoned that although the Indians had
suffered from the European discovery of America, they
had also benefited by the superior knowledge he felt they
had acquired. And, he maintained, they might have gained
far more had Europeans been half as zealous in spreading
the light of the gospel as they had in gratifying their avarice.
Norton acknowledged, however, that there were some good
men who had made a start in this work.[28] According to
John Hunter, who lived for many years among several
tribes, Indians were prejudiced against missionaries and
all white men except the Quakers, whom they held in great
esteem. The Society of Friends does seem to have fared
comparatively well in its work among the Indians, perhaps
because it endeavored to teach by example and tend to the
Indians' practical needs rather than to indoctrinate them
with religious dogma. The Quakers sought to ease the Indians' transition into the white man's world by exchanging
"the tomahawk and scalping knife for the plough and the
hoe," and the Clapham Sect used the American Quakers as
the example for their projected "Society for promoting the
Civilization and Improvement of the North American Indians Within the British Boundary." Even so, Quaker missionaries encountered problems, not the least among tribes
like the Shawnee who found their doctrine of nonresis-
tance difficult to accept.[29]

Despite generations of contact and change, Indian cultures demonstrated impressive persistence and resilience.
Britons who were concerned about the Indians' welfare
found their reluctance to change particularly frustrating
because they believed that Indians had to adapt or die. If
the Indian was to avoid extinction, he must succeed as a
settled farmer and become a white man in all but the color
of his skin. Britons in general adhered to the belief that
the Indian way of life would and should disappear before

the advancing tide of settlement and that the two could not coexist. The efforts of missionaries and philanthropists were often as much an attempt to save the Indian from the extinction that was the only alternative to assimilation, as they were to improve his moral and spiritual condition.[30]

Not everyone, however, viewed the ultimate extinction of the Indian as a calamity. Many people regarded it as but a necessary step in humanity's continual improvement and natural progression from what they considered a state of savagery to what they assumed was civilization. In 1814 the *New Annual Register* gave its opinion that "in the course of events, the Indians must give place to the inhabitants of the United States; and it is desirable on every account that it should be so."[31] A handful of pagan hunters could not be permitted to deprive a host of industrious Christians of their right and duty to cultivate the wilderness. The march of progress could not slow down to cater for peoples who were different and therefore adjudged inferior. Euro-Americans possessed the means and the motivation to establish theirs as the dominant culture before which other cultures would disappear and to which other peoples must adapt or die.

If the British in this period devoted any serious attention to the preservation of the native cultures with which they came into contact, their concern stemmed from self-interest and the realization that only with their lands and lifestyles intact could the Indians offer an effective check to American expansion or operate successfully in the fur trade. Such military and economic considerations aside, Britain showed no more interest than the United States in trying to preserve or protect native cultures, and most regarded their destruction as both necessary and inevitable.

Part Three

TRAPPERS, TRADERS, AND MIDDLEMEN

6

British Trade and Indian Trade

AT THE END of the American Revolution the fur trade was estimated to be worth some £200,000 per annum to Great Britain,[1] and the business underwent a rapid expansion over the next thirty years. The trade was concerned primarily with beaver pelts, but other skins were also sought, notably marten, mink, fox, wolverine, lynx, and wolf. These other skins were generally considered inferior, as were bear and buffalo skins. In the maritime trade of the Northwest Pacific Coast, the sea otter pelts were the prime article of commerce. The fur trade constituted the most important branch of commerce between British North America and the mother country. It was also of enormous political importance because it linked to the British Empire those Indian tribes whose loyalty was essential to the security of His Majesty's dominions in North America.[2] Trade was neither a European monopoly nor a European innovation in North America, and successful conduct of the British fur trade required that British merchants accommodate their business to Indian traders and Indian trading patterns.

Trade generally represented the first, and for long periods, the only, medium of contact between the European and Amerindian worlds. From the viewpoint of many western tribes in the eighteenth and early nineteenth century, to be white was to be a trader; there was no other kind of non-Indian in their universe. First contacts tended to be fairly amicable because there was no previous experience to mar relations. Although the fur trade carried disease, dependence, and degradation in its wake, it also offered attractive benefits to peoples living in stone-age material cultures. British traders provided not only goods hitherto unknown to the Indian but also European-made articles that the Indians used, thus saving the buyer the time and effort required to manufacture those articles by traditional methods. Indians who expressed contempt for European civilization as a whole often were eager to acquire the goods that that civilization produced, to the extent that the fur trade tended to create a uniform, pan-Indian material culture among tribes with whom Europeans dealt.[3] The fur trade offered the Indians the opportunity to secure some of the material advantages of the white world before that world destroyed their traditional ways of life. The Indians keenly sought the advantages that trade offered them, and trade with an Indian tribe often implied some kind of alliance.[4]

The English and Canadian fur companies had the best goods, the best organizations, and the most extensive connections and operations. Britain was the "workshop of the world." Lancashire cotton mills, Yorkshire textile mills, and Midlands ironworks produced high-quality goods for the Indian trade. British manufacturers and gunsmiths modified their products in response to Indian demands, catering to Indian tastes and to the needs of hunters in the far north. From the Arctic to the Gulf of Mexico and from the Atlantic to the Pacific, English trade guns were the Indians' first choice. Even in the late 1820s it was reported that Arapaho and Comanche Indians in Texas rejected all American firearms. In their eyes a gun was good only if it was of British manufacture. In addition, the North West Company traders demonstrated how to combine successfully British business tactics with an intimate knowledge of Indian customs.[5] Not surprisingly, Indians most often turned to the British when they sought to contract trading alliances.

In an age of Anglo-American tension, it was significant that Indian tribes were rendered dependent upon manufactured goods but kept independent of the United States by the British fur trade.[6] Lieutenant Governor John Graves Simcoe dismissed the fur trade as of no value whatsoever to Upper Canada, which he envisioned as a settled agricultural colony, but he was the exception.[7] Most Britons recognized the trade to be of tremendous importance in the influence it exerted over its Indian customers. The Sioux chief Wabasha acknowledged this influence in the critical year of 1812: "We live by our English Traders who have always assisted us, and never more so, than this last year, at the risk of their lives, and we are at all times ready to listen to them on account of the friendship they have always shewn us."[8]

Euro-Americans believed that Indian friendship was best maintained by continued trade. Indeed, Anglo-American competition for the fur trade was not so much a contest for profits as it was a struggle for the influence over the Indians which that trade brought. Control of the tribes lay with those who armed, fed, and clothed them, a fact that caused continual anxiety in the United States, since the fur trade remained predominantly in British hands after 1783, and tribes within, or bordering upon, the Republic's territory traded at will with former and potential enemies. Americans blamed many of their Indian troubles on the machinations of English traders. As one United States Indian agent maintained: "Every British trader among the Indians is a potential partisan, sowing the seeds of distrust and dislike against the Government and people of the United States."[9]

American emissaries among the tribes did little to frustrate such intrigues. The Lewis and Clark Expedition, so successful otherwise, managed, in its one skirmish with Indians, to initiate Blackfoot hostility toward the United States that was to last for a quarter century. Blackfoot, and especially Piegan, relations with British and Canadian traders, on the other hand, were relatively amicable and even continued peaceful when the fur companies began to supply guns to the Blackfeet's enemies.[10] Britons and Americans alike assumed that the Indians gave their loyalty to whomever last supplied their needs,[11] but the British best put that assumption into practice. When Zebulon Pike journeyed to the tribes of the Mississippi in 1806 in an effort to extend United States sovereignty, he took away the Indians' British flags and medals and presented them with American flags; he then departed and left the field open for British traders to resume their intercourse with the tribes. Indian friendship was bought with goods and guns, not with flags and speeches.[12]

The Britons came to dominate trade on the Upper Mississippi, the Missouri, and the Minnesota rivers. Even when the British government neglected the tribes between 1796 and 1808, traders helped to maintain and extend British influence by means of British goods and kinship ties among the tribes. During the War of 1812, the Americans aimed not so much to capture the fur trade itself as to oust Canadian traders and terminate their influence over the Indians. The British, however, managed to retain Indian loyalty, not the least in the region west of Lake Huron, where fur trader Robert Dickson was appointed agent for the tribes.[13] Dickson's immodest claim that his exertions had brought the western country under British dominion had more than a grain of truth to it. The Americans recognized Dickson's effectiveness in bringing the western tribes to Britain's aid, and they seized his brothers as hostages in an effort to put a stop to his work.[14] Indian traders, with their knowledge, experience, and connections, made ideal Indian agents. The nearest the Americans came to matching the British trader-agents was when Manuel Lisa of the Missouri Fur Company managed to keep the Missouri tribes loyal to the United States during the War of 1812.[15]

Indians who had become dependent on European manufactured goods could barely survive without trade. British trade was not only a means of winning Indian allegiance, it was also an instrument of control, with threats to cut off supplies made to tribes who proved uncooperative. The

British had used such ploys to encourage the Great Lakes tribes to greater efforts during the revolutionary war. The Spanish too attempted to bring troublesome tribes to obedience by depriving them of trade, but were unsuccessful because the Indians, if deprived of Spanish trade, could turn to the English on the Missouri for their supplies.[16]

Spaniards and Americans faced the same problems in trying to win Indian allegiance through trade. They could not compete with the expertise of the British trader-agents, or the organization and capital of the British companies, or the quality and price of British goods, but the Americans did seek to emulate British trading companies as well as British Indian administration.[17] The Northwest Pacific Coast maritime trade constituted an exception to the British domination of the North American trade, falling to the Americans after initial English predominance, but elsewhere Indian trade tended to be British trade in one form or another. Following the Revolution, the Spanish authorities in Florida, eager to secure Indian allegiance but lacking the means to do so, were obliged to permit the British firm of Panton, Leslie, and Company to continue its monopoly of the southern Indian trade. Panton and Leslie took an oath of loyalty to the Spanish Crown, but retained its British nationality. By the 1790s Panton's Indian trade extended from the Chickasaws along the Mississippi River to the Seminoles on Saint John's River in east Florida.[18] Both John Jacob Astor's Pacific Fur Company and the Spanish Missouri Company had their fair share of British or Canadian members, while to the north Britain enjoyed massive dominance through the Hudson's Bay and North West companies. In 1812 the British minister in Washington even reported that the Americans would have to break their own commercial restrictions because without the importation of British blankets they would be unable to fulfill their Indian treaty obligations.[19] British manufactures enjoyed an unequaled reputation for quality and low prices. William Augustus Bowles, who in the 1790s sought to rival Alexander McGillivray's leadership by building his own

power among the Lower Creeks, recognized that access
to British goods was vital to the success of his ventures.
Bowles passed himself off in England and elsewhere as the
leader of a mighty Indian confederacy, and he and his
Indian "State of Muskogee" persistently sought to open
free trade with Britain and break the monopoly of Panton, Leslie, and Company. The promise of British trading
houses being reestablished in Florida apparently constituted enough of an incentive to interest the Indians in a
proposed expedition to reconquer the region for Britain.[20]
    The influence that fur traders enjoyed among the In-
dians was sealed by the community of interests they shared
in trying to preserve the wilderness way of life from the
destructive tide of settlement. This community of interests, as well as the merchants' self-interest, was reflected in
frequent petitions on behalf of the Indians' rights. Fur-
trading concerns constantly stressed that the Treaty of
1783 and Jay's Treaty of 1794 were mistakes, that Britain
could not cede Indian lands to which it held no territorial
rights, and that security of Indian lands was vital to the security of Canada and the fur trade.[21] The fur trade thus
helped Canada to enjoy better relations with the Indians
than those which obtained in the United States, but the
situation also created tense relations with land-hungry
Americans as long as the conflict continued between settlement and the Indian fur trade. With the advance of settlement and the removal of Indian tribes westwards, the fur
trade likewise shifted its location, and Americans continued
to find themselves in competition with British traders until
the settlement of the Oregon boundary dispute in 1846.
By that time, Albert Gallatin was justified in claiming that
the British fur companies, because of their position, mo-
nopolizing character, and influence with both the Indians
and the British government, had been a source of annoyance to the United States for sixty years.[22] The English
had inaugurated trade with the Cree Indians when they
built trading posts on Hudson Bay in 1670. Not until more
than a century and a half later, with the erection of Fort

Union on the Missouri River, did the American Fur Company begin to attract some Crees to trade. A quarter century after the Lewis and Clark Expedition, American traders were just beginning to compete for the custom of tribes like the Blackfeet, Assiniboines, Chippewas, and Crees, who had been trading exclusively with the British for generations.[23]

Among Indian peoples, trade often took the form of reciprocal gift giving rather than formal market exchange. Europeans might regard trade as a simple matter of commerce, regulated by supply and demand, but for Indians it was hedged by important social and ceremonial occasions and often was undertaken to signify friendship rather than to secure profit. That is not to say that Indians operated without regard to commercial realities, nor that they were incapable of matching the European trader at his own game. To recognize that the Indians with whom British traders dealt were frontier businessmen rather than backwoods simpletons, it is important to appreciate the extent of Indian trade and the experience and expertise that the natives acquired in the course of that commerce.

The European fur trade stimulated, altered, and increased intertribal intercourse but did not necessarily create it. Europeans introduced horses and guns, but those commodities underwent their greatest diffusion by means of Indian-to-Indian rather than white-to-Indian exchange. Horses with Spanish brands found their way as far north as the Upper Missouri, following established routes of intertribal raiding and trade.[24] There were many interacting systems of trade in North America; some involved Indians and Europeans, others involved Indians only. The barter between Indian and British trader occurred as the final link in a chain of transactions that stretched from London to the northwest.[25] Yet this chain represented only half the picture. The Indian-trader point of contact was not just the final link in a single chain of transactions; it was a central link in a network of transactions. Goods traveled from London to Montreal to the point of British-Indian trade; from there they passed by way of Indian hands to more distant tribes. Furs passed through various Indian hands before reaching the trader who shipped them off to Montreal or London. A gun manufactured in Birmingham or London passed through many hands before it was fired on the Great Plains. Before the North West Company opened direct trade with them, the Flatheads and the Shoshones could acquire guns only from Crow middlemen who had gotten them from the Mandans and the Hidatsas; they in turn had traded the guns from the Crees and the Assiniboines, who had obtained them from Hudson Bay or North West Company traders. Different systems interlocked and overlapped and Indians participated in British trade and in Indian trade, acting as middlemen or as direct producers.

Trade was a vital factor in tribal intersocietal relations. Facilitated by sign language, whose use it doubtless increased, intertribal commerce was as common as intertribal war; indeed, intertribal diplomacy provided for cessations of hostilities in order that trade might take place. The Ottawas got their name, which means "traders," from their role as middlemen in the early French trade; the Kata or Arikara band of Kiowas took its name from a close trading connection with the Arikaras; and the name Arapaho may have derived from a Pawnee word signifying "buyer" or "trader."[26] Under the enormous stimuli of horses and guns, a network of intertribal trade developed and expanded. Just as British traders had to adjust to Indian political and cultural conditions, so the British fur trade had to fit into and take account of existing Indian commerce.

The fur trader's constant desire was to make direct contact with unsophisticated customers who would, he hoped, exchange their valuable pelts for trifles. In reality, however, he had to deal more often with consummate wilderness businessmen, who derived maximum profit from their trade, than with trinket-grasping innocents. The Indians who arrived at a trading post with furs were not necessarily the ones who had trapped them, and the role of middleman was an eagerly sought and jealously guarded position. Indian middlemen increased prices in passing European goods on to other tribes and in bringing the latter's furs to the trader, and they frequently dictated terms to British and Indians alike. Tribes sought to intrude themselves as middlemen as eagerly as British traders tried to exclude them. The Hudson's Bay Company previously had depended upon Indian intermediaries to convey furs to its posts on the Bay, and during the late seventeenth and early eighteenth century, the woodland Crees and Assiniboines had operated successfully in that role. When Montreal traders opened up direct trade with Indian producers by establishing posts in the fur country, the Crees and Assiniboines lost their lucrative middleman position.[27] Indian middlemen and Indian business acumen were inevitable by-products of the fur trade, however, and only rarely did British traders achieve the elusive goal of dealing with peoples who were unacquainted with European market values.

The successful plying of trade conditions was not a skill monopolized by whites, and the situation was complicated by the fact that Indian trade was tied up with Indian power politics. In earlier centuries the Iroquois had exploited and defended their favorable trade position as a source of power, and Indians continued to appreciate that those who possessed European goods, firearms in particular, enjoyed an enormous advantage over those who lacked them. The most keenly sought position was one that enabled a tribe to halt or control the flow of manufactured goods to other tribes. Indians competed for trade with white men as eagerly as whites competed for Indian trade. A tribe with access to European goods generally tried to deprive other tribes of those goods. They tried to prevent traders from reaching more distant tribes, either to preserve their own positions as middlemen or to maintain their dominance over neighbors who lacked firearms and manufactures. Indian determination to secure and retain a monopoly of trade caused enormous difficulties for traders from Saint Louis who endeavored to extend Spanish commerce to the strategically located tribes on the Upper Missouri in the 1790s. Jean Baptiste Truteau, on a mission to the Arikara and Mandan tribes in 1794–95, took precautions and made detours but nevertheless suffered losses at the hands of the Poncas, the Omahas, the Yanktons, and the Teton Sioux. As he found, "la politique des sauvages de cette rivièrre, est d'empecher la communication entre nous et les nations du haut du missouri, les priv(a)nt des munitions de guerre, et autres secours qu'ils receurcient De nous si nous y parvenions facilement. ils tiennent ces peuples Eloignes dans une crainte continuelle de leur armes a feu."[28]

The Osages too were determined that if they were not to receive Spanish trade, neither should any of the tribes beyond them. Nor was the practice restricted to the Missouri River tribes. On the Northwest Pacific Coast the Chinooks persistently tried to exclude upriver peoples from trade with European and American ships arriving at the mouth of the Columbia.[29] The Saint Louis traders seem to have acquiesced in payment of tribute to the warriors of the Lower Missouri. The Ponca and the Omaha tribes were particularly notorious pirates, surpassed only by the Sioux, who plundered Indians and non-Indians with equal enthusiasm.[30] Lewis and Clark appear to have been the first white voyagers up the Missouri to have refused to pay tribute, and their determination not to be imposed upon helped to open the river to traffic and end the Sioux's career as river pirates. Nevertheless, Sioux warriors remained a threat to parties ascending the Missouri as late as 1810.[31] The Indians, of course, saw their actions not as piracy but as the levy of legitimate payment for the right to cross their territory.

Indians adopted various ploys to prevent traders from reaching the tribes beyond, ranging from warning of the evil and hostile dispositions of those tribes to actual plundering and the threat or use of force. The Chinook chief Concomly, who impressed British and American traders as a devious and cunning character, sought to monopolize the trade of the recently arrived Astorians by telling them that the tribes farther inland were hostile and at the same time telling those tribes that the newcomers were their enemies, thus creating a situation in which the Chinooks could buy up all the furs and sell them to the whites at double the price they had paid.[32] Similarly, though more for military than economic motives, the Atsinas and the Blackfeet endeavored to prevent British trade with tribes west of the Rocky Mountains. The Piegans, the frontier tribe of the Blackfoot confederacy, remained on good terms with the traders as long as the latter's posts were confined to the eastern side of the mountains, thus enabling the Piegans to obtain goods and guns themselves but to bar them from their enemies farther west, especially the Kootenais. Armed with guns obtained from British traders, the Blackfeet had driven the comparatively defenseless Flatheads and Shoshones across the Rockies and preyed on their vast horse herds almost at will, besides pushing the Crows into the Yellowstone region.[33]

The Kootenais tried to reach the North West Company post at Fort George on the Saskatchewan, but their efforts were frustrated by the Piegans, who also managed to prevent the Flatheads and the Pend d'Oreilles from making contact with Canadian posts until 1806. In 1805, Piegans stopped David Thompson from crossing the Rockies and he did not manage to get across until 1807, when he built the first Kootenai trading post; even then he had to buy off a 300-strong Piegan war party who intended to destroy the post. Three years later, the Piegans suffered their first defeat at the hands of the now equally well-armed Kootenai and Flathead tribes. The enraged Piegans would have exacted vengeance on the British traders whom they held responsible for this defeat, but they realized that to do so would lose them their own supplies of firearms, ammunition, tobacco, and alcohol. Even so, Piegan opposition to Thompson's attempt to cross the Rockies in the winter of 1810–11 proved fatal to the North West Company's plan to

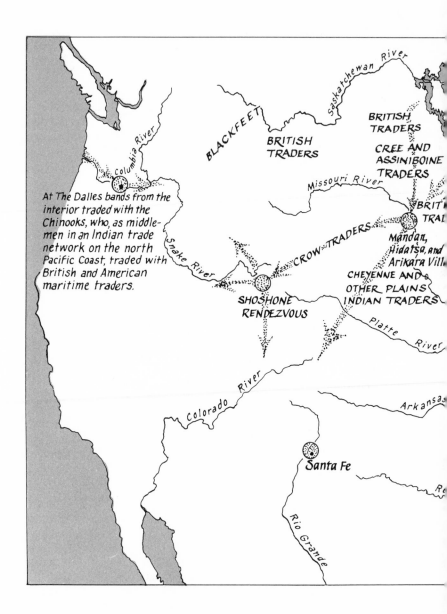

At The Dalles bands from the interior traded with the Chinooks, who, as middle-men in an Indian trade network on the north Pacific Coast, traded with British and American maritime traders.

BLACKFEET

BRITISH TRADERS

BRITISH TRADERS

CREE AND ASSINIBOINE TRADERS

BRIT TRAI

CROW TRADERS

Mandan, Hidatsa, and Arikara Vill

CHEYENNE AND OTHER PLAINS INDIAN TRADERS

SHOSHONE RENDEZVOUS

Santa Fe

Saskatchewan River

Missouri River

Columbia River

Snake River

Platte River

Colorado River

Arkansas

Rio Grande

Re

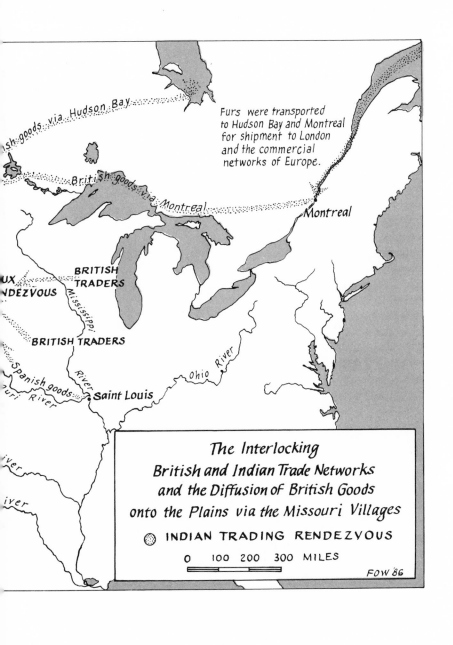

Furs were transported
to Hudson Bay and Montreal
for shipment to London
and the commercial
networks of Europe.

ish goods via Hudson Bay

British goods via Montreal

Montreal

BRITISH
TRADERS

UX
NDEZVOUS

Mississippi

BRITISH TRADERS

Ohio River

Spanish goods

River

uri River

Saint Louis

iver

iver

The Interlocking
British and Indian Trade Networks
and the Diffusion of British Goods
onto the Plains via the Missouri Villages

⊚ INDIAN TRADING RENDEZVOUS

0   100   200   300   MILES

FOW 86

reach the mouth of the Columbia River before John Jacob
Astor's American party and thereby to assert British title to
the region by right of prior settlement.[34]

The trade network that focused on the villages of the
Mandans, the Hidatsas, and to a lesser extent, the Arikaras illustrates the extent and character of intertribal intercourse, as well as the different roles and interests of
the tribes who participated. The Upper Missouri villages
became a rendezvous in Indian trade and a distribution
center for horses and European goods. Britons, French-
Canadians, Spaniards, and Americans all recognized the
importance of these villages. It was reckoned that a post
established among the Mandans would become a gath-
ering place for more than twenty Indian nations, and
the British had a fort there by the time Lewis and Clark
passed up the Missouri. Chippewas, Plains Crees, Assiniboines, Crows, Flatheads, Shoshones, Blackfeet, Cheyennes, Arapahos, Kiowas, Kiowa-Apaches, Comanches,
Plains Apaches, Pawnees, Poncas, and various bands of
Sioux visited the villages, either regularly or occasionally,
and the Upper Missouri villages became the center of an
Indian trade network that extended across half the continent and more, and linked up ultimately with European
trade networks.[35]

The trade operated as follows: the Arikaras, the Mandans, and the Hidatsas produced an agricultural surplus,
which they traded to the British, the Crees, and the Assiniboines on the north; to the Crows, the Shoshones, and the
Flatheads on the west; and to Plains Indians on the south
and west. From British traders they received manufactured goods, either directly or by way of the Crees and Assiniboines, while from the Plains Indians they received
horses, leather clothing, and dried meat. In this way the
semisedentary tribes of the Missouri became a market for
the exchange of British and Plains Indian produce and
were middlemen between the tribes on the south and west
and the British traders and forest tribes on the northeast.
As such they had the two most sought-after articles in the

Indian trade—horses and guns—at their disposal. The Indians who roamed the plains traded at this Missouri rendezvous and then acted as diffusion agents, transmitting British goods across the plains in exchange for more horses, which could be bartered for more goods. Horses, besides being a means of production in hunting, thus functioned as a medium of exchange in trade, and tribes like the Cheyenne Indians were able to play a profitable role as middlemen.

In fact, almost every tribe that was involved was able to secure itself an advantageous trading position. The Crees and Assiniboines traded with both the Mandans and Hidatsas and the British fur companies; the Mandans and Hidatsas traded with virtually everyone; and those tribes who came to trade at the Missouri villages passed on desired goods or horses at extortionate rates, as then did the tribes with whom they traded. This explains the eagerness of the Flatheads and the Kootenais to obtain direct trade with the British: the few guns and goods they received through the intertribal trade network had been repeatedly marked up in price by each tribe that handled them. For similar reasons, other tribes on the periphery sought to become involved in the trade network. In 1805 the Nez Percés apparently sent a delegation that accompanied the Crows on their annual trip from the Yellowstone to the Missouri villages.

With so many tribes occupying favorable economic positions, Indian efforts to preserve their privileged niches in the trading network were numerous. The Assiniboines traded with both the North West Company on the Assiniboine River and with the Mandans and Hidatsas on the Missouri, and therefore resented the traders who dealt directly with these agricultural tribes. The Mandans and the Hidatsas in turn understood the art and value of their middlemen role and tried to dissuade the white men from trading directly with their Crow customers. In 1806, Alexander Henry of the North West Company witnessed the Hidatsas or "Big Bellies" deriving full benefit from, and

jealously guarding, their Crow trade: "It was disgusting to
see how those impious vagabonds, the Big Bellies, keep
those poor inoffensive Crows in subjection, making their
own prices for horses and everything else; nor will they
allow a stranger to give the Crows the real value of their
commodities; the price once fixed by those scoundrels,
they permit no one to give more." Henry was probably
more envious of the Hidatsas' lucrative position than concerned with the plight of their customers. In any case, the
Crows would still have made a considerable profit on the
horses they had in turn traded from tribes farther west.
The Crows were themselves middlemen in a lucrative trade
and agents in the diffusion of horses and goods, operating
between the Mandans and Hidatsas and the Flatheads; it
was perhaps for this reason that they regarded the coming
of white traders with mixed feelings. Again, the Hidatsas
were greatly annoyed when North West Company clerk
Charles Mackenzie accompanied their Cheyenne customers back to their homes because they knew he would do a
more profitable trade there than on the Missouri.[36]

The whole Missouri trade situation was complicated by
the Teton Sioux, who offer a prime example of a tribe conscious of its favorable position and exploiting that position
to the full. Not only did they prevent traders from Saint
Louis from ascending the Missouri, they frequently plundered neighboring tribes and seem to have held the Arikaras in virtual vassalage. The Teton Sioux enjoyed a unique
position in the region that freed them from dependence
on the Missouri trade network for their supply of European goods. They got their manufactured goods, guns,
and ammunition from their Yankton and Sisseton kinsmen
on the east, who traded directly with British traders on the
Des Moines and Minnesota (Saint Peter's) rivers, respectively, or at an annual rendezvous at Prairie du Chien. The
annual Dakota rendezvous on the James River assured the
Tetons of the supplies they needed to maintain hegemony
over the Missouri.[37]

In such circumstances, British traders had to operate

within existing and developing Indian commercial networks and had to adjust to intertribal power politics and warfare. Traders complained that Indian wars disrupted business, but the fur trade itself intensified and in some cases created hostilities. Cree warriors, armed with British guns, came into increasing conflict with the Blackfoot and the Atsina tribes; the Blackfeet exploited their newly acquired firepower to prey on the Kootenais and the Shoshones. British traders preferred to trade with all tribes, irrespective of Indian politics, but to do so created difficulties. David Thompson incurred Piegan wrath by trading with the Flatheads and the Kootenais; and the Atsinas attacked traders on the Saskatchewan for doing business with the Crees.[38] Equally reluctant to become involved in Indian wars and to see rich fur grounds such as the Sioux-Chippewas' no-man's-land closed to trapping, British merchants endeavored to end the intertribal hostilities that were so bad for business. War and trade had become so interwoven in Indian society, however, that the traders' peace initiatives were doomed to failure. The traders, by their very presence, only increased the likelihood of intertribal competition and conflict.[39]

As fur traders had to fit into Indian societies and situations, so Indians found themselves a niche in the British scheme of trade. A relationship of mutual adaptation and interdependence developed between trader and Indian. Both had to live in a harsh and often dangerous environment. Indians became increasingly dependent for survival and an easier life upon the manufactures provided by the fur trade; the fur trade in turn relied heavily upon Indian cooperation and know-how. The Indian in the British fur trade was not a shadowy figure who emerged briefly from the forest to barter his furs and then disappeared for another season's hunting. He was an ever-present participant who fulfilled the roles of trapper, trader, scout, guide, ambassador, interpreter, laborer, porter, customer, partner, and competitor.

The extension of the fur trade into areas hitherto unexplored depended upon finding knowledgeable Indians as much as upon actual pathfinding by white explorers. Indian guides and interpreters earned frequent condemnation as troublesome and unreliable, but their services were indispensable to the fur trade.[40] Fur-trading and exploratory expeditions relied on Canadian voyageurs or Orkneymen for manpower, but they employed Indian modes of transport, notably canoes and snowshoes, as the best means of travel through the wilderness.

The Indians' main roles in the fur trade, however, were those of middlemen and producers. Indians proved to be capable intermediaries, but it was the native producers on whom the fur trade depended for its existence. Indian producers were of two general categories, those who provided furs and those who provided food. Under normal circumstances, of course, the fur companies were primarily concerned with the fur-producing tribes. As Duncan McGillivray pointed out, the division of Indians into those who had furs and those who had none was more important to traders than any distinctions of language or custom.[41] Northern forest tribes tended to produce the best furs, but the Plains Indians also acquired a useful and rewarding role in the business. As the fur trade expanded into remote northwestern regions its supply routes lengthened correspondingly. Buffalo-hunting Plains Indians then became useful because they supplied provisions of meat, grease, and fat to the isolated posts and to the fur brigades on their long canoe journeys. Thus, the very penetration inland by white traders, which had deprived the woodland Crees and Assiniboines of their lucrative position as middlemen between Hudson Bay and Indian hunters in the interior, now gave the plains branches of those two tribes a new economic role, that of providing food for the fur trade.[42] Alexander Henry complained that the Blackfoot trade in furs was of little or no value, that that tribe brought in nothing but trash, yet nevertheless realized how important the tribe's supplies of meat were for his post's sustenance, especially as the whites dared not risk sending out their own hunting parties while those same Blackfeet were around.[43] Hudson's Bay Company posts received both fish and geese from the neighboring Indians, and the smallpox epidemic of the early 1780s revealed the company's dependence on the Indians for food as much as furs.[44] The Chippewas seemed to the British to live under the constant threat of starvation, yet they still managed to provide food as well as furs for the posts in their country. The development of bands based around local trading posts was thus an arrangement advantageous to both parties, and the posts were apparently more often dependent on the Chippewas for food than vice-versa.[45]

Different tribes performed different roles and produced various commodities for the fur trade. Fur-producing tribes received preferential treatment from the traders, but they did not necessarily enjoy the most advantageous position in the trade. Forest bands who devoted all their energies to trapping beaver became dependent on the traders to supply their equipment and other necessities. The situation was very different on the plains; there, the fur traders depended on the Indians for provisions, but the equestrian tribes were not dependent upon the fur trade. Vast buffalo herds supplied the Indians' every need and enabled them to remain independent of traders. The Plains Indians even found their own bows and arrows better for hunting than any implements white men had to offer. When Plains Indians traded meat and horses, they bartered for firearms and luxuries rather than for necessities. In time, of course, luxuries, especially the addictive variety, became necessities, but observers frequently asserted that the plains Indians had the potential to be the happiest people on the continent.[46] The role of supplying food to the posts and traders was a by-product of the actual exchange of goods and furs, but it gave Plains Indians access to British trade without subjecting them to coercion.

In the actual trade, the fur companies tended to adapt their procedures to suit native custom and etiquette. Commercial transactions were cloaked in ceremony and conducted as exchanges of gifts, although the companies adopted the beaver pelt as the basic unit in order to standardize these exchanges. Traders did much of their business with individual Indians or with small family groups, but the procedure followed when a larger band arrived to trade best illustrates the mixture of elaborate ceremonial and hard-headed business practices that was characteristic of fur trading at the posts. As the Indian agent had to sit through exhaustive and exhausting Indian councils, so the fur trader had to tolerate the Indians' insistence that their visit to his post be treated as a social and ceremonial occasion rather than an impersonal economic activity. Duncan McGillivray, at Fort George on the Saskatchewan in the 1790s, painted the following picture:

> When a Band of Indians approach near the Fort it is customary for the Cheifs [sic] to send a few young men before them to announce their arrival, and to procure a few articles which they are accustomed to receive on these occasions—such as Powder, a piece of Tobacco and a little paint to besmear their faces, an operation which they seldom fail to perform previous to their presenting themselves before the *White People*. At a few yards distance from the gate they salute us with several discharges of their guns, which is answered by hoisting a flag and firing a few guns. On entering the house they are disarmed, treated with a few drams and a bit of tobacco, and after the pipe has been plyed about for some time they relate the news with great deliberation and ceremony relaxing from their usual taciturnity in proportion to the quantity of Rum they have swallowed, 'till at length their voices are drowned in a general clamour. When their lodges are erected by the women they receive a present of Rum proportioned to the Nation & quality of the Cheifs [sic] and the whole Band drink during 24 hours and sometimes much longer for nothing—a privilege of which they take every advantage— for in the seat of an Opposition profusion is absolutely necessary to secure the trade of an Indian. When the drinking match has subsided they begin to trade.[47]

It was customary to fire guns into the air on approaching a trading post or when meeting a friendly party because an empty gun was a sign of friendship and trust.

Besides the required ceremonial, however, traders needed to be vigilant and take precautions, especially when Indians became drunk. If a visiting tribe was proving troublesome, the Hudson's Bay Company tended to admit only a few Indians at a time to trade at its posts. Sometimes only the principal men of the tribe were allowed in, and frequently the Indians were permitted to trade only through a storeroom window, in an effort to curb pilfering. Peter Pond, however, recalled one trader who used the propensity for theft to his own advantage: he would leave small, inexpensive articles lying around on his counter for the Indians to steal, maintaining that Indians brought their trade to him because they could not resist such golden opportunities for pilfering. The Indians of the Northwest Coast were noted as particularly accomplished pilferers, but they were by no means the only people with a reputation for thieving.[48]

Throughout the fur trade, from London to the Far Northwest, transactions were based on credit, and the same system was employed at the posts. Indians pledged their hunt in advance in return for the supplies and equipment they needed to make that hunt, repaying their debts with the furs they trapped. Naturally, the amount of credit extended varied, depending on the reputation of the Indian hunter for honesty and ability. In order to safeguard their debts and regularize their business, traders sought to deal with the same chiefs each time, often holding the band leader responsible for the debts contracted by his followers. From this, it was but a small step to the appointment of Indians whom the traders thought suitable as "paper chiefs" for the purposes of trade. These chiefs were important intermediaries between trader and customers, advising their followers where to do business and often agreeing on prices with the trader beforehand. The recognition gained at the trading post was also important to the chiefs' position since the gifts they received both enhanced their prestige and increased their powers of munificence. The Chinook Concomly rose to preeminence on the Northwest Coast in this period largely because of his ability as a trading chief, acting as intermediary between his people and the white traders.[49] Indians perhaps accepted trader-made "chiefs" because they saw the advantage of having a good bargainer at the trading posts; but the practice had its disadvantages for both trader and Indian. The trading chief's influence rested on his having liquor, tobacco, and ammunition to hand out to his followers and, of course, lasted only so long as he had supplies to distribute. Moreover, under conditions of competition, the number of trading chiefs who were appointed increased to the extent that Alexander Henry complained there was scarcely a common buck to be seen; it seemed that all the Indians were wearing scarlet coats and carrying kegs of liquor. A single band of Indians could thus have several chiefs, each one contracted to a different trader and a different company. This same proliferation of chiefs, however, undermined the authority of the position because the chief was no longer the sole supplier of trade goods.[50] Thus, even with the appointment of chosen chiefs, the trader could not be sure the Indians would repay their debts.

The credit system was attacked for rendering the Indian indebted to and dependent on his trader,[51] but, to read fur traders' complaints, it appears to have been a source of as much, if not more, anxiety and trouble to the trader who gave the credit as it was to the Indians who received it. In a business where cash was short and returns on outlay could often take two to three years to materialize, the collection by the trader of furs pledged to him became the foundation of an extensive and complicated system of credit financing.[52] This partly explains the extreme measures to which traders sometimes resorted in order to secure the pelts owed to them, or even those owed to someone else. Indians were occasionally plundered of their furs and threatened with violence if they dared to trade with the opposition. In April 1804, for example, Alexander Henry intercepted a band of Indians on their return from hunting beaver and fought with the women until he got all their furs. "It is true," he admitted in his journal, "it was all my neighbor's debts."[53]

The years from the conquest of Canada until the merger of the Hudson's Bay and North West companies in 1821 saw the fur trade reach extremes of competition. Under the uncertainties and wilderness conditions of the trade, healthy competition was transformed into cut-throat rivalry that injured both the participants and the profits. The Nor'westers' penetration inland, the Hudson's Bay Company's following suit, the formation of the X.Y. and other lesser companies, and a sprinkling of free-lance operators, meant that traders and trading posts proliferated in the Indian country. One trading post sometimes stood within sight of another. With tribes like the Blackfeet around, rival posts were often built close together for mutual protection as well as for competition. In the winter of 1794–95, there were, for example, five different competitors in the area near the mouth of River Winnipeg, all working against one another. This proliferation of posts rendered the credit system virtually unworkable, and it often put the trader at the mercy of his customers because each rival trader represented an alternative market to the Indians. Some Indians contracted debts at one post in the autumn, only to take their hunt to another in the spring, thus securing double profits. Indians traded where goods were cheapest and where they received the best attention. Many became adept at playing one trader against another, having few qualms about switching allegiance in order to receive extra credits and gifts. Duncan Cameron lamented that Indians were "great cheats for their credits," but the trader was obliged to pander to them and pay extravagantly lest they take their business to the opposition; experience taught that to refuse one Indian credit could lose the trade of his whole band to a rival.[54] In effect, under conditions of intense competition, the fur trade became an auction in which each trader strove to outdo his rivals by paying higher prices for furs, extending more credit, and giving more gifts and drink to the Indians. Both English

and Canadian traders realized that such competition created turmoil and played into the Indians' hands. Monopoly
was regarded as the key to a more orderly and successful
trade. Not only would it render the Indians dependent and
make them industrious, loyal, and subordinate, but many
argued it meant that the Indians' morals and welfare could
be better looked after.[55] Consequently, the North West and
X.Y. companies merged in 1804 after five years of frenzied
competition and, following the union of 1821, the Hudson's Bay Company implemented new policies that reduced
credit, increased prices, and generally aimed to make the
Indians more dependent.

Cut-throat competition does seem to have accentuated
the worst abuses in the fur trade, with Indians and traders
alike sacrificing long-term interests for immediate gains.
The most glaring abuse was the use of alcohol. Because Indians tended to regard trading as a social occasion, rum
"according to imemorial [sic] usage is the indispensible
[sic] precursor of all bargains and negociations [sic] with
the savages."[56] Alcohol was admirably suited to the needs
of the trade; it was cheap and addictive and could be transported easily in concentrated form and then diluted for
the Indian customers. The strength of the liquor depended
on how accustomed to drink the recipient tribe was: that
given to the Chippewas, the Crees, or the Assiniboines was
nearly twice as strong as the rum diluted to form "Blackfoot milk."[57] Spirits served as an attraction and inducement
to trade more than an actual commodity of exchange, and a
gift of liquor usually put the customer in the right frame
of mind to do business. Indeed, Indians often considered
that drink was due to them out of ordinary hospitality,
an attitude that caused Alexander Henry considerable
trouble with the Piegans: "They appear fully as much as
addicted to liquor as the Crees, though, unlike the latter,
they will not purchase it. They cannot be made to comprehend that anything of value should be paid for what they
term 'water.' This is the cause of all our misunderstandings
with them; they will not pay for drinks, and will absolutely
insist upon our treating them with their favourite liquor."[58]

The Chipewyans were likewise reluctant to trade for liquor, while the Arikaras apparently refused to partake of it unless they were paid to do so, saying that the person who offered them drink wished to laugh at their expense and should therefore pay for the pleasure.[59] The Indians' reluctance to pay for drink is perhaps understandable in view of the poor quality of liquor used in the Indian trade. What one fur trader found surprising was not that a colleague should be so addicted to liquor that he went to bed drunk every night, "but I should Never have Believed that he would be fond enough thereof to Drink the Savages' Rum."[60]

Indians not yet fully acquainted with alcohol remained temporarily temperate: the Crows were averse to liquor until the 1860s. Others abstained in accordance with their religious observances. In 1807 trader John Askin, Jr., complained that, thanks to the teachings of the Shawnee Prophet, the Indians around Saint Josephs were not buying so much as a gallon of liquor a month and even refused it when it was offered to them for nothing.[61]

Among most tribes, however, alcohol seems to have served its purpose of securing furs, prompting the Indians to hunt, and attracting them to trade. According to Duncan McGillivray of the North West Company, the love of rum was the Indians' first inducement to work since they were prepared to undergo every hardship and fatigue to obtain it, "and when a Nation becomes addicted to drinking, it affords a strong presumption that they will soon become excellent hunters." Liquor was the Assiniboines' principal inducement in supplying dried meat to British posts on the Assiniboine River, while in September 1810 a fur brigade arrived at Alexander Henry's post and, according to trader Henry, "The Indians, like ravenous wolves on the scent of a carcass, came hotly after the canoes, attracted by the smell of liquor."[62]

Whatever the disastrous effects it had on Indian life and the difficulties it created for the trader, alcohol was an indispensable commodity in the fur trade, and its use increased dramatically in periods of stiff competition. Duncan McGillivray reckoned that during the North West–X.Y. Company struggle, nearly double the usual amount of alcohol was consumed in the Indian country. The North West Company certainly increased its liquor distribution from an annual average of 9,600 gallons to an average of 12,340 gallons for the years 1799–1804, reaching a high of 16,299 gallons in 1803, before declining to an average consumption of 10,700 gallons per annum from 1805 to 1808.[63] Not surprisingly, the use of such vast amounts of alcohol came under attack. The Reverend Edmund Burke, vicar-general of Upper Canada, denounced the use of rum in the Indian trade, maintaining that it destroyed more Indians in one year than all their wars with the yankees did in ten. Philanthropists in Parliament pressed for its prohibition in the face of North West Company opposition. Traders themselves generally seem to have regarded alcohol as the main cause of their problems and the root of all evil in the Indian country, yet frequently defended its use as a necessary evil in a business where competition was rife.[64]

The ill effects of the fur trade on the Indian tended to be cumulative rather than immediate, especially when conditions of competition offered him an advantageous economic position. The men who ran the fur trade sought to leave the Indian as an Indian, except perhaps for making him a more efficient and cooperative trapper, but the trade inevitably disrupted Indian societies and cultures. It rendered the Indian dependent on the trading posts, and then when the fur-bearing regions were exhausted, left him impoverished and demoralized to face the subsequent onslaught of white settlement.

The fur trade era saw an unprecedented slaughter of wildlife. White trappers were largely to blame, but the Indians also played a part. Whether Indians responded to new technology and market incentives to reap economic advantages or, as has been argued, resorted to overkill in a war of retaliation against animals they held responsible for the holocaust caused by epidemic diseases, the ecological re-

sults were disastrous and sacred symbiotic relationships between Indians and "persons-of-other-than-human-form"
were disrupted.[65]

Yet, in the actual scheme of the British fur trade, the Indian was a participant rather than a pawn and frequently
matched the profit-conscious trader in cheating, monopo-
lizing, and exploitation. The "gullible and unsophisticated
savage" existed in the wishful thinking of the trader rather
than in the reality of the fur trade. Occasionally, early
traders did find Indians who would hand over their furs
for a trifle, and for a time maritime traders on the Northwest Coast sought to emulate Captain James Cook and
reap a fortune in sea otter pelts. Even here the old stereo-
type of the avaricious trader buying Indian furs with trinkets may not have applied.[66] Indians soon came to realize
that a beaver skin or an otter pelt was worth more than a
two-penny knife or a six-penny trinket. In 1787, Captain
John Meares was warned of the need to practice strict
economy during his projected trading expedition to the
Northwest Coast. The Indians there were "such intelligent
traders" that, were Meares to be at all lavish, they would
drastically increase the price of their furs and not only
exhaust Meares's stock but also jeopardize any such ventures in the future. The coastal Indians appear to have
been particularly shrewd traders and displayed considerable commercial acumen in their dealings with British and
American traders.[67]

Indians generally were quick to learn the tricks of the
trade, and observers frequently commented that Indian
dishonesty and malpractice stemmed from contact with
white traders.[68] Whatever their actual condition, Indians
regularly pleaded hunger and poverty when they arrived
at a trading post. Writing from his knowledge of the Crees,
Andrew Graham asserted that Indians were sly and crafty,
and even the mild and friendly Eskimos were as bad: "They
glory in overreaching in trade, and think it no injury to
cheat, or thieve from a European."[69]

Traders on the plains found that valuable articles could

rarely be obtained for next to nothing, even at early dates and during initial contacts. Traders there were frustrated by the Indians' ignorance of, or refusal to abide by, white standards of trade as much as by any exercise of duplicity. Indians who were acquainted with the value of their goods tended not to give them away for worthless trinkets but rather to place an unrealistically high price on them and stick to it. The novitiate Crows preferred to deal with other Indians rather than with white men, and it was not unknown for one tribe to meddle in another's dealings. One French-Canadian trader was deprived of a potentially profitable trade with Arapahos on their first visit to the Arikara villages in 1804. A band of Cheyennes who were present had what the trader described as "a half knowledge" of the value of things, and were not only themselves difficult to trade with but also insisted on giving advice to the newcomers.[70] Alexander Henry, accustomed to dealing with the presumably more accommodating Chippewas, found infuriating the habit the Hidatsas and other Missouri Indians had of making a bargain and going away apparently satisfied, only to change their minds and return to demand a refund of their goods.[71] Indians' failure to repay debts was not always from duplicity but occasionally stemmed from a tendency to regard old debts as paid and to contract new ones without ever considering whether they would be able to repay them.[72] Nor did Indians always react as expected to economic enticements. The higher prices offered as a result of competition did not bring an increase and often caused a decrease in the amount of furs traded. Lacking the European's sense of and desire for property, the Indian took advantage of the improved terms to satisfy his limited material needs with less effort, instead of securing more goods by the same or extra effort. In British eyes the Indian wasted any additional time and profit that the situation brought him at leisure and on drink and tobacco.[73]

The value attached to an object is largely proportional to the amount of time and effort required to make or replace it, and until the Indians began to accept traders' prices as a measure of the value of commodities, Indians and whites had different notions of worth as well as of property. In early intercourse each gave the other things he valued lightly in exchange for things he valued highly, and each thought the other foolish for accepting. On the occasions when Indians did give freely, the trader might scoff at Indians who would trade a bundle of pelts for a few metal utensils. The Indian could not understand traders exchanging articles, which, it seemed to him, must have taken much time and labor to make, for skins that could be had for the hunting. To a man in the wilderness with many furs but no knife, a good knife was more valuable than prime beaver. David Thompson, preparing for a trading expedition to the Piegans, admitted that the goods he was taking were of little monetary value, but maintained they were of great utility to the Indians. The trade was profitable to both parties, but, Thompson reckoned, more so to the Indians, who exchanged useless furs for useful articles, than to the white traders whose pelts had then to undergo long distances and huge risks before being sold on the London market. The Indians of the Upper Missouri were cautious and seemed fickle when trading horses for what Britons considered trifles, but were quite the opposite when trading buffalo robes and wolf and fox skins. Wrote Alexander Henry: "They put little value on any of those skins, and cannot imagine what use we make of such trash, as they call it. They kill some beavers and a few grizzly bears, all of which they dispose of, and call the whites fools for giving them valuable articles for such useless skins."[74]

On the other hand, things that Europeans dismissed as trinkets could be of more than purely material value to Indians because they possessed symbolic, artistic, religious, or political significance that was often beyond European comprehension.[75] Indians quickly came to appreciate the value the traders put on things, however. While they might continue to regard a beaver pelt as of less value than an ax, they began to alter their prices in accordance with European values, asking more for their much-sought furs and giving less for goods with which white men seemed so willing to part.[76] Moreover, Indians realized that the value of their products increased with scarcity. The burning of large stretches of the northern plains, which received mention in many traders' journals, was often a deliberate Indian ploy to drive game away from the trading posts and thereby create a scarcity. This increased the value of the meat they alone could supply.[77]

The fur trade doomed the Indians to eventual poverty and dependence. Nevertheless, British traders in this period were not able to exploit ruthlessly and consistently and to impoverish peoples who had no experience with European values and trade practices. Traders who tried to swindle their Indian customers frequently found that the exploitation was mutual and that the Indian gave as good as he got, sometimes better. Indians used their traders to secure credit, goods, guns, and alcohol, just as the trader used them to obtain furs, food, and horses. Whether as hunters, trappers, traders, farmers, middlemen or producers, Indians succeeded in finding profitable roles in the British fur trade. The value of their role increased dramatically when cut-throat competition between fur companies made the Indian an ally much in demand and allowed him to play the market to his best advantage.

7

The Fur Trader and the Indian

THE FUR TRADE represented the major area of initial contact between Britons and American Indians and constituted a vital factor in determining Indian allegiance to the Crown. As a result, the relationships that developed between a trader and his Indian customers were as important as the profits the business secured. In the conditions of the fur trade, a European world was lightly superimposed upon existing tribal worlds. Traders and Indians alike found themselves in a new situation and were confronted with members of an alien culture who demanded their attention. Some attitudes and relationships developed specifically out of the fur trade and existed within its peculiar circumstances.[1]

Most fur traders were practical businessmen who went into the Indian country to make a profit, not to study the cultures they encountered in the process. An exception was trader George Keith, who devoted much of his time researching Indian tales and traditions.[2] The Indians and the traders inevitably formed opinions about one another, and whether they cooperated in the fur trade or not, Indians were ubiquitous in the country where that trade was conducted. The traders had to acquire a working knowledge of these natives, and this entailed learning to recognize different tribes, becoming familiar with some of their languages, and understanding their politics and customs. The successful trader had to acquaint himself with the various tribes' locations, numbers, and movements; he had to learn their economic pursuits and desires; he needed to know their dispositions toward white men and toward other tribes. In addition, the trader had to discern their willingness or ability to supply furs or food, the characters of their chiefs and principal men, and the overall state of inter- and intratribal politics.

The fur trade in this period provided first descriptions of many hitherto little-known peoples, notably the Haidas of the Northwest Coast, several of the Missouri tribes, and Plains Indians like the Kiowas and Crows. North West Company trader Antoine Larocque kept the first record of Crow customs as he traveled with the tribe from the Missouri to the Yellowstone in 1805. As the fur trade extended its operations into new areas, the trader was usually the first to meet and to mention different tribes, but he was also most likely to remain in contact with them thereafter. Alexander Henry of the North West Company was not unique in the range of his experiences, which included dealings with Chippewa, Sioux, Cree, Assiniboine, Mandan, Hidatsa, Cheyenne, Crow, Blackfeet, Blood, Piegan, Atsina, Sarcee, Flathead, Snake, Chinook, and Clatsop Indians.[3]

The knowledge traders acquired from such meetings was not usually superficial. Men who married Indian women and lived with, if not like, Indians, naturally became well acquainted with the people and their culture. In September 1791, Peter Fidler, a trader and surveyor with the Hudson's Bay Company, set out with four canoes of Chipewyans to spend the whole winter with them and learn their language. By the following February he was even dreaming in Chipewyan. The North West Company sent its partners and servants to live among the Indians while they were young enough to acquire a full knowledge of native languages and customs. Only then did the company entrust them with the management of its business.[4]

The traders had to try to understand the Indians if they were to do business with and live among the tribes. Traders soon came to recognize the diversity of the Indians' lives because they had to. Different tribes required different treatment and a trader learned that he could not always rely upon the reputation ascribed to them but had to form his own opinions from firsthand experience. One band of Indians might appear cooperative and friendly, the next troublesome and hostile, and a trader could hardly judge or treat all Indians in the same way.[5] Traders often tried to regard Indians objectively and sought explanations for their different characters and actions in such things as their environment and their varying degrees of contact with whites. Philip Turnor, observing that the Crees preyed on the Chipewyans, who in turn preyed upon the Eskimos, posited the theory that Indians were more peaceful the farther north they lived.[6]

More often than not, though, appraisals of Indians were subjective. Traders inevitably looked most favorably upon those who cooperated with them in their work. Alexander Henry's idea of a "good Indian" (and he thought there were few enough of them) was one who was informative, sober, quiet, and a good beaver hunter.[7] Those tribes appeared worst who fitted poorly into the scheme of trade, and, as has been seen, traders drew a sharp distinction between Indians with furs and those without. Blackfoot, Blood, Piegan, and Atsina Indians who brought horses, wolf skins, and meat to trade were treated with less liberality than were beaver hunters. But even beaver-hunting Indians were assured of a warm welcome only so long as they brought plenty of furs, and they met with indifference or contempt when they failed to do so.[8] Traders wanted Indians around only if they brought a good trade, and they had little time for Indians who refused to cooperate. In 1811 the Astorians established a post among the Nez Percé Indians, but when it became clear that those warriors would never take to trapping beaver, the trader "soon got sick of them" and the post was abandoned.[9]

Time and again, Indians were rated good or bad according to their degree of fur production and cooperation.
The Walla Wallas were described as good Indians except
that they had not yet acquired the knowledge or means to
trap furs. The Cheyennes were accounted clean, decent,
and modest, but "a very hard people to trade with." The
Assiniboines of the Red River produced only wolf, fox,
and buffalo skins, not beaver, otter, and other valuable
pelts. John MacDonnell dismissed them as "a very lazy,
indolent, perfidious set; & I believe the worst hunters of
any Indians in the NW who have traders amongst them."
Traders became exasperated with Plains Crees who were
known to be passionately fond of alcohol and tobacco but
refused to take to the woods to procure the furs with which
to buy those articles and persisted in hunting buffalo on the
open plains.[10]

On the other hand, Indian cooperation and fur production could fluctuate according to circumstances, and
traders could not afford to form inflexible opinions purely
on the basis of economic considerations. Like the Atsinas
or the Piegans, a tribe or band might prove hostile and re-
fractory one time, well disposed and cooperative another.[11]
The trader had to apply and adapt his knowledge and
opinions to specific cases, with the result that his recognition of the diversity of Indian life was being tested and re-
charged continually. When traders did indulge in invective
and sweeping condemnation of Indians, it was frequently
against the backdrop of an unfavorable trade situation, severe weather conditions, or depression brought about by
the monotony of life in the wilderness; it was an angry out-
burst in the face of adversity, rather than the expression of
a firmly and consistently held attitude.

Nevertheless, the majority of fur traders who gave vent
to their feelings seem to have been closer to Alexander
Henry and François Malhiot in their contempt for Indians
than to David Thompson and Charles Mackenzie, both of
whom appear to have had a genuine interest in, and even
liking for, Indians. Attitudes toward Indians as expressed

in traders' journals contrasted sharply with the mutual interest, concern, and friendship professed by merchants in the memorials they submitted to the government requesting privileges or protection. François Malhiot was extreme in his detestation of Indians, but most traders shared his sentiments at one time or another, if only briefly. Malhiot admitted that he might call some "good Indians," but, faced with frequent danger, trouble over liquor, and quarrels with Indians who pestered and crowded him so closely that he said they gave him their vermin, he denounced the majority: "As a rule, if I could put them all in a bag and know that Lucifer wanted them, I would give them all to him for a penny. . . . If they were lambs formerly, to-day they are rabid wolves and unchained devils. As a rule they possess all the vices of mankind and only think they are living well, when they live evil lives." Malhiot's North West Company employers, however, would not have endorsed his expressed hope that the flag which he had given one "black-hearted rogue" would serve as the Indian's winding sheet; the fur trade had little use for dead Indians, only for productive and cooperative live ones.[12]

British fur trade opinion in this period had little grasp of the attitude that maintained that the only good Indian was a dead Indian. Much less, however, did traders go to the other extreme and view the Indian as a "noble savage." Practical, profit-minded men themselves, traders regarded Indians as motivated purely by selfishness and maintained that it was impossible to get them to do anything without payment.[13] The Indians' preference for conducting trade as reciprocal gift giving instead of simple bartering strengthened rather than weakened this impression and gave rise to the phrase "Indian giving" to describe the practice whereby an Indian would present his trader with his gift, fully expecting to receive a more valuable present in return. Traders did much the same thing themselves, however. Antoine Larocque, for one, never gave Indians anything without making sure that they knew he expected something in return; he feared that Indians placed slight value upon things too freely given. Moreover, official policy encouraged "Indian giving." The Indian Department was under orders to give gifts of greater value in return for any presents received from the Indians. According to Moravian missionary John Heckewelder, Indians employed a double standard in their dealings with white traders. When they gave gifts to strangers, they expected only a token in return, but from their trader they expected at least double the value given, "saying that he could afford to do it since he had cheated them so often." [14]

Gift giving and the responsibility to return the favor worked to ensure an equitable distribution of property in many tribes. It also constituted a rudimentary kind of insurance against poverty and starvation. In an uncertain world the best way to guard against future misfortune often was to help those in need now, in the knowledge that they could be expected to return the favor when the tables were turned. Among peoples who combined economic communalism with an extreme degree of individual freedom, the ideal of generosity ensured that property was for use, not accumulation. Both prestige and wealth were measured in terms of the amount bestowed upon others. In part, this explains the Indians' distaste for "wealthy" European traders who refused to dole out their goods to the comparatively poor Indians.

Traders frequently complained that Indians were ungrateful, with no sense of loyalty. The trader thought it strange that Indians should expect to receive equally indulgent treatment whether they arrived with or without furs; but, at the same time, he denounced Indians for not caring for their trader once he had no more gifts to give them. [15] British traders argued that gratitude was foreign to the Indians' nature. If you gave Indians gifts one day, they would expect them as their due the next, and no matter how well you treated them, they would do nothing for you unless paid; yet to once refuse them anything would alienate them and cause all former obligations to be forgotten. According to Duncan Cameron, Indians were naturally ungrateful; they were shameless beggars who were deceitful and paid their debts not because they were honest but in expectation of a good reception and from fear of being refused when again in need. And, "Being themselves unacquainted with honor and honesty, they are very distrustful of us, thinking us worse than themselves." An example of Indian ingratitude that Alexander Henry thought worthy of note occurred in 1809. A Cree Indian arrived at Henry's post while a band of Blackfeet, sworn enemies of the Crees, were there trading. Henry quickly traded with the Cree and got him away before the Blackfeet had a chance to kill him. In return the Cree stole two of Henry's horses.[16]

It was galling to the trader that the Indian was not consistent in his self-interest; he might be shrewd and stubborn in trading and then appear foolish and wasteful with his profits. "Indolent" was a favorite word used by traders to describe Indians. Nothing, it was thought, could induce an Indian to work but absolute necessity. David Thompson, characteristically, sought an explanation: "The civilized man has many things to tempt him to an active life, the Indian has none, and is happy sitting still, and smoking his pipe."[17] Most traders, however, seem to have found such "improvidence" on the part of the Indians difficult to understand. Many Indians, especially those inhabiting the subarctic regions, who were dependent upon wandering herds of caribou, often lived on the verge of starvation. What most perplexed European traders was that when times were good, these Indians apparently made no attempt to provide for the lean times to come. Northern Indian life was thus a perpetual struggle for survival, punctuated by brief periods of plenty when the Indians ate well or, according to one trader, feasted, "wallowing up to the Eyes in good Meat."[18] Like many of their white counterparts in the fur trade, Indians would squander the profits from a season's hunt on drink. Alexander Mackenzie, the first white man to cross the North American continent, recalled seeing a village on the south shore of Lake Superior inhabited by some thirty Indian families, "who are one half the year starving, and the other half intoxicated." That the "eat-all feast" possessed important spiritual attributes thought to guarantee continued good hunting seems to have escaped most fur traders.[19]

Coupled with Indian improvidence, in the eyes of British traders, went Indian impracticality. Not only did the tribes fight seemingly petty wars when they could have been engaged in the profitable pursuit of trapping beaver, but tribal customs often made no sense to European merchants. In the winter of 1792, Peter Fidler watched in amazement as, despite freezing temperatures, a band of Chipewyan Indians cast off their clothes in mourning for the death of one of their number. The one Indian who retained his garments, and whom Fidler thought wise for doing so, was regarded as unfeeling by his fellows.[20]

Traders realized that the authority of Indian chiefs, and especially of trading chiefs, depended heavily on their having goods to distribute to their followers. Nevertheless, white men who went into the wilderness in the hope of making their fortune had little chance of understanding Indian cultures that viewed wealth and property as things to be disposed of, and which required a man virtually to impoverish himself if he wished to become great. The Dutch had commented on this aspect of Indian leadership among the Mohawks of New Netherland in the seventeenth century; John Bradbury explained the phenomenon among the Indians of the plains in the early nineteenth century: "The desire to acquire and possess more than others, is thought a passion too ignoble for a brave man: it often happens, therefore, that a chief is the poorest man in the community." Andrew Graham, formerly of the Hudson's Bay Company, thought that the liberality with which Indians provided for the needy partially excused the cunning and cheating to which he felt they resorted in trade. Nevertheless, people who lacked the Europeans' sense of property and who often were acquisitive only to be munificent remained an enigma to most fur traders.

What must have been equally puzzling was that Indian property could include not only material possessions but also intangible things like the exclusive right to perform a certain dance or song, almost a form of copyright.[21]

Traders operated in the belief that self-interest was the key to Indian behavior. Understanding Indians did not necessarily imply any sympathy with them nor any real appreciation of their cultures. For the trader, understanding Indians often meant no more than knowing when an individual was play acting, or anticipating what mood a band was likely to be in after suffering misfortune at the hands of enemies or nature, or predicting what the apparently capricious Indian might be expected to do in different situations. Following their attacks on North West and Hudson's Bay Company posts in 1793, the Atsina Indians sued for peace. The British interpreted this change of heart as an indication that the Atsinas had come to realize that a regular and peaceful trade was in their best interests. The Atsinas found themselves in a dilemma, however. They wished to renew intercourse with the British traders but, understandably, feared a bad reception, "for as they are naturally treacherous and vindictive themselves, it is reasonable to suppose that they suspect others of the same sentiments." Similarly, traders maintained that the Hidatsas, or Gros Ventres, of the Missouri refrained from killing and plundering white men only because they depended upon the traders for their supply of arms and ammunition.[22]

Traders considered Indians to be unreliable and to be artful actors. They made it a rule to be skeptical of the information Indians gave them and placed little reliance on Indian professions of friendship or poverty. Andrew Graham said that an Indian who was asked if any of his people were coming to the fort to do business would always reply in the affirmative, even if he knew nothing about it, in order to increase his own importance as the messenger of good news and to please the trader. If asked if he had had a good winter, however, the Indian would reply in the negative, always reckoning to be hungry when coming to the fort. Alexander Henry declared that when an Indian said he was starving, it really meant only that he was reduced to living on dried provisions. The traders quickly became immune to Indian attempts to evoke their pity.[23]

According to traders, Indians were not to be trusted, much less believed. Duncan McGillivray maintained that Indians were addicted to lying, always trying to impose upon the listener's credulity in the hope of securing a reward or increasing their prestige. Indians, however, seemed to be no more capable than Europeans of recognizing their own faults and forgiving them in others: "Notwithstanding this vice is so prevalent among all the Indians, it is rather remarkable that they cannot forgive it in Strangers. When a White Man is once detected in a lie they never believe him afterwards:—he is despised & neglected and subject to be insulted on every occasion for having once deviated from truth whilst his accusers themselves practice every species of deceit, without any shame or regret."[24]

Traders suspected Indian appearances of friendship and believed that it was vital to be on their guard continually. The need for caution and vigilance seemed to be particularly acute because Indians were feared to be most dangerous when they seemed least so. If offended, an Indian would rarely react violently at the time; rather, said traders, he would sulk and brood over it and wait, for years if necessary, for the opportunity to exact his vengeance when the offender least expected it. In traders' eyes, Indians often presented a contented appearance concealing "the most rancorous revenge lurking in their minds."[25]

Skepticism and distrust bred cynicism that occasionally found expression in written abuse of the Indians, sometimes in cold indifference to their plight or fate. During the smallpox epidemic of the 1780s, Hudson's Bay traders went among the dead Indians taking beaver robes from the corpses.[26] Such actions perhaps reflected the white merchants' concern with profits and that business continue almost as usual, rather than any lack of feeling for dead or dying Indians; living in Indian country, where death was a common occurrence and all life seemed to be held cheap, did breed a certain amount of callousness in the trader. Indian fatalities in drunken brawls occurred time and again and, as Alexander Henry commented when yet another Chippewa had been murdered by his own wife, "Murders among these people are so frequent that we pay little attention to them." In May 1802 the Chippewas, among whom Henry spent nearly sixteen years, had several of their number killed by Sioux. News of the tragedy, recorded Henry in his journal, had scarcely arrived before the Indians with whom he was camped "were in an uproar, bawling, howling, and lamenting the death of their relations, the end of which was to beg rum to wash the sorrow from their hearts. *15*th Indians sober. I began to sow garden seeds." Feeling, or rather not feeling, as he did about Indians, Henry could view with detached interest the plight of an old man whose wife had taken revenge for his stabbing her by thrusting a firebrand on his genitals: "The old gent with the roasted cods was in a sad condition, and appeared to be failing fast," but a similar case was recorded with like indifference in Hugh Faries' journal: "At night the indians got drunk, and the Cancre had his testicles pulled out by one of his wives, through jealousy. There was but a few fibres that held them, so that his life was almost despaired of. The men could not gum the canoe as the weather was cloudy and rainy." [27]

Traders were not incapable of decent feelings for the Indians, especially when, for example, they had to watch helplessly while men, women, and children suffered the ravages of smallpox. Some expressed concern at the probable fate of the Indian as doomed to extinction before the advance of civilization, and others even expressed admiration for the Indians. Usually, however, it was tribes that were far off or infrequently met who earned any such praise; an Indian's virtues seem to have increased in proportion to his distance. Matthew Cocking, journeying to the Blackfoot country for the Hudson's Bay Company in

the early 1770s, had described the Blackfeet, or "Equestrian Natives" as "certainly a brave people, & far superior
to any tribes that visit our Forts: they have dealings with no
Europeans, but live in a state of nature." Three or four
decades later, Alexander Henry thought no more highly
of the Blackfeet than he did of other nations with whom
he was in frequent contact.[28] Familiarity bred contempt,
and the trader not only saw Indians at their worst but also
saw the worst in those Indians whom he saw most often.
Initial contacts seem to have been generally friendly, but
the process of disillusion worked both ways. The French-
Canadian fur trader, Pierre-Antoine Tabeau, described it:

A new nation is always disposed in favour of the whites; it wor-
ships them, sometimes up to the point of superstition and especially fears to displease them. A little familiarity destroys the
illusion; the first ray of light convinces them that they are enlightened and that period is the most critical for the trader. Intercourse with the Savages has three ages:—the age of gold, that
of the first meeting; the age of iron, that of the beginning of
their insight; and that of brass, when a very long intercourse has
mitigated their ferocity a little and our trade has become indispensable to them.

According to Duncan Cameron, the North West Company
kept the Indians more respectful than did the Hudson's
Bay Company by keeping them at a greater distance. The
latter company's servants, apparently, had "the patience
of Job" and were slaves to the Indians who came to their
forts.[29]

To lose the Indians' respect was dangerous and could
prove fatal. The trader therefore geared his conduct and
behavior to maintain a pretense that he was neither at the
mercy of nor reliant upon the goodwill and cooperation of
the Indians by whom he was surrounded. To do so he believed that he had to maintain a bold front and strike the
correct balance between indulgence and severity in his
treatment of Indians. Traders feared that if once allowed
to do so, Indians would continually impose upon them.
Thomas Connor's life seems to have been a continual

struggle with drunken quarrelsome Indians, he refusing their demands for liquor and upbraiding them for not paying their debts.[30] Once Indians realized that they had the whip hand, the tables were turned and they would exploit their advantage to the full. Thus, according to the American explorer Meriwether Lewis, the willingness of Saint Louis traders to put up with the piracy of the Missouri tribes only increased Indian aggression, because Indians saw that it worked to their advantage and believed that "*the white man* [sic] *are like dogs, the more you beat them and plunder them, the more goods they will bring you and the cheaper they will sell them*"[31] (Lewis's italics).

British traders allowed no such liberties to be taken. The Indians were made to understand that any violence or molestation of the whites or their property would be followed by swift and sure retribution. It was believed that the respect of members of a warrior society could best be secured by the display or threat of force. On the one hand, the fur companies sought to foster intertribal peace so that trapping and trading were not disturbed by blood feuds, but on the other, they seem to have adopted the same eye-for-eye standard of justice in dealing with Indian crimes. Because it was "an universal maxim among Savages that Blood must pay for Blood," traders felt that the repentant Atsinas must be made to pay for the hostilities they committed in 1793 if the whites were not to lose their respect. Robert Dickson pointed out the need to make a severe example if traders were to be safe from the depredations of feuding tribes; and Alexander Mackenzie had to insist upon the return of a missing ax, not, he said, for the value of the thing itself, but because to have allowed the theft to go unchecked would have been to invite the Indians to take everything, possibly even his life.[32] Traders believed that a well-timed demonstration of force could be what was needed to make Indians behave themselves, or even to win their attachment. Duncan McGillivray gave Gros Blanc, a Blackfoot chief, a beating, yet that same Indian later adopted McGillivray as his "little brother" to replace one killed in war with the Snakes. Charles Chaboillez resorted to similar treatment as a means of keeping some drunken and troublesome Chippewas quiet for the rest of the night.[33]

It was equally important to be prepared for trouble. On more than one occasion, traders standing to arms made ill-disposed warriors think better of commencing hostilities. Alexander Henry kept his swivel gun loaded and pointed at the Indian camp when trading with the notorious Blackfeet, knowing that they would not relish the prospect of attacking someone so clearly ready and able to defend himself.[34] Fur-trade journals are sprinkled with stories of Indians threatening or attempting to plunder traders. The trader had to remain on his guard and dared not let the Indians act with impunity, yet he could not afford to take too extreme measures and risk alienating his customers.[35]

Violence was a final resort, to be avoided if possible. Since familiarity bred contempt, the best way to preserve the Indians' respect seemed to be to remain aloof. Traders felt that they should act like white men and not try to imitate Indians in either appearance or behavior. As Peter Fidler discovered, Indians showed no respect for a white man who tried to share their work and hardships; his best option was to refuse their requests for help as beneath his dignity.[36] Traders also had to retain the outward garb of their own culture, even in the wilderness, because Indians expected men of position to dress as befitted their importance. When the North West Company bourgeois, Alexander Henry and Charles Chaboillez, arrived at the Mandan villages in 1806, they reproached Charles Mackenzie, the resident clerk, for dressing like a savage. Yet, dressed in only leather and corduroy themselves, the visitors looked little better. The Indians saw nothing in their appearance, much less in their liberality, to command the respect that the two bourgeois were accustomed to receiving. In fact, the Upper Missouri peoples had nothing but contempt for Henry and Chaboillez, and the more Mackenzie said in praise of his superiors as chiefs, the more contempt he brought on himself. On the other hand, Alexander Henry, despite his prejudices against Indians in general and these Indians in particular, had to admit that the latter could look impressive on occasion.[37]

The trader believed that trouble arose when he lost the Indians' respect, when he failed to maintain the necessary balance between severity and indulgence in his treatment of them, and when he allowed them to see the weakness of his position and the strength of their own. He could usually keep the Indians under control by threatening to deprive them of trade or to punish misbehavior, but, to a trader isolated in the Indian country, the threat of violence was both immediate and real. Traders found fault with Indians for a variety of reasons, but their hatred seems to have been reserved for those who were dangerous. Empty-handed Indians might arouse the trader's scorn, beggarly Indians his contempt, but "treacherous" and hostile Indians were his primary worry. Far from the Indians being browbeaten by their trader, they often kept him in a state of constant consternation. Alexander Ross, from the safety of his retirement, reflected: "How precarious is the life of an Indian trader, if we take into consideration the habits of the country and the spirit of the people he has to live among; a people who feel no remorse in using the instruments of death; a people who delight in perfidy! Perfidy is the system of savages, treachery and cunning the instruments of their power, and cruelty and blood-shed the policy of their country." Alexander Henry would have agreed. He had several narrow escapes from death during his years as a trader.[38]

Anxiety about safety partly explains the vast amount of space devoted in traders' journals to Indian drunkenness. Under normal circumstances, Indians realized that to kill their trader would be to deprive themselves of trade, but when drunk they seemed to lose all reason and the ability to see where their best economic self-interest lay. Indians frequently refused to be held accountable for their behavior when intoxicated, since at such times they were pos-

sessed by the spirit of the bottle, and the normal mecha-
nisms of social restraint were unable to cope with their
aberrant behavior. Indians who appeared meek as lambs
when sober often seemed to be transformed into devils by
alcohol.[39] Since they got their liquor from the trader, he
was usually a witness to their drunken behavior (although
some traders insisted that their customers return to their
camps before getting drunk). It is virtually impossible to
read a journal of events at a trading post without coming across references to Indians drinking and doing so
generally in veritable bacchanalian orgies. In April 1795
no less than seven different Indian nations assembled at
Fort George on the Saskatchewan, but, according to Duncan McGillivray, they all agreed on one thing—to get heartily drunk. McGillivray described the ensuring scene:

Men, Women and children, promiscuously mingle together and
join in one diabolical clamour of singing, crying, fighting, & c.
and to such excess do they indulge their love of drinking that all
regard to decency or decorum is forgotten:—they expose themselves in the most indecent positions, leaving uncovered those
parts which nature requires to be concealed—a circumstance
which they carefully avoid in their sober moments, and the intercourse between the sexes, at any time but little restrained, is
now indulged with the greatest freedom, for as chastity is not
deemed a virtue among most of the tribes, they take very little
pains to conceal their amours, especially when they are heated
with liquor.

North West Company clerk Daniel Harmon presented a
similar picture of a houseful of drunken, fighting, stum-
bling, vomiting Indians, and it was common to liken an Indian "drinking match" to a scene out of hell.[40]

Stabbings occurred regularly, and even when Indian
women took the precaution of removing their menfolk's
weapons before a drinking bout, the Indians could not
part with their teeth, so noses were occasionally bitten
off.[41] Traders tried to prevent bloodshed on these occasions, and not for purely humanitarian reasons: murders
committed during drunken brawls could cause inter- and

intratribal blood feuds, which were bad for business. Duncan McGillivray particularly regretted that the Canoe Assiniboines got drunk and started quarrelling and killing because he reckoned that small tribe would soon destroy itself in the resultant blood feuds, and that would be a great loss to the area's trade since the Canoe Assiniboines were second only to the Crees as beaver hunters.[42] Drink may have been a necessity in the fur trade, but its use caused the trader unlimited trouble and anxiety. For, bad as Indians were when intoxicated, Canadian voyageurs were worse. Daniel Harmon maintained that he would rather have fifty drunken Indians than five drunken Canadians, while Alexander Ross thought that Michilimackinac would put Hogarth's "Gin Lane and "Beer Alley" to shame, with drunken Canadians everywhere. The trappers went there once a year to spend everything in a few days' orgy before returning to the wilderness. "In this manner these dissolute spendthrifts spin out, in feasting and debauchery, a miserable existence, neither fearing God nor regarding man, till the knife of the savage or some other violent death dispatches them unpitied."[43]

As with drink, so it was in sexual relations, with the whites in the British fur trade setting for the Indians few examples of irreproachable moral conduct. The British regarded most Indians as notoriously lax in their sexual behavior, the Cheyennes and the Flatheads being exceptions, acknowledged for their chastity and modesty. Britons regarded the Mandans and the Arikaras as particularly lascivious, but the Atsina and Blackfoot tribes were also described as "troublesome" in offering their women as articles of temporary barter. Chipewyans sold their women to white men; a Sioux husband, it was said, would guard the door while his wife was inside with a white man; and, among the Chinook, "Even the chief would boast of obtaining a paltry toy or trifle in return for the prostitution of his virgin daughter."[44] Indians, of course, lived by different standards and did not necessarily consider chastity in the European sense of the term to be a virtue. Ironically, the fur trade gave a boost to polygyny in some tribes since, by increasing the hunter's wealth, it meant he could afford additional wives to skin, tan, and transport the extra hides he was producing for the market. David Thompson explained that Plains Indians viewed the chastity of their wives as a question of property rather than of morals. Indeed, a wife's infidelity with a trader seemed less of a sin because she was seduced by the prospect of material gain and it denoted no preference for her new lover over her Indian husband.[45] Indian women who married white traders usually secured thereby a measure of prestige, a higher standard of living, and some escape from the drudgery that seemed to be the common lot of the wife of an Indian.

It is debatable, however, whether the lot of Indian women who married white traders improved to the extent that fur trade sources, colored by the European male perspective, claim. There was significant disparity between traders' perceptions of the role of Indian women and the reality of their lives. Indians used, and some no doubt abused, their women, but whites in the fur trade also tended to regard Indian women as primarily economic assets or sex objects. Efforts to curtail the taking of Indian wives *au façon du nord* proved ineffectual. The Hudson's Bay Company prohibited social contact between its servants and Indian women, but the chief factors themselves led the way in forming unions with Indian women, and by the mid-eighteenth century it had become an established custom for a company governor to take an Indian wife. The North West Company bourgeois who did not have "his girl" was rare. The North West Company readily adopted the attitude of their French predecessors, the coureurs de bois. All ranks were allowed to take a woman, and the company accepted responsibility for maintenance of Indian wives and families. Whatever the motivation for fur trade marriages, Indian women and marriage ties came to play an important role in the Canadian fur trade.[46]

An Indian wife gave her husband connections and the business of her relatives, especially if her father or brother was a chief. The arrangement also had its drawbacks. Although purchased for a small sum, an Indian bride could prove a costly investment, since those same relatives immediately became the new husband's dependents. Fur traders regularly complained about the impositions and expectations of their wives' families, but generally seem to have gone along with the custom.

Although few traders entered into marriage with Indian women with a view to establishing a binding arrangement, the growth of family ties sometimes caused a dilemma when the time came for the trader to leave the Indian country. The custom was for traders to leave Indian wives and children behind. When William McGillivray was a partner in the North West Company operating in the northwest Indian country he married a Cree or Métis woman *au façon du nord* and fathered a number of children by her. In 1799, McGillivray became chief superintendent of the North West Company; the following year he married Magdalen McDonald in London and began a new family. Daniel Harmon was exceptional. Not only did he express scruples about taking a mixed-blood wife in the first place, but also, when the time came for him to return home, he took his wife with him and married her according to the laws of white society. The Harmon family encountered considerable prejudice and endured hard times when they flouted convention and returned to Vermont.[47] Scots trader George Sutherland also formed a lasting attachment to his Indian women. He apparently became head of his own band, all of whom were descended from himself, as he fathered twenty-seven children by three Cree wives. British and Canadian traders seem to have considered Cree and mixed-blood women the most comely.[48]

Many traders, however, showed scant regard for their Indian women. Generally, white men in the fur trade seem to have regarded Indian women as a relief to their lust or their loneliness. Some northern tribes had their women abducted, Sabine-like, against their will, but the normal practice was to buy or hire female companionship. In the

William McGillivray and family, by William von Moll Berczy,
c. 1810. The family in the painting is the fur trader's second; he
had left his Cree or Métis wife and children in the Indian country when he returned east and assumed the position of chief superintendent of the North West Company. His English wife,
Magdalen, died in 1811, shortly after the portrait was painted.
(McCord Museum, McGill University, Montreal)

northwest the going price for an Indian wife was a horse, although the price varied, of course, according to the attributes of the woman and the desire of the suitor. A smaller outlay would usually secure a lady's favors. Alexander Henry was amazed that one of his men gave an expensive mare "for one single touch at a Slave girl."[49] Traders frequently expressed annoyance that their men were pestered to take Indian women, but Indians obviously recognized that there was an eager market for female company. In the Pacific northwest, Indian women of high status brought canoe loads of slaves to barter sexual services for European goods, and Indian women who were married to white traders often provided prostitutes at the forts.[50] Alexander Henry's men were in their glory when they found they could get both food and women on easy terms from the Blackfeet, while David Thompson wrote of his journey to the Missouri, "The curse of the Mandanes is an almost total want of chastity: this, the men with me knew, and I found it was almost their sole motive for their journey hereto." By 1814 venereal disease was so prevalent among fur company employees and Indian women on the Columbia that Alexander Henry feared the malady might seriously affect the trade and disable at least half of his men by the spring of that year.[51]

By the early nineteenth century, the replacement of Indian wives by women of mixed blood had become common in the fur trade. Indian-European intercourse in the trade produced a growing "synthetic" population that came to exert a significant social, cultural, and political influence on the frontier in both Canada and the United States.[52] The majority of these people grew up as Indians and considered themselves to be Indians, but many occupied an intermediary marginal position. Mixed-blood women, who were themselves often the daughters of fur traders, possessed familiarity with both the fur trade and the society of their Indian relatives. They could perform all the functions carried out by Indian women without becoming a source of friction between the races. Moreover, the lighter-skinned mixed-bloods more closely approximated European ideas of beauty than did full-blood Indian women. With the increase in the number of mixed-blood wives, the "custom of the country" gradually evolved toward white concepts of marriage, and many relationships between white traders and mixed-blood wives proved to be lasting. Missionaries exerted increasing pressure on the institution and, by the mid-nineteenth century, the custom of the country fell into disrepute in the society of the northern fur trade.[53]

If fur traders regarded the Indians as nuisances who had to be tolerated because they provided furs, food, horses, and women, then Indians held traders in similarly low esteem. Indian opinions, of course, received far less consideration in the records than those of the literate traders. Nevertheless, it is clear that few Indians in this period regarded their traders with the reverence those traders would have liked. In general, Indians seem to have looked upon traders as primarily a source of goods. Many apparently regarded the goods that traders brought as theirs by right and could not understand why the whites were not more liberal when they had so much. The traders' behavior seemed antisocial in Indian societies that stressed reciprocal generosity and eschewed individual accumulation of property.[54]

Acting on the assumption that the traders' goods were meant for them, Indians were not too particular about how they acquired those goods. Exceptional instances of Indian honesty were noted, but on the whole Indians acquired the reputation of being shrewd traders, great cheats, shameless beggars, and habitual thieves.[55] As Peter Grant wrote about the Chippewas, Indians generally seem to have operated according to a double standard, with one set of rules for conduct within the tribe, another for conduct toward outsiders: "These haughty people, though uncommonly reserved among themselves, are, with their traders, the meanest beggars and most abject flatterers on earth, and, though naturally honest in their dealings with one another, they often find many occasions to cheat their traders with impunity."[56]

Indians had few qualms about pestering, pilfering from, and even plundering their traders, and among people who regarded horse stealing as an honorable exploit, traders suffered almost continual losses of stock. The Assiniboines enjoyed a special notoriety as horse thieves in this period, and there was some truth to Alexander Henry's lament that "you are sure of your horse only when you are on his back." The reason the Blackfeet refrained from stealing his horses, thought Henry, was not because they were honest, but because they already had so many of their own, "acquired" from their as yet comparatively defenseless Snake and Flathead neighbors. With regard to anything else, claimed Henry, the Blackfeet were such great thieves that every piece of iron and every moveable article had to be locked away when a band of them were known to be coming to the fort. Inexperienced travelers apparently were often inconvenienced by Indians who stole their horses with a view to being hired to search for the "missing" animals.[57]

One way by which Indians seemed particularly reluctant to obtain goods was by "honest toil." The "Big" or "Long Arrowed" (possible Hare) Indians were reported to be great cheats, "being much fonder of acquiring things in this way than by procuring them at the sweat of their brows." The Nez Percés spurned beaver trapping as beneath their dignity and fit only for women or slaves. The Indians of the Missouri held similar views. Beavers were plentiful in their country, and the Indians told their trader that they would have been glad to supply him if beavers could have been caught in the same way as buffalo, by a chase on horseback, "but they considered the operation of searching for them in the bowels of the earth, to satisfy the avarice of the Whites, not only troublesome but very degrading." When Charles Mackenzie remarked to them that the northern Indian tribes were very industrious and friendly to the whites, one chief retorted that he and his people were not slaves, especially to a fur trade that had brought them as many evils as it had goods. The Piegans too were said to prefer war, women, liquor, and horses to the labor of hunting for furs. Not surprisingly, many western Indians held a low opinion of Iroquois trappers who came into their country as employees of the fur companies.[58]

Whatever professions they might make when poor, hungry, or thirsty, Indians generally seem to have thought themselves superior to the whites they encountered in the fur trade. Many tribes gave the impression of considering themselves the finest race on earth.[59] Indians not only thought themselves superior, but they also made sure the trader knew they thought so. The Chippewas, for example, made it clear that they thought traders came to their country either out of sordid avarice or because their own country was so poor. The highest honor they could bestow on a white man was to say he was like one of them. Alexander Henry warned, however: "Let no white man be so vain as to believe that an Indian really esteems him or supposes him to be his equal. No—they despise us in their hearts, and all their outward professions of respect and friendship proceed merely from the necessity under which they labor of having intercourse with us to procure their necessities." The trader merely tolerated the Indian for the furs and provisions he supplied; the Indian felt the same way about the trader on whom he relied for his goods, guns, and liquor.[60]

It was not only the white merchant who based his attitude toward an alien people largely on selfish economic considerations; by "avarice" Indians usually meant a trader's refusal to indulge their desires and distribute his goods more freely. Other factors also affected the formation of appraisals and opinions, however. A trader could be impressed with the nomadic independence or general character of a tribe even though that tribe refused to participate in the scheme of trade. Nor was openhanded generosity alone the best way to win an Indian's respect or attachment. Indian and white each thought the other judged him as he judged the other, governed by the same motives and forming opinions for the same reasons. Indians, we are told, thought the white men to be dishonest, treacherous, vengeful, and untrustworthy because they themselves were so;[61] the trader thought Indians were motivated by economic self-interest because he himself was. In a business venture that both parties entered into for what they could get out of it, economic considerations were naturally uppermost in deciding the mutual attitudes of those parties. Fur traders had few illusions about the basis of their relationship with the Indians. In March 1802, following a brief disagreement, Daniel Harmon and some Indians parted "nearly as good friends as civilized People and Savages generally are for that friendship seldom goes further than *their* fondness for our property and *our* eagerness to obtain their Furs—which is I am persuaded (with a few exceptions only) all the friendship that exists between the Traders and Savages of this Country"—and Harmon was by no means the most cynical of fur traders. In 1805, Alexander Henry recorded that the Indians with whom he had been associated for many years appeared to be truly affected at his departure, but whether their regret was occasioned by the loss of a trader rather than of a friend is not clear; in any case, Henry had no regrets about leaving them.[62]

The fur trade was not only the first area of extensive contact between Britons and Indians but may also have been the least strained since traders sought to exploit and operate within existing Indian societies, rather than to alter or eradicate them. Nevertheless, it was not an ideal medium for the formation of objective cultural appraisals. Judgments were made from a self-interested economic viewpoint and, by its nature and its effects, the fur trade often seemed to reveal the worst in both Indians and white men. Those tribes who enjoyed a good reputation irrespective of their role in the fur trade—notably the Cheyennes, the Nez Percés, and the Flatheads—lived far from the main areas of Indian-white contact. Tribes with whom the traders dealt more regularly were closer at hand and therefore more acculturated and dependent. As a result, traders derived a poor impression of Indians in general from those whom they saw most often. Some traders lived as Indians among their customers, accompanying the bands to their villages for a season. More often, traders saw the Indians when they came to the fort, at which times they appeared indolent, drunken, and troublesome. There were many facets to tribal life but, despite his close proximity, the trader normally saw but one. Occasionally he was impressed by the Indians' appearance and abilities. Alexander Henry thought the sight of the Missouri tribes on the move was impressive, and Francois Antoine Larocque, Charles Mackenzie, and Robert Stuart each acknowledged the skill and the magnificent appearance demonstrated by Crow warriors on horseback.[63] Basically, though, the fur trader was interested in procuring furs, and that business more often exposed him to what he viewed as the filth, the brutality, and the inhumanity of Indian life.

In the same way, the fur trade did not present Indians with an ideal, or even a representative, picture of white civilization. Even from their own writings, fur traders do not emerge as paragons of virtue. Neither the literate trader who took the trouble to record his sentiments on paper, nor the wealthy merchant in Montreal or London, was typical of the men the Indians encountered in the fur trade and on whom they based their impressions of white society in general. The man who went to the frontier could hardly be considered typical of the society he had chosen, or been obliged, to leave. The Earl of Selkirk believed that, under conditions of competition, traders behaved more like the savages by whom they were surrounded than like civilized white men. In the 1780s, Governor Haldimand, at least privately, regarded merchants who traded in the Indian country as "get-rich-quick" types, and he advised the Earl of Shelburne "that the generality of the Merchants here, are not such men as you meet with in London, whose

Honor is superior to every Temptation, but are young Adventurers upon Credit who have all their Fortunes to make, and are not Solicitous about the means." Haldimand may have been unduly prejudiced against the Canadian traders, but his comments were apt. After the revolutionary war, disbanded soldiers seeking to avoid the restraints of law and "every idle fellow" entered the Indian trade, and their conduct gave the Indians an unfavorable impression of the British in general. David Thompson, commenting on the "want of chastity" among the Mandans, acknowledged that the white men who had visited their villages were not themselves particularly virtuous, educated, or religious.[64] The men of the fur trade may have been forerunners of white civilization, but they were no more representative of British culture and society than was the Indian hanging around the trading post typical of more distant tribal societies.

With some few exceptions, the British fur trade in this period was a business of mutual exploitation. The participants, both Indian and white, derived maximum profit from their economic advantages, made judgments based upon economic considerations, and viewed one another with thinly veiled contempt or necessity inspired toleration, rather than with any real respect or admiration. The view that Indians were motivated by greed and self-interest governed the conduct of British fur traders toward the Indians. It also permeated British Indian policy and linked that policy firmly to the fur trade as a means of binding Indian loyalty to the Crown with strong economic ties.

Unfortunately, British-Indian relations rested on foundations of sand. Britons and Indians alike sought to preserve a world that was fast disappearing. Each advance of the American frontier represented a victory of settlement over the fur trade. The Canadian fur trade itself was divided by cut-throat competition at the very time when expanding American settlements in the west offered new markets for British goods and new sources of grain for England's growing urban population, while the South, after the invention of the cotton gin in 1790, provided raw material for Britain's textile mills. As the Industrial Revolution gathered momentum, Britain's commitment to the Indians and the fur trade dwindled. Even as British diplomats negotiated in vain for the creation of an Indian barrier state, other voices called for a policy of encouraging American settlement in the heart of the continent. Anglo-American commerce was worth far more to British manufacturers and the British Empire than were all the furs and Indians of Canada. Time was running out for the fur trade and the influence of the fur-trade lobby in London declined accordingly, dwarfed by the strident demands of the new industrial order.

For the Indians, the fur trade was a Trojan horse, unleashing catastrophic forces at the same time as it delivered desirable gifts. The fur trade tied the Indians into the European, and ultimately into a world, economy. European manufactured goods made life easier but in the process killed many traditional craft skills. European guns increased the extent and deadliness of intertribal warfare. Alcohol and epidemic diseases wrought social and demographic havoc. The community of interests that bound Britons and Indians in the fur trade doomed them both to defeat because the fur trade helped to destroy the very world they sought to preserve.[65] British and Indian attempts to defend that world placed them in an uneasy military alliance against the expansion of American settlement.

Part Four

AN UNEASY ALLIANCE

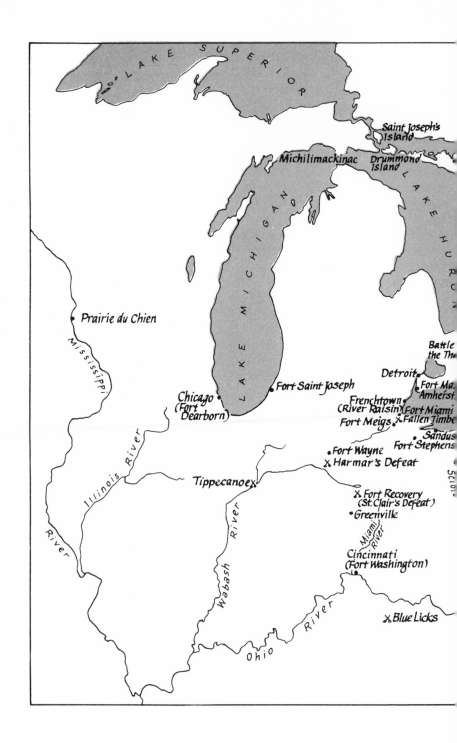

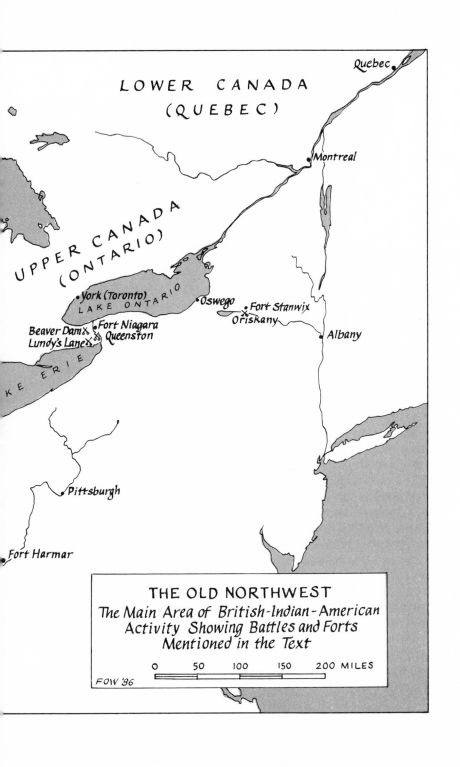

THE OLD NORTHWEST
The Main Area of British-Indian-American
Activity Showing Battles and Forts
Mentioned in the Text

0   50   100   150   200 MILES

FOW '96

8

Indians as Allies

FROM THE ERA of the American Revolution to the end of
the War of 1812, Britons and Indians found that they were
to a large extent natural, if often uneasy, allies against
their common enemy, the United States. There was no
official alliance in arms between the Indian tribes and the
Crown, but Britain regarded American expansion as a
threat both to its North American colonies and to its political traditions, while Indians saw their lands, culture, and
existence imperiled by the growth of the new nation. During the Indian wars against the Republic, Britain watched
from the wings, prompting the tribes with advice and supplies. In almost every tribe there were pro-American as
well as pro-British factions; but many Indians, and the
British authorities generally, recognized that in unity lay
their best hope of restricting American expansion. The
community of objectives was underlined by British fur-
trading interests that wished to see the Indians preserve
their lands against the tide of American settlement.
Strengthening the bonds of this natural alliance, Britain
possessed a number of advantages that its former colonists
lacked. It had a tradition of relatively good dealings with
the Indians and had made some attempts to restrain rather
than give free rein to white land hunger. It could draw
upon the reputation, the expertise, and the organization

of the Indian Department. It had fur-trading companies whose organization, experience, merchandise, and influence far surpassed anything that the United States had to offer. And it had an industrial and commercial superiority that produced goods of a quality and quantity the Americans could not match.

In addition, the Indians themselves generally realized the fate awaiting them if American expansion were allowed to go unchecked. American actions intensified this awareness. The United States government often endeavored to pursue humane policies toward the Indians, but it was impotent to implement those policies. American frontiersmen and soldiers, on the other hand, frequently perpetrated treacherous and barbaric acts that inflamed the Indians. These served to drive the tribes to unusually united action and into the arms of the British, and they confirmed British warnings that the Americans sought only to exterminate the Indians.[1]

Americans seemed to gear their actions toward alienating the tribes at a time when they could least afford to do so because Indian warriors posed a powerful threat to the frontier, if not the nation, especially when backed by the supplies and sympathy of a foreign power. After the Revolution, Indian power continued to limit and condition American development, and the need to meet and overcome that power played a vital part in the creation of a peacetime army and the foundation of the military establishment in the United States.[2]

Nor was Indian warfare in this period exclusively an affair of raiding for horses and burning isolated cabins. On several occasions, virtual armies of Indians fought pitched battles with American forces that the infant Republic could ill afford to maintain, let alone lose. Whites persistently underrated the Indians' ability to pursue strategy and tactics. The Indians were never defeated in open battle where the numbers on each side were anything like equal, but American forces suffered defeat after defeat at the hands of inferior Indian forces. The most notable Indian victory occurred in November 1791 when Little Turtle and the united northwestern tribes routed General Arthur St. Clair's army, inflicting a disaster that cost the Americans some nine hundred casualties (including about six hundred dead) and was their worst defeat ever by Indians. By contrast, American victories over Indians were modest affairs indeed. Although Anthony Wayne broke the western Indian confederacy at Fallen Timbers in 1794, the actual losses inflicted were relatively small. As will be seen, the Indians were dispirited as much by British inaction as by their own defeat. In 1811, Governor William Henry Harrison led a preemptive strike against Tecumseh's growing confederacy and, while the Shawnee chief was away, defeated the Indians at the Battle of Tippecanoe. Harrison's victory received great acclaim, but his success was small. Matthew Elliott reported Indian losses in the battle as twenty-five dead from an attacking force of which never more than a hundred were actually engaged, but said that the warriors inflicted more than a hundred casualties on the Americans before giving way when their ammunition ran out. American reports suggested that Indians and Americans each lost "upwards of fifty." On his return, Tecumseh dismissed the battle as a scuffle between children.[3] Even so, the engagement was a telling blow for Indians who were accustomed to sustaining minimal casualties, even in their crushing defeats of Braddock and St. Clair.

In view of their poor military record against the Indians, and with Britain supporting the hostile tribes, Americans could hardly fail to see the Indians as a powerful menace, locally and nationally. The extent of the perceived threat posed by the Anglo-Indian alliance is perhaps best indicated by the fact that the two American commanders who inflicted defeats on both the British and the Indians— William Henry Harrison in the north and Andrew Jackson in the south—both later attained the presidency largely on the basis of these military achievements.

On the other hand, the Indians' fear and hatred of Americans attached them more firmly to the British (or the Spanish in some southern regions), as both Britons and Americans realized.[4] British goods, interests, reputation, and policy, on the one hand, and American actions and ambitions, on the other, generally made the Indians' choice an easy one. For their part, the British recognized that Indians possessed a number of advantages over regular troops and were sufficiently valuable as allies or dangerous as enemies that King George should be sure to have them on his side if and when war broke out.

The British had to come to terms with the fact that in employing Indians in war they were allying themselves to people whose concept and conduct of war seemed radically different from anything practiced by European armies. Indian methods of warfare had changed considerably under the impact of European contact. Throughout North America, European firearms rendered obsolete traditional Indian tactics. Ritualistic battles fought between ranks of warriors armed with stone-age weapons gave way to deadly guerrilla warfare waged by warriors armed with guns.[5] In addition, European invasion sparked tribal migrations, competition for trade and firearms, and contests for hunting territories, while European imperial rivalry embroiled the tribes in debilitating colonial wars. By the late eighteenth century, war appeared to observers to be the normal state of affairs in tribal society, and the deadliness of that warfare was interpreted as peculiarly Indian rather than a product of devastating new forces.

In the guerrilla and predatory warfare of the North American wilderness, there was little place for tactical movements and military drill in the European manner. The colonial wars demonstrated the importance of light troops, but the British light infantryman remained heavily encumbered in comparison with the Indian warrior. Moreover, guerrilla tactics implemented in forest terrain frequently nullified any advantages possessed by regular troops. In forest fighting, where British troops were no match for backwoods riflemen, the Indians were indispensable auxiliaries, enjoying as much advantage over

American frontiersmen as did the latter over British regulars. One witness doubted whether anyone who had not seen it firsthand could have any concept of the appalling nature of Indian warfare when the warriors were fighting in their native forests.[6] Trader John Askin thought that in the woods one Indian was the equal of three white men; Indians themselves tended to rate their superiority more highly.[7]

War was an institution and a means of advancement in most Indian societies. Young men in search of plunder, revenge, or personal glory took to the warpath as individuals, and military operations were largely voluntary affairs. That is not to say that Indians fought as disorganized mobs, however. Fear of disgrace often operated as a more effective rein than did the British soldier's discipline and fear of punishment. Yet, despite his warrior training, the Indian was rarely able to match, or even comprehend, the dreadful determination of his Euro-American adversaries. Indians readily and regularly gave way in the face of determined resistance or if their enemies displayed stronger war medicine. To incur heavy casualties in achieving an objective was a concept foreign and repulsive to Indian peoples whose relatively small numbers meant that any losses were severely felt. Fur trader Peter Grant noted that the Chippewas generally displayed great bravery if compelled to stand and fight and would seldom ask or give quarter, but that they thought nothing of retreating if they found their enemies too strong, preferring to try to pick off a straggler and thereby procure a scalp without sustaining any casualties. "Their ideal of a good warrior," he suggested, "is to know how to attack an enemy unawares and, in retreat, to know how to baffle his pursuers by his superior cunning."[8] Euro-American armies, by contrast, frequently sustained appalling casualties. Indians preferred to fight in lightning raids and skirmishes; Indian armies rarely stayed together for longer than a battle or a brief season. White armies defeated them by sustained and systematic campaigns, carried out regardless of season or suffering, which destroyed Indian crops, villages, and non-combatants. Military organization and bloody determination demoralized the Indians as much as did the superior numbers and technology of the whites.

Men and women who had witnessed Indian attacks saw evidence of what to them seemed sadistic savagery, and some observers dismissed Indian warfare as no more than robbery and assassination. Some commentators recognized and explained that Indians fought according to different standards, but complaints leveled against Indians as fighters are legion in the records.[9] British officers complained frequently that Indians were interested only in scalps and plunder (though regulars and militia seem to have been equally given to plundering).[10] Many observers assumed that scalps and plunder, revenge and glory constituted the purposes of Indian wars, and that Indians were warlike by nature. Although many Indian cultures required war, the majority of tribes who fought against the Americans did so from a recognition that they were fighting for their land and the survival of their way of life. Europeans frequently overlooked the causes of Indian wars in their preoccupation with the nature of Indian warfare.

British observers, trained to think of warfare in conventional European terms of honor, discipline, heroism, and strategy, saw Indian warfare as at worst cowardly murder, at best a baffling series of contradictions. Indian warfare, like the tribal societies, offered variety and diversity. Indian warriors ritually tortured prisoners and murdered noncombatants; they also on occasion treated captives with kindness and respect and successfully adopted them into the tribe as a means of maintaining the population level. Indians sometimes refused to meet an enemy in open combat; at other times, when their war medicine was strong, they performed daredevil exploits that left their white enemies open-mouthed in wonderment. Indians might turn and flee at the approach of the enemy; yet, in 1814 eight hundred Creek warriors fought fanatically almost to the last man at the Battle of Horseshoe Bend. Some tribes attached great importance to the killing of enemies and the taking of scalps, but most Plains Indians placed scalping relatively low on the scale of war honors and accorded greater recognition to feats that involved a higher personal risk, such as touching an enemy. Protecting women and children, even at great risk, was taken for granted and did not merit special recognition among plains warriors; on the other hand, horse raiding, which whites dismissed as simple theft, represented one of the highest forms of achievement. Indian warfare involved social, cultural, and religious elements of which British observers had little perception or knowledge.

Britons were not usually blind, however, to the potential of employing Indian warriors as both a destructive and a diversionary force. In the War of 1812, Admiral Alexander Cochrane planned to use Indians in concert with British troops to conquer Louisiana and Florida, declaring that theirs was the most effective kind of war to wage against such perfidious enemies as the Americans and that the Indians represented the cheapest means of providing a diversion for the defense of Canada.[11]

The Indians' effectiveness in war could be further enhanced by adequate support and suitable employment. Lieutenant Colonel Robert McDouall, often a severe critic of Indians as allies, had far more respect for them once the possibility arose that they might turn against him as enemies. He could think of no more terrible foe, in a country like Upper Canada, than a powerful force of Indian warriors properly managed and led. In 1814 a force of Sauks, Foxes, Winnebagos, and Sioux demonstrated just how effective they could be when amply supported, especially with artillery. The Indians fought a determined action at Rock River, defeating an American gunboat flotilla under the command of Major Zachary Taylor.[12]

After five years of frontier warfare during the Revolution, Major Arent De Peyster still felt it necessary to point out to his superiors that Indians were most effectively employed when it was remembered that they *were* Indian war-

riors and not British regulars.[13] The British military, however, did not always heed this reminder, as evidenced by
some of the complaints made by British officers in subsequent years. Indians and British alike seem to have agreed
that the best way to use Indian warriors was in concert with
a corps of soldiers, led by officers who had knowledge of
the Indians and their languages. In this way, it was said,
the British could prevent atrocities and direct operations
most effectively, unless the Indians were accompanying an
army, in which case they could be more easily influenced
and were encouraged by the numbers and example of the
British troops. Such methods had proved effective during
the revolutionary war when Butler's Tory Rangers had terrorized the New York frontier. The Indians requested that
such a corps be sent to serve with them in the War of 1812,
but to no avail. Lieutenant Colonel Cecil Bishoppe, for
one, lamented the failure to raise a corps of light troops
attached to the Indians as this would have encouraged
the warriors, rendered their operations more effective,
and saved regular troops from having to support and assist them.[14]

For thirty years after the Revolution, Britain advised and
encouraged the Indians in their struggle against the United
States, but only in the War of 1812 did British troops officially fight alongside Indian warriors against their common
American enemies. During that conflict, Britain perhaps
did not employ its Indian allies to the best advantage, but it
nevertheless derived considerable service from them as forest soldiers. Despite frequent complaints that the information they provided was unreliable, Indians performed admirably as scouts. They also had a devastating effect as
guerrillas, as when they cut General Hull's lines of supply
and communication at Detroit in 1812.[15]

Perhaps the Indians' greatest asset in the war, however,
was as a psychological weapon. Brigadier General Isaac
Brock said he expected no great service from the Iroquois
once they joined him, but he knew they would be useful for intimidating the enemy. On occasion, British and

Sir Isaac Brock, painted by J. W. L. Forster. Brock and Tecumseh became personal friends in the early months of the War of 1812. Brock's death at the Battle of Queenston Heights was a severe blow to the British-Indian alliance. (Public Archives of Canada, Ottawa; C-7760)

American soldiers turned and ran at the very sight or sound of enemy Indians.[16] The British and Indian leaders exploited this psychological factor to the full in the capture of Detroit in 1812. Tecumseh adopted the ruse of marching his men repeatedly through a clearing in view of the garrison, thus conveying an exaggerated impression of Indian numbers. Meanwhile Brock, who was well aware of Hull's apprehension thanks to dispatches captured by Indian scouts, called on the American commander to surrender, making the usual veiled threat that he would be unable to restrain his Indian allies if the fort had to be taken by storm.[17] Brock presented Tecumseh with an engraved compass as a mark of his esteem and the understanding and mutual respect that developed between the two men augured well for the success of British-Indian operations. Unfortunately, both fell in battle the following year.

It appears that Indians generally were perceived to be more terrible as enemies than useful as allies, and much of their effectiveness stemmed from the terror they inspired. American reports frequently convey the impression that the Indians, not the British, were the main enemy to be feared. General James Winchester's Kentucky Volunteers certainly were preoccupied with the Indian menace during the expedition that ended in disaster and massacre at the River Raisin in 1813. In their constant anxiety, the Kentuckians gave exaggerated reports of Indian numbers, went off on wild goose chases, and even fired upon their own men. The frontier inhabitants' dread of Indian warfare had thus abated little since the beginning of the Revolution.[18]

British complaints notwithstanding, Indians fought gallantly in battle after battle, winning praise for their valor at Fallen Timbers, Tippecanoe, Detroit, Michilimackinac, Queenston Heights, River Raisin, the Thames, Beaver Dam, Rock River, and Horseshoe Bend, as well as inflicting crushing defeats on Generals Harmar and St. Clair. The Battle of Beaver Dam in 1813 was an Indian victory, but, as John Norton indicated, credit did not always go to the deserving party: "The Cognauga Indians fought the battle, the Mohawks got the plunder, and [Lieutenant James] Fitzgibbon got the credit."[19]

Certain tribes were regarded as particularly valuable as allies or displayed exceptional tenacity in the struggle against American expansion. During the Revolution the Cherokees fought courageously and suffered greatly, and in the years following Dragging Canoe and his Chickamauga band led hostilities against the United States, although by 1814 the Cherokees were fighting with Andrew Jackson against the Red Stick Creeks.[20] In the decade following the Revolution, the Miamis emerged as a bulwark of Indian resistance against American expansion, and eight expeditions were sent against them between 1786 and 1794. The Wyandots, a senior tribe of considerable influence, enjoyed a remarkable reputation for bravery and frequently suffered the highest proportion of casualties in battle.[21] The Kickapoos were an acknowledged power in the Illinois region and became steady allies of the British after 1783, and many of the tribes of the Great Lakes regularly supplied warriors to fight in King George's wars.[22]

As has been seen, the Six Nations and the Shawnees were each of paramount importance to the British alliance. Farther west, the dominant power was the Sioux. By the early nineteenth century, the Sioux had defeated the Omahas, the Poncas, the Arikaras, the Cheyennes, and the Kiowas, besides being at continual variance with the Chippewas, and seemed to epitomize the warrior society, confident of their power and superiority.[23] Nor does their confidence appear to have been unfounded. British officers praised the Sioux who came to fight for them during the Revolution as excellent and disciplined warriors, led by "a prince of an Indian," a chief named Wabasha who possessed uncommon abilities.[24] In 1799, Alexander McKee, agent among the Shawnees, recognized the potential of the Sioux as allies; not only were six thousand mounted warriors a force to be reckoned with, he said, but the Sioux were considered "the best Indian Warriors in America."

Americans too recognized that the Sioux held the balance of power in the Missouri-Mississippi region, and during the War of 1812, it was crucial for the United States that, though most Sioux bands and the Mississippi Dakotas in particular espoused the British cause, those on the Missouri remained pro-American. As it was, the British acknowledged those Sioux who did serve with them as a valuable asset.[25]

If the Sioux dominated the northwest, the most powerful force in the southeast in this period was the Creek Confederacy. Though divided between upper and lower towns and between peace and war factions, the Creeks were strong in warriors and constituted a formidable force in an area where the United States, Britain, and Spain vied for their allegiance. Unfortunately, the British seem to have overestimated Creek potential, especially in view of the hammerblows suffered by the confederacy in the Creek–American War of 1813–14. From the Revolution to the War of 1812, private petitioners, government officials, Indian agents, traders, adventurers, the military, and at least one admiral, all, at one time or another, believed that the Creeks would be able, almost single-handedly, to take Florida and Louisiana for Britain. William Augustus Bowles saw no reason to stop there; he extended his ambitions to include the liberation of Mexico from Spain. One proposal even suggested employing Creek warriors in the West Indies since their physical constitution and mode of warfare would be ideally suited to the task and thus save the lives of great numbers of British soldiers.[26]

The British government displayed brief and varying degrees of interest in such schemes, but did not prepare to act in that direction until the later stages of the War of 1812. Supplies, agents, marines, and finally a British expedition were sent to the area, but by that time it was already too late. The British, and some of the Indians themselves, failed to realize that the enterprise had little chance of success after the disastrous losses sustained by the Creeks in a war that was as much civil as racial. Andrew Jackson, after a string of crushing victories culminating in the annihilation of more than eight hundred Red Stick warriors at Horseshoe Bend, realized that Creek power had been broken forever.[27] Nevertheless, about a thousand Creek intransigents sought refuge with the Florida Indians who had been fighting the Americans since 1811. The British Admiral Cochrane and his subordinates persistently overestimated the potential of these warriors. Although they reported on the Indians' sorry plight, they failed to appreciate the shattered condition of the Creek Confederacy. The Creeks had had little hope of success without securing the allegiance of the powerful Choctaws on their western border; but Choctaws, Chickasaws, Cherokees, and pro-American Creeks all fought alongside the American forces. The British had high hopes of dramatic success, but the Creek threat remained a threat only. Major Edward Nicholls failed to create the expected uprising on the Florida frontier, and ambitious British projects for the conquest of Louisiana petered out in dismal failure at Fort Bowyer, Pensacola, and New Orleans. Nevertheless, plans for coordinated British-Indian offensives continued to receive serious attention until the war was officially over.[28] Even after the traumas of racial and civil war, Creek warriors inspired British observers with hopes of easy victory and won praise for conduct while on service.[29]

Whatever advantages an Indian alliance offered, it was not an unmixed blessing for the British. Indian character, politics, society, and modes of warfare posed many problems for the British military. Britain expended considerable effort and expense in securing and maintaining the allegiance of the tribes, but Britons repeatedly questioned whether that allegiance was worth the trouble and complained that the Indians' defects outweighed their military value. British military thinking held that Indians were neither reliable nor manageable in war, and complaints that Indian allies had "as usual" proved of little benefit occurred time and again in military dispatches. Indeed, instances of Indians serving with "spirit" and "discipline" were sufficiently rare as to merit special mention.[30]

In fact, the British believed that the advantages offered by Indian allies tended to be negative: if an Indian was fighting for you, at least he was not fighting against you. Accepted wisdom held that in the event of war, Indians had to be employed because they had no concept of neutrality. During the Revolution, Sir Frederick Haldimand had warned that, to Indians, neutrality was "little better than a Declaration of War against the weakest Party," and successive Canadian governors tended to agree that neutrality was something of which Indians had no concept.[31] This belief governed British Indian policy during the crisis in Anglo-American relations which occurred in 1807–08, and in the years immediately preceding the outbreak of war in 1812. The Indians might be of limited value as allies, but it was better that they should be fighting with rather than against the British. Therefore, while the Indians should not be encouraged to engage in hostilities against the United States, nor that power be provoked, they should be made to understand that Britain expected their active support if and when war did break out. If Britain did not secure their help, the enemy would.[32] The employment of Indians as allies in the War of 1812 was thus a necessary measure of self-preservation upon which Canada's survival depended.[33]

Not surprisingly, the British in Canada became alarmed when, after war broke out in 1812, the Iroquois on the Grand River seemed reluctant to join them and expressed a desire to stay out of the conflict. From the Iroquois' point of view, to have fought in the war would have embroiled them in conflict with those of their New York kinsmen who sided with the United States; but the British thought it absurd to expect this "fickle race" to remain neutral in the midst of war. Anxiety spread throughout the country, and the militia used the situation as a pretext for staying at home rather than leaving their families to the mercy of "savages" who might at any moment turn on them.[34]

The British displayed better understanding of Indian reactions to the war than did the American general and governor of Michigan Territory, William Hull. As late as July 1812, Hull felt confident that the Indians in his region would remain neutral. He based this confidence on the assurances of the Wyandot and Shawnee chiefs, the Crane, Walk-in-the-Water, Black Hoof, and Blue Jacket. Unfortunately, by this time, Hull was talking to the wrong men. This older generation of leaders had been superseded by younger warriors such as Roundhead and Tecumseh. In any case, once the Indians learned of the easy victory at Michilimackinac, when a force of British traders and Indian warriors called for and received the surrender of the startled American garrison, promises to remain neutral were forgotten in the rush to share in the British-Indian success.[35] Robert Dickson, British agent for the tribes west of Lake Huron and a trader with extensive experience of Indians, placed no such faith in Indian professions: "I have told the Sauks and Renards [Foxes] that they sleep too long. If they do not get up, that I shall rouse them with the hatchet, and that Britain suffers no neutrals."[36]

The British in general placed little reliance on Indian professions of sincerity or loyalty unless backed by actions.[37] They maintained that Indians were least reliable and most to be feared when things were going badly. Governor Haldimand's fears that the Indians would turn against the British after the 1783 treaty lingered throughout the next decade and revived strongly when the western posts were finally given up in 1796. Lieutenant Governor Simcoe was haunted by the prospect that Upper Canada's strongest defenders could become its worst enemies and turn their terrible warfare against the colony whenever the British betrayed signs of weakness.[38]

Similar fears arose anew during the War of 1812, even influencing British strategy at times. Major General Isaac Brock dreaded the prospect of having several hundred "fickle" Indians of dubious loyalty hanging on his flanks in the event of a retreat. Many of the Indians serving with the

Right Division of the British army in Canada belonged to
"wild" tribes from the west who had rarely seen a white man
before. Henry Procter, the division commander, found
himself obliged to alter his plans to accommodate his rather
volatile allies. In the summer of 1813, he yielded, against his
better judgment, to Indian clamor for an attack on Fort
Stephenson. The attack failed dismally. The following autumn, Procter had to explain to Tecumseh and his followers his decision to retreat to the Thames River. The Indians seemed to be on the verge of defecting, owing to the
British failure to keep them supplied.[39] The British military feared that the Indians were likely to desert or turn
against the redcoats whenever the army had to retreat.[40]
Procter was court-martialed for misconduct during the operations culminating in the British defeat at the Battle of
the Thames in October 1813. He defended his actions in
delaying the retreat and making a stand where he did on
the grounds that he had to conciliate between two and
three thousand Indian warriors lest they turn on his retreating army for what they regarded as a betrayal. The
prosecution attacked Procter for endangering his entire
division, but witnesses with experience among Indians
concurred that the need to conciliate these allies was a primary consideration in making military decisions.[41] Even
so, when Procter did decide to retreat, many warriors,
notably the Ottawas and Chippewas, deserted him, some
immediately changing sides. Some Potawatomis and the
Miamis followed suit after the defeat at the Thames, although Main Poc's Potawatomi warriors, who had not retreated with Procter, continued independent operations
against the Americans.[42]

Indians naturally interpreted actions as indicators of
strength or weakness and reacted accordingly. Even before the outbreak of war in 1812, Brock realized that the
amount of support the Indians gave in the coming conflict
would depend on whether the British were strong enough
to take Detroit, the capture of which, he foresaw, would be
the signal for enthusiastic cooperation from the Indians.[43]

The British and American governments alike sought to impress successive delegations of Indians with visits to Quebec and Washington, and Simcoe maintained that a British military presence was necessary in Upper Canada because "nothing will intimidate the Indian but the reality or appearance of a formidable Force."[44]

Judging in terms of power, Indians saw an indication of both the inclination and the ability of the British to support them in the amount of supplies they received. Normally scattered tribes, with farming and hunting economies, could hardly be expected to secure their own food when on service for the British, and they depended on regular supplies to keep them assembled in any numbers.[45] Consequently, during the War of 1812, the northern Indians had to fight a war based at the Great Lakes, where they could be provisioned by the British, just as in the south the Creeks depended on the British shipping on the Gulf Coast for supplies.[46] Since the Great Lakes constituted both Canada's border and her major communication line to the west, the naval defeat suffered on Lake Erie in 1813 was a double blow to the British. It allowed William Henry Harrison to advance into Canada and also broke the line of supply to Malden and the Indians, thus endangering the whole structure of Indian alliances that had been erected in the west. Brock, recognizing the importance of the water line, had aimed earlier to defend by launching a series of offensive thrusts each at a point essential to intercourse with the Indians.[47]

Not only did the Indians need British supplies, but it was generally believed that they were a mercenary people who sold their services to the highest bidder and could not be relied upon to act without presents. After the recapture of Prairie du Chien from the Americans in 1814, the British commander complained bitterly about the Winnebagoes, who "despise the idea of receiving Orders from an Officer that [does] not hold a Blanket in one hand and a piece of Pork in the other to pay them to listen to what he may have to say."[48] The Winnebagoes were one of Robert Dickson's

favored tribes and therefore accustomed to ample supplies. Many Britons complained that Indian allies were
very expensive for what they actually did; that the Crown
had to look after the families of the warriors who were
away at war, and that it even cost money to stop Indians
fighting once a war was over.[49] Others pointed out that, despite the cost, employing Indians constituted a relatively
cheap way of waging war.[50]

The British realized that revenge constituted a major
factor in Indian warfare. Retribution often operated as a
system of justice in kinship societies and the British used it
as a means of spurring on their allies to greater efforts.
The bloody Battle of Oriskany in August 1777 had pitted
Senecas against Oneidas in a conflict that widened the
growing divisions in the Iroquois Confederacy; and the
exertions of Loyalist Iroquois increased noticeably as they
sought to avenge their losses. After the Revolution, the
British continued to take into account Indian determination to exact vengeance for any losses or injuries suffered.
In 1814, Brevet Major Edward Nicholls of the Royal Marines worked to build up an Indian force in Florida to
create a diversion in the south and also to aid any British
expeditions in the region. He tried to ensure that the
Choctaws, whom he wished to win over but who were serving with Andrew Jackson at that time, would not clash with
his own Creeks because it would be virtually impossible to
reconcile the two tribes if they once had a battle.[51]

Britons frequently attributed what they viewed as the
Indians' cruelty in war to this implacable spirit of revenge.
Nevertheless, the British in general found Indian cruelty
difficult to excuse or to defend. British defenses of atrocity
committing Indians on the grounds that Americans also
employed them or else committed the atrocities themselves, reflected some of the guilt a supposedly civilized nation felt when employing "savages" to fight its wars, as well
as indignation at American hypocrisy in condemning that
employment.[52] The British believed that cruelty was inherent in Indian warfare, but Indian atrocities generally oc-

curred despite, rather than because, of British efforts.[53] Following the massacre of the American garrison at Fort Dearborn in 1812 by Potawatomi, Ottawa, and Chippewa warriors acting alone, the British dispatched troops post-haste to Fort Wayne to prevent a similar tragedy from occurring there; and, far from bounties being paid for scalps during that war, a reward of five dollars was offered for every prisoner brought in alive.[54]

Indian barbarities were a source of constant anxiety to the British, whose attempts at restraint were not always successful. Instances of Indians *not* committing atrocities merited special mention in reports, indicating that they were exceptions to the rule.[55] On at least one occasion, British soldiers could only stand and watch as their Indian allies murdered prisoners, and at Fort Meigs in 1813, Indians killed a soldier of the Forty-first who intervened to try and save an American prisoner.[56] It was not the British but an Indian, however, who prevented a massacre of prisoners at Fort Meigs. Potawatomi warriors had painted their faces black and were about to slaughter the prisoners when Tecumseh arrived on the scene, brandishing his sword, and ordered them to desist. Tecumseh's humane treatment of prisoners and noncombatants earned him the admiration of the British, while Kentuckian Robert McAfee, who had little good to say about Indians or British, pronounced that: "In this single act, Tecumseh displayed more humanity, magnanimity, and civilization, than Proctor with all his British associates in command, displayed through the whole war on the northwestern frontiers."[57]

In the seventeenth century the Iroquois exploited their reputation for cruelty as a terror tactic against neighboring tribes. For all their complaints about Indian atrocities, European commanders readily employed similar tactics during the colonial wars and the War of 1812. Besieged garrisons were frequently threatened with Indian massacre as the alternative to surrender. The Indians held no monopoly in the committing of barbarities, though. As Francis Jennings has shown, the idea that atrocity and tor-

Tecumseh (1768?–1813). This portrait by an unknown artist is thought to be the only painting of the Shawnee war chief, although sketches and imaginative representations survive. (Courtesy Field Museum of Natural History, Chicago)

ture belonged exclusively to so-called savage warfare was a myth produced by Europeans whose own civilization was characterized by brutality and violence.[58] Scalping was virtually universal in frontier warfare and white men had little to learn from their supposedly savage foes. Indians and Britons leveled innumerable complaints against American frontiersmen. At the end of the revolutionary war, Iroquois chiefs complained that while they were trying to restrain their young men, the rebels were committing atrocities, "and if we had the means of publishing to the World the many Acts of Treachery and Cruelty committed by them on our Women and Children, it would appear that the title of Savages wou'd with much greater justice be applied to them than to us."[59] Indeed, the notorious torture of Colonel William Crawford in 1782 (Crawford was scalped, had hot ashes poured over his bleeding head, and was finally roasted alive over a slow fire) was an act of retaliation by the Delawares for the massacre of their Moravian relatives by American militiamen at Gnadenhütten earlier in the year.[60] Mutilation of Indian corpses seems to have been a favorite pastime among American frontiersmen, even if the practice required them to open graves. The story that American soldiers flayed the skin from Tecumseh's body after death at the Battle of the Thames is probably inaccurate only in that the mutilated corpse may not have been Tecumseh's.[61] In view of American denunciations, the British were enraged that not only was the United States not averse to employing Indians, but on at least one occasion held out the attraction of fighting free from restraint as a means of winning over the tribes.[62]

The British found it hard to accept that Indians, whom they assumed to be born warriors, should display such unsoldierly traits. Torture of prisoners and killing of noncombatants were contrary to British ideals of how a soldier should act (although Scottish Highlanders were not unmindful that English redcoats had committed atrocities at the Battle of Culloden in 1746). In addition, Indian warriors seemed incapable of conducting themselves with the order and discipline expected of a British soldier. Indian armies, especially those composed of warriors from various tribes, were prone to division and dissension. In 1794 warriors from Mackinac and Saguina, en route to join the Indian army opposing Wayne, committed depredations in the villages they passed, whose men, their allies, were already away.[63] British and Indian leaders both realized that the Indians' strength lay in unity; as Brant said, "without being United we are nothing." Multitribal expeditions frequently faltered as a result of disharmony, to the chagrin of British agents and officers. Moreover, British observers had little comprehension and much less patience with Indians' concern that their war medicine be strong and the omens propitious. One fur trader reckoned that 75 percent of all Indian war expeditions ended without ever reaching their goal. Frustrated British officers saw such behavior as evidence of military incompetence rather than as a different concept of war.[64]

Intertribal wars and feuds posed a recurrent problem for the British and for farsighted Indian leaders who strove for unity. Throughout North America, intertribal hostilities plagued Indian nationalist movements and played into the hands of Euro-American invaders. Throughout the 1780s, the British made concerted efforts to curb hostilities between the Sioux, the Menominees, and the Chippewas lest the Crown should require their assistance and also because the Sioux-Chippewa no-man's-land constituted an untapped and inaccessible fur-bearing region. But, as late as 1825, the United States was still endeavoring in vain to end hostilities between the Sioux and the Chippewas, the Sauks, and Foxes, and the Iowas. Sioux-Chippewa conflicts did not finally end until 1858.[65] During the War of 1812, those Sioux bands that were committed to the British cause kept breaking off to fight the Chippewas, especially toward the end of the war, and the Sioux seemed eager for any opportunity to strike against the Sauks and Foxes.[66] Septuagenarian Indian agent Matthew Elliott advised that care be taken in the selection of tribes to compose an expedition since intertribal jealousies could jeopardize the success of any undertaking.[67] Robert Dickson's tendency to favor the Menominees, Winnebagoes, and Sioux worried officers who had to deal with other tribes who felt themselves deprived because Indian jealousies seemed quickly aroused.[68] The schism that occurred in the Indian confederacy in 1793 had its roots in a tradition of distrust stemming from the Treaty of Fort Stanwix in 1768 when the Iroquois had sold lands belonging to the Shawnees, the Delawares, and the Miamis, who subsequently developed a confederacy of western tribes unwilling to accept Iroquois leadership.[69]

Even influential Indian leaders had problems controlling and directing their warriors. In the autumn of 1790, Little Turtle and Blue Jacket tried in vain to keep a sufficient force assembled to strike the retreating American army a second blow. The tribes followed the lead of the Ottawas, who withdrew after their medicine men had convinced them that another battle would cause them heavy casualties. Alexander McGillivray was well aware of his warriors' shortcomings when military discipline and order were required; and not even Tecumseh could dissuade his followers from returning to their villages to celebrate after a victory.[70] But, in British eyes, Indian leaders themselves rarely set a good example to their warriors. The Shawnee chief Blue Jacket sported a scarlet frock coat with gold epaulets, a sash, and a large medallion of George III, but Colonel Richard England, commanding at Detroit, had little respect for him. Blue Jacket, he said, had been drunk for two days in the summer of 1793 and was more likely to cause trouble than to do any good. Colonel England was not the most friendly commentator on Indians, but he was considerably impressed with the Miami war chief Little Turtle, who had already masterminded the defeats of Harmar and St. Clair. Significantly, overall leadership of the Indian forces passed from Little Turtle to Blue Jacket before the defeat at Fallen Timbers.[71]

The British thought that Indians were so deficient in the

areas of supply and discipline that they could be effective only when supported by British aid and British troops, and Indians leaders often concurred, especially when requesting supplies.[72] Commanders did face enormous difficulties in leading a combined force of British and Indians. By British standards, Indians could not be relied upon to follow strategy and seemed fickle and disloyal. Lieutenant Colonel Robert McDouall feared that Ottawa warriors who had shown great determination in the capture of Michilimackinac in July 1812 were behaving suspiciously less than two weeks later, and they seemed ready to return the fort to the Americans within the month.[73] Two years later McDouall's attitudes remained unchanged: "I am now fully convinced of the great danger of depending upon these people for the defence of this Island—they are as fickle as the wind, a most difficult task to keep them with us." He maintained that one could never tell whether Indians were disposed to fight, nor predict how they would perform if they did fight.[74]

Many British officers believed that Indian warriors were generally impetuous and impatient of control. Before the Battle of Fallen Timbers, the Indians launched an ill-advised attacked on Fort Recovery and were repulsed with losses. Some warriors returned home while those that remained were dispirited before their vital clash with Wayne. In 1811, while Tecumseh was away in the south, the northern Indians under his brother the Prophet allowed themselves to be drawn into premature battle at Tippecanoe, thereby frustrating the Shawnee war chief's plan of holding back until the combined Indian forces could obtain British aid and strike a crushing blow against the United States. In 1813, Creek warriors likewise initiated hostilities before the British were ready to support them, and they suffered appalling casualties. In such instances, Indians seemed to display religious fanaticism rather then sound military judgment.[75]

Once in action, Indians proved difficult to control, especially if exposed to enemy fire or confronted with a for-

tified position. Tecumseh expressed the Indians' reluctance to attack fortifications, declaring: "It is hard to fight
people who live like ground hogs."[76] Indians refused to incur heavy losses taking an objective by storm, and British
officers and traders commented and complained time and
again that Indians lacked the perseverance to be of use in a
siege or the courage to face determined resistance.[77] Some
observers pointed to the difference between the Indians'
prowess when fighting in the woods and their refusal to
stand up to fire in open country.[78] Others maintained that
Indians who reproached their British allies for exposing
themselves to unnecessary danger and who "fled like hares"
when action became heated were quick to abandon cover
when the enemy retreated, bounding forward and toma-
hawking their fleeing foes from behind, or to return and
plunder the dead and dying.[79] The battles at Fallen Timbers and Tippecanoe suggested that Indians were unable
to withstand bayonet and cavalry charges.[80] Indians preferred to attack at dawn, as they did at Tippecanoe and
with devastating effect against St. Clair in 1791.[81]

British officers who thought in terms of campaigns and
military objectives found most frustrating the Indian practice of returning home after each action. The Indian concept of the warpath as leading to and from a single engagement was unsuited to the demands of a prolonged
campaign as envisaged and executed by the British. Indian
warriors who had attacked Fort Recovery in 1794 went
home after the engagement, although they left runners to
recall them should Wayne advance. After the victory at
Fort Meigs in 1813, the Indians streamed back to their villages, only Tecumseh and a handful of warriors remaining
with the disconcerted Procter.[82] Some observers thought
that Indian warfare was little more than a kind of seasonal
pastime in which there was much ado about nothing and
the taking of a scalp or a prisoner constituted sufficient victory to end hostilities for the year.[83]

The British fought an uphill struggle to remedy what
they regarded as the Indians' military defects. Not only did

they send troops to support, direct, and when necessary, restrain their Indian allies, they also, from the Revolution to the end of the War of 1812, endeavored to induce the Indians to adopt more "regular" methods of fighting. Wrote Governor Haldimand in 1783: "they Must in Some Measure adopt our Systems and be advised by Officers of knowledge and Experience Who May be Sent to Conduct them." Other plans were less practical; British attempts to train Florida Indians in the use of the bayonet in 1814 met with little success.[84]

The British redcoat generally had little respect for his Indian allies. The attitude of the common soldier toward the Indian (at least insofar as expressed by the uncommon soldiers who committed their opinions to paper) seems to have been a mixture of fear and loathing. Creek and Choctaw chiefs who visited the British fleet prior to the expedition against New Orleans inspired ridicule rather than respect.[85] Rumors of Indians turning on their red-coated allies or digging up British corpses for scalps heightened soldiers' suspicions, and they viewed Indians as dubious allies at best.[86] The decision of the British military to use Indians to bring back deserters hardly served to improve the opinions of the men in the ranks who often feared the Indians more than they did the enemy.[87]

British soldiers frequently found Indian treatment of prisoners and wounded abhorrent. After the Battle of Lundy's Lane, one soldier shot and killed an Indian who tried to throw a wounded American officer onto a fire. The soldier promptly threw the Indian's body on the same fire.[88] The men in the ranks saw little in Indian conduct or character to impress them. When they expressed their thoughts on their Indian allies, the result was usually a denunciation of them as treacherous savages. A captain in the Nova Scotia Fencibles dismissed the Indians as shameless cowards who "undoubtedly murder many of our wounded officers for the sake of plunder." Sergeant James Commins, Eighth Foot, was more explicit: "Their General Character is that of a Cowardly, Pusillanimous Filthy Crew, it matters not what others have said of them, I shall give them their due. So far from being those brave warriors and have [sic] such a Contempt of Death as you may have heard before, I conceive them to be the most cowardly despicable characters I ever saw (except scalloping [sic] a defenceless man or plundering the wretched inhabitants be an act of bravery) their cruelty exceeds everything I have seen among enemies." Perhaps recognizing his own inconsistency in acknowledging the contribution of the Caughnawagas at the Battle of Beaver Dams, Commins pointed out that they were "the most civilized of the Indians."[89] From the little documentary evidence available, it appears that British soldiers found little in their Indian allies to merit risking the death penalty that General William Hull proclaimed awaited any white man found fighting alongside Indians, nor to lend support to Major General Isaac Brock's counterproclamation that the brave Indians were brother sufferers defending invaded rights.[90]

Whereas the British soldier condemned the Indian as a savage, the higher ranks in the army tended to condemn the Indian for not being a soldier. The British military held irregular auxiliaries of any kind in low esteem. General James Wolfe, the hero-to-be of Quebec, had denounced the American militia during the Seven Years War as contemptible cowards who could not be relied upon in action: "They fall down dead in their own dirt and desert by battalions, officers and all. Such rascals as those are rather an incumbrage than any real strength to an army."[91] Similar contempt sent British regulars on a frontal assault against the American guns defending New Orleans in January 1815, with disastrous results.

The American service was not the kind of war relished by British professionals, especially those accustomed to victory over Napoleon's forces on the Peninsula.[92] British officers who were sent to serve in the North American wilderness did not necessarily lack experience of irregular warfare, but often they were inclined to compare Indian warriors with, and expect them to act like, regular troops in a European theater of war. A few officers knew how to make best use of Indians and militia, and they lamented the "deplorable ignorance and stupidity" of those who believed that nobody but a regular soldier could fight well.[93] Yet the latter remained the predominant opinion among British officers, while Indian warriors had neither the training nor the inclination to emulate the British redcoat.

In sum, when making general appraisals, the British criticized and denounced Indians as fighters far more than they commended them. Reports of Indian conduct in specific actions, however, seem to have been as often favorable as not. The British complained that Indians were unreliable and cruel, but they sought their help time after time. The frustrations and disadvantages involved in employing Indian allies were outweighed by the fact that once the Indians went to war, they did so as allies, not as enemies.

One writer summed up the contribution of the tribes in the War of 1812 with a fair degree of accuracy: "Of the Indian people generally, as our allies in the late war in America, those dwelling in Lower Canada were entirely useless; the Six Nations higher up, in the country lying between the Lakes Huron and Ontario, were of some service; but to the tribes at the head of Lake Erie, on the western shores of Huron, and from thence towards the Mississippi, is the preservation of Upper Canada in the first years of the war, mainly to be attributed." He was not alone in recognizing the value of the Indian alliance to Canada; the fur traders and the military agreed on that.[94] The Napoleonic Wars imposed tremendous demands on Britain's small army, and the regimental force that could be spared for North America was slight. At the beginning of the War of 1812, Canada's defenses comprised 5,500 regular troops and a militia force that was stronger on paper than in fact: only 4,000 of Upper Canada's 11,000 militia were thought reliable enough to arm. This, in addition to the bad disposition of the colony's population, gave credibility to Henry Clay's claim that Canada could be had for the marching.[95]

Britain relied on Indian auxiliaries to bolster its regimental presence and prevent such a catastrophe. In the event, the Indian alliance and American incompetence saved Britain's North American colonies. British policy among the western tribes, implemented by fur traders, ensured that at the outbreak of war Indian support was available at strategic positions. The first definite news that the American commander at Michilimackinac received of his government's declaration of war was when he was called upon to surrender by a force of Indians and British fur traders. This, along with the Indian-aided British capture of Detroit and the Potawatomis' capture of Fort Dearborn, prevented the early American victory that had seemed likely in the west. After helping to hold back the Americans for a whole year on the Detroit frontier, some warriors continued to serve in the Niagara campaigns after the British defeat and the death of Tecumseh at the Thames, but they were mainly displaced refugees dependent upon British supplies. By mid-1814, Indian support was mainly concentrated west of Lake Michigan, and it enabled Britain to maintain control of that area until the end of the war. As Robert Dickson pointed out in defense of one of his favorite tribes, although everyone seemed to hate the Winnebagoes, they would do well to remember that it was thanks to that tribe that Prairie du Chien had not fallen to the Americans. Similarly, as Edward Nicholls reminded Admiral Cochrane, Creek hostility to the United States had at least done as Britain had intended it should, keeping some five thousand enemy troops and the best American general occupied in the south and unable to reinforce the invasion of Canada.[96] After the war, the British government was sufficiently grateful to have a special medal struck in appreciation of the services rendered by their Indian allies while later Canadian historians were inspired to write nonsense about Indian patriotism in the heroic defense of Canada.[97]

Indian resistance to American expansionism in the postrevolutionary decades gave the British some idea of their military worth.[98] British realization of just how effective Indians could be as allies came only with fear of how deadly they would be as enemies. Joseph Brant was able to exploit the Canadian authorities' anxiety over rumors of an Indian uprising in 1797 to get his own way in the dispute over the Grand River lands.[99] Nor was the tendency to fear Indian enmity, rather than to value Indian friendship, restricted to those in close proximity to the Indians. In 1809, Foreign Secretary Castlereagh approved Governor Craig's proposals for conciliating the tribes on the principle "that if in a Contest they are not employed to act with us, they will be engaged to act against us; and that we are to consider not so much their use as Allies as their destructiveness if Enemies."[100] With such an attitude prevailing, those who faced Indians as enemies perhaps better appreciated their worth as fighters than did their allies, who saw occasional examples of Indian effectiveness and instances of Indian brutality against a backdrop of expense, unreliability, and frustration.

9
The British as Allies

THE Indians' allegiance to Britain was never guaranteed, especially after the tribes had had some experience of what loyalty to George III entailed. Between 1783 and 1815, the Indians became increasingly wary of committing themselves to a power that regarded them as expendable and they were understandably suspicious of British policies, which varied between encouragement and restraint, support and desertion. The Indians were engaged in a continual struggle to preserve their lands and their cultures, and they expected the support of their avowed allies to be similarly constant. British conduct toward the Indians, however, was influenced by forces beyond the bounds of the alliance and fluctuated as the demands of the international situation altered. As a result, Britons who complained that Indians were unreliable often seemed equally capricious to the Indians.

Changes in British policy and the signing of treaties contrary to promises constituted betrayal not only of Indian allies but also of those British officers and agents who had implemented previous policies and who now had to explain the about-face. White men who lived and worked among the Indians shared their dismay at British breaches of faith. That these men sometimes had given unauthorized and exaggerated assurances of support made it even more

difficult for the Indians to understand Britain's reluctance
to help them against the Americans, although the Canadian authorities explained that, as only a part of the king's
domains, they could not take it upon themselves to start a
war that might engulf half the world.[1]

In addition to having commitments elsewhere that might
dictate its North American policies, Britain also experienced periodic changes in government, notably in the
critical years 1782–83. Moreover, it had conflicting interests in America; a proposed policy of encouraging American settlement as a market for British manufactures hardly
was compatible with the preservation of Indian lands for
the fur trade.[2] Consequently, actual or implied promises of
help made by British representatives to the Indians were
not necessarily acts of deliberate deception. Changes in
ministry, in policy, or in the international or North American situation could cause assurances given in good faith to
become lies in effect. Few Indians showed as much understanding as those Winnebago chiefs who absolved the British commanding officers of responsibility for the cession of
Michilimackinac in 1815, contrary to promises, because
they realized that the officers had done their best but were
subject to the will of a distant king.[3] To the majority of Indians, it mattered little that agents exceeded their authority
or were impotent to alter higher policy decisions. Those
agents had been introduced as the king's representatives
and the Indians accepted them as such. Concerns of policy
or empire carried little weight with people who saw themselves betrayed in their struggle for survival against an enemy they considered to be Britain's as much as their own.

In addition to Britain's retention of the western posts
through the 1780s and early 1790s, British supplies, advice,
and presence at councils gave the Indians good reason to
think that King George was still their ally and protector.
Signs of British encouragement increased significantly in
the critical year 1794. The British rebuilt a fort on the
banks of the Maumee River, and Lord Dorchester delivered a bellicose and controversial speech to a group of Indian delegates who assembled at the Castle of Saint Lewis

in Quebec in February. Referring to the conduct of the
Americans, the governor declared, "I shall not be surprised if we are at war with them in the course of the
present year." He said that, if such proved to be the case,
the disputed boundary line between British and American
possessions would have to be drawn by the warriors.[4] As
Anthony Wayne led his army into the Northwest, it seemed
to the Indians that Britain was ready at last to give them
open assistance against the Americans.[5] Not surprisingly,
as Wayne advanced, the Indians made repeated requests to
the British to honor their promises and lend support because time was running out.[6]

In the event, the Indians received only further and more
convincing proof that the British were not to be trusted.
Concerned with developments in revolutionary France,
Britain was not prepared to engage in war with the United
States for the sake of its Indian allies. As the American
army approached, the confederated tribes issued a proclamation requiring all traders and residents in the area to
don Indian dress and join the Indian army in resisting the
common enemy. A "great number of British soldiers with
their faces Blacked" reputedly joined in the Indian attack
on Fort Recovery, and Wayne's Choctaw and Chickasaw
scouts reported that a considerable number of white men,
all with their faces blackened except for three red-coated
officers, urged the Indians on from the rear. At the Battle
of Fallen Timbers, 20 August 1794, Canadian and Detroit
militia men apparently fought in the Indian ranks, and
Wayne reported that the bodies of white men lay strewn in
the woods after his victory. However, those British subjects
who fought alongside the Indians did so as individuals,
perhaps under compulsion and without the approval of
their government. Alexander McKee, Matthew Elliott, and
Simon Girty watched the battle from a safe distance, and
the Indians received no military support from the garrison of the British fort on the Maumee. Fleeing from the
Americans after the battle, they found the gates of the fort
barred against them.[7]

Most accounts agreed that the Indians fought gallantly

against superior odds, but Colonel Richard England, at Detroit, declared, "The Indians on this occasion have forfeited every pretension to a Warlike or Gallant Character." He even denounced the Indians for leaving unprotected the very fort that denied them refuge after the battle. Colonel England's lone condemnation of the Indians' conduct may have stemmed from the precariousness of his position at Detroit. Alternatively, he may have sought to pin the whole blame for the defeat squarely on the Indians. He knew that the warriors should have been better supplied, and he himself had evaded Little Turtle's plea for help a month previously.[8]

Having refused asylum to the fleeing Indians, the English garrison stood by and watched as the Americans destroyed Indian crops and villages right beneath the guns of the fort. The victorious General Wayne declared that this lack of action proved that the British had neither the power nor the inclination to afford the Indians the protection they had led them to expect.[9] The British desertion at such a critical moment, rather than the battle itself, proved to be the vital factor in subduing the Indians. Writing in retrospect, Mohawk chieftain John Norton concluded: "The conduct of the British Fort dispirited the Confederates much more than the issue of the battle, which they fought with very inferior number, and in a disadvantageous position, without considerable loss: this they considered as a misfortune which might be repaired with glory,— another time; but the former, they did not know how to remedy." The Indians were still prepared to fight as late as the autumn of 1794, if the British supported them.[10]

The Indians were angry and confused at the conduct of the British. Joseph Brant maintained that the Indians would have fared better if Britain had not interfered at all, as they then would either have made an equitable peace or have remained united against the enemy.[11] The tribes became further discouraged during the winter of 1794–95, and they seemed to have little option but to make peace with the United States. This they did at Greenville in August 1795. Signatories to the treaty included the formerly militant Shawnee, Blue Jacket; the Miami war chief, Little Turtle; the Delaware, Buckongahelas; and Tarhe (known as the Crane), a Wyandot chief who had been wounded at Fallen Timbers and who, though more than seventy years of age, was to fight for the United States against Britain during the War of 1812.[12] The Treaty of Greenville brought to a close one phase of the wars for the northwest and ended a generation's struggle for survival on its own terms.

When, under the terms of Jay's Treaty of 1794, Britain finally handed over the disputed frontier posts to the United States, Britons once again feared that the Indians would make reprisals. This act of desertion on the part of the British was heightened by the fact that the posts were yielded in exchange, not for territorial concessions to the Indians, but for commercial concessions to British and Canadian merchants. Once again, the British made considerable efforts to convince the tribes that they were not really being abandoned. The Indians were not easily convinced, and Joseph Brant complained that "this is the second time the poor Indians have been left in the lurch." Nevertheless, the British once more escaped the Indian vengeance they so dreaded.[13] Even so, British conduct at Fort Miami in the summer of 1794 earned the redcoats a reputation for perfidy that was to cast a shadow of suspicion and bitterness over Anglo-Indian relations; it ensured that when the time came for Britain to seek Indian aid in war, the tribes were far less eager to commit themselves to such unreliable allies.[14]

Between 1796 and 1807, Britain tended to neglect the Indians as she focused her attention on developments in Europe. Speaking before an audience of Chippewas, Ottawas, and Potawatomis in 1802, Joseph Brant declared that "the British Government altogether has shown great ingratitude to those who have rendered it the greatest service." When John Johnson learned of his "Poor Old friend, Brants Death" in 1807, he praised him as "a faithful and Brave Servant of the Crown."[15] Brant certainly remained

loyal to Britain to the end, but his final years were marked
by growing disillusionment. He had seen his people betrayed in the Peace of Paris, he had felt himself excluded
from councils with the western tribes, he had fought and
fueled factional battles in the Indian Department, and he
had been a constant thorn in the government's side on the
issue of the Grand River lands. When he complained about
British ingratitude, Brant no doubt had his own services
and the disputes over the Grand River lands in mind.
Nevertheless, British concern and support did seem to
be in short supply in those years. Meanwhile, increasing
American population stepped up the demand, the Louisiana Purchase provided the means, and the United States
government and military increased the pressure for the
expulsion of Indians from their lands east of the Mississippi River.

Then, in June 1807, the British ship *Leopard,* in search
of deserters from the royal navy, fired on the American
frigate *Chesapeake* and initiated an international crisis. As
the likelihood of war increased, the British in Canada
made frantic efforts to renew their connections with the
Indian tribes to whom they had to turn for help in the
event of war. The British dared not provoke the warriors
into opening hostilities with the United States, but they
had to ensure that the tribes would be ready and willing to
fight for the Crown if war did break out.[16] This was no easy
task. Potawatomi warriors in 1807 remained as bitter toward the British as they had been in 1795 and were not
about to put their trust in allies who had proved faithless
in the past.[17]

The *Chesapeake* crisis passed, but four years later the
British again faced the dilemma of trying to secure the
support of the Indians in readiness for a possible war
while at the same time restraining the warriors from any
action that might provoke that conflict. Such a policy can
have seemed little more than duplicity to the Indians, and
it also placed British agents in the almost impossible position of trying to preserve good relations with both the In-

Joseph Brant, by Ezra Ames. This oil portrait on canvas, 1806, was the last painted of Brant (1743–1807). In the thirty years since he had sat for Romney in London, Brant had become increasingly disenchanted with his British allies. (New York State Historical Association, Cooperstown)

dians and the United States.[18] The Indians, of course, were
not content to be mere tools of British policy. Increasingly,
the British found themselves dealing with the capable
Shawnee leaders, the Prophet and Tecumseh, at the head
of a growing Indian confederacy that was directed toward
securing Indian, not British, ends.[19] The Indians refused
to be restrained, and by the time war broke out in 1812,
many tribes already were engaged in hostilities against the
United States. Brigadier General Isaac Brock thought it
hardly surprising that the Indians should go to war: "Our
cold attempt to dissuade that much-injured people from
engaging in such a rash enterprize could scarcely be expected to prevail, particularly after giving such manifest
indications of a contrary sentiment by the liberal quantity
of military stores with which they were dismissed."[20] Governor James Craig, however, demonstrated the contradictory nature of the British position. In an effort to preserve
Britain's avowed neutrality, Craig, in early 1811, felt obliged
to warn the United States government against projected Indian hostilities. He did so on the grounds that he wished to
save the frontier from the horrors of Indian attacks; but
these were the same Indians he had intended to unleash
upon the Americans in the event of the latter declaring
war on Britain.[21]

British traders and agents succeeded in maintaining or
reviving their country's influence among the tribes, but
nagging doubts remained as to how much trust the Indians would place in allies who had let them down in the
past. Isaac Brock realized that American pressure made it
an act of policy for the Indians to disguise their suspicions
of the British. Tecumseh had as much reason as any to distrust the redcoats, having fought at Fallen Timbers and
lost a brother there. But Tecumseh pressed for Indian
unity with a renewed British alliance. Fully aware of British shortcomings, he had suffered far more at the hands
of Americans who had killed his father and two brothers,
destroyed his home, and murdered the Shawnee chief
Cornstalk. For Tecumseh, as for most Indians, distrust of
faithless redcoats was far outweighed by hatred of Ameri-

cans who seemed only too willing to implement the extermination of the Indians which the expansion of their settlements demanded.[22]

The western tribes Robert Dickson had mustered had not felt the full effects of earlier British betrayals, but several of the eastern tribes showed a marked and understandable reluctance to commit themselves to another British war. In June 1812, the Senecas, Cayugas, and Onondagas living in the United States sent a deputation to the Mohawks north of the border, predicting war and counseling noninvolvement. Why, they asked, should Indians become involved when neither power had any regard for them, as had been made clear in 1783? "Experience has convinced us of their neglect, except when they want us. Why then should we endanger the comfort, even the existence of our families, to enjoy their smiles only for the Day in which they need us?"[23] As Joseph Brant remarked in another context, "the Indians were not always to be fools because they had once been such." The Grand River Iroquois in particular showed little wish to rally to the British cause. They had experienced the effects of British policy or perfidy in 1783 and 1794 and, in addition, were involved in dispute with the government over lands which they felt they had earned in full by their loyal services in the revolutionary war.[24] Britons complained that only success, a show of strength, and a steady flow of presents would win Indian allegiance; but the Indians regarded these things as indications of the redcoats' sincerity and commitment. Fortunately for the British, it was they and not the Americans who won the early victories, and this, in addition to the energy and determination displayed by Isaac Brock, drew many Indians from their shell of distrust. Even so, the New York Iroquois reversed their historic role and fought against the Crown in the War of 1812. Several other tribes joined them when the war swung in favor of the Americans.[25]

Once the fighting began, the Indians seem to have had a fairly high opinion of the British soldiers who fought alongside them. They frequently requested that British troops be sent to serve with them, and they certainly con-

sidered them to be superior to irregular troops and militia.[26] As the British decried many Indian modes of warfare, however, so Indians looked askance at some of the
redcoats' practices. An army that ordered that "Crouch-
ing, ducking, or laying down when advancing under fire
are bad habits, and must be corrected,"[27] may have been
better pleased with the disciplined dying of its troops before New Orleans on 8 January 1815, but it was hardly
likely to win the emulation of Indian warriors accustomed
to fighting on the principle that victory went to the side
without casualties. As one observer recalled, "The Indians
regarded the indifference with which our troops fearlessly
exposed themselves to fire with much admiration; but this
feeling, notwithstanding, always appeared qualified with
some mixture of wonder, and perhaps contempt, at our
folly and ignorance of what they deemed the immutable
principles of warfare."[28]

Black Hawk, the Sauk war chief, fought for the British
in the War of 1812 at River Raisin and Fort Meigs and then
returned home after the abortive attack on Fort Stephenson. Later, in an autobiography obviously written for a
white audience, Black Hawk gave an account of what he
had seen to his people (the emphases supposedly are his):

> I explained to them the manner the British and Americans
> fought. Instead of stealing upon each other, and taking every
> advantage to *kill the enemy* and *save their own people*, as we do,
> (which, with us is considered good policy in a war chief), they
> march out, in open daylight, and *fight*, regardless of the number
> of warriors they may lose! After the battle is over, they retire to
> feast, and drink wine, as if nothing had happened; after which,
> they make a *statement in writing*, of what they have done—*each
> party claiming the victory!* and neither giving an account of half
> the number that have been killed on their own side. They all
> fought like braves, but would not do to *lead a war party* with us.
> Our maxim is, *"to kill the enemy, and save our own men"*. Those
> chiefs would do to *paddle* a canoe, but not to *steer* it.[29]

Indians often found British treatment of prisoners to be
equally puzzling. While British soldiers could not accept

the Indians' killing prisoners, most Indians found it difficult to understand why an enemy should cease to be regarded as such the moment he stopped fighting. The parole and exchange of prisoners meant that Indians sometimes met enemies they had captured previously in battle a second time. It made no sense to them for the British to capture enemies only to set them free to fight another day. Moreover, as Joseph Brant pointed out, white men applied the prisoner-of-war concept only to fellow whites; captured Indians were put to death.[30]

The main cause of the Indians' dissatisfaction with their British allies, however, lay not in the redcoats' behavior in the field but in their absence. The British were keen to have Indians do their fighting for them, but seemed reluctant to support and supply the warriors in their struggle. The frequency of requests for troops indicates not only that the Indians wanted assistance but also that the British were often unwilling or unable to give it, promises to the contrary notwithstanding. British failures to match promise with performance during the Revolution continued in later years and gave substance to Brant's complaint about British lack of action and support, as usual.[31] Britons might feel contempt for what they interpreted as the Indians' mercenary character, but Indian impressions of their British paymasters were little better. In 1784 the British officer at Michilimackinac refused a Chippewa chief's request for supplies and found himself subjected to a torrent of abuse. The enraged Chippewa denounced all Englishmen as liars and impostors who had encouraged his people to go to Canada to fight and to lose their brothers and children, but who left the Indians to starve now that the fighting was done. All this, remarked the officer, from an Indian who was not even drunk.[32]

The British did cut back on their supply of presents when the Indians' services were no longer required. This, as Lieutenant Governor Francis Gore realized, was neither just nor sound policy because it jeopardized the chances of securing Indian assistance in the future by convincing the

Indians that: "You are very kind, when you want us to fight
for you but when that Service is performed, you shut the
Store Door in our Faces."[33] The Indians expected not only
to be supplied with the means to wage war but also to be
rewarded for past services and compensated for losses suffered.[34] Indeed, the Indians felt that the English were
largely responsible for their heavy losses. At Quebec, in
1814, Neywash, leader of the pro-British Ottawas and a
veteran of the retreat from Malden with Procter and Tecumseh, complained to the governor that the Indians had
been told they were to fight on the army's flanks and rear,
but instead they had always gone in front and this was why
so many warriors had been lost. In a council held the following spring, an Onondaga speaker declared that the
reason the Shawnees had suffered so much and lost Tecumseh was because "the red Coated Officers were always
pressing them forward on Service."[35]

Having once persuaded the Indians to do their fighting
for them, the British often were as slow to provide supplies
as they were to give support. Long supply lines and severe
Canadian winters made regular provisioning of the tribes
enormously difficult, but the Indians expected the British
to honor their promises and placed little value in excuses,
however justified, for failing to do so. Their patience became exhausted when the same promises and the same excuses were made year after year.[36] Joseph Brant reproached
the deputy superintendent of Indian affairs at Niagara in
1786: "I am sorry to say that You the English has been always too slow of sending up of Indian Presents, always
some excuse or other of delays, when there is goods enough
at Montreal, when there is so much wanted here. You
better say at once that those goods are not for the Indians,
then You have a right to keep them where they are."[37]

The Mohawk spoke from bitter experience: the British
failure to support and supply the Six Nations in 1779 had
left the Iroquois' crops and villages open to destruction at
the hand of Sullivan's expedition, which in turn threw the
Indians on to the British at Niagara for sustenance.[38] It has

been pointed out that during the Revolution, the best that the rebels could hope for in the war on the frontier was stalemate. Britain, with its Indian allies, had the potential for victory, but persistent shortages of supplies prevented that potential from being realized.[39] The same problem seems to have limited Indian military effectiveness throughout the period, not the least in 1794 when lack of supplies caused some of the warriors to disperse before the Battle of Fallen Timbers.[40] In the southern theater during the War of 1812, observers noted that only lack of supplies prevented the Indians from inflicting greater damage than they did on the enemy. Even on their scanty rations, the Indians performed considerable achievements.[41]

Requests for Indian supplies were frequent during the war and came not only from the Indians. In 1813 the inhabitants of Prairie du Chien pointed out that the neighboring Sioux, Sauks, and Winnebagos remained faithful to Britain but were short of guns and supplies. With the Americans increasing their presents, it was feared that English influence among the nations of the Mississippi could be lost for want of supplies. Moreover: "It is extraordinary that our Government asks the Indians help in this War, and that it refuses the furnishing them the necessary quantity of powder—May this want of Energy not put them under the necessity of turning those arms that are disposed to serve us, against us."[42] According to Robert Dickson, who probably understood as well as anybody the importance of Indian supplies in wartime, the small quantity of presents sent to the western tribes was not only totally inadequate for their protection, but it also gave the Indians a poor impression of the resources of the British Empire. Dickson, however, seems to have made sure that *his* western tribes received ample supplies, even if it meant depriving other tribes of their fair share.[43]

To allow the Indians to derive a poor impression of British power was dangerous. British policy required that the Indians retain a proper sense of awe for the might of King George. British forces in North America might appear

small, but the Indians must never be allowed to forget
the greatness of the empire. Indians, however, quickly
realized that British actions did not match their proud
words. News of General Burgoyne's surrender in 1777 had
reached the Indians only a short time after the British had
gathered many of them together in council at Niagara and
assured them that "the King is too powerful to be conquered by his undutiful Children the Americans."[44] In
1814 the British heralded their initiative in the south with
declarations to the Indians that the king, who had already
soundly defeated his French enemies, was now turning his
attention to America in order to chastise President Madison.[45] The British efforts came to nothing, however, with
Jackson's unopposed capture of Pensacola, the failure of
the attempt to take Fort Bowyer, and the lemminglike attack on New Orleans.

Perhaps the most glaring example of British military
failure occurred in the retreat and subsequent defeat at
the Battle of the Thames. The untimely death of Isaac
Brock at the Battle of Queenston Heights robbed the British-Indian war effort of a pivotal figure. No one else in the
British military enjoyed similar standing with the Indians,
and Tecumseh and his followers found themselves dealing
with the uninspiring Henry Procter. The British defeat on
Lake Erie in 1813 compelled Brigadier General Procter
to withdraw his army from Malden. Procter had often
condemned Indians for cowardice and unreliability, but
he became the target for abuse himself when Tecumseh
learned that he intended to abandon his position: "You always told us, that you would never draw your foot off British Ground; but now, Father, we see you are drawing back,
and we are sorry to see our Father doing so, without seeing
the Enemy—We must compare our Father's conduct to a
fat Animal that carries its tail upon its back, but when af-
frighted, it drops in between its legs and runs off—." Fearing another British desertion, Tecumseh requested that if
the redcoats would not stand and fight, they at least give
the Indians guns and ammunition so that they could defend their lands and, if necessary, die upon them.[46]

The Shawnee war chief was eventually persuaded the retreat was necessary, and acceded to it, but the Indians had no confidence in the British, and the British troops had little in Procter. The enraged warriors were said to have threatened the life of Matthew Elliott, and the old Indian agent was apparently reduced to tears at the state of affairs. When the army did turn and face William Henry Harrison's pursuing American force, the British troops broke at the first charge. In all, 601 British soldiers were taken prisoner. Procter fled the field, leaving the Indians to put up the only real resistance, which they did until Tecumseh was killed. Matthew Elliott described the battle: "The Conduct of the Troops was Shameful in the highest degree a great part of them never firing one round until the[y] retreated, this threw the Indians in the Centre into Confusion and they broke [;] on the right they remained firm and Compelled the Enemys left wing to retreat for about a Mile and a half." Returning from the pursuit, the Indians "were much Surprised to find we had not been equally Successful on the left," and victory turned into retreat. Tradition holds that Tecumseh had a premonition of death on the night before the battle and discarded his uniform of an English brigadier general to fight and die in Indian dress.[47] In view of such British performance, it was not surprising that many tribes saw a better chance of survival in coming to terms with the Americans than in fighting alongside the redcoats.

Many British subjects were well aware of the ill feelings the Indians harbored following repeated betrayals. From almost the beginning of the War of 1812, people sent petitions, warnings, and recommendations to the authorities, advising the government not to neglect the Indians again when peace was made. Preferably, they argued, the government should rectify the errors of earlier treaties by securing a new boundary for the Indian lands, which would also help to protect Britain's North American colonies.[48] Unfortunately, Britain was to show no more concern for its Indian friends at the end of the War of 1812 than it had at the end of the Revolution. In the peace settlement negoti-

ated at Ghent in 1814, Britain showed once again, as it had
in 1783, 1794, and in 1813 at the Battle of the Thames,
that it was a perfidious ally who could be trusted only to let
the Indians down in their hour of need.

Despite these betrayals, Indian speakers in council regularly expressed their faith in their British father. The pro–
British Black Hawk claimed, in later years, that whereas
Americans made many promises but never kept them, the
British made few promises but could always be relied upon
to keep their word. Nevertheless, other Indians placed far
less faith in British promises. Indians were no more willing
than whites to forgive and forget; indeed, warned one officer at the end of the War of 1812, "A breach of faith, is
with them an utter abomination & never forgotten."[49]
When British Ambassador Robert Liston visited the Indian village at the Lake of the Two Mountains in Lower
Canada, the inhabitants presented their grievances to him,
"observing that their complaints were more likely to reach
th *ears* of their Father, as the Ambassador's *Coat* was *not
red.*"[50]

Britons feared and Americans hoped that each successive breach of faith would finally alienate the Indians
from the British.[51] Nevertheless, despite deterioration in
confidence and understandable hesitation on the part of
some tribes in the War of 1812, the Indians adhered to
their British friends with surprising persistence. They did
so not from any love of George III. The Indians generally
had a greater awareness of the realities of their situation
than they have received credit for. They entered into military, political, and commercial relations with the British
with a fair idea of what they stood to gain and to lose, and
of what the alternative was likely to be if they remained un-
supplied and unsupported by the redcoats. Confronted
with the prospect of being overwhelmed by American expansionism, Indians found that British support, supplies,
and presence temporarily strengthened their military and
bargaining position and helped to postpone defeat and expulsion at the hands of the Big Knives. British conduct dis-

appointed and disgusted the Indians time and again, but Indian leaders had few illusions about the nature of their "alliance" with the Crown, and most understood clearly the position in which the tribes found themselves. The Reverend John Heckewelder heard Indians compare the English and the Americans to the blades of a pair of scissors which, in closing, did not destroy each other but only the Indians who were caught between the cutting edges. Seneca chief Cornplanter reminded Joseph Brant in 1794 that whites on both sides, in Canada as in the United States, despised the Indians, wanting only to increase their own power and rule over the Indians.[52]

Indian attitudes toward their red-coated allies varied according to tribe and individual and fluctuated according to time and circumstance. On the whole, however, Indian confidence in the British declined, and Indians looked upon British actions in 1783, 1794, and 1814 as a trilogy of betrayals. Indian loyalty to the British rested upon a realistic appraisal of British, American, and Indian interests. What Lieutenant Governor Simcoe said about Joseph Brant in 1793 could be applied to most Indians throughout the period. Brant declared in public council "that for years He had made it his business to become acquainted with the Politicks of Great Britain and the United States; that they were both actuated by a regard to self Interest." Simcoe accurately assessed the Mohawk's sentiments: "I believe that He considers the Indian Interests as the first Object—that as a second, tho' very inferior one, He prefers the British, in a certain degree, to the people of the United States."[53] Caught between the British and the American millstones, most tribes sided with the British as the lesser of two evils.

Conclusion: 1815

WHEN peace negotiations began at Ghent in 1814, Britain demanded as a sine qua non that its Indian allies be included in the treaty and first proposed that a new Indian boundary be established on the basis of the Greenville Treaty line of 1795. The Americans, however, refused to accept such terms. After a generation of global war against France, Britain was tired of fighting and eager to be rid of "the millstone of an American war." Financial difficulties at home and dramatic events in Europe demanded the full attention of Lord Liverpool's Tory government, and the Indian question became an embarrassment. Consequently, despite the dissatisfaction of one of the commissioners, Henry Goulburn, Britain backed down on the boundary issue and accepted a reciprocal undertaking to restore the Indian tribes to their prewar situation. Britain did, however, secure American recognition that the Indians should be included in the treaty and that separate treaties should be made with the tribes who had been involved in the war.[1] Some regarded the Treaty of Ghent as an honorable end to the war, but the London *Times* denounced it as yielding all Britain's conquests and abandoning its Indian allies to the mercy of the United States. Americans did not find it too difficult to accept inclusion of the Indians in the peace because they realized that the stipulations made were "little more than would have been the case had the treaty not contained them."[2]

Article IX of the Treaty of Ghent required that the Indians be restored to their situation as of 1811 and that separate treaties of peace be made with the various tribes. Consequently, the United States made a string of treaties: with the Potawatomis, the Piankeshaws, and various bands of Sioux, Omahas, Kickapoos, Wyandots, Chippewas, Ottawas, Senecas, Shawnees, Delawares, Miamis, Osages, Iowas, Kansas, Sauks and Foxes, in 1815; with the Sauks, Sioux, and Winnebagoes in 1816; and with the Menominees, Otos, and Poncas in 1817. These treaties established peace and pardoned hostilities, and supposedly restored the Indians to their prewar situation while acknowledging them to be under United States protection.[3] Despite the fine words to the Indians that they were included in a peace that was to last forever and that they could return to their lands,[4] the Indian article was largely an empty gesture. The British knew that American expansion would not cease and that the United States had little or no intention of returning anything to the Indians. As the still unhappy Goulburn was told, the Treaty of Ghent stated only that the Indians should be restored to their prewar situation; it did not stipulate that they were to be maintained forever in that situation. If the Americans allowed the Indians to return to their lands for only a week or a month, they complied with the treaty literally. The Americans might be bound by the laws of justice to maintain the Indians in, as well as restore them to, their former situation, but they were not so bound by the Treaty of Ghent. Earl Bathurst, secretary for war and the colonies, agreed: the treaty required only that the Indians be given back what they had held before the war. "It does not nor was it ever intended on the part of Great Britain to guarantee those territories and possessions against future Invasion after they had been restored."[5] In short, Article IX was a facade, affording the Indians no security against conquest by their enemies. If the British government ever believed that

Captain W. Andrew Bulger Saying Farewell at Fort Mackay, Prairie du Chien, Wisconsin, 1815, by Peter Rindisbacher. Pen and water-color on paper, c. 1823. The British evacuated Fort McKay in

May 1815, less than a year after they had captured it with the help of some 500 Menominee, Winnebago, Chippewa, and Sioux warriors. (Amon Carter Museum, Fort Worth, Texas)

the Americans would act with justice in honoring the terms, the Winnebagoes knew better: "*Father!*—The peace made between you and the Big Knives, may be a lasting one; but it cannot be for us, for we hate them; they have so often deceived us that we cannot put any faith in them."[6]

When the peace negotiations had foundered on the Indian boundary question, Lieutenant Colonel Robert McDouall at Michilimackinac had told the various tribes that the war was now being continued solely on their behalf because the king was determined to fulfill his promises to the Indians and to have their lands restored to them as an independent state.[7] The Iroquois had apparently been given similar assurances. At a council held after the war, the Mohawk speaker reminded the British that they had promised not to make peace until the ancient boundary line was restored, but now that peace was made nothing was said about where the boundary was fixed.[8] Ironically, by the time McDouall was telling the Indians that the war was being continued for their sake, the Treaty of Ghent had already been signed. Report of the settlement reached McDouall in mid-March 1815, and his incredulity was matched by his bitterness at having been let down by his government: "It is a little hard upon officers commanding to be made the channel of these vacillating communications, having so strong a tendency to make the Indians believe they were purposely deceived & trifled with upon subjects of such peculiar interest & consequence to them."[9]

Exposed to the reproaches of the disappointed Indians, McDouall suffered the old fears that the warriors would wreak vengeance when they saw that Michilimackinac was to be given up. That post was the key to the whole western country, and to give it up would be such conclusive proof of British submission to the United States and so contrary to the promises that McDouall had only recently been instructed to make, as to constitute a breach of faith, which, like the betrayal at Fort Miami twenty years earlier, would never be forgotten.[10] Moreover, McDouall complained, what was happening on the Mississippi in no way conformed with the Treaty of Ghent. The Americans had no right to be seizing the Indian country and be building forts therein because they had never possessed it until after 1812.[11] McDouall saw this American fort building as an effort to separate the British from the Indians, who had relied upon repeated assurances of protection and of their remaining lands being secured to them by treaty. He could not believe that Great Britain, "the mistress of the World," could make concession after concession to the United States. If, as he had heard, Britain had also yielded its right to trade with the Indians within that country, that would sever its final link with the western tribes, and "after what I have told them what a superlative and unequalled——they must think me—." In addition, McDouall feared that the American activities were geared toward bringing a renewal of the Indian war, and, in view of Indian hostility to the building of the forts, seemed likely to succeed. This, he feared, would give the Americans the opportunity and excuse to totally subjugate the western tribes. That task would possibly be entrusted to the "Merciless Jackson"; "if so I shall to the latest period of my life, bewail the hapless Destiny of those devoted Nations who listened to our solicitations and confiding in our promises faithfully adhered to us during the war, but found the Peace which *promised* security to them and their Country only led to their utter ruin and annihilation."[12]

Nevertheless, while he might complain that the Indians had been deceived by a distant government, McDouall was not above continuing the work of deception himself. He knew full well that the treaty was a disaster for Indians who had expected, and had been led to expect, so much more; yet, with "dexterous & judicious management," he wrote, "it may be made to appear a prudent and judicious peace, & really conducive to their interest and advantage." He suggested telling the Indians that the king had wanted to continue the war, but that peace had been made because the tribes were divided and Britain did not want to involve its allies in fratricidal strife. This from the man who, not three months before, had declared: "Sincerity with an Indian, as it ought to be with all mankind, is the only mode!"[13]

In the south, Britain's Indian allies secured even less from their involvement in the war and the subsequent Treaty of Ghent. Anglophobe Robert McAfee placed the blame for the Creek War squarely on the shoulders of the British. They had bribed and deluded the Creeks into taking up arms against the United States, and then left them to face the inevitable American retribution. Reflecting on the carnage of Horseshoe Bend, McAfee wrote: "We cannot forbear to compassionate [the Creeks'] misfortunes while we execrate with indignation, the brutal barbarism of the British, whose cold blooded policy could doom this nation to inevitable ruin, merely in the hope that it would produce some temporary and inconsiderable benefit to the unhallowed cause in which they were engaged."[14]

When hostilities ended, the British assured their allies that by adhering to the peace they would become prosperous and populous, with their interests watched over by the British government.[15] The situation was complicated in the south by the fact that the Treaty of Fort Jackson (whereby Andrew Jackson confiscated the lands of the Lower Creeks, who had fought with him, as well as of the hostiles; in all, about two-thirds of the Creek domain) had been signed on 9 August, well before the Ghent Treaty of Christmas Eve, 1814.[16] The United States, therefore, took the line that the Treaty of Ghent did not apply to the Creeks because that tribe had already made peace. Some Creeks and Britons, on the other hand, maintained that the Ghent settlement rendered Jackson's treaty null. Moreover, of the thirty-six chiefs who signed the latter treaty, only one had been hostile, the rest being friendly to the United States. Consequently, the intransigent Red Sticks who had not attended Fort Jackson expected to be restored to their lands under the terms of the Ghent agreement, whereas the United States regarded them as outlaws under the Jackson treaty. Whatever the legal situation, British agents led the Indians to believe that their lands would be returned to them; something which the Americans had no intention of doing.[17] The British government did not even ensure that the Indians kept possession of the lands they still held, let alone secure restoration of territory taken since 1811. The British were well aware that the Peace of Ghent was no peace for the Indians they were abandoning. On their departure, the British informed their former allies of the peace settlement and advised them to abide by it, but at the same time left them arms with which to defend themselves against the Americans.[18]

It was not long before complaints began to come in from Indians who could not believe that the king and his ministers knew what was happening and yet did nothing to prevent it. Far from restoring lands, Americans were making further encroachments, which seem to have developed into a renewed racial war for Creek and Seminole land.[19] Affairs came to a head when Jackson treacherously captured and executed the Creek chief Hidlis Hadjo (otherwise known as the Prophet Francis) and then arrested and executed the British traders Alexander Arbuthnott and Robert Ambrister during a raid into Spanish-claimed Seminole country in 1817.[20] Jackson's conduct gave rise to a storm of protest, not least in the columns of the *Times,* which progressed from defending the right of British agents to be among the Indians to demanding whether the British government meant to honor its pledges to its former allies. The Treaty of Ghent's stipulation that Indian lands and rights be restored implied, said the *Times,* a bona fide restoration. To have restored the lands one day, only to take them back the next, would not have complied with the spirit of the treaty. In fact, there had been no restoration at all, and contrary to assurances given to the Indians, Britain made no effort to see the treaty enforced. As the *Times* pointed out: "It is nonsense to talk in this case of the treaty containing no guarantee. All treaties *imply* guarantees of their own conditions, otherwise, they bind to nothing."[21] The British government, though, was eager to be rid of its troublesome allies, and visiting Creek and

Seminole chiefs now met with a decidedly cold reception.[22] The government was not prepared to risk renewed war in order to secure compliance with an article they had made as the least dishonorable, yet practicable, way of disentangling Britain from its Indian alliances, and which, in any case, was of doubtful legality as applied to the Creeks. As usual, British agents had exceeded instructions, and that enabled the government to deny and evade responsibility, either to an angry American government or to deserted Indian allies.[23]

In the war of 1812, as in the American War of Independence, Britain's Indian allies won considerable victories in the west. On both occasions, however, these local victories were sacrificed by the government in London and its diplomats in Europe for what they deemed more valuable concessions elsewhere. Hence, the terms of neither the 1783 nor the 1814 treaty were a true reflection of the situation in the west. Britons often condemned Indians for actions the motives behind which they did not understand; so too, Indians, unaware of and unconcerned with Britain's European and imperial problems, regarded English conduct as betrayal.

In the postwar years, as Britain handed back its conquests and withdrew its garrisons, the United States established a chain of forts from Lake Michigan to the Mississippi River as a means of protecting its growing settlements and disrupting communications between the British and the Indian tribes. Evacuating posts captured during the war and running down the Union Jack symbolized Britain's humiliation and its inability to afford the Indians continued protection against American expansion. The British Indian Department resumed operations at Malden and Drummond Island, but Robert McDouall warned that, when the Indians found themselves hemmed in by their enemies and deprived of their traders, they would remember past instances of British misconduct and would blame the redcoats for their present suffering. In that case, McDouall

SIR JOS JEBB.

Two Ottawa Chiefs who with others lately came down from Michilli-machinac [sic] *Lake Huron to have a talk with their great Father the King or his representative.* Watercolor sketch by Sir Joshua Jebb. (Courtesy Peabody Museum, Harvard University; photographed by Hillel Burger)

feared, the Indians would "exact their own revenge and become the terrible assailants of the frontier which they before defended and of which they are the natural defenders."[24] Once again, however, as they had in 1783 and 1796, the British escaped the Indian vengeance that they dreaded. The British-Indian alliance that had dominated the North American frontier for half a century did not explode in violence and vengeance; it petered out in anger and recrimination as disgruntled Indians and embarrassed redcoats came to terms with the new situation. Indians continued to trek to the British posts to seek relief from American mistreatment and economic hardship. The redcoats continued to supply them, but British largess fell far short of Indian expectation, and postwar councils revealed the strains in British-Indian relations. In June 1816, Winnebago delegates stalked out in disgust from a meeting with the British, declaring that the government had deceived them and abandoned them to their enemies. In the summer of 1817 delegates from the Sauks, the Winnebagoes, and the Foxes assembled in council with Lieutenant Colonal William McKay at Drummond Island. Black Hawk spoke for them all when he reminded the British of the Indians' miserable situation: "We have not Slept either in peace or tranquility since we laid down the Hatchet and smoked the pipe with the Big Knives as you desired us." He recalled how promptly the British had supplied the Indians with ammunition when there was fighting to be done, and how shocked he had been to learn that the British had made peace: "At this news I many times rubbed my Eyes and cleared my ears before I could believe what I saw or what I heard." The redcoats had assured him that all would be well and that the king would never forget his Indian children; instead, Black Hawk found that the Americans were taking over the Indians' lands and he looked for British help in defending them. McKay made an evasive reply, and the Indians were given clothing and supplies. Black Hawk persisted in his demands and urged McKay to empty his stores of guns, ammunition, and blankets "that I may convince our brethren that the word of the English is like thunder." The British had promised the Indians that they would receive compensation for their losses but, Black Hawk pointed out, there were wounded warriors present and many widows and orphans at home in their villages who were still in mourning and had received nothing. Pointing angrily at Captain Thomas Anderson, the

Black Hawk, Prominent Sauk Chief, by George Catlin. Oil on canvas, 1832. A staunch supporter of the Crown, Black Hawk (1767– 1838) was nonetheless reduced to tears of rage in 1817 by the British failure to help his people in their hour of need. (National Museum of American Art, Smithsonian Institution; gift of Mrs. Joseph Harrison, Jr.; L.1965.1.2)

Sauk chief declared: "You was not afraid to bring us our Great Fathers bounty when our Hatchet was still red with blood. Why can you not do it now when our Women and Children are poor and we are threatened with the loss of our Lands by the bad Spirits."

Exasperated by the Indians' demands and unable to provide a satisfactory answer, McKay brought the proceedings to an abrupt conclusion and refused to give the Indians any more except some powder and tobacco, saying, "I have my Great Fathers orders to obey and all the Indians in the universe will not make me deviate from them—The Council is Ended and you must withdraw." Black Hawk by this time was "crying with rage." He promised not to trouble McKay again for the moment, but swore to return next year "with a great many canoes & if I cannot get assistance on this side of the Great Lake, I will cross to the other side to seek the Great Father's help." The angry Sauk shook hands with the officers and strode away from the council.[25]

The next year McKay again had to endure a barrage of demands and denunciations. Some 350 Ottawa, Chippewa, and Winnebago Indians gathered in front of his marquee on Drummond Island. An Ottawa chief, named Ocaita, laid down the wampum belt that Sir William Johnson had given them in 1764, proceeded to review the history of British-Indian relations, culminating in the British betrayal of 1814, and begged the British to provide the help that they had promised. Tired of delays and evasive replies, the Ottawa confronted McKay, saying, "You McKay, it is to you our chiefs speak when they request you to put your parole in a fair road to our new Father at Quebec." The harassed superintendent made the usual promise to do what he could, but added: "[e]very year, you are so loud to me with reproaches, I can no longer bear the burden, and if I have not some good news to tell you next Spring I will not come here."[26] Such was the condition of British-Indian relations in the post-war years.

Americans continued to be worried by British activities among the tribes within United States territory. The specter of a revived, British-backed, Indian confederacy haunted the imaginations of American agents and officials on the frontier, who saw evidence of British intrigue behind every manifestation of Indian discontent. Reports of the British distributing unprecedented quantities of supplies and urging the warriors to remain on the alert for a renewal of hostilities fueled American suspicions, and Governor Lewis Cass of the Michigan Territory was convinced that the British were using the Shawnee Prophet as a major instrument for preserving influence and sowing dissatisfaction among the tribes.[27] Far from cultivating the Prophet, the British found him to be something of an embarrassment, and the Shawnee visionary became increasingly alienated. In 1825 he proclaimed that the British had deceived him and all the Indians, that it was the redcoats, not the Americans, who were to blame for his brother's death, and that "he detested them and looked upon them like dust under his feet."[28]

Indian visits to the British posts remained a source of contention well into the 1830s. Gradually, American policy of distributing annuities in accordance with the treaty provisions of land cessions largely supplanted the Indian practice of going to the British for presents, and the Upper Canadian Indian Department pledged not to give gifts to Indian visitors from the United States. Finally, in 1852, the Canadian government stopped giving presents to its own Indian wards. Indians from below the border no longer had any reason to go to Canada, and the problem of British interference among the tribes of the United States was ended.[29] Never again after the War of 1812 did Britain require Indian allies to fight against the United States.

By 1815, Indian power east of the Mississippi River had been broken. Left largely to their own devices, and with their cultures significantly weakened, the tribes suffered a rapid decline in fortunes, culminating in the mass re-

movals to lands beyond the Mississippi in the 1830s. The
Miamis, the Delawares, the Shawnees, the Six Nations, and
the Creeks were no longer significant military powers. In
1832 a band of Sauk Indians under their aged chief Black
Hawk caused a brief attack of anxiety on the frontier when
they refused to evacuate their Illinois villages and migrate
across the Mississippi. Regular troops and militia brought
the "Black Hawk War" to a swift conclusion when they
massacred the harassed Indians at Bad Axe on the Mississippi that August. Seminoles continued to defy the United
States army in the swamplands of southern Florida, but,
on the whole, Indian wars became a thing of the past in the
east. Powerful and independent tribes inhabited the trans–
Mississippi west and resisted the Americans until the end
of the century, but the age of Indian confederacies, united
against their common enemy and supported by foreign
power, was dead. With it died any hope of limiting American expansionism. Western tribes threw up messiahs and
leaders of ability who enjoyed local success and deserved
renown but no one came forward to fill the role left vacant
by Brant and Tecumseh.

Those tribes who lived in or removed to Canada generally fared better than those in the United States. Brant's
Mohawks secured asylum from American expansion by removing to British soil, and though their relations with the
British government were far from untroubled, they did receive some aid and certainly suffered no more than their
Seneca and other Iroquois relatives who elected to take
their chances and remain in the United States. The comparatively better treatment that Indians in Canada experienced stemmed from differing circumstances rather than
from superior British virtue. The Canadian frontier lacked
the rapidly expanding and land-ravenous population that
doomed to failure the efforts of the United States government to deal honorably with its Indian inhabitants. Despite
its flawed record, Britain continued to enjoy a reputation
for better dealings with Indians long after 1815. Many
tribes had suffered as a result of cynical British policies,

but it is doubtful if British interference and conduct did much more than protract an inevitable and bloody process of dispossession of the Indians. Some tribes actually profited for a time from their connection with the British, taking advantage of supplies of guns and merchandise to lord it over less fortunate tribes. On the whole, the British connection was eagerly sought and jealously guarded more often than it was imposed and resented.

Nevertheless, British-Indian relations were part of a wider contact situation between European and Amerindian worlds. When cultures collided, misunderstanding and conflict occurred. Most Europeans failed to see beyond what they regarded as the filth, the brutality, and the superstition of tribal life. Indians rarely saw anything but greed, viciousness, and hypocrisy in the white invaders. Some marginal individuals transcended racial and ethnic barriers and functioned as cultural brokers, but for the most part, Indians and Europeans failed to understand one another. Some Indians enjoyed a measure of temporary success in a rapidly changing world, but all Indians faced the inescapable fact that the superior power and purposefulness of the white invaders guaranteed the ultimate destruction of their traditional ways of life. From the Euro-American point of view, Indians were a doomed and defeated people. The only alternative to extinction was for the Indian to cease being an Indian and to follow the white man's road.

The Indians, however, held their own views of things. Certainly in the thirty years or so following the American Revolution, few Indians tamely accepted the white man's prediction of destruction. Rather, they sought ways to preserve their lands and cultures from American encroachment, and many embraced the British as a means to that end. Indians and Britons alike expected their relationship to serve certain purposes, and they formed opinions according to how well those purposes were realized. Soldiers' opinions tended to be favorable or not depending upon Indians' military abilities and conduct. Fur traders' based their attitudes on Indians' fur-producing capabilities and cooperation. Missionaries, philanthropists, and others eager to extend the blessings of their civilization to the "untutored heathen" naturally were most heartened by those who seemed most receptive to their overtures. The few who saw virtue in Indian life tended to think that those Indians who were least affected by the corrupting influence of white civilization were most admirable. Indians likewise judged according to their own interests. They preferred allies who supported and supplied them regularly, traders who gave good prices and quality merchandise, and white men who offered them some of the benefits of their world without demanding that they give up their lands and cultures in return. British and Indians alike saw the best in those who most resembled themselves, took for granted that their way of life was superior to any other, and judged alien societies in terms of their own cultures and by their own standards.

Contrary to British assumptions and predictions, all Indians did not disappear before the advance of civilization. Many migrated; others survived behind the frontier through strategies of cultural adaptation and social change and clung tenaciously to their ancestral homelands. White observers who saw defeated and demoralized Indians hanging around frontier settlements, drinking, begging, prostituting their women, and wearing the discarded clothing of the white invaders, identified only degeneration and erosion of what they took to be true Indianness.

Even at the best of times, British-Indian relations were uneasy and unstable. Indian tribes were employed in the Crown's wars, exploited in the British fur trade, and sacrificed to British policy. Britain made little or no provision for the tribes' future welfare and security. The British in the postrevolutionary era wanted the Indian for two things—his furs and his firepower. As long as the fur trade offered a profit and the Americans posed a threat, Britain was prepared to give the tribes varying degrees of assistance in their fight against American settlement. But growing American settlements represented lucrative markets for British manufactures. The fur trade declined in economic and political importance and British interest in the Indians diminished as the tribes ceased to be a military factor. For thirty years, Britons and Indians had joined in a common endeavor to preserve the fur trade and limit American expansion. Old connections and mutual interests survived, but the Treaty of Ghent marked the end of an era. By 1815, Britain looked to North America for markets, grain, and raw materials rather than for furs and allies.

American officials testified vociferously to the enduring strength of the British-Indian alliance in the postwar years, but British-Indian relations were in disarray and the bonds of that alliance were strained and thin. Indian spokesmen denounced the redcoats as faithless allies who had led them to destruction and then abandoned them in their hour of need. British agents and officers countered with evasive replies, placatory statements, and gifts. The damage was done, though. The Treaty of Ghent may not have reflected the situation in the west in 1814, but it did accurately reflect the position occupied by the Indians in the global thinking of the British government. Viewed from London, the significant events of 1814–15 occurred at Waterloo and Vienna, not at New Orleans and Ghent, and certainly not at Malden and Michilimackinac. Britain went on to build the greatest empire the world had seen; the Americans translated their nominal hegemony into reality; and the Indians were left to survive as best they could in a world made foreign and hostile by Euro-American enemies and allies.

Notes

Add. Mss.
: Additional Manuscripts (British Museum)

Adm. Papers
: Admiralty Papers, Public Record Office

A.H.R.
: *American Historical Review*

Am. Philos. Soc.
: The American Philosophical Society

Ann. Rept.
: Annual Report

Ann. Rept. Am. Hist. Ass'n
: Annual Report of the American Historical Association

A.S.P.I.A.
: Walter Lowrie and Matthew St. Clair Clarke, eds., *American State Papers. Class II. Indian Affairs, 1789–1827*, 2 vols. (Washington, 1832–34)

B.A.E.
: Bureau of American Ethnology, Smithsonian Institution

B.M.
: British Museum

Brock Correspondence
: Ferdinand Brock Tupper, ed., *The Life and Correspondence of Major-General Sir Isaac Brock, K.B.*, 2d ed. (London, 1847)

Les Bourgeois
: L. R. Masson, ed., *Les Bourgeois de la Compagnie du Nord Ouest*, 2 vols. (Quebec, 1889–90)

Carleton Papers
: Carleton Papers or Headquarters Papers of the British Army in America, Public Record Office, P.R.O. 30/55

C.H.R.
: *Canadian Historical Review*

C.O.
: Colonial Office Records, Public Record Office

Cochrane Papers	Cochrane Papers, National Library of Scotland
Doc. Hist. Niagara Campaigns	E. A. Cruikshank, ed., *The Documentary History of the Campaigns on the Niagara Frontier, 1812–1814,* 9 vols. (Welland, Ont., 1896–1908)
Draper Mss.	Draper Manuscripts, Wisconsin State Historical Society
F.O.	Foreign Office Records, Public Record Office
Haldimand Papers	Haldimand Papers, British Museum, Add. Mss.
H.M.C.	(Great Britain), Historical Manuscripts Commission, London
M.A.E.S.	*Monographs of the American Ethnological Society*
M.P.H.S.C.	*Collections of the Michigan Pioneer Historical Society*
M.V.H.R.	*Mississippi Valley Historical Review*
Nat.Lib. Scot.	National Library of Scotland, Edinburgh
New Light	Elliott Coues, ed., *New Light on the History of the Greater North West: The Manuscripts Journals of Alexander Henry and David Thompson,* 2 vols. (Minneapolis, 1965 reprint)
Ont. Hist. Soc.	Ontario Historical Society
P.A.C.	Public Archives of Canada, Ottawa
Procs.	Proceedings
Pubns.	Publications
P.R.O.	Public Record Office, London
R.S.C.	Royal Society of Canada
Russell Papers	E. A. Cruikshank and A. F. Hunter, eds.; *The Correspondence of the Honourable Peter Russell, With Allied Documents: . . . ,* 3 vols. (Toronto, 1932–36)
Select Brit. Docs.	William Charles Henry Wood, ed., *Select British Documents of the Canadian War of 1812,* 3 vols. (Toronto, 1920–28)
Simcoe Papers	E. A. Cruikshank, ed., *The Correspondence of Lieutenant Governor John Graves Simcoe, with Allied Documents . . . ,* 5 vols. (Toronto, 1923–31)
S.P.G.	Society for the Propagation of the Gospel in Foreign Parts

S.S.P.C.K.	Society in Scotland for Propagating Christian Knowledge
Trans.	Transactions
W.C.J.A.	Western Canadian Journal of Anthropology
W.O.	War Office Records, Public Record Office
W.S.H.S.C.	Collections of the Wisconsin State Historical Society

INTRODUCTION: *1783*

1. Francis Parkman, *The Jesuits in North America in the Seventeenth Century* (Boston, 1867), 1:131.
2. Colin G. Calloway, "Suspicion and Self-Interest: The Peace of Paris and British-Indian Relations," *The Historian* 48 (Nov. 1985): 41–60. Much of the introduction is taken from the article.
3. J. Leitch Wright, *Britain and the American Frontier, 1783–1815*, 1, 13–16; Barbara Graymont, *The Iroquois in the American Revolution*, 260–61; *The Parliamentary History of England*, 23 (May 1782–Dec. 1783):381–82, 410.
4. W. C. Ford and G. Hunt, eds., *The Journals of the Continental Congress 1774–89*, 34 vols. (Washington, 1904–37), 25:681–93; George Washington to James Duane, 7 Sept. 1783 in John C. Fitzpatrick, ed., *The Writings of George Washington*, 37 vols., 27:134–36.
5. Frederick Haldimand to Lord North, 27 Nov. 1783, Haldimand Papers, 21717:178.
6. Speech of Cornplanter, Half Town and Great Tree . . . , Dec. 1, 1790, *A.S.P.I.A.*, 1:140–42; Message from the Western Indians to the U.S. Commissioners, 13 Aug. 1793, *Simcoe Papers*, 2:17–20.
7. Thomas Townshend to Haldimand, 28 Feb. 1783, Haldimand Papers, 21705:93; Haldimand to Major John Ross (private), 6 Apr. 1783, ibid., 21783:30; Haldimand to North, 2 June 1783, ibid., 21717:60–61.
8. Haldimand to Townshend, 23 Oct. 1782 and 7 May 1783, Haldimand Papers, 21717:146–47; 160; Extract of a Council of Six Nations & Confederates, 2 July 1783, ibid., 21779:115–16; Haldimand to Sir John Johnson, 12 Apr. 1784, ibid., 21723:65–66; Major Wall's Speech to the Shawanese, 7 July 1783, ibid., 21779:117.
9. Brigadier General Allan Maclean to Haldimand, 18 May 1783,

Haldimand Papers, 21756:138–40, also printed in Charles M. Johnston, ed., *The Valley of the Six Nations: A Collection of Documents on the Indian lands of the Grand River*, 35–38; Proceedings with the Indians of the Six Nations Confederacy, July, 1783, Haldimand Papers, 21779:123–29, esp. 123–24; Speech of the Mohawks to Daniel Claus, 4 Jan. 1784, Claus Papers, PAC, MG19, F1, 4:1, Reel C-1478.

10. Louis De Vorsey, Jr., *The Indian Boundary Line in the Southern Colonies, 1763–1775* (Chapel Hill: University of North Carolina Press, 1966).

11. Thomas Brown to Townshend, June 1, 1783, C.O.5/82:367–76; Brown to Lord Sydney, May 20, 1784, Foreign Office Records, United States of America, Series I, 1782–1794, F.O. 4/1:143–44; Jn. Douglas to Lord North, Feb. 5, 1784; Substance of Talks . . . , C.O. 5/82:372–73, 430, 448–49; Talk from the Head Warrior of the Euphalies, May 10, 1783, Carleton Papers or Headquarters Papers of the British Army in America, P.R.O., Gifts and Deposits, P.R.O. 30/55/69:7654; Talk . . . by the Headman of the Cherokees, Carleton Papers, 30/55/60:6742(4–6).

12. Townshend to Brown, 14 Feb. 1783, Carleton Papers, 30/55/62:6908; Brown to Guy Carleton, 26 Apr. 1783, ibid., 30/55/68:7556; Brown to Lieutenant-Colonel A. McArthur, 15 May 1783, and McArthur to Carleton, 19 May 1783, ibid., 30/55/69:7688 (6); 7717; Carleton to McArthur, 19 June 1783, ibid., 30/55/72:8084(3); Brown to Carleton, 12 Sept. 1783, ibid., 30/55/81:9098; Brown to Townshend, 1 June 1783, C.O. 5/82:432; Carleton to Brown, 4 Oct. 1783, C.O. 5/111:45.

13. Alexander McGillivray for the Chiefs of the Creek, Chickasaw and Cherokee Nations, 10 July 1785, in John W. Caughey, *McGillivray of the Creeks*, pp. 90–93; McGillivray to Brown, 30 Aug., C.O. 5/82:405; Substance of a Talk from the Little Turkey and the Headmen and Warriors of the Overhill Cherokees to Brown, 17 Nov. 1783, C.O. 5/82:446–47.

14. Carleton to Governor Patrick Tonyn, 4 Oct. 1783, C.O. 5/111:39–40; The Representation of William Augustus Bowles . . . , F.O. 4/9:9.

15. Haldimand to North, 20 Aug. 1783, Haldimand Papers, 21717:168–69; Haldimand to Ross, 26 Apr. 1783, ibid., 21785:130. A. C. McLaughlin, "The Western Posts and the British Debts," *Annual Report of the American Historical Association*, 1894, 413–44; A. L. Burt, "A New Approach to the Problem of the Western Posts," *Report of the Annual Meeting of the Canadian Historical Association*, 1931, 61–75; G. S. Graham, ed., "The Indian Menace and the Retention of the Western Posts," *Canadian Historical Review*, 15 (1934):46–48, supports the view that Britain kept the posts to avert an Indian war. S. F. Bemis, *Jay's Treaty: A Study in Commerce and Diplomacy*, 6–14, argues that the fur trade and fear of the Indians constituted the real reason for the refusal to give up the posts, and that the debts issue provided the excuse.

16. Extracts of Sundry Letters to Mr. Thomas Forbes, Merchant, P.R.O. 33/8/344:10–11; Lawrence J. Kinnaird, ed., "Spain in the Mississippi Valley, 1756–94: Translations of Materials from the Spanish Ar-

chives in the Bancroft Library," *Annual Report of the American Historical Association*, 1945, 3:114–16; Memorial of Merchants to Earl Bathurst . . . , May 7, 1814, C.O. 42/59:173–76.

17. On the Grand River lands, see *Simcoe Papers*, passim; *Russell Papers*, passim; Johnston, ed., *Valley of the Six Nations*, esp. 41–58, 70–119; Douglas Brymner, ed., "Indian Lands on the Grand River," *Report on the Canadian Archives*, 1896, note A, 1–23; Charles M. Johnston, "Joseph Brant, the Grand River Lands and the Northwest Crisis," *Ontario History*, 45 (1963):267–82.

18. Colin G. Calloway, "The Intertribal Balance of Powers on the Great Plains, 1760–1850," *Journal of American Studies*, 16 (1982):25–47. On the impact and extent of the 1781–82 smallpox epidemic see E. E. Rich, ed., *Cumberland and Hudson House Journals, 1775–82*, 224 ff; Richard Glover, ed., *David Thompson's Narrative, 1784–1812*, 234–38.

19. Minutes of Transaction with the Indians at Sandusky, 26 Aug.–8 Sept. 1783, Haldimand Papers, 21779:132–39; Maclean to Haldimand, Sept. 27, 1783, ibid., 21756:150–51; Bert Anson, *The Miami Indians*, ch. 4; J. M. Sosin, "The British Indian Department and Lord Dunmore's War," *Virginia Magazine of History and Biography*, 74 (1966):34–50.

20. Robert Mathews to Joseph Brant, 12 Apr. 1784, Haldimand Papers, 21725:6–10; Lord Sydney to Henry Hope, 6 Apr. 1786 and enclosures; Sydney to Brant, 6 Apr. 1786, in A. Shortt and A. G. Doughty, eds., *Documents Relating to the Constitutional History of Canada, 1759–1791*, 2 vols. (Ottawa, 2d ed., 1918), 2:805–9.

21. Henry Dundas to Lord Dorchester, 16 Sept. 1791, C.O. 42/21:283–87, or C.O. 42/83:134–42; ibid., 15 Mar. 1794, C.O. 42/89:47–50; Precis of proposed Indian boundary line, Chatham Papers, P.R.O., Gifts and Deposits, P.R.O. 30/8/344:47–48; Robert F. Berkhofer, Jr., "Barrier to Settlement: British Indian Policy in the Old Northwest, 1783–1794," in David M. Ellis, ed., *The Frontier in American Development: Essays in Honor of Paul Wallace Gates*, 249–76; Orpha E. Leavitt, "British Policy on the Canadian Frontier, 1782–1792: Mediation and an Indian Barrier State," *Proceedings of the Wisconsin State Historical Society*, 63 (1916):151–85; G. G. Hatheway, "The Neutral Indian Barrier State: A Project in British North American Policy, 1754–1815," Ph.D. dissertation, University of Minnesota, 1957; "Instructions and Despatches of the British Ghent Commission," *Proceedings of the Massachusetts Historical Society*, 47 (1914):139–50

22. Council at Niagara, 1 Apr. 1783, Haldimand Papers, 21779:111–12.

23. The translations of the Gospels and Norton's book are discussed in chapter 5; for mention of Brant's attempt to write an Indian history, see Brant to Kirkland, 8 Mar. 1791, *Simcoe Papers*, 5:2–4; Donald Jackson, ed., *Black Hawk: An Autobiography*, 37.

24. For example, John D. Hunter, *Memoirs of a Captivity among the Indians of North America. . . .* I have used Hunter only to reinforce or

illustrate points made in, or impressions gained from, other sources. See Richard Drinnon, *White Savage: The Case of John D. Hunter* (New York, 1972).

25. Indian Council held at Drummond Island, 29–30 June 1816, *M.P.H.S.C.*, 16 (1890):479–87, esp. speech of little Corbeau, 481–82; Speech of Little Crow at Drummond Island 1816, V. I. Armstrong, comp., *I Have Spoken: American History Through the Voices of the Indians* (New York, 1972), 57–58; Doane Robinson, *History of the Dakota or Sioux Indians*, 98–100.

26. Minutes of the Indian Council held at Burlington Heights, 24–27 Apr. 1815, Murray Papers, Nat. Lib. Scot., Advocate Mss., 46.6.5:164.

27. Reverend John Heckewelder, *History, Manners, and Customs of the Indian Nations Who Once Inhabited Pennsylvania and the Neighbouring States*, 321–22.

28. Glover, ed., *David Thompson's Narrative*, 240–51.

CHAPTER 1
Contact and Change Across a Continent

1. For discusson of the cataclysmic effects of European epidemics and dramatic upward revisions of proto-historic Indian population estimates, see: Henry F. Dobyns, *Their Numbers Become Thinned: Native American Population Dynamics in Eastern North America;* Russell Thornton, "American Indian Historical Demography: A Review Essay with Suggestions for Future Research," *American Indian Culture and Research Journal*, 3 (No. 1, 1979):69–74, and the works discussed therein.

2. Calvin Martin, "Ethnohistory: A Better Way to Write Indian History," *Western Historical Quarterly*, (1978):41–56.

3. J. B. Tyrrell, ed., *Journals of Samuel Hearne and Philip Turnor between the years 1774 and 1792;* Lawrence J. Burpee, ed., "An Adventurer from Hudson Bay: Journal of Matthew Cocking, from York Factory to the Blackfoot Country, 1772–73," *Transactions of the Royal Society of Canada*, 3d Series, 2 (1908), sec. 2:89–121; Arthur J. Ray, *Indians in the Fur Trade: Their Role as Hunters, Trappers, and Middlemen in the Lands Southwest of Hudson Bay, 1660–1870*, chs. 3 and 4; Abraham P. Nasatir, *Borderland in Retreat, from Spanish Louisiana to the Far Southwest*, 18, 39–40, 119.

4. Edward M. Bruner, "Mandan," in Edward H. Spicer, *Perspectives in American Indian Culture Change* (Chicago & London, 1961), 203–4.

5. Annie H. Abel, ed., *Tabeau's Narrative of Loisel's Expedition to the Upper Missouri*, 123–24; John C. Ewers, ed., *Edwin Thompson Denig's Five Indian Tribes of the Upper Missouri*, 41n–42n.

6. George E. Hyde, *Red Cloud's Folk: A History of the Oglala Sioux Indians* (Norman, 1976), 41–42; Thomas Douglas, Fifth Earl of Selkirk, *A Sketch of the British Fur Trade in North America*, 42–43; Arthur S. Morton, ed., *The Journal of Duncan McGillivray of the North West Company, at*

Fort George on the Saskatchewan, 1794–95, 47; W. Kaye Lamb, ed., *Sixteen Years in the Indian Country: The Journal of Daniel Williams Harmon, 1800–1816*, 72.

7. Frank R. Secoy, "Changing Military Patterns on the Great Plains," *M.A.E.S.*, 21 (1953):92; Richard Glover, ed., *David Thompson's Narrative*, 240–43, 300, 330–34, 345.

8. Anthony R. McGinnis, "Intertribal Conflict on the Northern Plains, 1738–1889," Ph.D. dissertation, University of Colorado, 1974, 69; Glover, ed., *David Thompson's Narrative*, 240ff; George E. Hyde, *Indians of the High Plains: From the Prehistoric Period to the Coming of Europeans*, 194, 197.

9. Oscar Lewis, "The Effect of White Contact upon Blacfoot Culture," *M.A.E.S.*, 6 (1942):34, 54; Glover, ed., *David Thompson's Narrative*, 240; Ross Cox, *Adventures on the Columbia River*, 2 vols., 1:152, 154, 236–38; Philip A. Rollins, ed., *The Discovery of the Oregon Trail: Robert Stuart's Narratives . . .*, 151.

10. Richard White, "The Winning of the West: The Expansion of the Western Sioux in the Eighteenth and Nineteenth Centuries," *Journal of American History*, 65 (1978):319–43; Hyde, *Red Cloud's Folk*, chs. 1–4.

11. W. A. Sloan, "The Native Response to the Extension of the European Traders into the Athabasca and Mackenzie Basin, 1770–1814," *C.H.R.*, 60 (1979):286, 292.

12. Eric R. Wolf, *Europe and the People Without History;* William E. Meyer, "Indian Trails of the Southeast," *42d Ann. Rept., B.A.E.*, (1924–25), 735.

13. Glover, ed., *David Thompson's Narrative*, 269; Alice M. Johnson, ed., *Saskatchewan Journals and Correspondence*, 298. Arthur J. Ray and Donald B. Freeman, *"Give Us Good Measure": An Economic Analysis of Relations Between the Indians and the Hudson's Bay Company before 1763*, 45.

14. E. E. Rich, ed., *Cumberland and Hudson House Journals, 1775–82*, 224 ff.; Glover, ed., *David Thompson's Narrative*, 234–38; Ray, *Indians in the Fur Trade*, ch. 5.

15. Memorials on the subject of Upper Canada and the Indians, 23 and 30 Dec., 1794, F.O. 5/7:209–11, 464–65; Ferdinand Smyth Stuart to the Earl of Liverpool, 18 March 1814, Liverpool Papers, B.M. Add. Mss., 38257:6. [John Ferdinand Smyth added Stuart to his name in 1793.]

16. Milo M. Quaife, ed., *John Long's Voyages and Travels*, 40; "Journal of Jean Baptiste Truteau on the Upper Missouri," *A.H.R.*, 19 (1914), pt. 2:312; Abel, ed., *Tabeau's Narrative of Loisel's Expedition*, 105–6.

17. Edwin James, ed., *A Narrative of the Captivity and Adventures of John Tanner*, 197.

18. John R. Swanton, "Social Organization and Social Usages of the Indians of the Creek Confederacy," *42d Ann. Rept., B.A.E.* (1924–25), 279–80.

19. Major Gordon J. Smith, "Captain Joseph Brant's Status as a Chief," *Ontario Historical Society, Papers and Records*, 12 (1914):89–101. Isabel Thompson Kelsay, *Joseph Brant, 1743–1807: Man of Two Worlds.*

20. Milo M. Quaife, ed., *Alexander Ross: Adventures of the First Settlers on the Oregon or Columbia River*, 345.

21. Haldimand to John Johnson, 6 Feb. 1783, Haldimand Papers, 21775:65; Extract of a Letter from Sir James Craig to Lieutenant Governor Francis Gore dated 28 Dec. 1807, C.O. 42/136:158.

22. Haldimand to Lord George Germaine, 13 Sept. 1779, Haldimand Papers, 21717:39; George Ironside to Alexander McKee, 6 Feb. 1795, *Simcoe Papers*, 3:288–89. See also Mr. H. Franklin to his Brother, n.d., in Priscilla Wakefield, *Excursions in North America* . . . , 215.

23. Susan R. Sharrock, "Crees, Cree-Assiniboines, and Assiniboines: Interethnic Social Organization on the Far Northern Plains," *Ethnohistory*, 21 (1974):95–122.

24. Lawrence J. Kinnaird, ed., "Spain in the Mississippi Valley, 1765–1794"; Kinnaird, "International Rivalry in the Creek Country," *Florida Historical Quarterly*, 10 (1931):59–79; J. Leitch Wright, "British Designs on the Old Southwest: Foreign Intrigue on the Florida Frontier, 1783–1803," *Florida Historical Quarterly*, 44 (1966):265–84.

25. Governor William Harrison to War Dept., 6 Aug. 1811, in Carl F. Klinck, ed., *Tecumseh: Fact and Fiction in Early Records*, 88–89.

26. D. Claus to Haldimand, 12 Oct. 1779, Claus Papers, P.A.C., MG19, F1, 26:120–21, Reel C–1485; Maclean to Haldimand, 9 May 1783, Haldimand Papers, 21763: 99; on Brant's second visit to England, see C.O. 42/49:1–80, passim; R. Mathews to Haldimand, 9 Aug. 1786, Haldimand Papers, 21736:215–19.

27. Charles M. Johnston, ed., *The Valley of the Six Nations*, xxxviii–xli, 48.

28. Ibid., esp. 41–58, 70–119; Douglas Brymner, ed., "Indian Lands on the Grand River," *Report on the Canadian Archives*, 1896, esp. Maitland to Bathurst, 22 Feb. 1821, 1–3; *Simcoe Papers*, passim; *Russell Papers*, passim.

29. E. A. Cruikshank, "The Coming of the Loyalist Mohawks to the Bay of Quinte," *Papers and Records of the Ontario Historical Society*, 26 (1930):390–430.

CHAPTER 2
The Indian Department and the Indian Agent

1. Robert S. Allen, "The British Indian Department and the Frontier in North America, 1755–1830," *Canadian Historic Sites: Occasional Papers in Archaeology and History* (1975), 5–125.

2. Shelburne to Haldimand, 22 Apr. 1782, Haldimand Papers, 21705: 23; Standing Orders, 6 Feb. 1783, Haldimand Papers, 21775:57–60.

3. Haldimand Papers, 21770 passim; Haldimand to John Johnson, 6 Feb. 1783, Haldimand Papers, 21775:65.

4. Proceedings with the Indians of the Six Nation Confederacy and Sir John Johnson, July 1783, Haldimand Papers, 21779:123–29 (esp. 123–24).

5. Haldimand to John Johnson, 6 Feb. 1783, Haldimand Papers, 21775:65–66.

6. Daniel Claus to Matthews, 7 July 1783, Haldimand Papers, 21774: 320–21; Gary Clayton Anderson, *Kinsmen of Another Kind: Dakota-White Relations in the Upper Mississippi Valley, 1650–1862*, ch. 4.

7. Colonel Guy Johnson to Haldimand, 10 Oct. 1781, Haldimand Papers, 21767:238–41; Claus to Haldimand, 15 May 1780, ibid., 21774: 120–21; Extract from James Goddard to Alexander Davison, 15 Dec. 1785, C.O. 42/17:164; Haldimand to Sydney, 16 Mar. 1785, C.O. 42/48:251.

8. Gore to Craig, 8 Apr. 1808, C.O. 42/136:163; Extract from Craig to Gore, dated 11 May 1808, C.O. 42/136:163–65. On Elliott's corruption and dismissal, see Ernest J. Lajeunesse, ed., *The Windsor Border Region*, 221–25; on his reinstatement, see Craig to Viscount Castlereagh, 15 July 1808, plus enclosures, C.O. 42/136:147–71, passim; [Castlereagh] to Craig, 8 Apr. 1809, C.O. 42/138:77–78.

9. Instructions for Robert Dickson Appointed Agent for the Indians of the Nations to the Westward of Lake Huron, 14 Jan. 1813, from George Prevost, *M.P.H.S.C.,* 25 (1890):219–21; Louis Arthur Tohill, "Robert Dickson, British Fur Trader on the Upper Mississippi," *North Dakota Historical Quarterly*, 3 (1928–29):14; Ernest Alexander Cruikshank, "Robert Dickson, the Indian Trader," *W.S.H.S.C.,* 12 (1892):138.

10. See also Glyndwer Williams, ed., *Andrew Graham's Observations on Hudson's Bay 1767–1791*, 297–98.

11. Thomas Forsyth to William Clark, 22 Sept. 1815, *W.S.H.S.C.,* 11 (1888):343; see also [Thomas Forsyth] "The French, British and Spanish Methods of Treating Indians & c.—," *Ethnohistory*, 6 (1957):214–17.

12. Louise P. Kellogg, "Wisconsin Indians during the American Revolution," *Trans. Wisconsin Academy of Sciences, Arts and Letters*, 24 (1929), 48; Cornelius J. Jaenan, *Friend and Foe: Aspects of French-Amerindian Cultural Contact in the Sixteenth and Seventeenth Centuries* (New York, 1976); Lewis O. Saum, *The Fur Trader and the Indian*, ch. 4.

13. Lieutenant Colonel Henry Hope to Evan Nepean, 9 Nov. 1785; Johnson to Hope, 6 Nov. 1785; Hope to Johnson, 30 Oct. 1785; Johnson to Nepean, 7 Nov. 1785, C.O. 42/17:188, 190, 192, 208–9; Gore to Castlereagh, 4 Sept. 1809, C.O. 42/349:88–92; Gore to Bathurst, 27 Dec. 1815, & enclosures, C.O. 42/356:159–70.

14. Instructions for Johnson, 6 Feb. 1783, Haldimand Papers, 21775: 61–63; Medicines Wanted for the use of the Indian Department, ibid., 21772:92; (Account), ibid., 21772:114–15; (Account), ibid., 21769: 36–42; Matthew Elliott to McKee, 20 Oct. 1793, *Simcoe Papers*, 5:78–79. Ironically, Amherstburg was named after the general who had considered distributing smallpox-infected blankets among the Indians in the 1760s. See Bernhard Knollenburg, "General Amherst and Germ Warfare," *M.V.H.R.*, 41 (1954–55):489–94, and Donald Kent's rebuttal, ibid., 762–76.

15. Extract of a letter from Montreal, dated 1 Aug. 1785, C.O. 42/17: 115–18 (esp. 116).

16. Robert Dickson to Robert Hamilton, n.d., *Simcoe Papers*, 1 : 390–91.

17. To Haldimand from the citizens of Quebec; Haldimand's reply, 5 Aug. 1784, Haldimand Papers, 21880 : 169, 171.

18. Maclean to Haldimand, 20 Apr. 1783, Haldimand Papers, 21763 : 48–49; Haldimand to Maclean, 22 May 1783, ibid., 21764 : 366–67. For the verdict and proceedings of the inquiry into this murder, see ibid., 21763 : 54, 56–59.

19. Lieutenant Colonel John Campbell to Haldimand, 24 Dec. 1781; Campbell to Mathews, 14 Jan. 1782, Haldimand Papers, 21772 : 126–27, 132–33.

20. In Council, Detroit, 1 Dec. 1782 (Speech of the Seneca Chief), Haldimand Papers, 21783 : 276–77.

21. Wilbur R. Jacobs, *Wilderness Politics and Indian Gifts: The Northern Colonial Frontier, 1748–1763;* Draper Mss., 1YY15; Return of Indian presents delivered from 1 Oct. to 30 Nov., Niagara, Dec. 20, 1782, Haldimand Papers, 21762 : 234–35; also Outfit Commonly Given to Indians, n.d., *W.S.H.S.C.,* XII (1892): 100–104; William Knox to Nepean, 28 Dec. 1782, Haldimand Papers, 21705 : 109; Governor Lewis Cass to Secretary of War, 3 Sept. 1814, Carter, ed., *Territorial Papers,* 10 : 476; Carl P. Russell, *Guns on the Early Frontiers,* 55, 59; "Forsyth's Voyage, 1819," *W.S.H.S.C.,* 6 (1872): 214; also, *Times,* 6 Aug. 1791, 4.

22. Maclean to Haldimand, 24 Dec. 1782, Haldimand Papers, 21762 : 238; e.g., Haldimand to Shelburne, 17 Aug. 1782, ibid., 21717 : 142–44.

23. MacLean to Haldimand, 8 Aug. 1783, Haldimand Papers, 21763 : 225–26.

24. Haldimand to Maclean, 11 Mar. 1783, Haldimand Papers, 21756 : 131; Haldimand to Johnson, 5 Sept. 1781, ibid., 21767 : 220; Major Arent Schuyler De Peyster to Haldimand, 1 June 1779, ibid., 21756 : 12; Haldimand to De Peyster, 10 Aug. 1780, ibid., 21781 : 38–39; Standing Orders to be observed at the several posts in the Upper Country, 6 Feb. 1783, ibid., 21775 : 59; Haldimand to John Johnson, 6 Feb. 1783, ibid., 21775 : 65–68; William McKay to Lieutenant Colonel Robert McDouall, 1 Aug. 1814, *W.S.H.S.C.,* 12 (1892): 116; William Claus to Lieutenant Colonel Harvey, 15 Aug. 1813, *Doc. Hist. Niagara Campaigns,* 7 : 23; Isaac Weld, Jr. gives a description of the delivery of Indian presents at Malden, in *Travels Through the States of North America. . . ,* 356–59.

25. Joseph Brant to Joseph Chew, 5 Mar. 1795, *Simcoe Papers,* 3 : 315; Proceedings of a Council with the Six Nations, Niagara, July 1783, Haldimand Papers, 21779 : 125.

26. Reuben G. Thwaites, ed., "The Bulger Papers," *W.S.H.S.C.,* 13 (1895): 10–153 passim; C. M. Johnston, "William Claus and John Norton: A Struggle for power in Old Ontario," *Ontario History,* 57 (No. 2, June 1965): 101–108: Answer of Neywash on the Part of the Western Indians (to Colonel Caldwell), *Select Brit. Docs.,* 3 : 726–27. In Indian metaphor, milk and mammary glands signified liquor and the source of its supply; here it may mean presents generally. D. Claus to ?, 4 Dec. 1813, Claus Papers, P.A.C., MG19 F1, 10 : 87–110.

27. For example, Instructions for Johnson, & Haldimand to Johnson,

6 Feb. 1783, Haldimand Papers, 21775:61–63, 65–68; Instructions for the Good Government of the Indian Department: Sir George Prevost to Sir John Johnson, 1 May 1812, C.O. 42/146:180–86.

28. Maclean to Haldimand, 26 June 1783, Haldimand Papers, 21763: 162; Maclean to De Peyster, 26 June 1783, ibid., 21763:164; Elizabeth Cometti, ed., *The American Journals of Lt. John Enys*, 143.

29. Minutes of Transactions at Sandusky, 26 Aug.–8 Sept. 1783, Haldimand Papers, 21779:132–39.

30. For numerous examples of such councils, see Haldimand Papers, 21779 passim.

31. Haldimand to Johnson, 6 Feb. 1783, Haldimand Papers, 21775:65.

32. Haldimand Papers, 21779 passim.

33. "Names by which the different Indian Nations address each other in public conferences," McKee Papers, P.A.C., MG19, F16:1; Powell to Haldimand, 17 Aug. 1782, Haldimand Papers, 21762:128–29.

34. At a meeting held at Niagara, 6 Mar. 1784, Haldimand Papers, 21779:154.

35. [Mathews] to Powell, 31 May 1782, Haldimand Papers, 21764: 293; James Cochran to De Peyster, 22 Apr. 1781, ibid., 21761:53; Thomas Welch to Acting Surveyor General, 12 June 1797, *Russell Papers*, 1:187; Instructions for Johnson, 6 Feb. 1783, Haldimand Papers, 21775: 62–63; Captain Prichard's verbal information to General de Riedesel, 17 Nov. 1782, Hald. Papers, 21797:348.

36. D. Claus to ?, 4 Dec. 1813, Claus Papers, P.A.C., MG19, F1, 10:98.

37. ? to Dorchester, 4 May (say June) 1788, C.O. 42/59:238; Gore to William Windham, 24 Apr. 1807, C.O. 42/343:119.

38. Ironside to McKee, 6 Feb. 1795, *Simcoe Papers*, 3:288–89.

39. Lieutenant Duncan Graham to Lieutenant Lawe, 14 Mar. 1815, *W.S.H.S.C.*, 10 (1882):127–32.

40. Lieutenant Colonel William McKay to Lieutenant Colonel Robert McDouall, 27 July 1814, *W.S.H.S.C.*, 11 (1888):266; Dickson to Lawe, 6 Feb. 1814; ibid., 10 Mar. 1814, *W.S.H.S.C.*, 11 (1888):292–93, 299.

41. John Graves Simcoe to McKee, 10 July 1794, *Simcoe Papers*, 5:97; cf. Dundas to Simcoe, 4 July 1794, ibid., 2:300; Simcoe to England, 15 Nov. 1794, ibid., 3:184; cf. Duke of Portland to Simcoe, 19 Nov. 1794, ibid., 185–86.

42. Smith's Answer to Blue Jacket, C.O. 42/73:40–41 (enclosed in Dorchester to Grenville, 23 Jan. 1791).

43. Brigadier General Isaac Brock to Craig, 27 Feb. 1811; Brock to Major Taylor, 4 Mar. 1811, *Brock Correspondence*, 96, 97.

44. Simcoe to McKee, 23 July 1793, *Simcoe Papers*, 5:62–63, (two letters); Simcoe to Alured Clarke, 29 July 1793, ibid., 1:392–93.

45. Brant's Journal of Proceedings at the General Council held at the foot of the Rapids of the Miamis, May 1793, ibid., 2:5–17; Brant to Simcoe, 2 Sept. 1793, ibid., 47; Simcoe to Dorchester, 10 Nov. 1793, ibid., 101–04. See also Brant's letter of complaints to McKee, Aug. 4,

1793, Draper Mss. 11F205; Brant to ?, 23 May 1793; Brant to McKee, 4 Aug. 1793, Claus Papers, MG19, F1, 5:95–96, 285–87; Reel C–1479.
46. McKee to Simcoe, 22 Aug. 1793, *Simcoe Papers*, 2:34–35.
47. Simcoe to Dundas, 20 Sept. 1793, ibid., 61–62; and Simcoe to Dorchester, 10 Nov. 1793, ibid., 101–04.
48. Extracts from a "Journal of a Treaty Held in 1793 with the Indian Tribes Northwest of the Ohio, by Commissioners of the United States," ibid., 30.
49. Simcoe to Portland, 22 Dec. 1794, ibid., 3:238–40.
50. Simcoe to Dorchester, 9 Mar. 1795, ibid., 320; see also Reginald Horsman, "The British Indian Department and the Abortive Treaty of Lower Sandusky," *The Ohio Historical Quarterly*, 70 (No. 3, July 1961):189–213.
51. Gore to Claus, 26 Feb. 1811, C.O. 42/351:32.
52. Instructions to Jay as Envoy Extraordinary, 6 May 1794, Henry P. Johnston, ed., *The Correspondence and Public Papers of John Jay*, 4 vols., 4:15; Letter from Vincennes to War Dept., 6 Feb. 1811, *A.S.P.I.A.*, 1:800; Governor Cass to Sec. of War, 3 Aug. 1819, Clarence Edwin Carter, ed., *The Territorial Papers of the United States*, 28 vols., 10:853; John Quincy Adams to Richard Rush, Dec. 1, 1818, in William R. Manning, ed., *Diplomatic Correspondence of the United States: Canadian Relations 1784–1860*, Vol. 1, 1784–1820, p. 287.

CHAPTER 3
British Views of Indian Life

1. For white perceptions of and preconceptions about Indians, see Roy Harvey Pearce, *The Savages of America: A Study of the Indian and the Idea of Civilization;* Robert F. Berkhofer, *The White Man's Indian: Images of the American Indian from Columbus to the Present;* Bernard Sheehan, *Seeds of Extinction: Jeffersonian Philanthropy and the American Indian.*
2. Berkhofer, *White Man's Indian*, 25–27; John Ferdinand Dalziel Smyth, *A Tour in the United States of America . . .*, 2 vols., 1:340.
3. E. A. Benians, intro., *A Journal by Thos. Hughes . . .*, 175; cf. Major Amos Stoddard, *Sketches, Historical and Descriptive, of Louisiana*, 427–28.
4. G. Imlay, *A Topographical Description of the Western Territory of North America . . .*, 261; F. W. Hodge, ed., "Handbook of American Indians North of Mexico," B.A.E., Bulletin 30, 1:38–39.
5. John Pinkerton, *Modern Geography . . .*, 654, 656.
6. W. Kaye Lamb, ed., *Sixteen Years in the Indian Country . . .*, 257.
7. Richard Glover, ed., *David Thompson's Narrative, 1784–1812*, 178; *New Light*, 2:530–31, 734–35.
8. *Quarterly Review*, 1 (1809):302–3; *Times*, 11 Jan. 1808, 3; *Quarterly Review*, 12 (1814–15):325.
9. Mackenzie, in *Les Bourgeois*, 2:372; L. Draper, ed., "Narrative of Captain Thomas G. Anderson," *W.S.H.S.C.*, 9 (1882):152.

10. Glover, ed., *David Thompson's Narrative*, 258–59.

11. Jack D. L. Holmes, ed., *Journal of a Tour in Unsettled Parts of North America in 1795 & 1797. By Francis Baily*, 212; *Boswell's Life of Johnson* (Oxford, 1965), 309, 405, 912, 1227.

12. *Leeds Intelligencer*, 8 Mar. 1791, 1.

13. Warren Barton Blake, ed., *Letters from an American Farmer by Hector St. John De Crèvecoeur*, 214–15.

14. James Axtell, "The White Indians of Colonial America," *William and Mary Quarterly*, 3d Series, 32 (1975):55–58; J. Norman Heard, *White Into Red: A Study of the Assimilation of White Persons Captured by Indians;* Erwin H. A. Ackernecht, "White Indians: Psychological and Physiological Peculiarities of White Children Abducted and Reared by North American Indians," *Bulletin of the History of Medicine*, 15 (1944): 15–36; "Thomas Ridout's Narrative of Captivity Among the Shawanese in 1788," in Matilda Edgar, ed., *Ten Years of Upper Canada in Peace and War, 1805–1815* . . . , 358, 370.

15. Colin G. Calloway, "Neither White nor Red: White Renegades on the Anglo-American Indian Frontier," *Western Historical Quarterly*, 17 (Jan. 1986):43–66.

16. The Newberry Library in Chicago has the world's largest collection of captivity narratives. Richard Van Der Beets, ed., *Held Captive by Indians: Selected Narratives, 1642–1836*, intro; Richard Slotkin, *Regeneration Through Violence: The Mythology of the American Frontier, 1600–1860*, (Weslyan University Press) chs. 4 & 5, 241–59.

17. Mackenzie, in *Les Bourgeois*, I:382.

18. G. R. Gleig, *Narrative of the Campaigns of the British Army at Washington and New Orleans* . . . , 266, my italics.

19. Milo Milton Quaife, ed., *Alexander Ross: Adventures of the First Settlers* . . . , 353–54.

20. Glover, ed., *David Thompson's Narrative*, 92, 74.

21. George W. Woodbine to Lieutenant Colonel Edward Nicolls, 27 Oct. 1814, Cochrane Papers, Ms. 2328:99.

22. Isaac Weld, Jr., *Travels Through the States of North America* . . . , 402; Milo Milton Quaife, ed., *War on the Detroit* . . . , 24; Philip Ashton Rollins, ed., *The Discovery of the Oregon Trail* . . . , 161. Cf. *Gentleman's Magazine*, 90 (1820), pt. 2:399.

23. Lamb, ed., *Sixteen Years in the Indian Country*, 43; Lamb, ed., *Letters and Journals of Simon Fraser, 1806–1808*, 71; Edwin James, ed., *A Narrative of the Captivity and Adventures of John Tanner* . . . , 24; (Alexander Mackenzie), *Journal of a Voyage*, B.M., Stowe Mss., 793:44; Quaife, ed., *Alexander Ross: Adventures*, 142; cf. Reuben Gold Thwaites, ed., *Original Journals of the Lewis and Clark Expedition*, 7 vols., 4:341, 343, 347, 354.

24. Quaife, ed., *Alexander Ross: Adventures*, 354; James, ed., *Tanner's Narrative*, 26.

25. Glyndwer Williams, ed., *Andrew Graham's Observations on Hudson's Bay 1767–1791*, 150.

26. Mary Quayle Innis, ed., *Mrs. Simcoe's Diary*, 114.

27. George Landmann, *Adventures and Recollections of Colonel Land-mann* . . . , 160, 152; Gleig, *Narrative of the Campaigns of the British Army*, 269; Milton W. Hamilton, ed., "Guy Johnson's Opinions on the American Indian," *Pennsylvania Magazine of History and Biography*, 77 (July 1953):322; Weld, *Travels*, 398–99; Richard Beale Davis, ed., *Jeffersonian America* . . . , 41; Glover, ed., *Thompson's Narrative*, 254; Lamb, ed., *Journals and Letters of Sir Alexander Mackenzie*, 249, 256; Lamb, ed., *Sixteen Years in the Indian Country*, 221.

28. George Heriot, *Travels through the Canadas* . . . , 421; Weld, *Travels*, 389; Lamb, ed., *Journals and Letters of Mackenzie*, 364; also Glover, ed., *David Thompson's Narrative*, 73; Holmes, ed., *Journal of a Tour*, 241; Innis, ed., *Mrs. Simcoe's Diary*, 107.

29. M. Francois, Perrin du Lac, *Travels through the Two Louisianas* . . . , 66; Smyth, *A Tour in the United States of America*, 1:341.

30. John Lambert, *Travels Through Canada and the United States of America* . . . , 2 vols., 1:369; Hugh Gray, *Letters from Canada* . . . , 161–62.

31. Holmes, ed., *Journal of a Tour*, 236.

32. Gray, *Letters from Canada*, 157–59.

33. Lambert, *Travels through Canada*, 357–58.

34. Annie Heloise Abel, ed., *Tabeau's Narrative of Loisel's Expedition to the Upper Missouri*, 172.

35. Reverend J. E. Strickland, ed., "Journal of a Tour in the United States of America, 1794–1795. By William Strickland," *Collections of the New York Historical Society*, 83 (1950):135; Weld, *Travels*, 260; Lambert, *Travels through Canada* . . . , 354; L. Draper, ed., "The North West in 1817: A Contemporary Letter," *W.S.H.S.C.*, 6 (1872):179.

36. Samuel Cole Williams, ed., *Adair's History of the American Indians* (New York, 1930), 11–230; Account of Visits to the Indians in 1802 and 1803 by Ann Mifflin, Central Library Warrington, Ms. No. 45, n.p.; Gwyn A. Williams, *Madoc: The Making of a Myth* (London, 1979); David Williams, "John Evan's Strange Journey," *A.H.R.*, 54 (1948–49):227–95, 508–29.

37. Hamilton, ed., "Guy Johnson's Opinions on the American Indian," 316; *Scots Magazine*, 48 (1786):242–44; [John Maude], *Visit to the Falls of Niagara in 1800*, 51; Heriot, *Travels through the Canadas*, 272; Burpee, ed., "Journal De Larocque," *Pubns. of the Canadian Archives*, No. 3 (1911):60.

38. *New Light*, 2:525; Ross Cox, *Adventures on the Columbia River* . . . , 112.

39. Liston Papers, Nat. Lib. Scot., Ms. 5697:26; Gleig, *Narrative of the Campaigns of the British Army*, 267.

40. Weld, *Travels*, 249; Glover, ed., *Thompson's Narrative*, 357.

41. Cameron, in *Les Bourgeois*, 2:247–48; Lambert, *Travels through Canada* . . . , 533–34; *Quarterly Review*, 1 (1809):303.

42. Louis B. Wright and Marion Tinling, eds., *Quebec to Carolina in 1785–1786* . . . , passim; *New Light*, 2:849.

43. *New Light*, 1 : 348; 399.
44. Harold Driver, *Indians of North America* (Chicago and London, 1969), 222.
45. Glover, ed., *Thompson's Narrative*, 82; Quaife, ed., *Alexander Ross: Adventures*, 318; also Williams, ed., *Andrew Graham's Observations* . . . , 175.
46. Liston Papers, Nat. Lib. Scot., Ms. 5701 : 23; Bradbury, in Reuben Gold Thwaites, ed., *Early Western Travels 1748–1846*, 32 vols., 5 : 109; see also Heriot, *Travels through the Canadas*, 309; Smyth, *Tour in the United States of America*, 193.
47. Lamb, ed., *Journals and Letters of Mackenzie*, 155; Grant, in *Les Bourgeois*, II : 366.
48. For example, Glover, ed., *David Thompson's Narrative*, 72–73.
49. Bradbury, Thwaites, ed., *Early Western Travels*, V : 177; H. M. Brackenridge, *Views of Louisiana; Together with a Journal of a Voyage up the Missiouri River, in 1811*, (Ann Arbor: University Microfilms, 1966), 256; Stoddard, *Sketches, Historical and Descriptive of Louisiana*, 423–25; Donald Jackson, ed., *Journals of Zebulon Montgomery Pike* . . . , 2 vols., 2 : 372.
50. Heriot, *Travels through the Canadas* . . . , 25; Priscilla Wakefield, *Excursions in North America* . . . , 122; Grant, in *Les Bourgeois*, 2 : 258–59.
51. McKenzie, in *Les Bourgeois*, 2 : 414.
52. Edward Umfreville, *Present State of Hudson's Bay* . . . , 40.
53. Weld, *Travels*, 294; McKenzie, in *Les Bourgeois*, 2 : 419.
54. *New Light*, 1 : 351; 2 : 772; 1 : 371, 383, 391; Arthur S. Morton, ed., *Journal of Duncan McGillivray* . . . , 43.
55. Lambert, *Travels through Canada* . . . , 370; Arthur M. Schlesinger, "Food in the Making of America," in *Paths to the Present* (New York, 1949), 235.
56. Weld, *Travels*, 415–16.

CHAPTER 4
Indian Views of the British

1. Liston Papers, Nat. Lib. Scot., Ms. 5701 : 19–20.
2. Hoxie N. Fairchild, *The Noble Savage: A Study in Romantic Naturalism* (New York, 1928), 2.
3. John Ferdinand Dalziel Smyth, *A Tour in the United States of America:* . . . , 2 vols. 1 : 344; Isaac Weld, Jr., *Travels Through the States of North America* . . . , 361.
4. Mary Quayle Innis, ed., *Mrs. Simcoe's Diary*, 72; Liston Papers, Nat. Lib. Scot., Ms. 5703 : 20; Glyndwer Williams, ed., *Andrew Graham's Observations on the Hudson's Bay 1767–1791*, 150; Milo Milton Quaife, ed., *Alexander Ross: Adventures of the First Settlers* . . . , 108; Richard Glover, ed., *David Thompson's Narrative, 1784–1812*, 314; Jack D. L. Holmes, ed., *Journal of a Tour* . . . , 217.
5. Carolyn Thomas Foreman, *Indians Abroad, 1493–1938*, 94–99; 101–9; 114–20; Charles Ryskamp and Frederick A. Pottle, eds., *Bos-*

well: The Ominous Years, 1774–1776, in the Yale editions of the *Private Papers of James Boswell* (Melbourne, London, & Toronto, 1963), 341–42; Captain Houghton to ?, 23 Jan. 1786, C.O. 42/18:28; *Daily Universal Register*, 6 Apr. 1786, 3; *Leeds Intelligencer*, 29 Mar. 1791, 3; 5 Apr. 1791, 2; *Times*, 17 Mar. 1791, 3; 18 Mar. 1791, 3. On Bowles, see J. Leitch Wright, Jr., *William Augustus Bowles, Director General of the Creek Nation;* Gore to Castlereagh, 4 Sept. 1809; C.O. 42/349:89; W.O. 1/143:60–66; 78; F.O. 5/108:59–61; F.O. 5/140:74–148 passim; *Times*, 25 Sept. 1818, 3.

6. *The Times*, 5 Feb. 1805, 3. See also, Colin G. Calloway, "The Wild Indian Savages in Leeds," in *The Thoresby Miscellany* (published by the Thoresby Society, Leeds, England), 16 (1979):305–15, for press coverage of the visit of a band of Senecas to Great Britain in 1818.

7. Weld, *Travels*, 396; Richard Beale Davis, ed., *Jeffersonian America . . .*, 41.

8. Grant, in *Les Bourgeois*, 2:325.

9. Charles A. Stuart, ed., *Memoir of Indian Wars and Other Occurrences; By the late Colonel Stuart, of Greenbrier . . .* (New York; Arno Press, 1971), 49; *New Light*, 1:347; 350; 2:722.

10. Smyth, *Tour in the United States . . .*, 185–86; Weld, *Travels*, 403; George Heriot, *Travels through the Canadas . . .*, 116; Patricia Wakefield, *Excursions in North America, . . .*, 137; Robert Sutcliff, *Travels in Some Parts of North America . . .*, 203.

11. Council at Onondaga, Grand River, 9 Nov. 1806, Newberry Library, Ayer Mss. 654; Weld, *Travels*, 171; Haldimand to Germaine, 13 Sept. 1779, Haldimand Papers, 21717:39.

12. Sutcliff, *Travels in Some Parts of North America*, 133–34; John D. Hunter, *Memoirs of a Captivity . . .*, 254.

13. Cameron, in *Les Bourgeois*, 2:263–64; Grant in ibid., 325; *New Light*, 1:264.

14. Weld, *Travels*, 349–50.

15. John Henry Cooke, *Narrative of Events in the South of France . . .*, 167.

16. Heriot, *Travels*, 354.

17. Edwin James, ed., *A Narrative of the Captivity and Adventures of John Tanner . . .*, 193; W. Kaye Lamb, ed., *Sixteen Years in the Indian Country . . .*, 49; Hunter, *Memoirs*, 20, 40–41; 119–21; 361.

18. Brant to Reverend Samuel Kirkland, 8 Mar. 1791; Charles M. Johnston, ed., *Valley of the Six Nations: . . .*, 269–70; Dr. Kempe to Dr. Wheelock, 22 Feb. 1802, S.S.P.C.K. Records, Scottish Records Office, G.D. 95/3/1:74–78 (see also Account of Visits to the Indians in 1802 & 1803, by Ann Mifflin, Warrington Central Library, Ms. 45, n.p.); David J. Jeremy, ed., "Henry Wansey and his American Journal 1794," *Memoirs American Philosophical Society*, 82 (1970):117; Smyth, *Tour in the United States*, 2:107–8; John Norton to an Unknown Correspondent [Wilberforce], 1 Sept. 1808, Johnston, ed., *Valley of the Six Nations*, 278–79.

19. Louis B. Wright and Marion Tinling, eds., *Quebec to Carolina in 1785–1786: . . .*, 37; Davis, ed., *Jeffersonian America*, 34, 43.

20. M. Francois Perrin du Lac, *Travels through the Two Louisianas . . .* , 51; Glover, ed., *Thompson's Narrative,* 127.
21. Glover, ed., *Thompson's Narrative,* 87–88; Lamb, ed., *Sixteen Years in the Indian Country,* 143, 183.
22. McKenzie, in *Les Bourgeois,* 2:419.
23. W. C. Vanderwerth, comp., *Indian Oratory: Famous Speeches by Noted Indian Chieftains* (Norman: University of Oklahoma Press, 1972), 40–41.
24. Cameron, in *Les Bourgeois,* 2:263–64; see also Milo Milton Quaife, ed., *John Long's Voyages and Travels, . . . ,* 39.
25. Robert F. Berkhofer, Jr., *Salvation and the Savage: An Analysis of Protestant Missions and American Indian Response, 1787–1862,* 107 and ch. 6.

CHAPTER 5
"Savagery" and "Civilization"

1. Robert F. Berkhofer, Jr., *The White Man's Indian . . . ,* esp. 29–30, 113–14; Francis Jennings, *Invasion of America . . . ,* passim.
2. Louis B. Wright and Marion Tinling, eds., *Quebec to Carolina in 1785–1786: . . . ,* 57.
3. Jack D. L. Holmes, ed., *Journal of a Tour in Unsettled Parts of North America . . . ,* 106; Isaac Weld, Jr., *Travels Through the States . . . ,* 371; Michaux, in Reuben Gold Thwaites, ed., *Early Western Travels 1748–1846,* 32 vols., 3:262–63; Washington to Humphreys, 20 July 1791, in John C. Fitzpatrick, ed., *Writings of George Washington,* 37 vols., 31:320; Craig to Knox, 6 Mar. 1791, in William Henry Smith, ed., *The St. Clair Papers: . . . ,* 2 vols., 2:201–2; John D. Hunter, *Memoirs of a Captivity . . . ,* 363.
4. G. E. Fussel, "An Englishman in America in the 1790's," *Agricultural History,* 47 (April 1973):117; "Journal of John Mair, 1791," *A.H.R.* 12 (1906–07):80; Dorchester to Sydney, 13 June 1787, C.O. 42/50:399; John Ferdinand Dalziel Smyth, *Tour in the United States of America . . .* 1:130–32, 179–81; Weld, *Travels,* 371; Reverend R. E. Strickland, ed., "Journal of a Tour in the United States of America . . . ," *Collections of the New York Historical Society,* 83 (1971):60; Milo Milton Quaife, ed., *Alexander Ross: Adventures of the First Settlers . . . ,* 187, 314.
5. W. Kaye Lamb, ed., *Sixteen Years in the Indian Country: . . . ,* 136, 147–48.
6. George Landmann, *Adventures and Recollections of Colonel Landmann, Late of the Corps of Royal Engineers,* 136 (see also 27–28); H. H. Langton, ed., *Travels in the Interior Inhabited Parts of North America in the Years 1791 and 1792 by P. Campbell,* 164–65, 167; D'Arcy Boulton, *Sketch of His Majesty's Province of Upper Canada,* 67; W. S. Wallace, ed., "Captain Miles Macdonell's 'Journal of a Jaunt to Amherstburg' in 1801," *C.H.R.,* 25 (1944):168. Francis Hall, *Travels in Canada, and the United States in*

1816 and 1817 (London: Longman, Hurst, Rees, Orme and Brown, 1818), 212.

7. From Thomas Scott, n.d., David Douglas, ed., *Familiar Letters of Sir Walter Scott*, 2 vols., 1:345–46; Carl F. Klinck and James J. Talman, eds., *The Journal of Major John Norton 1816*, esp. 3; Brant to Kirkland, 8 Mar. 1791, *Simcoe Papers*, 5:3; Walter Scott to George Canning, 28 June 1816; John Norton to George Canning, 1 Aug. 1816, Leeds Public Libraries, Archives Dept., Canning Mss., 66A; From Wm. Pitt, 11 July 1814, F.O. 5/103:274–75; William Wilberforce to Mr. Norton, 13 Aug. 1805; Norton to William Wilberforce, 29 Aug. 1805: *The Correspondence of William Wilberforce*, edited by his sons, Robert Isaac and Samuel Wilberforce (London, 1840), 2:36–39; Norton to Wilberforce, 1 Sept. 1808, C.O. 42/140:180–82 (the same letter is printed as Norton to an Unknown Correspondent, in C. M. Johnston, ed., *Valley of the Six Nations*, 278–79). For an account of Norton's translation of the Gospel of St. John into Mohawk, see *Quarterly Review*, 36 (1827):9–11. From Daniel Claus, 27 June 1778, S.P.G. Archives, C. Mss., C/CAN/PRE, 14; Journals of the Proceedings of the S.P.G., 31 (1815–18):318; Brant's translation of the Gospel of St. Mark is in the 1787 edition of the *Mohawk Book of Common Prayer*, a copy of which is in the Archives Dept. of the U.S.P.G., London. Letter Book of John Norton, Newberry Library, Ayer Mss. 654: 135, 141; Norton to Rev. John Owen, Aug. 17, 1805, Ayer Mss. 654. Also: Sketch of the career of John Norton, Claus Papers, P.A.C. MG18, F1, 13:58–59.

8. William Priest, *Travels in the United States of America: . . .*, 43; M. M. Quaife, ed., "Henry Hay's Journal from Detroit to the Mississippi," *Proceedings of the Wisconsin State Historical Society*, 62 (1914):257; Langton, ed., *Travels . . . by P. Campbell*, 225; Glyndwer Williams, ed., *Andrew Graham's Observations on Hudson's Bay 1767–1791*, 145; Selkirk to Drummond, 11 Nov. 1815, C.O. 42/163:197; *New Light*, 2:488.

9. Arrell M. Gibson, *The Chickasaws* 80–81; Henry Knox to the President of the United States, 6 Dec. 1792, *A.S.P.I.A.*, 1:322.

10. Edward Umfreville, *The Present State of Hudson's Bay*, 29–30; Smyth, *A Tour in the United States of America*, 1:342; Lamb, ed., *Sixteen Years in the Indian Country*, 200; *ibid.*, ed., *Journals and Letters of Sir Alexander Mackenzie*, 134; Pond, in Charles M. Gates, ed., *Five Fur Traders of the Northwest: . . .*, 40; Hunter, *Memoirs of a Captivity*, 362; Points to which Lord Castlereagh desired to be informed . . . (with Gore's answers, 4 Sept. 1809), C.O. 42/349:94; Lady Liston's Journals, Liston Papers, Nat. Lib. Scot., Mss. 5697:25, 5699:19, 5603:16; Edmund Burke to Littlehales, 14 Aug. 1795, *Simcoe Papers*, 4:63–64; Elizabeth Cometti, ed., *The American Journals of Lt. John Enys*, 144.

11. John Lambert, *Travels Through Canada . . .*, 358 & picture opp.; Lady Bourchier, ed., *Memoir of the Life of Admiral Sir Edward Codrington . . .*, 2 vols., 1:329–30; John Henry Cooke, *Narrative of Events . . .*, 166; William Surtees, *Twenty-Five Years in the Rifle Brigade*, 334–35; Benson Earle Hill, *Recollections of an Artillery Officer: . . .*, 2 vols., 1:299–

300; George Catlin, *Letters and Notes on the Manners, Customs, and Conditions of the North American Indians* (New York, 1973), 1:56, 2:194, 200.

12. Quaife, ed., *Alexander Ross: Adventures of the First Settlers*, 353; see also Strickland, ed., "Journal of a Tour in the United States of America . . . ," 116.

13. Hector Maclean to James Green, 12 July 1799, *Russell Papers*, 3: 269; [George Proctor], *The Lucubrations of Humphrey Ravelin Esq.*, . . . , 263; William Dunlop, *Recollections of the American War, 1812-14*, 78; Hugh Gray, *Letters from Canada* . . . , 160-61; M. Francois Perrin du Lac, *Travels Through the Two Louisianas* . . . , 63-64; Smyth, *Tour*, 1:344-45; Weld, *Travels*, 260; Richard Glover, ed., *David Thompson's Narrative 1784-1812*, 305, 356, 359; *New Light*, 2:710-11. Lewis O. Saum, *The Fur Trader and the Indian*, 55-57, suggests a fur trader's "scale" of preference.

14. Lambert, *Travels through Canada* . . . , 1:370, 384.

15. Mackenzie, in *Les Bourgeois*, 1:380, 383; W. Kaye Lamb, ed., *Journals and Letters of Sir Alexander Mackenzie*, 65; Quaife, ed., *Alexander Ross: Adventures of the First Settlers* . . . , 314.

16. Minutes of the Executive Council, 22 Oct. 1798, *Russell Papers*, 2:290-91; Patrick C. White, ed., *Lord Selkirk's Diary, 1803-04:* . . . , 115-16; the Representation of William Augustus Bowles . . . & the chiefs deputed from the United Nation of Creeks and Cherokees, F.O. 4/9:5-17; "Letters of Benjamin Hawkins, 1796-1806," *Collections of the Georgia Historical Society*, 9 (1916), passim; Richard A. Preston, ed., *Kingston Before the War of 1812:* . . . , cxii, 41-42; cf. 361; *Gentleman's Magazine*, 78 (1808):1031; Anthony F. C. Wallace, *The Death and Rebirth of the Seneca*, 313.

17. Kirkland to Brant, 3 Jan. 1792, *Simcoe Papers*, 5:5-6; Simcoe to Phineas Bond, 7 May 1792, ibid., 1:153; Lambert, *Travels through Canada* . . . , 1:375, 381-82; An Estimate of the Annual Expenditure of the Indian Department at Detroit (1814), Clarence Edwin Carter, ed., *The Territorial Papers of the United States*, 28 vols., 10:478; William Coates, intro., "A Narrative of An Embassy to the Western Indians, From the Original Manuscript of Hendrick Aupaumut," *Memoirs of the Historical Society of Pennsylvania*, 2 (1827), pt. 1:127.

18. Alex Dalrymple, *Plan for Promoting the Fur Trade* . . . , 32.

19. Dr. Kempe to Dr. Morse, 22 July 1803, S.S.P.C.K. Records, Scottish Records Office, G.D. 95/3/1:91-94; *Ann. Repts of the S.P.G.*, 1788: xxii, 1789:xxv-xxvi, 1815:18-19; *Proposal for Forming a Society for Promoting the Civilization and Improvement of the North American Indians, Within the British Boundary*, 21-24; Quaife, ed., *Alexander Ross: Adventures of the First Settlers* . . . , 361-62; Hunter, *Memoirs*, 364; Account of Visits to the Indians in 1802 and 1803, by Ann Mifflin, Ms. 45, Warrington Central Library, n.p.

20. Richard Beales Davis, ed., *Jeffersonian America:* . . . , 46.

21. Lamb, ed., *Journals and Letters of Sir Alexander Mackenzie*, 67; *Quarterly Review*, 26 (1821-1822):416; *Edinburgh Review*, 1 (1802-03):

146–47; Major Amos Stoddard, *Sketches, Historical and Descriptive of Louisiana*, 447–49.

22. Stuart to Bishop Inglis, 6 July 1788, Richard A. Preston, ed., *Kingston Before the War of 1812: . . .* , 136; S.P.G. *Journals*, 27 (1796–1799): 235.

23. S.P.G. *Journals*, 28 (1799–1804): 126–27, 414; *Ann. Rept. of the S.P.G. for 1796*: 53; for 1797: 17–19; S.S.P.C.K. Records, Scottish Record Office, G.D. 95/3/1 passim.

24. Points to which Lord Castlereagh desired to be informed . . . (with Gore's Answers, 4 Sept. 1809) C.O. 42/349: 94–95; "Some Account of the Trade carried on by the North West Company," Rept. of P.A.C. for 1928: 63; Klinck & Talman, eds., *Journal of Major John Norton*, 11.

25. Hunter, *Memoirs*, 42–43.

26. Norton's comments on Religion in the Indian Settlements, 1806, in Johnston, ed., *Valley of the Six Nations*, 243; Norton to Mr. Owen, Aug. 12, 1806, Newberry Library, Ayer Mss. 654: 36.

27. Liston Papers, Nat. Lib. Scot., Ms. 5703: 21; Lambert, *Travels through Canada . . .* , 1: 361; Weld, *Travels*, 409.

28. Klinck and Talman, eds., *Journal of Major John Norton*, 48.

29. Hunter, *Memoirs*, 370; Account of Visits to the Indians, Warrington Central Library, Ms. 45, n.p.; *Edinburgh Review*, 8 (1806): 442–50; *Gentleman's Magazine*, 77 (1806): 1129; *Two Attempts Towards the Civilization of Some Indian Natives* (London, 1806), 43–45; *Proposal for Forming a Society for Promoting the Civilization and Improvement of the North American Indians, within the British Boundary*, 14–15, 18–19; Weld, *Travels*, 409–10.

30. Lambert, *Travels through Canada . . .* , 1: 380; Smyth, *Tour*, 1: 351–52; Weld, *Travels*, 360.

31. *New Annual Register* for 1814: 346; see also *Quarterly Review*, 1 (1809): 293–94; 303–4.

CHAPTER 6
British Trade and Indian Trade

1. Memorandum relative to the Trade in the Upper Country . . . , Haldimand Papers, 21759: 140. This estimate was for the upper countries only. Also C.O. 42/21: 57. For the value of products from Hudson's Bay, see Paul Chrisler Phillips, *The Fur Trade*, 3, n. 1; cf. also Shelburne's low estimate of £50,000 per annum, *Hansard's Parliamentary Debates*, 13: 408–10.

2. "Some Account of the trade carried on by the North West Company, 1809," Rept. of P.A.C. for 1928, 58. Written by Duncan McGillivray with corrections and additions by his brother William, the original manuscript is held by the Library of the Royal Commonwealth Society, London.

3. George Irving Quimby, *Indian Culture and European Trade Goods.* . . . Edward Bruner, "Mandan," 208–209.

4. A. Rotstein, "Trade and Politics: An Institutional Approach," *W.C.J.A.*, 3 (No. 1, 1972): 15. The idea that trade represented and re-affirmed a political alliance between traders and Indians may hold true for western Canada, but it does not seem to have applied to Hudson Bay or eastern James Bay. Daniel Francis and Toby Morantz, *Partners in Fur: A History of the Fur Trade in Eastern James Bay, 1600–1870*, 46–47; Arthur J. Ray and Donald B. Freeman, *'Give Us Good Measure'*: . . . .

5. John C. Ewers, ed., *The Indians of Texas in 1830. By Jean Louis Berlandier* (Washington, D.C., 1969), 110, 119; W. L. Morton, "The North West Company: Pedlars Extraordinary," *Minnesota History*, 40 (Winter 1966): 157–65.

6. Lewis to Secretary of War, 1 July 1808, in Clarence Edwin Carter, ed., *The Territorial Papers of the United States*, 28 vols., 14: 196–208.

7. Simcoe to Dundas, 28 Apr. 1792, *Simcoe Papers*, 1: 141.

8. Speeches of Indian Chiefs assembled in Council, *Select Brit. Docs.*, 1: 425.

9. Memorial of Montreal Merchants, 20 Oct. 1808, F.O. 5/61: 304; "Some Account of the trade carried on by the North West Company," Rept. of P.A.C. for 1928, 63–64. American complaints at intrigues of British traders are legion; From John Johnson, 6 Sept. 1815, *A.S.P.I.A.*, 2: 82–83.

10. Reuben Gold Thwaites, ed., *Original Journals of the Lewis and Clark Expedition, 1804–1806*, 7 vols., 5: 219–25, 334–35; Richard Glover, ed., *David Thompson's Narrative, 1784–1812*, 273; John C. Ewers, *The Blackfeet* . . . , 45–48.

11. Frances Lebaron's Answers to Queries . . . (24 Dec. 1816), Carter, ed., *Territorial Papers*, 17: 294.

12. Donald Jackson, ed., *Black Hawk* . . . : *An Autobiography*, 59–60; Lewis Cass to Sec. of War, Sept. 3, 1814, Carter, ed., *Territorial Papers*, 10: 476.

13. Gary Clayton Anderson, *Kinsmen of Another Kind* . . . , chs. 4 and 5; Julis Pratt, "Fur Trade Strategy and the American Left Flank in the War of 1812," *A.H.R.*, 40 (Jan. 1935): 253; Instructions for Robert Dickson Appointed Agent for the Indians of the Nations to the West-ward of Lake Huron, 14 Jan. 1813, from George Prevost, *M.P.H.S.C.*, 15 (1890): 219–21; for the enormous importance of Dickson in the region, see Draper, ed., "Captain Anderson's Journal at Fort McKay, 1814," *W.S.H.S.C.*, 9 (1882): 207–61.

14. Robert Dickson to Captain Bulger, 8 Feb. 1815, *W.S.H.S.C.*, 13 (1895): 69; Statement sent by the Lord President to Lord Melville, 7 Aug. 1813, Scottish Record Office, Melville Castle Muniments, G.D. 51/1/588.

15. Manuel Lisa to Clark, 1 July 1817, in Hiram M. Chittenden, *A History of the American Fur Trade of the Far West*, 2 vols. (Stanford, Cal.: Academic Reprints, 1954 rep.), Appendix B, 2: 899–902.

16. Haldimand to Lieutenant Governor Sinclair, 31 May 1781, Haldimand Papers, 21758:51; Haldimand's Speech to Indians . . . , 2 July 1779, ibid., 21779:34−35; Lawrence J. Kinnaird, ed., "Spain in the Mississippi Valley," Ann. Rept. Am. Hist. Ass'n, 171−73, 201−3, 286−87; and Perez to Miro, 5 Oct. 1791, ibid., 416.

17. Trudeau to Governor Carondelet, 20 May 1793, in A. P. Nasatir, ed., *Before Lewis and Clark: Documents Illustrating the History of the Missouri, 1785−1804*, 2 vols., 1:174−79; Ninean Edwards to William H. Crawford, ? Nov. 1815, *A.S.P.I.A.*, 2:62−67; J. Mason to Crawford, 6 Mar. 1816, ibid., 70; and ibid., 26−88 passim.

18. Extracts of Sundry Letters to Mr. Thomas Forbes, Merchant, P.R.O. 30/8/344:10−11; Kinnaird, ed., "Spain in the Mississippi Valley," 108−12, 114−16; Daniel J. J. Ross and Bruce S. Chappell, eds., "Visit to the Indian Nations: The Diary of John Hambly," *Florida Historical Quarterly*, 54 (1976):69n.

19. Augustus Foster to Marquis Wellesley, 16 Jan. 1812, F.O. 5/84:71−72.

20. Representation of William Augustus Bowles, F.O. 4/9:5−17; Bowles to Grenville, 1791, F.O. 4/9:69−74; Robert Liston to Grenville, 13 Feb. 1797, F.O. 5/18:64; Unheaded, 29 Dec. 1796, Liston Papers, *Nat. Lib. Scot.*, Ms. 5583:107.

21. For example, Memorial of Merchants to Earl Bathurst, 7 May 1814, C.O. 42/159:173−76; John Richardson & James Irvine to Prevost, 14 & 24 Oct. 1812, C.O. 42/159:133−36.

22. "The Oregon Question," in Henry Adams, ed., *The Writings of Albert Gallatin*, 3 vols. (New York: Antiquarian Press, Ltd., 1960 rep.), 3:514.

23. John C. Ewers, ed., *Five Indian Tribes of the Upper Missouri . . . , By Edwin Thompson Denig*, 112n.

24. Bradbury, in Reuben Gold Thwaites, ed., *Early Western Travels 1748−1846*, 32 vols., 5:176−77.

25. Wayne E. Stevens, "The Organization of the British Fur Trade, 1760−1800," *M.V.H.R.*, 3 (1916):183−86.

26. F. W. Hodge, ed., "Handbook of American Indians North of Mexico," B.A.E., Bulletin 30, 2:167; Mildred P. Mayhall, *The Kiowas* (Norman: University of Oklahoma Press, 1971), 14; Virginia C. Trenholm, *The Arapahoes* (Norman: University of Oklahoma Press, 1973), 32.

27. Arthur J. Ray, *Indians in the Fur Trade: . . . , 104, 126.

28. "Truteau's Journal," *A.H.R.*, 19 (1914), pt. 2:301, 305−7, 309−17, 321−25.

29. Perez to Miro, 8 Nov. 1791, Nasatir, ed., *Before Lewis and Clark: . . . , 1:149−50; Robert H. Ruby and John H. Brown, *The Chinook Indians: . . . , 121−22.

30. Kinnaird, ed., "Spain in the Mississippi Valley," 166; "Truteau's Journal," *A.H.R.* 19 (1914), pt. 2:328, 332; Annie Heloise Abel, ed., *Tabeau's Narrative of Loisel's Expedition . . . , 100−101; James H. Howard, "The Ponca Tribe," *B.A.E.*, Bulletin 195 (1965):25−26.

31. Thwaites, ed., *Journals of the Lewis and Clark Expedition*, 1:162–74, 5:365–68, 7:61–65; Bradbury, in Thwaites, ed., *Early Western Travels*, 5:103–9, 142.

32. Philip Ashton Rollins, ed., *Discovery of the Oregon Trail:* . . . , 4; Quaife, ed., *Alexander Ross: Adventures of the First Settlers* . . . , 84.

33. *New Light*, 2:526.

34. Arthur S. Morton, ed., *The Journal of Duncan McGillivray* . . . , 56; Narrative of the Expedition to the Kootenae and Flat Bow Indian Countries . . . , by D. Thompson, Ms. Held by the Royal Commonwealth Society, London, n.p.; *New Light*, 2:643–44, 646, 655, 713; Glover, ed., *David Thompson's Narrative*, 273, 277–79, 296–97, 306; Oscar Lewis, "The Effects of White Contact upon Blackfoot Culture . . . ," *M.A.E.S.*, 6 (1942):18–20.

35. Information on the Missouri-centered trade network is contained in: Thwaites, ed., *Journals of the Lewis and Clark Expedition*, esp. 6:80–120; Abel, ed., *Tabeau's Narrative of Loisel's Expedition;* L. Burpee, ed., "Journal De Larocque," *Pubns. of the Canadian Archives*, 3 (1911), or in *Les Bourgeois*, 1:299–313; Charles Mackenzie, "The Missouri Indians, 1804–1806," in *Les Bourgeois*, 1:315–93; "Truteau's Journal," *A.H.R.*, 19 (1914):299–333; Nasatir, ed., *Before Lewis and Clark; New Light*, esp. 1:324–404; Annie Heloise Abel, ed., "Trudeau's Description of the Upper Missouri," *M.V.H.R.*, 8 (1921):1149–79; and in W. Raymond Wood and Thomas D. Thiessen, eds., *Early Fur Trade on the Northern Plains: Canadian Traders Among the Mandan and Hidatsa Indians, 1738–1818*. Secondary works that describe and analyze the network include: Joseph Jablow, "The Cheyenne in Plains Indian Trade Relations, 1795–1840," *M.A.E.S.*, 19 (1950); John C. Ewers, *Indian Life on the Upper Missouri*, 14–31; Roy W. Meyer, *The Village Indians of the Upper Missouri* . . . ; Preston Holder, *The Hoe and the Horse on the Plains* . . . ; and Donald J. Blakeslee, "The Plains Interband Trade System: An Ethnohistoric and Archaeological Investigation," Ph.D. dissertation, University of Wisconsin-Milwaukee, 1975.

36. Glover, ed., *David Thompson's Narrative*, 162–63; Francis Haines, *The Nez Perces* (Norman: University of Oklahoma Press, 1972), 25–26; Abel, ed., "Trudeau's Description of the Upper Missouri," *M.V.H.R.* 8 (1921):173–74; Larocque, in *Les Bourgeois*, 1:301; Lawrence J. Burpee, ed., "Journal De Larocque . . . ," *Pubns. P.A.C.* 3 (1911):15–20; Mackenzie, in *Les Bourgeois*, 1:343, 347–49, 374–75; *New Light*, 1:399, John C. Ewers, "The Horse in Blackfoot Indian Culture," *B.A.E. Bulletin* 159 (1955):7–11.

37. Thwaites, ed., *Journals of the Lewis and Clark Expedition*, 5:356, 6:45, 89, 96; M. Francois, Perrin du Lac, *Travels through the Two Louisianas* . . . , 49, 63; "Lewis and Clark's Expedition, 1806," *A.S.P.I.A.*, 1:710, 714; "Truteau's Journal," *A.H.R.*, 9 (1914):310–17; *New Light*, 1:314; Abel, ed., *Tabeau's Narrative of Loisel's Expedition*, 121–23, 132, 151.

38. Morton, ed., *Journal of Duncan McGillivray*, passim, e.g, 62–64; Narrative of the Expedition to the Kootenae . . . by D. Thompson,

Royal Commonwealth Soc. Ms. n.p.; Glover, ed., *David Thompson's Narrative*, 273, 277–79, 296–97; *New Light*, 2 : 540, 643, 646, 655, 713.

39. Grant, in *Les Bourgeois*, 2 : 346–47; Memorial of Indian Traders . . . , 4 Apr. 1786, *W.S.H.S.C.*, 12 (1892) : 76–78; Memoranda Relative to the Indian Trade, 13 Apr. 1786, ibid. : 78–82; Journal of Peter Fidler, in Alice M. Johnson, ed., *Saskatchewan Journals and Correspondence*, 299, 306, 313.

40. R. Douglas, ed., *Nipigon to Winnipeg: A Canoe Voyage Through Western Ontario by Edward Umfreville in 1784*, 15–22; Alexander Mackenzie, Journal of a Voyage Performed by Order of the North West Company, B.M., Stowe Mss., 793 : 20, 35, 44, 55, 68, 76; W. Kaye Lamb, ed., *Letters and Journals of Simon Fraser 1806–1808*, 169–70.

41. "Some account of the trade carried on by the North West Company," Rept. of P.A.C. for 1928, 68.

42. Thwaites, ed., *Journals of the Lewis and Clark Expedition*, 1 : 306–7.

43. *New Light*, 2 : 541, 544.

44. Edwin Rich, ed., *Cumberland and Hudson House Journals, 1775–82*, 2d series, 1779–82, passim; ibid., ed., *Moose Fort Journals, 1783–85*, passim; cf. Francis and Morantz, *Partners in Furs*.

45. Edwin James, ed., *A Narrative of the Captivity and Adventures of John Tanner, . . .* , passim. Harold Hickerson, ed., "Journal of Charles Baptiste Chaboillez, 1797–98," *Ethnohistory*, 6 (1959) : 265–316, 363–427 passim; ibid. "The Genesis of a Fur Trading Band: The Pembina Chippewa," *Ethnohistory*, 3 (1956) : 289–345; Charles A. Bishop, *The Northern Ojibwa and the Fur Trade: . . .* , 235.

46. "Some account of the trade carried on by the North West Company," Rept. of P.A.C. for 1928, 69; Abel, ed., *Tabeau's Narrative of Loisel's Expedition*, 72; Thomas Douglas, Fifth Earl of Selkirk, *A Sketch of the British Fur Trade in North America, . . .* , 42–43; Morton, ed., *Journal of Duncan McGillivray*, 47.

47. Morton, ed., *Journal of Duncan McGillivray*, 30. For similar accounts see *New Light*, 2 : 728–30; Edward Umfreville, *The Present State of Hudson's Bay*, 56–65; Glyndwer Williams, ed., *Andrew Graham's Observations on Hudson's Bay . . .* , 315–24.

48. Johnson, ed., *Saskatchewan Journals and Correspondence*, 313; Williams, ed., *Andrew Graham's Observations*, 318–19; Pond, in Charles M. Gates, ed., *Five Fur Traders of the Northwest*, 45–46; (William Beresford), *A Voyage Round the World . . .* , 161–62, 225.

49. McDonnell, in *Les Bourgeois*, 1 : 293; Mackenzie, in ibid., 1 : 334; Bradbury, in Thwaites, ed., *Early Western Travels*, 5 : 130–32; *New Light*, 1 : 241, 2 : 541; Beresford, *Voyage*, 187; Minutes of Council of the Account given by Captain Meares of his Voyages . . . 1st Minute, 8 Feb. 1791, P.R.O., Privy Council Office Records, P.C. 1/63/B. 22, n.p.; Ruby and Brown, *Chinook Indians*, 113.

50. Duncan Cameron, "The Nipigon Country 1804," *Les Bourgeois*, 2 : 278; *New Light*, 1 : 256, 2 : 550.

51. Selkirk, *Sketch of the British Fur Trade*, 44–46.

52. P. A. Prendergast, "The Economics of the Montreal Traders," *W.C.J.A.*, 3 (No. 1, 1972): 34−42; W. Kaye Lamb, ed., *Journals and Letters of Sir Alexander Mackenzie*, 81.

53. William Tomison to James Swain, 26 Apr. 1796; same to same, 10 May 1796, in Johnson, ed., *Saskatchewan Journals and Correspondence*, 57−60; *New Light*, 1: 239−40.

54. *New Light*, 1: 256, 2: 452, 597; Cameron, in *Les Bourgeois*, 2: 274, 277−78, 296; McDonnell, in *Les Bourgeois*, 1: 294; Hickerson, ed., "Journal of Charles Jean Baptiste Chaboillez," 290.

55. "Some account of the trade carried on by the North West Company," Rept. of P.A.C. for 1928, 61−63; Selkirk, *Sketch of the British Fur Trade*, 128 & passim; Wentzel to McKenzie, 27 Mar. 1807, in *Les Bourgeois*, 1: 96; Mackenzie, in ibid., 336; *New Light*, 1: 256, 268.

56. "Some account of the trade carried on by the North West Company," Rept. of P.A.C. for 1928, 59.

57. Lewis, "Effects of White Contact upon Blackfoot Culture," 21; *New Light*, 2: 542.

58. *New Light*, 2: 723.

59. Lamb, ed., *Journals and Letters of Sir Alexander Mackenzie*, 153; J. B. Tyrrell, ed., *Journals of Samuel Hearne and Philip Turnor . . .* , 452−53; James Parker, "The Fur Trade and the Chipewyan Indian," *W.C.J.A.*, 3 (No. 1, 1972): 51; Abel, ed., *Tabeau's Narrative of Loisel's Expedition*, 171; Thwaites, ed., *Journals of the Lewis and Clark Expedition*, 1: 186, 199.

60. R. G. Thwaites, ed., "A Wisconsin Fur Trader's Journal, 1803−04, by Michel Curot," *W.S.H.S.C.*, 20 (1911): 451.

61. John C. Ewers, "The Influence of the Fur Trade upon the Indians of the Northern Plains," in Malvina Bolus, ed., *People and Pelts: Selected Papers of the Second North American Fur Trade Conference*, 18; Lewis O. Saum, *The Fur Trader and the Indian*, 213; Milo Milton Quaife, ed., *The John Askin papers*, 2 vols., 2: 568−70.

62. Morton, ed., *Journal of Duncan McGillivray*, 47; Thwaites, ed., *Journals of the Lewis and Clark Expedition*, 1: 306; *New Light*, 2: 628.

63. "Some account of the trade carried on by the North West Company," Rept. of P.A.C. for 1928, 62−63. Figures reflecting the keenness of the X.Y. and North West companies' competition are also given in Gordon Charles Davidson, *The Northwest Company*, 91.

64. The Reverend Edmund Burke to E. B. Littlehales, 14 Aug. 1795, *Simcoe Papers*, 4: 63−64; Minutes of the Transactions of the N.W. Co. at Fort William, W. Stewart Wallace, ed., *Documents Relating to the North West Company*, 268−69; Selkirk, *Sketch of the British Fur Trade*, 53−54; R. Douglas, ed., *Nipigon to Winnipeg: . . .* , 42−43; *New Light*, 1: 209.

65. Calvin Martin, *Keepers of the Game: Indian-Animal Relationships and the Fur Trade;* cf. Shepard Krech, ed., *Indians, Animals and the Fur Trade: A Critique of Keepers of the Game* (Athens, Ga.: University of Georgia Press, 1981).

66. For example, Beresford, *Voyage Round the World*, 201, 225, 228−29; cf. Robin Fisher, *Contact and Conflict: Indian-European Relations in British Columbia, 1774−1890*, 4.

67. Hugh Gray, *Letters from Canada* . . . , 217–18; Instructions of the Merchant Proprietors to Captain John Meares, 24 Dec. 1787, in Vincent Harlow and Frederick Madden, eds., *British Colonial Developments, 1774–1834: Select Documents*, 32; Quaife, ed., *Alexander Ross: Adventures*, 84, 96.

68. Quaife, ed., *Alexander Ross: Adventures*, 96, 218; Umfreville, ed., *Present State of Hudson's Bay*, 180–81; Captain George Vancouver, *A Voyage of Discovery to the North Pacific Ocean*, . . . , 3 vols., 2 : 364–65.

69. Williams, ed., *Andrew Graham's Observations*, 152–53, 219.

70. Mackenzie, in *Les Bourgeois*, 1 : 346; *New Light*, 1 : 383; Abel, ed., *Tabeau's Narrative of Loisel's Expedition*, 153.

71. *New Light*, 1 : 354–55.

72. Oppelt to Askin, 6 May 1801, Quaife, ed., *John Askin Papers*, 2 : 335–37.

73. E. E. Rich, "Trade Habits and Economic Motivation among the Indians of North America," *Canadian Journal of Economics and Political Science*, 26 (No. 1, Feb., 1960) : 46–53; Ray, *Indians in the Fur Trade*, 68, 141–42; Ray and Freeman, *'Give Us Good Measure'*, ch. 14.

74. Glover, ed., *David Thompson's Narrative*, 45; *New Light*, 1 : 356.

75. Wilcomb E. Washburn, "Symbol, Utility, and Aesthetics in the Indian Fur Trade," *Minnesota History*, 40 (Winter, 1966) : 198–202.

76. *New Light*, 1 : 356; Cameron, in *Les Bourgeois*, 2 : 296.

77. Morton, ed., *Journal of Duncan McGillivray*, 38; *New Light*, e.g., 1 : 210; cf. Chittenden, *History of the American Fur Trade of the Far West*, 2 : 756.

CHAPTER 7
The Fur Trader and the Indian

1. For a broader consideration of trader-Indian relations, see Lewis O. Saum, *The Fur Trader and the Indian*.

2. Keith, in *Les Bourgeois*, 2 : 88.

3. (William Beresford), *A Voyage Round the World* . . . , esp. 224–29; "Truteau's Journal," *A.H.R.*, 19 (1914) : 299–333; Annie Heloise Abel, ed., *Tabeau's Narrative of Loisel's Expedition*, passim; Lawrence J. Burpee, ed., "Journal De Larocque . . . ,"; *New Light*, passim.

4. "Journal of a Journey with the Chipewyan or Northern Indians . . . by Peter Fidler," in J. B. Tyrrell, ed., *Journals of Samuel Hearne and Philip Turnor* . . . , 495–555, esp. 495, 543; "Some account of the trade carried on by the North West Company," Rept. of P.A.C. for 1928, 60.

5. R. G. Thwaites, ed., "A Wisconsin Fur Trader's Journal, 1804–05, by Francois Victor Malhiot," *W.S.H.S.C.*, 19 (1910) : 188 (the original French version of this journal is in *Les Bourgeois*, 1 : 223–63); Richard Glover, ed., *David Thompson's Narrative, 1784–1812*, 356; cf. 359.

6. Tyrrell, ed., *Journals of Samuel Hearne and Philip Turnor*, 458.

7. *New Light*, 2 : 647.

8. "Some account of the trade carried on by the North West Company," Rept. of P.A.C. for 1928, 68; Arthur S. Morton, ed., *The Journal*

of Duncan McGillivray of the North West Company, . . . , 8:53—54; *New Light,* 2:575—76.

9. Milo Milton Quaife, ed., *Alexander Ross: Adventures of the First Settlers* . . . , 235—36.

10. Philip Ashton Rollins, ed., *The Discovery of the Oregon Trail:* . . . , 62; *New Light,* 1:383; McDonnell, in *Les Bourgeois,* 1:281; *New Light,* 2:512—13.

11. Morton, ed., *Journal of Duncan McGillivray,* 13—16, 56—57, 61, 63—64, 73—74; *New Light,* 2:529—30, 600, 713, 723—24.

12. Thwaites, ed., "Wisconsin Fur Trader's Journal, 1804—05," 199, 203—04.

13. *New Light,* 1:342.

14. Burpee, ed., "Journal De Larocque," 49; Instructions for Johnson, 6 Feb. 1783, Haldimand Papers, 21775:62; The Reverend John Heckewelder, *History, Manners, and Customs of Indian Nations* . . . , 102.

15. *New Light,* 2:575—77.

16. Ibid., 1:125, 342, 2:452; Glyndwer Williams, ed., *Andrew Graham's Observations on Hudson's Bay* . . . , 153; Cameron, in *Les Bourgeois,* 2:249; *New Light,* 2:574.

17. Glover, ed., *David Thompson's Narrative,* 16, 73.

18. Tyrrell, ed., Fidler, in *Journals of Samuel Hearne and Philip Turnor,* 529, 536; Edward Umfreville, *The Present State of Hudson's Bay,* 38.

19. W. Kaye Lamb, ed., *The Journals and Letters of Sir Alexander Mackenzie,* 93; Calvin Martin, *Keepers of the Game,* . . . , 80—82.

20. Tyrrell, ed., Fidler, in *Journals of Samuel Hearne and Philip Turnor,* 542—43.

21. J. Franklin Jameson, ed., *Narratives of New Netherland, 1609—1664* (New York: Barnes & Noble, 1959), 179; Bradbury, in Reuben Gold Thwaites, ed., *Early Western Travels 1748—1846,* 32 vols., 5:176; Williams, ed., *Andrew Graham's Observations,* 153; Abel, ed., *Tabeau's Narrative of Loisel's Expedition,* 134—35.

22. Morton, ed., *Journal of Duncan McGillivray,* 64, 73—74; *New Light,* 1:347.

23. Williams, ed., *Andrew Graham's Observations,* 153; *New Light,* 2:725.

24. Morton, ed., *Journal of Duncan McGillivray,* 70.

25. Quaife, ed., *Alexander Ross: Adventures,* 352—53; Alice M. Johnson, ed., "Journal of Peter Fidler, 1801—02," in *Saskatchewan Journals and Correspondence,* 312.

26. Glover, ed., *David Thompson's Narrative,* 236.

27. *New Light,* 1:105—6, 156, 159, 197, 429; Faries, in Charles M. Gates, ed., *Five Fur Traders of the Northwest:* . . . , 200.

28. Edwin Rich, ed., *Cumberland and Hudson House Journals 1775—82,* 2d series, 232, 267; *New Light,* 2:710—11; Lawrence J. Burpee, ed., "Journal of Matthew Cocking from York Factory to the Blackfoot Country, 1772—73," *Transactions R.S.C.,* 3d series, 2 (1908):110; *New Light,* 2:523 ff.

29. Abel, ed., *Tabeau's Narrative of Loisel's Expedition,* 153—54; Cam-

eron, in *Les Bourgeois*, 2:273; see also W. Kaye Lamb, ed., *Letters and Journals of Simon Fraser*, 88.

30. Gates, ed., *Five Fur Traders*, 245–78.

31. Thwaites, ed., *Journals of the Lewis and Clark Expedition*, 7:372.

32. Journal of George Sutherland, in Johnson, ed., *Saskatchewan Journals and Correspondence*, 76; Morton, ed., *Journal of Duncan McGillivray*, 57; Dickson to Hamilton, n.d., *Simcoe Papers*, 1:390–91; Lamb, ed., *Journals and Letters of Alexander Mackenzie*, 370.

33. Morton, ed., *Journal of Duncan McGillivray*, 45–46, 73; Harold Hickerson, ed., "Journal of Charles Jean Baptiste Chaboillez, 1797–98," *Ethnohistory*, 6 (1959):384.

34. Connor, in Gates, ed., *Five Fur Traders*, 260; Hickerson, ed., "Journal of Chaboillez," 291, 293; *New Light*, 2:546.

35. *New Light*, 1:257, 2:452–53.

36. Tyrrell, ed., Fidler, in *Journals of Samuel Hearne and Philip Turnor*, 535.

37. Mackenzie, in *Les Bourgeois*, 1:383–86.

38. Quaife, ed., *Alexander Ross: Adventures*, 182; *New Light*, 1:251, 2:452.

39. R. Douglas, ed., *Nipigon to Winnipeg: . . .*, 42–43.

40. Morton, ed., *Journal of Duncan McGillivray*, 72; W. Kaye Lamb, ed., *Sixteen Years in the Indian Country: . . .*, 38; "Reminiscences by Hon. Roderic Mckenzie," in *Les Bourgeois*, 1:12; Milo Milton Quaife, ed., *The War on the Detroit: . . .*, 27–28.

41. Williams, ed., *Andrew Graham's Observations*, 155; Connor, in Gates, ed., *Five Fur Traders*, passim, esp. 277–78.

42. Morton, ed., *Journal of Duncan McGillivray*, 71–72.

43. Lamb, ed., *Sixteen Years in the Indian Country*, 65; Quaife, ed., *Alexander Ross: Adventures*, 186–87.

44. Abel, ed., *Tabeau's Narrative of Loisel's Expedition*, 178, 180–81; *New Light*, 2:710; *Quarterly Review*, 1 (1809):302; Glover, ed., *David Thompson's Narrative*, 305; *New Light*, 1:342, 2:735; James Parker, "The Fur Trade and the Chipewyan Indian," *W.C.J.A.*, 3 (No. 1, 1972):50; Tyrrell, ed., *Journals of Samuel Hearne and Philip Turnor*, 446n, 448–49; Quaife, ed., *Alexander Ross: Adventures*, 100.

45. Glover, ed., *David Thompson's Narrative*, 178; Abel, ed., *Tabeau's Narrative of Loisel's Expedition*, 180.

46. Sylvia Van Kirk, *"Many Tender Ties": Women in Fur Trade Society, 1670–1870*, 6–7; W. Stewart Wallace, ed., *Documents Relating to the North West Company*, 210–11; Jennifer S. H. Brown, *Strangers in Blood: Fur Trade Company Families in Indian Country*.

47. Marjorie Wilkins Campbell, *McGillivray, Lord of the Northwest*, xi, 49, 54–59, 111–112; Lamb, ed., *Sixteen Years in the Indian Country*, xv, 28–29, 62–63, 98, 194; Walter O'Meara, *Daughters of the Country: The Women of the Fur Traders and Mountain Men* (New York: Harcourt, Brace & World, 1968), 271–72.

48. David G. Mandlebaum, "The Plains Cree," *Anthropological Papers*

of the American Museum of Natural History, 37, pt. 2 (1940): 167; Lamb, ed., *Sixteen Years in the Indian Country*, 62-63.
49. James Mckenzie, in *Les Bourgeois*, 2:388; Tyrrell, ed., *Journals of Samuel Hearne and Philip Turnor*, 446n, 448-49; *New Light*, 1:235 (by "slave," Henry meant Blackfoot).
50. Mary C. Wright, "Economic Development and Native American Women in the Early Nineteenth Century," *American Quarterly*, 33 (1981):534.
51. *New Light*, 2:577; Glover, ed., *David Thompson's Narrative*, 177; *New Light*, 2:836. See also Bradbury, in Thwaites, ed., *Early Western Travels*, 5:61, 140, 180; Wright, "Economic Development and Native American Women," 525.
52. *The American Indian Culture and Research Journal*, 6 (1982):2; Special Metis Issue; Jacqueline Peterson and Jennifer S. H. Brown, eds., *The New Peoples: Being and Becoming Métis in North America* (Lincoln: University of Nebraska Press, 1985).
53. John C. Ewers, "Mothers of the Mixed Bloods," in *Indian Life on the Upper Missouri*, 57-73; Van Kirk, *"Many Tender Ties."*
54. Abel, ed., *Tabeau's Narrative of Loisel's Expedition*, 134-35; Quaife, ed., *Alexander Ross: Adventures*, 130.
55. (Alexander Mackenzie), Journal of a Voyage performed by Order of the N.W. Company, . . . B. M. Stowe Mss., 793:44-46; Quaife, ed., *Alexander Ross: Adventures*, 142; Reuben Gold Thwaites, ed., *Original Journals of the Lewis and Clark Expedition . . .*, 7 vols., 4:341, 343, 345, 347.
56. Grant, in *Les Bourgeois*, 2:325.
57. Morton, ed., *Journal of Duncan McGillivray*, 26-27; Diary of Archibald McLeod in Charles M. Gates, ed., *Five Fur Traders of the Northwest: . . .*, 167, 170; McDonnel, in *Les Bourgeois*, 1:281; Larocque, in ibid., 308; Mackenzie, in ibid., 328-29; *New Light*, 2:493, 517, 579, 620; Glover, ed., *David Thompson's Narrative*, 158; *New Light*, 1:295, 2:526; John Francis McDermott, ed., "The Western Journals of Dr. George Hunter 1796-1805," *Trans. Am. Philos. Soc.*, New Series, 53, Pt. 4 (July 1963):33.
58. Keith, in *Les Bourgeois*, 2:119; Quaife, ed., *Alexander Ross: Adventures*, 235-36; *New Light*, 2:724; Mackenzie, in *Les Bourgeois*, 1:331; Glover, ed., *David Thompson's Narrative*, 233; Lamb, ed., *Sixteen Years in Indian Country*, 193.
59. For example, *New Light*, 1:347, 350; Quaife, ed., *Alexander Ross: Adventures*, 235-36, Rollins, ed., *Discovery of the Oregon Trail*, 82.
60. Grant, in *Les Bourgeois*, 2:325; *New Light*, 1:264; also Milo Milton Quaife, ed., *John Long's Voyages and Travels . . .*, 39; Mackenzie, in *Les Bourgeois*, 1:384; *New Light*, 1:347.
61. Cameron, in *Les Bourgeois*, 2:249; Morton, ed., *Journal of Duncan McGillivray*, 73; Tyrrell, ed., *Journals of Samuel Hearne and Philip Turnor*, 479.
62. Lamb, ed., *Sixteen Years in Indian Country*, 55; *New Light*, 2:447, 452-53.

63. Mackenzie, in *Les Bourgeois*, 1:386, 345; Burpee, ed., "Journal De Larocque," 23; Rollins, ed., *Discovery of the Oregon Trail*, 285.

64. Thomas Douglas, Fifth Earl of Selkirk, *A Sketch of the British Fur Trade in North America . . .* , 5; Haldimand to Germaine, 25 Oct. 1780, Haldimand Papers, 21717:90–92; Haldimand to Shelburne, 17 July 1782, ibid., 21717:137–38. For the opinion that the Haldimand administration was unjustly prejudiced against the Canadian merchants, see Allan Maclean to Andrew Stewart, 24 Oct. 1779, Nat. Lib. Scot., Ms. 8250:34–36; Dease to Hamilton, 16 Sept. 1785, Rept. on P.A.C. for 1890, 65; Glover, ed., *David Thompson's Narrative*, 177; see also Donald Jackson, ed., *The Journals of Zebulon Montogomery Pike, . . .* , 2 vols., 1:198.

65. Colin G. Calloway, "Foundations of Sand: The Fur Trade and British-Indian Relations, 1783–1815." Paper presented at the Fifth North American Fur Trade Conference, Montreal, June 1, 1985, and in press.

CHAPTER 8
Indians as Allies

1. Reginald Horsman, *Expansion and American Indian Policy, 1783–1812;* Patrick Henry to William Fleming, 19 Feb., 1778, in Reuben Gold Thwaites and L. P. Kellogg, eds., *Frontier Defense on the Upper Ohio, 1777–78* (Madison, 1912), 207–8; Haldimand to Shelburne, 17 July 1782, Haldimand Papers, 21717:135–36; Extract of a Speech Delivered . . . by the Six Nations, 11 Dec., 1782, ibid., 21756:94; McDouall to Drummond, 16 July 1814, *Select Brit. Docs.*, 3:253–56; Prevost to Bathurst, 2 Aug., 1814, C.O. 42/157:97–98; Langan to Claus, 14 Dec. 1786, Claus Papers, P.A.C., MG19, F1, 4:134, Reel C-1478.

2. Major John Butler to Captain Le Maistre, 28 Jan. 1778, Haldimand Papers, 21756:31–32; McKee to De Peyster, 28 Aug. 1782, ibid., 21762:149–50; Richard H. Kohn, *Eagle and Sword: The Federalists and the Creation of the Military Establishment in America, 1783–1802* (New York, 1975).

3. Elliott to Brock, 12 Jan. 1812; *Select. Brit. Docs.*, 1:281–83; Robert B. McAfee, *History of the Late War in the Western Country*, 33–34; Speech . . . Delivered by Tehkumthai, *Select. Brit. Docs.*, 1:312–14.

4. McKee to John Johnson, 28 Jan. 1792, C.O. 42/90:154; Clinton Rossiter, ed., *The Federalist Papers* (New York, 1961), Publius, no. 24, Hamilton, 161; [George Proctor], *The Lucubrations of Humphrey Ravelin*, 263.

5. For example, Richard Glover, ed., *David Thompson's Narrative, 1784–1812*, 241–42.

6. [Proctor], *Lucubrations of Humphrey Ravelin*, 267; George W. Spragge, ed., *The John Strachan Letter Book: 1812–1834*, 6.

7. John Askin to William D. Powell, 25 Jan. 1813, *Doc. Hist. Niagara Campaigns*, 5:50; Evidence of Captain Caldwell, W.O. 71/243:164;

General Gaines to Secretary of War, 15 Dec. 1817, *British and Foreign State Papers*, 5:1107.

8. [Proctor], *Lucubrations of Humphrey Ravelin*, 267; Peter Grant, "The Sauteux Indians," in *Les Bourgeois*, 2:348–49.

9. John Ferdinand Dalziel Smyth, *A Tour in the United States of America . . .* , 2 vols., 2:165–66; George Heriot, *Travels through the Canadas . . .* , 423, 448.

10. For example, McKay to McDouall, 27 July 1814, *Select Brit. Docs.*, 3:261–62; *Doc. Hist. Niagara Campaigns*, 9:26–29; Proctor to Sheaffe, 1 Feb. 1813, *M.P.H.S.C.*, 15 (1890):236.

11. Sir Alexander Cochrane to Croker, 20 June 1814, Cochrane Papers, Ms. 2348:32–34; Cochrane to Governor Cameron, 25 Mar. 1814, Cochrane Papers, Ms. 2346:2–3.

12. McDouall to Forster, 15 May 1815, *Select Brit. Docs.*, 3:534; Graham to Thomas G. Anderson, 3 Sept. 1814, *W.S.H.S.C.*, 9 (1882):224–25; same to same, 7 Sept. 1814, ibid., 226–28; Anderson to McDouall, 14 Sept. 1814, ibid., 230–32.

13. De Peyster to Haldimand, 26 Jan. 1782, Haldimand Papers, 21781:81.

14. Guy Johnson to Haldimand, 20 Nov. 1780, Haldimand Papers, 21767:151; Proctor to Major General Sheaffe, 13 Jan. 1813, *Select Brit. Docs.*, 2:4; Spragge, ed., *John Strachan Letterbook*, 7.

15. Hull to Eustis, 26 Augs. 1812, John Brannan, ed., *Official Letters of the Military and Naval Officers of the United States . . .* , 44–49.

16. Brock to Prevost, 7 Sept. 1812, *Select Brit. Docs.*, 1:587; McDouall to Proctor, 14 June 1813, *Doc. Hist. Niagara Campaigns*, 6:82; Captain James Fitzgibbon to Captain William J. Kerr, 30 Mar. 1818, ibid., 120–21; Extract from a letter . . . , 17 Aug. 1813, ibid., 7:28; Handbill printed at Montreal, 28 Dec. 1813, ibid., 9:16; From a Diary in the Handwriting of Charles Askin, ibid., 28.

17. Captain W. H. Merritt's Journal, *Select Brit. Docs.*, 3:554; Brock to Hull, 15 Aug. 1812, ibid., 1:461.

18. Elias Darnell's account, in John Gellner, ed., *Recollections of the War of 1812: . . .* , 108–53 passim; (Germain) to Burgoyne, 23 Aug. 1776, Mss. of Mrs. Stopford-Sackville, *H.M.C.* Report, 49, 3 (1910):40.

19. McKee to John Johnson, 5 Dec. 1791, C.O. 42/89:192–93; *Gentleman's Magazine* for 1791, 61:668; Simcoe to Dundas, 30 Aug. 1794, *Simcoe Papers*, 3:19–20; Harrison to William Eustis, 18 Nov. 1811, F.O. 5/84:130; General Order, 16 Aug. 1812, *Select Brit. Docs.*, 1:465; General Order, 21 Oct. 1812, *Doc. Hist. Niagara Campaigns*, 4:151; Proctor to Sheaffe, 25 Jan. 1813, *Select Brit. Docs.*, 2:7–9; Proctor to Major General De Rottenburg, 23 Oct. 1813, C.O. 42/152:66–69 (esp. 69); General Order, 24 Nov. 1813, *Select Brit. Docs.*, 2:294; Floyd to Pinckney, 4 Dec. 1813, Brannan, ed., *Official Letters*, 283–85; Jackson to Blount, 31 Mar. 1814, John Spencer Bassett, ed., *The Correspondence of Andrew Jackson*, 2 vols., 1:489–92; McKay to McDouall, 27 July 1814, C.O. 42/157:199–202; McDouall to Lieutenant General Drummond, 2 Oct. 1814, C.O. 42/157:339–40; Merritt's Journal, *Select Brit. Docs.*,

3:585; also, *Doc. Hist. Niagara Campaigns*, 4:110, 112, 115–16, 120–21, 122–23.
    20. Brown to Carleton, 9 Oct. 1782, Report on American Mss., *H.M.C.* 59; 3:157; Brown to Germaine, 6 Apr. 1782, C.O. 5/82:277; A Talk from the Cherokee Nation . . . , 1 Sept. 1781, C.O. 5/82:287–88; Brown to Shelburne, 25 Sept. 1782, C.O. 5/82:343–45; Brown to Lord North, 30 July 1783, C.O. 5/82:392–93.
    21. Bert Anson, *The Miami Indians*, 95–96, 118–19; McKee to Chew, 27 Aug. 1794, *Simcoe Papers*, 3:7–8; Brant to Colonel R. G. England, 28 Sept. 1794, ibid., 106–07; William Campbell to England, 20 Aug. 1794, ibid., 2:395–96; Proctor to Brock, 11 Aug. 1812, *M.P.H.S.C.*, 15 (1890): 129; Proctor to Sheaffe, 25 Jan. 1813, *Select Brit. Docs.*, 2:7–9; [Proctor], *Lucubrations of Humphrey Ravelin*, 269–70.
    22. Arrell M. Gibson, *The Kickapoos: Lords of the Middle Border* (Norman, 1975), p. 33.
    23. Royal B. Hassrick, *The Sioux: Life and Customs of a Warrior Society*, 71–74; Richard White, "The Winning of the West: . . . ," *Journal of American History*, 65 (1978):329–43.
    24. Sinclair to Captain D. Brehm, 15 Feb. 1780, Haldimand Papers, 21757:289; Sinclair to Haldimand, 15 Feb. 1780, and Lieutenant Philips to Lieutenant Clowes, 27 Apr., 1780, ibid., 21757:292; 332; De Peyster to Campbell, 14 June 1779, ibid., 21771:108–9.
    25. Prideaux Selby to Peter Russell, 23 Jan. 1799, *Russell Papers*, 3:60–62; Nicholas Boilvin to Secretary of War, 2 Aug. 1809, in Clarence Edwin Carter, ed., *Territorial Papers of the United States*, 28 vols., 14:288; Doane Robinson, *A History of the Dakota or Sioux Indians*, 85, 88; [Proctor], *Lucubrations of Humphrey Ravelin*, 282.
    26. Brown to Carleton, 23 Feb. 1783, Carleton Papers, 63, 6953 (no. 2): Representation of William Augustus Bowles . . . , F.O. 4/9:5–17; Bowles to Grenville, 13 Jan. 1791, F.O. 4/9:69–74; Unaddressed, 1801, Liverpool Papers, B.M. Add. Mss., 38356:101–4; Unheaded, 29 Dec. 1796, Liston Papers, Nat. Lib. Scot., Ms. 5583:105–7; Cochrane to Croker, 20 June 1814, Cochrane Papers, Ms. 2348:32–34;·Cochrane to Bathurst, 2 Sept. 1814, W.O. 1/141:67; A proposal for the Conquest of Louisiana, 10 Dec. 1812, Leeds Public Libraries, Archives Dept., Canning Mss., 49; F. B. Johnson (to Melville), 1 Nov. 1796, Melville Castle Muniments, Scottish Record Office, G.D. 51/1/521.
    27. Brannan, ed., *Official Letters*, 255–56, 264–66, 281–82, 283–85, 294–96, 298–305, 319–20; Jackson to Blount, 31 Mar. 1814, Bassett, ed., *Correspondence of Andrew Jackson*, 1:489–92; Frank L. Owsley, ed., *The Creek War of 1813 and 1814, by H. S. Halbert and T. H. Ball*, 269–78.
    28. Creek chiefs to Cochrane, Adm. 1/506:402 (for British high hopes); Nicolls's details of his proceedings, 12 Aug. 1814, Cochrane Papers, Ms. 2328:59–66; Owsley, ed., *Creek War*, 120–21, 211–18; William Lattimore to Secretary of War, 9 Mar. 1814, Carter, ed., *Territorial Papers*, 6 (1938):424; John K. Mahon, "British Strategy and the Southern Indians, War of 1812," *Florida Historical Quarterly*, 44 (1966): 285–302; Cochrane to Major General Lambert, 17 Feb. 1815, Coch-

rane Papers, Ms. 2349:270–72; John Sugden, "The Southern Indians in the War of 1812: The Closing Phase," *Florida Historical Quarterly*, 60 (1982):273–312.

29. For example, Captain Pigot to Cochrane, 6 June 1814, Cochrane Papers, Ms. 2326:149–52; G.W. to Hope, 31 May 1814, ibid., Ms. 2328:13; Woodbine to Cochrane, 25 July 1814, ibid., Ms. 2328:35; Memorial of Major Edward Nicolls to Bathurst, n.d., ibid., Ms. 2275: 120–21.

30. Prevost to Sir Gordon Drummond, 17 Feb. 1814, *Doc. Hist. Niagara Campaigns*, 9:188–89; Drummond to Prevost, 10 July 1814, *Select Brit. Docs.*, 3:121; McKay to McDouall, 27 July 1814, ibid., 257–63; Grahame to Carleton, 20 July 1782, Report on American Institution Manuscripts, *H.M.C.*, 59, 3:30.

31. Haldimand to Germaine, 13 Sept. 1779, Haldimand Papers, 21717:34–38; Observations on the Posts on the Lakes: Simcoe to Dundas, 26 Aug. 1791, *Simcoe Papers*, 1:51.

32. Craig to Castlereagh, 15 July 1808, plus enclosures, C.O. 42/136: 147–58, 167–71; (Castlereagh) to Craig, 8 Apr. 1809, C.O. 42/138: 177; *New Annual Register* for 1812, 33:342.

33. Strachan to Wilberforce, 1 Nov. 1812, Spragge, ed., *John Strachan Letter Book*, 21–23; Alexander Clark Casselman, ed., *Richardson's War of 1812*, 6; [Proctor], *Lucubrations of Humphrey Ravelin*, 266–67; [Nathaniel Atcheson], "A Compressed View of the Points To Be Discussed in Treating With the United States of America," *The Pamphleteer*, 5 (No. 9, Feb. 1815):133; Draper Mss., 6YY:118.

34. Prevost to Liverpool, 26 Aug. 1812, C.O. 42/147:160; Brock to Colonel Edward Baynes, 4 Aug. 1812, *Select Brit. Docs.*, 1:408–10; Brock to Prevost, 25 July 1812, *Brock Correspondence*, 216–17.

35. Speech of Tekumthai . . . , C.O. 42/351:42–43, Hull to Eustis, 14 July 1812; same to same, 21 July 1812 and 26 Aug. 1812, *M.P.H.S.C.*, 40:413–14, 419–20, 460–63.

36. Dickson to Lawe, 20 Mar. 1814, *W.S.H.S.C.*, 10 (1888):115–16; same to same, 31 Mar. 1814, ibid., 11 (1888):302.

37. Prevost to Brock, 27 July 1812, *Select Brit. Docs.*, 1:382; McDouall to Bulger, 26 Feb. 1815, *W.S.H.S.C.*, 13 (1895):96; De Peyster to Powell, 3 Sept. 1782, Haldimand Papers, 21762:160; Haldimand to Guy Johnson, 24 July 1780, ibid., 21767:99.

38. Haldimand to North, 20 Aug. 1783, Haldimand Papers, 21717: 168–68; Haldimand to Ross, 26 Apr. 1783, ibid., 21785:130; Russell to Robert Prescott, 29 Aug. 1796, *Russell Papers*, 1:33; Memorandum from Simcoe to Dundas, n.d., *Simcoe Papers*, 1:29–30; Simcoe to Dundas, 26 Aug. 1791, ibid.:51–53.

39. Prevost to Bathurst, 10 July 1814, C.O. 42/157:7–9; Brock to Prevost, 3 July 1812, *Select Brit. Docs.*, 1:348; Proctor to Prevost, 9 Aug. 1813; [Prevost] to Proctor, 22 Aug. 1813, ibid., 2:44–49; Proctor to De Rottenburg, 23 Oct. 1813, ibid., 323; Proctor to Freer, 6 Sept. 1813, ibid., 269–70; Draper Mss., 6YY:116.

40. Major General Vincent to De Rottenburg, 18 Oct. 1813, *Doc.*

Hist. Niagara Campaigns, 8:78; De Rottenburg to Vincent, 23 Oct. 1813, ibid., 88–89.

41. The 450 pages of Procter's court-martial proceedings are in W.O. 71/243. See especially the testimonies of Lieutenant Colonel Baby, 145–54; Captain William Caldwell, 154–65; Colonel William Caldwell, 175–77; Mr. William Jones, 177–81; the prosecution's summing up, 293–95, and Procter's defense, Appendix 6:346–80. For a comprehensive study of Procter's retreat and the death of Tecumseh, see John Sugden, *Tecumseh's Last Stand.*

42. Brannan, ed., *Official Letters*, 225; A Proclamation by General Harrison, 16 Oct. 1813, ibid., 246; E. A. Cruikshank, "Robert Dickson, The Indian Trader," *W.S.H.S.C.*, 12 (1892):148.

43. Brock to Prevost, 16 May 1812, *Select Brit. Docs.*, 1:301–3.

44. Haldimand to Campbell, 21 June 1779, Haldimand Papers, 21773:49–50; Memorandum from Simcoe to Dundas, n.d., *Simcoe Papers*, 1:30; also, ibid., 82–83, 114, 142, 170; ibid., 2:100.

45. McKee to Chew, 8 May 1794, *Simcoe Papers*, 2:234; Memorial to Sir George Prevost, 26 Feb. 1813, *M.P.H.S.C.*, 15:250–52.

46. Cochrane Papers, Nat. Lib. Scot., Ms. 2328:125, 138, 180–81, 183; Ms., 2336:67–68.

47. John K. Mahon, "British Command Decisions in the Northern Campaigns of the War of 1812," *C.H.R.*, 46 (1965):221.

48. Haldimand to Germaine, 24 Oct. 1779, Haldimand Papers, 21717: 52–53; Haldimand to Knox, 20 Oct. 1781, ibid., 21718:10; De Peyster to Haldimand, 24 Oct. 1778, ibid., 21756:7–8; Outline for a reformation of Expenses in the Indian Dept., n.d., ibid., 21758:362; Bethune to Cameron, 27 Aug. 1780, C.O. 5/82:95–96; Butler to Johnson, 13 June 1791, C.O. 42/82:357–58; McKay to McDouall, 27 July, 1814, *Select Brit. Docs.*, 3:261.

49. Haldimand to Powell, 24 June 1781, Haldimand Papers, 21756: 136; De Peyster to Maclean, 18 June 1783, ibid., 21763:145.

50. Cochrane to Cameron, 25 Mar. 1814, Cochrane Papers, Ms. 2346:2–3; Nicholls to Cochrane, 26 July 1816, ibid., Ms. 2575:157; Guy Johnson to Haldimand, 10 Oct. 1781, Haldimand Papers, 21767: 238–41 (esp:241); Narrative of Captain Thomas G. Anderson, *W.S.H.S.C.*, 9 (1882):198.

51. Claus to Haldimand, 15 May 1780, Haldimand Papers, 21774: 120–21; C. E. Cartwright, ed., *Life and Letters of the Late Hon. Richard Cartwright . . .* , 29; Nicoll's details of his proceedings, 12 Aug. 1814, Cochrane Papers, Nat. Lib. Scot., Ms. 2328; 59; see also, Milo Milton Quaife, ed., *Alexander Ross' Adventures of the First Settlers . . .* , 352; Hamilton to Simcoe, 4 Jan. 1792, *Simcoe Papers*, 1:98–99; McDouall to Drummond, 16 July 1814, *Select Brit. Doc.*, 3:253–56.

52. For example, Bathurst to Lords Commissioners of the Admiralty—1814, W.O. 6/2:49–50; [Nathaniel Atcheson], "A Compressed View of the Points To Be Discussed in Treating With the United States of America," 131; Strachan to Wilberforce, 1 Nov. 1812, Spragge, ed., *John Strachan Letter Book*, 21–23.

53. Haldimand to North, 14 Oct. 1783, Haldimand Papers, 21717: 170; e.g., George Hammond to Grenville, 19 Dec. 1791 (and enclosure, 24 Nov. 1791), F.O. 4/11:250; Craig to Gore, 6 Dec. 1807, C.O. 42/136: 156; Craig to Liverpool, 29 Mar. 1811, C.O. 42/143:31–32; Lieutenant Colonel Harvey to Elliott, 17 Dec. 1813, *Select Brit. Docs.*, 2:484; Casselman, ed., *Richardson's War of 1812*, 6–8; Instructions to Nicolls, 4 July 1814, Cochrane Papers, Ms. 2333:138–39; Haldimand to Powell, 7 Sept. 1781, Haldimand Papers, 21764:232–33; De Peyster to McKee, 6 Aug. 1782, *M.P.H.S.C.*, 20 (1892):37–39.

54. General Order, 26 July 1813, *Select Brit. Docs.*, 2:170–71; Harvey to William Claus, 15 July 1813, *Doc. Hist. Niagara Campaigns*, 6:236; Casselman, ed., *Richardson's War of 1812*, 7–8.

55. Gilbert Tice to Guy Johnson, 15 Nov. 1781, Haldimand Papers, 21767:254; Brown to Germaine, 9 Mar. 1781, C.O. 5/82:211–12; Captain Charles Roberts to Brock, 17 July 1812, *Select Brit. Docs.*, 1: 433–34; General Order, 16 Aug. 1812, ibid., 463–65; Gaines to Secretary of War, 23 Aug. 1814, *Doc. Hist. Niagara Campaigns*, 1:156. De Peyster to McKee, 22 June 1780, in J. Watts De Peyster, ed., *Miscellanies by An Officer . . . 1774–1813 . . .* , xxv.

56. Milo Milton Quaife, ed., *War on the Detroit: . . .* , 91–93; Shadrach Byfield, "A Narrative of a Light Company Soldier's Service in the 41st Regt. of Foot," *The Magazine of History*, Extra No. 11 (1910):70; Casselman, ed., *Richardson's War of 1812*, 154.

57. Casselman, ed., *Richardson's War of 1812*, 154–55; William James, *A Full and Correct Account of the Military Occurrences of the Late War Between Great Britain and the United States of America*, 2 vols., 1:201; Chambers to Proctor, 24 Aug. 1812, *Select Brit. Docs.*, 1:498–99; Robert Breckinridge McAfee, *History of the Late War in the Western Country*, 272.

58. Francis Jennings, *The Invasion of America*, ch. 9, "Savage War," 146–70.

59. Council at Niagara, 1 Apr. 1783, Haldimand Papers, 21779: 111–12.

60. Haldimand to Shelburne, 17 July 1782, ibid., 21717:135–36; Extract of a Letter from Captain Caldwell to Major De Peyster, dated 13 June 1782, ibid., 21762:80.

61. Extract of Speech to Maclean by the Six Nations in Council at Niagara, 11 Dec. 1782, C.O. 42/15:383; A. H. Young, ed., "Letters from William Jarvis," in *Women's Canadian Historical Society of Toronto*, Transaction No. 23 (1922–23):37–38; Address from Blackbird . . . to Claus, 15 July 1813, *Doc. Hist. Niagara Campaigns*, 6:242; Proctor to De Rottenburg, 23 Oct. 1813, *Select Brit. Docs.*, 2:327; McKee to Chew, 27 Aug. 1794, *Simcoe Papers*, 3:7–8; Casselman, ed., *Richardson's War of 1812*, 212–14; James, *A Full and Correct Account of the Military Occurrences*, 1:295–96; [Nathaniel Atcheson], "A Compressed View of the Points To Be Discussed . . . ," 117; Carl F. Klinck, ed., *Tecumseh: Fact and Fiction in Early Records*, 200–19. Draper Mss., 1YY:66–67; 7YY passim.

62. Bathurst to Lords Commissioners of the Admiralty, 1814, W.O. 6/2:49–51; General Porter to the Six Nations, n.d., (May 1814), *Doc. Hist. Niagara Campaigns*, 2:392–93.

63. [Joseph Chew], "Diary of an Officer in the Indian Country in 1794," *American Historical Magazine*, 3 (1908):641; and in Claus Papers, P.A.C., MG19, F1, 6:164, Reel C-1479.

64. Brant to McKee, 25 Feb., 1795, *Simcoe Papers*, 5:33; Brant to McKee, 4 Aug. 1793, ibid., 66–67; Butler to Chew, 27 Apr. 1794, ibid., 2:218; McKee to England, 10 July 1794, ibid., 315; Edwin James, ed., *Narrative of the Captivity and Adventures of John Tanner*..., 195–200; Mc-Douall to Anderson, 23 Sept. 1814, *W.S.H.S.C.*, 9 (1882):267; Muir to Proctor, 30 Sept. 1812, *M.P.H.S.C.*, 15 (1890):151–54; Annie Heloise Abel, ed., *Tabeau's Narrative of Loisel's Expedition*..., 206.

65. Harold Hickerson, *The Chippewa and Their Neighbours*, passim, esp. 64–119; De Peyster to Haldimand, 8 June 1780, Haldimand Papers, 21781:74; *W.S.H.S.C.*, 12 (1892):76–95.

66. Roy W. Meyer, *History of the Santee Sioux*..., 28–29; for information on one Sioux band, the Fireleaf, who became pro-American, see *W.S.H.S.C.*, 13 (1895):23, 36–37, 45–52; De Peyster to Haldimand, 1 June 1779, Haldimand Papers, 21756:12–13; Anderson's Journal, *W.S.H.S.C.*, 9 (1882):238.

67. Elliott to Clegg, 31 Jan. 1814, *Doc. Hist. Niagara Campaigns*, 9:158.

68. "Bulger Papers," *W.S.H.S.C.*, 13 (1895):10–153 passim; Proposed Plan for the Future Government of the Indian Department, enclosed in McKee to Dorchester, 7 June 1796, *Simcoe Papers*, 4:294–95.

69. Simcoe to Dundas, 10 Nov. 1793, *Simcoe Papers*, 2:99–101; Anthony F. C. Wallace, *The Death and Rebirth of the Seneca*, 154.

70. The Information of Blue Jacket, 1 Nov. 1790, C.O. 42/73:37; McGillivray to Miro, 20 Sept. 1788, in John Walton Caughey, *McGillivray of the Creeks*, 201; McGillivray to Brown, 10 Apr. 1783, C.O. 5/82:376; [Proctor], *Lucubrations of Humphrey Ravelin*, 278.

71. Milo M. Quaife, ed., *The Indian Captivity of O. M. Spencer*, 91; England to McKee, 15 July 1793, *Simcoe Papers*, 5:59; England to Simcoe, 22 July 1794, ibid., 2:333–34. On Blue Jacket, see Draper Mss., 2YY:166–69.

72. Creek deputies to Governor Cameron, 16 Dec. 1816, F.O. 5/127:157–58; Creeks to King George, n.d., F.O. 5/138:198; McKee to John Johnson, 7 Nov. 1790, C.O. 42/73:47; Creek chiefs to Cochrane, n.d., Cochrane Papers, Ms. 2328:180; or Adm. 1/506:402; Foster to Wellesley, 12 Nov. 1811, F.O. 5/77:77; Foster to James Monroe, 13 Dec. 1811, F.O. 5/77:159; Brock to Prevost, 3 Dec. 1811, *Brock Correspondence*, 130; Craig to Gore, 2 Feb. 1811, C.O. 42/143:45–46. Roger Lamb, *An Original and Authentic Journal of Occurrences during the Late American War*..., 146; Gore to Craig, 5 Jan. 1808, C.O. 42/136:170; Proctor to Brock, 30 Sept. 1812, *Select Brit. Docs.*, 1:524; McDouall to Prevost, 14 Aug. 1814, ibid., 3:276–77.

73. John Askin, Jr. to William Claus, 18 July 1812; Roberts to Clegg, 29 July 1812, Roberts to ?, 16 Aug. 1812; *Select Brit. Docs.*, 1:436–37, 438–41, 444–47.

74. McDouall to Prevost, 14 Aug. 1814, ibid., 2:273–77; cf. De Peyster to Haldimand, 26 Jan. 1782, Haldimand Papers, 21781:81.

75. England to Simcoe, 7 July 1794, *Simcoe Papers*, 2:308; Brock to

Prevost, 3 Dec. 1811, *Brock Correspondence*, 130; McAfee, *History of the Late War in the Western Country*, 31.

76. Speech of Tecumseh to Proctor, n.d., W.O. 71/243 (Appendix 7):318; the speech is also reproduced in Klinck, *Tecumseh: Fact and Fiction in Early Records*, 184–85, and in Casselman, ed., *Richardson's War of 1812*, 205–6.

77. Proctor to Prevost, 9 Aug. 1813, *Select Brit. Docs.*, 2:46; Prevost to Bathurst, 26 Aug. 1813, *Doc. Hist. Niagara Campaigns*, 7:63; McKay to McDouall, 27 July 1814, *Select Brit. Docs.*, 3:257; Arthur S. Morton, ed., *Journal of Duncan McGillivray* . . . , 14.

78. Thomas Anburey, *Travels Through the Interior Parts of America* . . . , 2 vols., 1:294; Louis B. Wright and Marion Tinling, eds., *Quebec to Carolina in 1785–86:* . . . , 73–74; E. A. Benians, ed., *A Journal by Thos. Hughes* . . . , 183.

79. William Dunlop, *Recollections of the American War, 1812–1814*, 77; Norman C. Lord, ed., "The War on the Canadian Frontier, 1812–14 . . . ," *Journal of the Society for Army Historical Research*, 18 (1939):209.

80. Harrison to Eustis, 18 Nov. 1811, F.O. 5/84:129A; Dresden W. Howard, ed., "The Battle of Fallen Timbers as told by Chief Kin-jo-i-no," *Northwest Ohio Quarterly*, 20 (Jan. 1948):47; Tackle to Bathurst, 24 Nov. 1812, *W.S.H.S.C.*, 20 (1911):9–10; Proctor to Prevost, 4 July 1813 (P.S.), *M.P.H.S.C.*, 15 (1890):333.

81. De Rottenburg to Baynes, 14 July 1813, *Doc. Hist. Niagara Campaigns*, 6:233; Elliott to Brock, 12 Jan. 1812, *Select Brit. Docs.*, 1:281; Brant to Chew, 30 Dec. 1791, C.O. 42/89:195.

82. Proctor to Prevost, 14 May 1813, *Select Brit. Docs.*, 2:35; McKee to Chew, 7 July 1794, *Simcoe Papers*, 2:310; Simcoe to Dundas, 5 Aug. 1794, ibid., 353; see also Caldwell to De Peyster, 11 June 1782, Haldimand Papers, 21762:62.

83. Thomas Duggan to Chew, 5 July 1796, *Simcoe Papers*, 4:325; Narrative of Captain Thomas G. Anderson, *W.S.H.S.C.*, 9 (1882):190.

84. Haldimand to Maclean, 10 Feb. 1783, Haldimand Papers, 21756:130; Pigot to Cochrane, 6 June 1814, Cochrane Papers, Ms. 2326:149–52; G.W. to Hope, 31 May 1814, ibid., Ms. 2328:13; Cochrane to Chiefs, 29 June 1814, ibid., Ms. 2346:7; Cochrane to Nicolls, 3 Dec. 1814, ibid., Ms. 2346:16–17.

85. William Surtees, *Twenty-Five years in the Rifle Brigade*, 334–35; John Henry Cooke, *A Narrative of Events in the South of France* . . . , 165–67; Lady Bourchier, ed., *Memoir of the Life of Admiral Sir Edward Codrington* . . . , 2 vols., 1:329–30; Benson Earle Hill, *Recollections of an Artillery Officer:* . . . , 2 vols., 1:299–300.

86. Quaife, ed., *War on the Detroit*, 242–43; Byfield, "Narrative of a Light Company Soldier's Service in the 41st Regt. of Foot," 70; Casselman, ed., *Richardson's War of 1812*, 154; "Recollections of the War of 1812, from the Manuscript of the Late Hon. James Crooks," *Niagara Historical Society*, 28 (1915):37.

87. Gellner, ed., *Recollections of the War of 1812*, 106–7; De Rottenburg to Prevost, 17 Sept. 1813, *Doc. Hist. Niagara Campaigns*, 7:140; Bulger to McDouall, 15 Jan. 1815, *W.S.H.S.C.*, 13 (1895):56.

88. Byfield, "Narrative," 90; Lord, ed., "War on the Canadian Frontier," 209.

89. Colonel C.P. Stacey, ed., "Upper Canada at War, 1814 . . . ," *Ontario History*, 48 (1956):42; Lord, ed., "War on the Canadian Frontier," 200, 206.

90. Proclamation by Brigadier General Hull; Brock's Answer to Hull's Proclamation, *Select Brit. Docs.*, 1:355–57, 371–74.

91. General Wolfe to Lord George Sackville (July 1758), Mss. of Mrs. Stopford-Sackville, *H.M.C.* Report 49, 2 (1910):266.

92. G. C. Moore Smith, ed., *Autobiography of Sir Harry Smith, 1787–1819*, 251; E. M. Pakenham to Mother, and Sir Hercules Pakenham to Earl of Longford, 6 June 1814, and Dec. 20, 1814, in Thomas Longford, Earl of Pakenham, ed., *Pakenham Letters, 1800–1815*, 248–51.

93. Peter E. Russell, "Redcoats in the Wilderness: British Officers and Irregular Warfare in Europe and America, 1740–1760," *William and Mary Quarterly*, 3d Series, 35 (1978):629–52; Spragge, ed., *John Strachan Letter Book*, 6–8.

94. [Proctor], *Lucubrations of Humphrey Ravelin*, 263; Askin to Powell, 25 Jan. 1813, *Doc. Hist. Niagara Campaigns*, 5:49–51; Richardson and Irvine to Prevost, 14 & 24 Oct. 1812, C.O. 42/159:133–36; Prevost to Bathurst, 5 Oct. 1812, C.O. 42/147:207–11; Memorial to Merchants, 7 May 1814, F.O. 5/103:187–92; John Johnson to William Claus, 16 Mar. 1813, De Peyster, ed., *Miscellanies by an Officer*, lxi–lxii.

95. Prevost to Liverpool, 18 May 1812, C.O. 42/146:198; Brock to Baynes, 29 July 1812, *Select Brit. Docs.*, 1:396–97 (on Canada's defenses in 1812, see also Sir John W. Fortescue, *History of the British Army*, 13 vols. (London and New York: Macmillan & Co., 1899–1930), 8:515–21); Speech on Proposed Repeal of Non-Intercourse Act, 22 Feb. 1810, James F. Hopkins, ed., *The Papers of Henry Clay*, 2 vols., (Lexington: University of Kentucky Press, 1959), 1:450.

96. Reginald Horsman, *The Causes of the War of 1812*, 214; Horsman, "The Role of the Indian in the War," in Philip Mason, ed., *After Tippecanoe: Some Aspects of the War of 1812*, 65–68, 75; Dickson to Lawe, 23 Jan. 1814, *W.S.H.S.C.*, 9 (1888):285–87; Nicolls to Cochrane, 25 July 1816, Cochrane Papers, Ms. 2575:157.

97. Donald Jackson, ed., *Black Hawk . . . : An Autobiography*, 48n–49n; Melvill Allan Jamieson, *Medals Presented to North American Indian Chiefs . . .* , 28–31.

98. Charles Stevenson to Dundas, n.d. (rec. 13 July 1793), *Simcoe Papers*, 1:411; Brock to Prevost, 2 Dec. 1811, *Select Brit. Docs.*, 1:273.

99. Minutes of Executive Council, 29 June–1 July 1797, in Charles M. Johnston, ed., *Valley of the Six Nations: . . .* , 87–88; Liston to Prescott, 8 Apr. 1797, *Russell Papers*, 1:160; Liston to Grenville, 6 May 1797, Liston Papers, Nat. Lib. Scot., Ms. 5587:114–15.

100. For example, Burke to Littlehales, 27 May 1795, *Simcoe Papers*, 4:22; (Castlereagh) to Craig, 8 Apr. 1809, C.O. 42/138:77–78.

CHAPTER 9
The British as Allies

1. Dorchester to John Johnson, 27 Nov. 1786, C.O. 42/50:78–79.
2. Considerations on the Propriety of Great Britain Abandoning the Indian Posts and Coming to a Good Understanding with America, July 1794, in Vincent Harlow and Frederick Madden, eds., *British Colonial Developments 1774–1834: Select Documents*, 477–80.
3. Winnebagoes at the Peace of 1814, (Council at Mackinaw, 3 June 1815), *W.S.H.S.C.*, 10 (1888):144.
4. Dorchester to the Seven Nations of Lower Canada, 10 Feb. 1794, *Simcoe Papers*, 2:149–50; Randolph to Hammond, 20 May 1794, ibid., 239.
5. Reginald Horsman, "The British Indian Department and the Resistance to General Anthony Wayne, 1793–1795," *M.V.H.R.*, 49 (1962–63):269–90.
6. Message delivered by two Delaware chiefs who arrived at the Foot of the Rapids with Six Scalps . . . , 25 May 1794, *Simcoe Papers*, 2:249–50; and McKee Papers, P.A.C., MG19, F16:2–3; A Speech Delivered to Colonel England (by the principal Wyandot chiefs), 5 Aug. 1794, *Simcoe Papers*, 2:357.
7. Isaac Weld, Jr., *Travels Through the States of North America . . .* , 364; A. H. Young, ed., "Letters from William Jarvis," *Women's Canadian Historical Society of Toronto*, Transaction No. 23 (1922–23):37–38; *The Times*, 17 Oct. 1794:3; Draper Mss. 1YY17; (Joseph Chew), "Diary of an Officer in the Indian Country," *American Historical Magazine*, 3 (1908):640; and "Diary of J.C. an Officer at the Glaize, 14 June–2 July 1794," Claus Papers, MG19 F1:164; Wayne to Knox, 7 July and 28 Aug. 1794, in Richard C. Knopf, ed., *Anthony Wayne: A Name in Arms*, 347–48, 351–55; Examination of Antoine Laselle, 28 Aug. 1794, *Simcoe Papers*, 3:13.
8. England to Simcoe, 24 Aug. 1794, *Simcoe Papers*, 2:419; same to same, 30 Aug. 1794, ibid., 3:20–22; McKee to England, 10 July 1794, ibid., 2:315; England to Simcoe, 22 July 1794, ibid., 333–34.
9. General Order by Wayne . . . , 23 Aug. 1794, *Simcoe Papers*, 2:409–10; Simcoe to Portland, 24 Oct. 1794, ibid., 3:145–46; Wayne to Pickering, 15 May 1795, Knopf, ed., *Anthony Wayne: A Name in Arms: . . .* , 415–19.
10. Carl F. Klinck and James J. Talman, eds., *The Journal of Major John Norton 1816*, 186; Proceedings of a Council at Brownstown, 11–14 Oct. 1794, C.O. 42/101:172–76 (esp. 175); and M. M. Quaife, ed., "General James Wilkinson's Narrative of the Fallen Timbers Campaign," *M.V.H.R.*, 16 (1929–30):89.
11. Brant to Chew, 22 Oct. 1794, *Simcoe Papers*, 3:140–41; William J. Chew to Joseph Chew, 24 Oct. 1794, ibid., 150–51.
12. The Treaty of Greenville is in *British and Foreign State Papers*, 3:402–9; Charles J. Kappler, ed., *Indian Treaties, 1778–1883*, 39–45; on Tarhe, see F. W. Hodge, "Handbook of American Indians," *B.A.E. Bulletin* 30, (1907–10):694.

13. Hawkesbury (to Grenville), 17 Oct. 1794, Liverpool Papers, British Museum, Add. Mss., 38230:68; Dorchester to Portland, 18 June 1796, C.O. 42/105:311; Portland to Simcoe, 19 Nov. 1794, *Simcoe Papers*, 3:185–86; Simcoe to Dorchester, 22 Dec. 1795, ibid., 4:164–65; Brant to Chew, 19 Jan. 1796, ibid., 177–78.

14. For example, Gen. William Hull to Dearborn, ? Nov. 1807, *M.P.H.S.C.*, 40 (1927):247–52; Brock to Prevost, 2 Dec. 1811, *Select Brit. Docs.*, 1:273–74; same to same, 28 Sept. 1812, ibid., 596–98; Proctor to Brock, 30 Sept. 1812, ibid., 524; Evidence of Captain Caldwell, W.O. 71/243:163; Evidence of Lieutenant Colonel Francis Baby, W.O. 71/243:151.

15. Speech of Captain Joseph Brant (probably 1802) to the Chippewas, Ottawas, and Pottawatomies, *M.P.H.S.C.*, 23 (1893):19–20. John Johnson to ?, 15 Dec. 1807, Claus Papers, P.A.C., MG 19 F1:165–67, Reel C-1480.

16. C.O. 42/136:147–86 passim, esp. Craig to Castlereagh, 15 July 1808, C.O. 42/136:147–52; Craig to Gore, 6 Dec. 1807, C.O. 42/136:153–57; At a Private Meeting Between Colonel Claus . . . and Three Principal Shawanoe Chiefs, 25 Mar. 1808, C.O. 42/136:180–81.

17. Minutes of Treaty . . . Greenville, 16 June to 10 Aug. 1795, Speech of New Corn, *A.S.P.I.A.*, 1:564–82 (p. 580); Reply of Nanaume, a Pottawatomie Chief to Governor Hull's Speech, ? Nov. 1807, ibid., 745 (also in Hull to Dearborn, Nov. 1807, *M.P.H.S.C.*, 40 (1920):247–52).

18. Gore to Claus, 26 Feb. 1811, C.O. 42/351:32.

19. R. David Edmunds, *The Shawnee Prophet*.

20. Brock to Craig, 27 Feb. 1811, *Brock Correspondence*, 94–96.

21. Craig to Liverpool, 29 Mar. 1811, C.O. 42/143:31–32; Craig to Gore, 2 Feb. 1811, C.O. 42/143:45–46.

22. Brock to Prevost, 28 Sept. 1812, *Select Brit. Docs.*, 1:596; Glenn Tucker, *Tecumseh: Vision of Glory*, 26–28, 41–42, 64, 70.

23. Klinck & Talman, ed., *Journal of Major John Norton*, 289.

24. Simcoe to Dorchester, 6 Dec. 1793, *Simcoe Papers*, 2:114; Baby to Clegg, 27 July 1812, *Select Brit. Docs.*, 1:387–89; Brock to Baynes, 4 Aug. 1812, ibid., 408–10; also, ibid., 348, 378, 507.

25. Arthur C. Parker, "Seneca Indians in the War of 1812," *The Southern Workman*, 45 (Feb. 1916):116–22.

26. Bulger to McDouall, 30 Dec. 1814, *W.S.H.S.C.*, 13 (1895):33.

27. District General Order, 5 Aug. 1814, *Doc. Hist. Niagara Campaigns*, 2:427.

28. [George Proctor], *The Lucubrations of Humphrey Ravelin . . .* , 277–78.

29. Donald Jackson, ed., *Black Hawk . . . : An Autobiography*, 80.

30. Maclean to Haldimand, 16 Dec., 1782, Haldimand Papers, 21756:88; In Council, 1 Dec. 1782 (Speech of Seneca chief), ibid., 21783:276; [Proctor], *Lucubrations of Humphrey Ravelin*, 279.

31. Daniel Claus to Haldimand, 15 May 1780, Haldimand Papers, 21774:120–21, for an example of Indian complaints. On British failures to supply, see Maclean to Stewart, 24 Oct. 1779, Stuart Stevenson Papers, Nat. Lib. Scot., Ms. 8250:34–36; Talk of Choctaw Chief to

Cameron, 1 Apr. 1781, C.O. 5/82:210; A Talk from the Cherokee Nation . . . , 1 Sept. 1781, C.O. 5/82:287–88; Brant to Butler, 10 Sept. 1786, C.O. 42/49:434.

32. Robertson to Mathews, 7 Sept. 1784, Haldimand Papers, 21758, 321–22.

33. Gore to Castlereagh, 4 Sept. 1809, C.O. 42/349:92.

34. For example, Indian Council held at Burlington Heights, 24–27 Apr. 1815, Murray Papers, Nat. Lib. Scot., Advocate Ms. 46.6.5:165–66.

35. *The Times*, 2 June 1814:2; Indian Council, 24–27 Apr. 1815, Murray Papers, Nat. Lib. Scot., 46.6.5:164.

36. Bulger to McDouall, 30 Dec. 1814, *W.S.H.S.C.*, (1895):26.

37. Brant to Butler, 10 Sept. 1786, C.O. 42/49:434–35.

38. Maclean to Stewart, 24 Oct. 1779, Stuart Stevenson Papers, Nat. Lib. Scot., Ms. 8250:34–36; Frederick Cook, ed., *Journals of the Military Expedition of Major John Sullivan against the Six Nations of Indians in 1779* (Auburn, N.Y.: Knapp, Peck & Thomson, 1887), 296–305. Mary Jemison, a white captive, witnessed the sufferings the campaign produced among the Seneca. James Everett Seaver, *De-he-wa-mis; or, A Narrative of the Life of Mary Jemison . . .* , (Batavia, N.Y.: 2d ed., 1842), 87–89.

39. R. Arthur Bowler, *Logistics and the Failure of the British Army in America, 1775–1783*, (Princeton, N.J.: Princeton University Press, 1975), 238.

40. McKee to Chew, 8 May 1794, *Simcoe Papers*, 2:234; McKee to Chew, 7 July 1794, ibid., 310; McKee to England, 10 July 1794, ibid., 315; Simcoe's Diary . . . , Sept. 1794, ibid., 3:99–100.

41. Nicolls to Morier, 25 Sept. 1815, W.O. 1/143:60–61; Nicolls to Malcolm, ? Feb. 1815, Cochrane Papers, Ms. 2336:67–68; Cochrane to Melville, 25 Mar. 1814, ibid., Ms. 2345:2–5; Captain Rawlins to Senior Officer of H.M.'s Ships . . . , 16 Jan. 1815, ibid., Ms. 2328:138.

42. For example, (Indian speeches), *Doc. Hist. Niagara Campaigns*, 9:271–74; Inhabitants of Prairie du Chien to Captain Roberts, 10 Feb. 1813, *Select Brit. Docs.*, 3:251–52; Polier et al. to Roberts, n.d., *M.P.H.S.C.*, 15 (1890):246–47.

43. Dickson to Military Secretary Freer, 17 Jan. 1815, *M.P.H.S.C.*, 16 (1890):43; John Askin to ?, n.d., ibid., 32–33; McDouall to Bulger, 18 Feb. 1815, *W.S.H.S.C.*, 13 (1895):78–82.

44. Council at Niagara, n.d., Haldimand Papers, 21779:189–92 (esp:190, 192).

45. Cochrane to Indian chiefs, 29 June 1814, Cochrane Papers, Ms. 2346:7 (or Adm. 1/505:163–64).

46. Speech of Tecumseth . . . , W.O. 71/243, Appendix 7:381–82.

47. Procter's Court Martial, W.O. 71/243, esp. 11, 18, 154–65, 286–87, 293–95; Harrison to Armstrong, 9 Oct. 1813, in John Brannan, ed., *Official Letters . . .* , 233–39; Strachan to Richardson, 12 Oct. 1813, in George W. Spragge, ed., *The John Strachan Letter Book*, 50; Fortescue, *History of the British Army*, 9:335n. Elliott to Claus, 24 Oct. 1814, Claus Papers, P.A.C., MG19, F1, 10:111–13, Reel C-1480; Draper Mss. 2YY51, 57; John Sugden, *Tecumseh's Last Stand*, ch. 5.

48. John Richardson and James Irvine to Prevost, 14 & 24 Oct. 1812, C.O. 42/159:133–36; Merchants' Memorial to Bathurst, 7 May 1814, C.O. 42/159:173–76; (Bathurst) to Prevost, 9 Dec. 1812, C.O. 42/147: 237–38; Prevost to Bathurst, 10 July 1814, C.O. 42/157:8; [Nathaniel Atcheson], "A Compressed View of the Points To Be Discussed . . . ," 105–39.

49. Indian council at the Glaize 1792, *Simcoe Papers*, 1:218–19, Speech of Painted Pole, 228; Speech of Indian (Sioux) Chiefs Assembled in Council, n.d., *Select Brit. Doc.*, 1:425–26; Jackson, ed., *Black Hawk*, 68; cf.: Anderson to McDouall, 18 Oct. 1814, *W.S.H.S.C.*, 9 (1882):269; McDouall to Forster, 15 May 1815, *Select Brit. Docs.*, 3:534.

50. Lady Liston's Journal, Liston Papers, Nat. Lib. Scot., Ms. 5703:22.

51. McDouall to Forster, 15 May 1815, *Select Brit. Docs.*, 3:532–36; William Henry Puthuff to Cass, 14 May 1816, *W.S.H.S.C.*, 19 (1910): 408–13.

52. The Reverend John Heckewelder, *History, Manners, and Customs of the Indian Nations . . . , 104;* O'Beale to Brant, 25 Oct. 1794, *Simcoe Papers*, 3:154.

53. Simcoe to Henry Dundas, 20 Sept. 1793, *Simcoe Papers*, 2:59.

CONCLUSION: *1815*

1. Material relating to the negotiations at Ghent can be found in the following collections: F.O. 5/101–2; "Instructions and Dispatches of the British Ghent Commission," *Massachusetts Historical Society, Proceedings*, 47 (Dec. 1914):138–62; Charles William Vane, ed., *Correspondence, Despatches, and Other Papers, of Viscount Castlereagh*, vol. 10; Duke of Wellington, ed., *Supplementary Despatches, Correspondence, and Memoranda of Field Marshal Arthur Duke of Wellington*, vol. 9; Elizabeth Donnan, ed., "The Papers of James A. Bayard, 1796–1815," *Ann. Rept. Am. Hist. Ass'n.* for 1913, 2, or H.M.C. Report, 11 (1913); James F. Hopkins, ed., *The Papers of Henry Clay*, 2 vols., (Lexington, Ky.: University of Kentucky Press, 1959), 1:857–1013. See esp. Castlereagh to Commissioners, 28 July 1814, Vane, ed., *Castlereagh Correspondence*, 10:67–72; same to same, 14 Aug. 1814, ibid., 86–91; Goulburn to Bathurst, 21 Aug. 1814, Wellington, ed., *Supplementary Despatches*, 9:188–89; same to same, 26 Sept. 1814, ibid., 287–88; Liverpool to Wellington and Castlereagh, 27 Sept. 1814, ibid., 290; Liverpool to Castlereagh, 28 Oct. 1814, ibid., 382–83; same to same, 18 Nov. 1814, ibid., 438; also Liverpool to Bathurst, 14 Sept. 1814, Francis Bickley, ed., "Report on the Manuscripts of Earl Bathurst," *H.M.C.* 76 (1923):286–88; Liverpool to Canning, 28 Dec. 1814, Canning Mss., 69, Leeds Public Libraries, Archives Dept.

2. *New Annual Register* for 1814, 346; *Edinburgh Annual Register*, 7 (1814):343; cf. *The Times*, 2 Feb. 1815:3; Dallas to Harrison et al., 19 June 1815, *A.S.P.I.A.*, 2:13.

3. Charles J. Kappler, ed., *Indian Treaties 1778–1883*, 110–24, 126–

31, 138–40, or, *British and Foreign State Papers*, 3:437–60, 465–71, or, *A.S.P.I.A.*, 2:1–25, 91–123, 127–28.

4. (Copy of speech to be delivered to the Indians), Mar. 1815, C.O. 42/161:76–77.

5. E. Cooke to Henry Goulburn, 20 May 1816, F.O. 5/118:210–11; Bathurst to Sherbrooke, 31 Oct. 1816, F.O. 5/119:142–43.

6. Council at Mackinaw, 3 June 1815, *W.S.H.S.C.*, 10 (1888):143.

7. McDouall's Speech to the Indians, ibid., 12 (1895):97–100.

8. Minutes of Indian Council held at Burlington Heights, 24–27 Apr. 1815, Murray Papers, Nat. Lib. Scot., Adv. Mss., 46.6.5:165.

9. McDouall to Bulger, 19 Mar. 1815, *W.S.H.S.C.*, 13 (1895):118–22.

10. McDouall to Forster, 15 May 1815, *Select Brit. Docs.*, 3:532–36; McDouall to ?, 7 Aug. 1816, *M.P.H.S.C.*, 16 (1890):510–11; (spelled McDonall in *M.P.H.S.C.*,).

11. McDouall to Robinson, 24 Sept. 1815, *W.S.H.S.C.*, 13 (1895): 152–53.

12. McDouall to Sir George Murray, 25 June 1815, *M.P.H.S.C.*, 16 (1890):136–39; Speech of Black Hawk, ibid., 196–97; McDouall to Robinson, 22 Sept. 1815, ibid., 283–85; same to same, 4 Oct. 1815, ibid., 309–10; McDouall to ?, 19 June 1816, ibid., 468–69; (Indian speeches) in council, June 1816, ibid., 479–83.

13. McDouall to Bulger, 1 May 1815, *W.S.H.S.C.*, 13 (1895):138; same to same, 16 Feb. 1815, ibid., 76.

14. Robert Breckinridge McAfee, *History of the Late War in the Western Country*, 483–84.

15. Cochrane to Rear Admiral Malcolm, 17 Feb. 1815, Cochrane Papers, Ms. 2350:191–92; same to same, 8 Mar. 1815, ibid., Ms. 2349:287.

16. Treaty of Fort Jackson is in Kappler ed., *Indian Treaties*, 107–10; *British and Foreign State Papers*, 3:434–37; *A.S.P.I.A.*, 1:826–27.

17. Secretary of State to Erving, 28 Nov. 1818, *British and Foreign State Papers*, 6:331–48.

18. Cochrane to Malcolm, 17 Feb. 1815, Cochrane Papers, Ms. 2450: 191–92; Cochrane to Nicolls, 14 Feb. 1815, ibid., Ms. 2349:266–68.

19. Head chiefs of Creeks, Cherokees, Choctaws, & Chickasaws to Governor of Bahamas (enclosed in Cameron to Bathurst, 23 Mar. 1816), F.O. 5/118:207; Nicolls to Hamilton, 27 June 1818, F.O. 5/139:173, and enclosures, 175–203.

20. *British and Foreign State Papers*, 6:326–502, for documents on the Seminole War.

21. *The Times*, 12, 13, 15, 24, 26 Aug.; 3, 4 Sept., 1818, especially 15 Aug. 1818:2.

22. F.O. 5/140:74–148 passim.

23. Baker to Monroe, 15 Dec. 1815, F.O. 5/112:3–4.

24. McDouall to ?, 7 Aug. 1816, *M.P.H.S.C.*, 16 (1890):510–11.

25. McDouall to Military Secretary, 17 June 1816, *M.P.H.S.C.*, 16 (1890):464; Council with the Western Indians, Aug. 1817, William McKay Papers, P.A.C., MG 19 F29:1–9.

26. Council with the Ottawa, Chippewa, and Winibago Indians at Drummond Island, 7 July 1818, McKay Papers, P.A.C., MG 19 F29 : 9–13.

27. Clarence Edwin Carter, ed., *The Territorial Papers of the United States*, 28 vols., 10:852–55, 867–73, and Cass to Secretary of War, 24 Apr. 1816, ibid., 629–31.

28. R. David Edmunds, *The Shawnee Prophet*, 156–64; George Ironside to William Claus, ? Dec. 1825, *M.P.H.S.C.*, 23 (1895): 129.

29. Sheridan Warrick, "The American Indian Policy in the Upper Old Northwest following the War of 1812," *Ethnohistory*, 3 (1956): 118–20; Colin G. Calloway, "The End of an Era: British-Indian Relations in the Great Lakes Region after the War of 1812," *Michigan Historical Review*, 2 (Fall, 1986).

Bibliography

MANUSCRIPTS

British Museum, London

Deciphers of Diplomatic Papers. vol. 51. America 1780–1841; Add. Mss., 32, 303.

Dropmore Papers. Correspondence and Papers of William Wyndham Grenville. Add. Mss., 58855–59494.

Haldimand Papers. Correspondence and Papers of Governor-General Sir Frederick Haldimand, 1758–1791; Add. Mss., 21661–892.

Journal of a Voyage performed by Order of the N.W. Company, in a Bark Canoe in search of a Passage by water through the N.W. Continent of America from Athabasca to the Pacific Ocean in summer 1789 (by Alexander Mackenzie); Stowe Mss., 793.

Liverpool Papers. The Papers of Charles Jenkinson, First Earl of Liverpool (1728–1808), and of Robert Jenkinson, Second Earl of Liverpool (1770–1828), and supplement; Add. Mss., 38190–38489; 38564–81.

Melville Papers. Letters and Papers from the correspondence of Henry Dundas, First Viscount Melville, and of Robert Saunder Dundas, Second Viscount Melville; Add. Mss., 40100–102; 41079–85.

Miscellaneous American Papers (1718–1796); Add. Mss., 24, 322.

Windham Papers. Official and private correspondence and papers of William Windham; Add. Mss., 37842–935.

Edinburgh University Library

Andrew Brown. (Unfinished) History of North America (dealing mainly with the Indians and the latter half of the eighteenth century) and his notes relating thereto: 7 boxes, GEN. 154–59.
Curiosities presented to the Edinburgh Royal Society by Andrew Graham, late factor to the Honble Hudson's Bay Company with a true account of them, Jan. 1787; in Ms. Dc. 1.57.

Leeds Public Libraries, Department of Archives

George Canning Papers.

National Library of Scotland, Edinburgh

Cochrane Papers. Correspondence and papers, private and official, of Admiral the Hon. Sir Alexander Forrester Inglis Cochrane, G.C.B., and of his son Admiral Sir Thomas John Cochrane, K.C.B., from 1779 to 1856; Mss., 2264–505; 2568–608 (material relating to the North American Station is in Mss., 2326–49, 2450, 2574–75).
Correspondence and papers of the Eighth Marquis of Tweedale, including correspondence and military returns connected with his service in the Peninsular War, 1811–1813, and in Canada, 1814–1815; Mss., 7100–1 (in Yester Papers).
Letter of Colonel Allan Maclean at Montreal concerning the conduct of the Governor of Canada and the British alliance with Iroquois, 1779; Ms. 8250, ff. 34–36 (in Stuart Stevenson Papers).
Liston Papers. Mss., 5510–721 (The Papers of Sir Robert Liston in Philadelphia (incorrectly catalogued as Washington) 1796–1801 are in Mss., 5583–93; the Journals of Lady Liston in North America are in Mss., 5696–704).
Melville Papers. Mss. 3841; 3847–49, 3851.
Murray Papers. Correspondence and papers of General Sir George Murray; Advocate Mss., 46.6.5–6.

Newberry Library, Chicago

Letter Book of John Norton (Teyoninhokarawen), Ayer Mss. 654.
Memorandum of several things wished by the Mohocks . . . by Jos. Brant, Ayer Mss. 106.

Public Archives of Canada, Ottawa

Claus (Family) Papers. MG 19, F1, Reel C–1478–1485.
Brant Family Papers. MG 19, F6, Reel C–6818.
McKee Papers. MG 19 F16 (1 folio).
William McKay Papers. MG 19 F29 (1 folder).

Public Records Office, Kew, England

Admiralty Papers. In-Letters; Adm. 1 (Adm. 1/480–509. Letters
    from Admirals on the North American Station 1745–1815).
Admiralty Papers. Out-Letters; Adm 2. (Adm. 2/114–68. Orders
    and Instructions 1783–1815; Adm. 2/932–33: Letters to
    Commanders in Chief at Stations Abroad: North America,
    1808–1815; Adm. 2/1342–82. Secret Orders and Letters
    1783–1815).
Admiralty Papers. Various; Adm. 49.
Admiralty Papers. Out-Letters; Adm. 98 (1742–1816).
Colonial Office Records. Class 5: America and the West Indies
    C.O. 5.
Colonial Office Records. Class 42: Canada; C.O. 42.
Colonial Office Records. Class 43: Entry Books; C.O. 43.
Foreign Office Records. America, United States of, Series 1,
    1782–1792; F.O. 4.
Foreign Office Records. America, United States of, Series 2,
    1793–; F.O. 5.
Foreign Office Records. Protocols of Treaties, United States of
    America; F.O. 93/8.
Foreign Office Records. Ratifications of Treaties, United States
    of America; F.O. 94.
Foreign Office Records. Miscellanea, Series 1; F.O. 95 (F.O. 95/1:
    Miscellanea 1781–1815; F.O. 95/512–15).
Foreign Office Records. Supplement to General Correspon-
    dence, America, United States of; F.O. 97 (vols. 1–9).
Foreign Office Records. America, United States of, Correspon-
    dence 1791–; F.O. 115.
Foreign Office Records. America, United States of, Letter Books
    1791–1823; F.O. 116.
Gifts and Deposits. Carleton Papers or Headquarters Papers of
    the British Army in America; P.R.O. 30/55.
Gifts and Deposits. Chatham Papers; P.R.O. 30/8.
Privy Council Office. Unbound Papers; P.C. 1 (P.C. 1/58–66: Co-
    lonial Papers 1677–1799).

Privy Council Office. Privy Council Register; P.C. 2 (P.C. 2/128–97: Oct. 1782–Jan. 1816).
War Office. In-Letters; W.O. 1 (esp. vols. 14, 96, 141–43).
War Office. Out-Letters, Commander in Chief; W.O. 3 (W.O. 3/602–8).
War Office. Out-Letters, Secretary at War: W.O. 4 (W.O. 4/275–81).
War Office. Out-Letters, Secretary of State; W.O. 6 (esp. vol. 2).
War Office. H.Q. Records; W.O. 28 (esp. vol. 10).
War Office. American Rebellion: Entry Books, 1773–1783; 1798–1799, 4 vols.; W.O. 36.
War Office. Commissariat, In-Letters; W.O. 57 (vols. 10, 14, 15).
War Office. Commissariat, Out-Letters; W.O. 58 (vols. 63–65).
War Office. Courts-Martial Proceedings; W.O. 71 (W.O. 71/243: Brigadier General Henry Procter's court-martial).

Royal Commonwealth Society, London

Journal of a Journey in North-West Canada, commencing 21st July 1794 by Duncan McGillivray.
Narrative of the Establishment on the Sources of the Columbia. . . (or) Narrative of the Expedition to the Kootenae & Flat Bow Indian Countries, on the Sources of the Columbia River, Pacific Ocean by D. Thompson on behalf of the N.W. Company 1807.
Remarks on the Countries westward of the Rocky Mountains with reference to the Rough Chart.—by D[avid] T[hompson] 1813.
Some account of the trade carried on by the North West Company.—by W. McGillivray.

Scottish Records Office, H. M. General Register House, Edinburgh

Letter book containing the American correspondence of the S.S.P.C.K. (Society in Scotland for Propagating Christian Knowledge); G.D./95/3/1.
Melville Castle Muniments. G.D. 51

United Society for the Propagation of the Gospel, London

"C. Mss." Canada.
Journals of the Proceedings of the Society for the Propagation of the Gospel.

Warrington Central Library

Account of Visits to the Indians in 1802 and 1803, by Ann Mifflin. Philadelphia. Ms. No. 45.

Wisconsin State Historical Society

Draper Mss. On microfilm. Series F. Brant Manuscripts; G: Brant Miscellanies; YY: Tecumseh Papers.

NEWSPAPERS AND OTHER CONTEMPORARY PERIODICALS

The Annual Register, 1776–1819
The Daily Universal Register, 1785–1787
The Edinburgh Annual Register, 1808–1814
The Edinburgh Review, 1802–1822
The Gentleman's Magazine, 1782–1820
The Leeds Intelligencer, 1780–1818
The Leeds Mercury, 1780–1818
The New Annual Register, 1780–1818
The Quarterly Review, 1809–1825
The Scots Magazine, 1780–1817
The Times, 1785–1820

DISSERTATIONS

Allen, Robert S. "Red and White: The Indian Tribes of the Ohio Valley and Anglo-American Relations, 1783–1796." M.A. thesis, Dalhousie University, Halifax, Nova Scotia, 1970.

Blakeslee, Donald J. "The Plains Interband Trade System: An Ethnohistoric and Archaeological Investigation." Ph.D. dissertation, University of Wisconsin–Milwaukee, 1975.

Chalou, George Clifford. "The Red Pawns Go to War: British-American Indian Relations, 1810–1815," Ph.D. dissertation, Indiana University, 1971.

Chernow, Barbara Ann. "American Indian Policy and Great Britain, 1789–1796." M.A. thesis, Columbia University, 1969.

Gotz, Herbert Charles Walker, Jr. "Tecumseh, The Prophet and the Rise of the Northwest Indian Confederation." Ph.D. dissertation, University of Western Ontario, 1973.

Hatheway, Glover G. "The Neutral Indian Barrier State: A Project in British North American Policy, 1754–1815." Ph.D. dissertation, University of Minnesota, 1957.

Horsman, Reginald. "British Opinion and the United States of America 1806–1812." M.A. thesis, Birmingham University, 1955.

Humphreys, B. "Sir Alexander Cochrane and the Conclusion of the American War, 1813–1815." M.A. thesis, University of Liverpool, 1960.

McGinnis, Anthony Robert. "Intertribal Conflict on the Northern Plains, 1738–1889." Ph.D. dissertation, University of Colorado, 1974.

Mitcham, Peter. "The Attitude of British Travellers to North America Between 1790 and 1850." Ph.D. dissertation, Edinburgh University, 1958.

Monahan, Forrest Dewey, Jr. "Trade Goods on the Prairie: The Kiowa Tribe and White Trade Goods, 1794–1875." Ph.D. dissertation, University of Oklahoma, 1965.

Stevens, Paul Lawrence. "His Majesty's 'Savage' Allies: British Policy and the Northern Indians During the Revolutionary War. The Carleton Years, 1774–1778." Ph.D. dissertation, State University of New York at Buffalo, 1984.

PRINTED PRIMARY SOURCES

Abel, Annie Heloise, ed. *Tabeau's Narrative of Loisel's Expedition to the Upper Missouri*. 2d ed. Norman: University of Oklahoma Press, 1968.

———. "Trudeau's Description of the Upper Missouri." *Mississippi Valley Historical Review*, 8 (1921): 149–79.

Accounts of Two Attempts Towards the Civilization of Some Indian Natives. London: Phillips & Fardon, 1806.

Anburey, Thomas. *Travels Through the Interior Parts of America. In a Series of Letters. By an Officer*. Reprint of 1789 ed. 2 vols. New York: New York Times & Arno Press, 1969.

Ashe, Thomas. *Travels in America, Performed in the year 1806*. . . . London: Richard Phillips, 1809.

[Atcheson, Nathaniel]. "A Compressed View of the Points to be Discussed in Treating With the United States of America. . . . By the author of 'American Enchroachments on British Rights.'" *The Pamphleteer*, 5, no. 9, (Feb. 1815): 105–39.

Bassett, John Spencer, ed. *The Correspondence of Andrew Jackson*. Vols. 1–2. Washington: Carnegie Institution, 1926–27.

Baynton, Benjamin. *Authentic Memoirs of William Augustus Bowles, Esquire, Ambassador From the United Nations of Creeks and Cherokees, to the Court of London.* London: R. Faulder, 1791.

Benians, E. A., ed. *A Journal by Thos. Hughes. For his Amusement & Designed Only for his Perusal by the Time He Attains the Age of 50 If He Lives So Long (1778–1789).* Cambridge: University Press, 1947.

Beresford, William. *A Voyage Round the World: But More Particularly to the North-West Coast of America: Performed in 1785, 1787, and 1788. . . .* London: Geo. Goulding, 1789.

Blake, Warren Barton, ed. *Letters from an American Farmer by Hector St. John De Crèvecoeur.* Everyman ed. London: J. M. Dent & Sons, Ltd., 1945.

Boulton, D'Arcy. *Sketch of His Majesty's Province of Upper Canada.* London: 1805.

Boyce, Douglas W., ed. "A Glimpse of Iroquois Culture and History Through the Eyes of Joseph Brant and John Norton." *Proceedings of the American Philosophical Society,* 117 (1973): 286–94.

Brannan, John, ed. *Official Letters of the Military and Naval Officers of the United States, During the War with Great Britain in the Years 1812, 13, 14, & 15. . . .* Reprint of Washington, 1823 ed. New York: New York Times & Arno Press, Inc., 1971.

Burpee, Lawrence J., ed. "An Adventurer from Hudson Bay: Journal of Matthew Cocking, From York Factory to the Blackfeet Country, 1772–73." *Trans R.S.C.,* 3d ser., 2 (1908), section 2:89–121.

————. "Journal De Larocque de la Rivière Assiniboine Jusqu'à la Rivière 'Aux Roches Jaunes,' in 1805." *Publications of the Public Archives of Canada,* 3 (1911).

Butterfield, Consul Willshire, ed. *Journal of Captain Jonathon Heart, on the March With His Company from Connecticut to Fort Pitt . . . 1785 . . . To Which is Added the Dickinson-Harmar Correspondence of 1784–5.* Albany, N.Y.: Joel Munsell's Sons, 1885.

Byfield, Shadrach. "A Narrative of a Light Company Soldier's Service in the 41st Regiment of Foot, during the late American War: Together With Some Adventures Amongst the Indian Tribes from 1812 to 1814." Bradford, Wilts; John Bubb, 1840. Reprinted New York: William Abbot, 1910, being extra no. 11 of the *Magazine of History* with Notes and Queries (1910): 57–95 (345–84 fac.). (Also in John Gellner, ed., *Recollections of the War of 1812.* Toronto: Baxter Publishing Co., 1964, 1–45.)

[Canada]. *Indian Treaties and Surrenders. From 1680 to 1890.* 2 vols. Ottawa: The Queen's Printer, 1891 (Facsimile ed. reprinted by Coles Publishing Co., Toronto, 1971).

————. Reports on the Canadian Archives. Ottawa, 1872–.

Carter, Clarence Edwin, ed. *The Territorial Papers of the United States.* 28 vols. Washington: U.S. Government Printing Office, 1934–1975.

Cartwright, C. E., ed. *Life and Letters of the Late Hon. Richard Cartwright, Member of Legislative Council in the first Parliament of Upper Canada.* Toronto: Belford Brothers, 1876.

Cass, Lewis. "Policy and Practice of the United States and Great Britain in Their Treatment of Indians. . . ." *North American Review,* 24 (1827): 365–442.

Casselman, Alexander Clark, ed. *Richardson's War of 1812.* Toronto: Historical Publishing Co. (The Bryant Press), 1902.

Clark, William. "William Clark's Journal of General Wayne's Campaign." *Mississippi Valley Historical Review,* 1 (1914–15): 418–44.

Coates, William. "A Narrative of An Embassy to the Western Indians, From the Original Manuscript of Hendrick Aupaumut." *Memoirs of the Historical Society of Pennsylvania,* 2 (1827), pt. 1: 61–131.

Cometti, Elizabeth, ed. *The American Journal of Lt. John Enys.* New York: Syracuse University Press, 1976.

[Connolly, John]. "A Narrative of the Transactions, Imprisonment, and Sufferings of John Connolly, an American Loyalist and Lieut. Col. in His Majesty's Service." *Pennsylvania Magazine of History and Biography,* 12 : 310–24, 407–20; 13 : 61–70, 153–67, 281–91.

Cooke, John Henry. *A Narrative of Events in the South of France, and of the Attack on New Orleans, in 1814 and 1815. By Captain John Henry Cooke, Late of the 43rd Regiment of Light Infantry.* London: T. & W. Boone, 1835.

Cooper, John Spencer. *Rough Notes of Seven Campaigns in Portugal, Spain, France, and America, During the Years 1809–10–11–12–13–14–15. By John Spencer Cooper, Late Sergeant in the 7th Royal Fusiliers.* London: John Russell Smith; Carlisle: Geo. Coward, 1869.

Cooper, Thomas. *Some Information Respecting America, Collected by Thomas Cooper, late of Manchester.* Dublin and London, 1794. Reprinted New York: Augustus M. Kelley, 1969.

Coues, Elliott, ed. *New Light on the Early History of the Greater Northwest: The Manuscript Journals of Alexander Henry and David Thompson, 1799–1814. . . .* 2 vols. Reprint ed. Minneapolis: Ross & Haines, Inc., 1965.

Cox, Ross. *Adventures on the Columbia River, Including the Narrative of a Residence of Six Years on the Western Side of the Rocky Mountains, Among Various Tribes of Indians Hitherto Unknown: Together*

With a Journey Across the American Continent. 2 vols. London: Henry Colburn & Richard Bentley, 1831.

Cruikshank, Ernest A., ed. *The Correspondence of Lieutenant Governor John Graves Simcoe. With Allied Documents Relating to His Administration of the Government of Upper Canada* 5 vols. Toronto: Ontario Historical Society, 1923–31.

————. ed. "The Diary of an Officer in the Indian Country in 1794." *American Historical Magazine.* 3 (1908):639–43.

————. *The Documentary History of the Campaigns on the Niagara Frontier, 1812–1814.* 9 vols. Welland, Ont.: Lundy's Lane Historical Society, 1896–1908.

————. "Documents Relating to the Invasion of Canada and the Surrender of Detroit, 1812," *Publications of the Public Archives of Canada,* 7 (1912).

Cruishank, E. A., and Hunter, A. F., eds. *The Correspondence of the Honourable Peter Russell. . . .* 3 vols. Toronto: Ontario Historical Society, 1932–36.

Dalrymple, Alex. *Plan for Promoting the Fur-Trade, and Securing It to This Country, by Uniting the Operations of the East India and Hudson's Bay Companys.* London: George Bigg, 1789. Reprint ed. Montreal: I. Ehrlich, 1975.

Davis, Richard Beale, ed. *Jeffersonian America: Notes on the United States of America Collected in the Years 1805–6–7 and 11–12 by Sir Augustus John Foster, Bart.* San Marino, Calif.: The Huntington Library, 1954.

De Peyster, J. Watts, ed. *Miscellanies by an Officer, By Colonel Arent Schuyler de Peyster, 1774–1813. With an Appendix, Explanatory Notes & c., Original Letters of Col. De Peyster, Brig. Gen. Sir John Johnson Bart., Col. Guy Johnson, and others from 1776 to 1813 Never Before Published. . . .* New York: A. E. Chasmer & Co., 1888.

Donnan, Elizabeth, ed. "The Papers of James A. Bayard, 1796–1815." *Annual Report of the American Historical Association* for 1913, 2. Also, *Historical Manuscripts Commission,* 11 (London: His Majesty's Stationary Office, 1913).

Doughty, Arthur G., ed. "Some Account of the Trade Carried On By the Northwest Company (1809)." *Report of Public Archives of Canada,* 1928, Appendix E: 56–73.

Douglas, David, ed. *Familiar Letters of Sir Walter Scott.* 2 vols. Edinburgh: David Douglas, 1894.

Douglas, R., ed. *Nipigon to Winnipeg: A Canoe Voyage Through Western Ontario by Edward Umfreville in 1784. With Extracts From the Writings of Other Earlier Travellers Through the Region.* Ottawa: R. Douglas, 1929.

Dunlop, William. *Recollections of the American War, 1812–14.*

Toronto: The Historical Publishing Co. (The Bryant Press, Ltd.), 1905.

Edgar, Matilda, ed. *Ten Years of Upper Canada in Peace and War, 1805–1815; Being the Ridout Letters, . . . Also an Appendix of the Narrative of the Captivity Among the Shawanese Indians, in 1788, of Thos. Ridout, After Surveyor-General of Upper Canada; . . .* London: T. Fisher Unwin, 1891.

Einstine, Lewis, ed. "Recollections of the War of 1812 by George Hay, Eighth Marquis of Tweeddale." *American Historical Review,* 32 (1927): 69–78.

Fitzpatrick, John C., ed. *The Writings of George Washington.* 37 vols. Washington: U.S. Government Printing Office, 1931–44.

Forsyth, Thomas. "The French, British and Spanish Methods of Treating Indians & c.—" *Ethnohistory,* 4 (1957): 210–17.

Gates, Charles M., ed. *Five Fur Traders of the Northwest: Being the Narrative of Peter Pond and the Diaries of John Macdonnel, Archibald N. McLeod, Hugh Faries, and Thomas Connor.* Minneapolis: University of Minnesota Press, 1933. Reprinted. Saint Paul: Minnesota Historical Society, 1971.

Gellner, John, ed. *Recollections of the War of 1812: Three Eyewitnesses' Accounts.* Toronto: Baxter Publishing Co., 1964.

Gleig, G. R. *A Narrative of the Campaigns of the British Army at Washington and New Orleans, Under Generals Ross, Pakenham, and Lambert, in the Years 1814 and 1815; With Some Account of the Countries Visited. By An Officer Who Served in the Expedition.* London: John Murray, 1821.

Glover, Richard, ed. *David Thompson's Narrative, 1784–1812.* Toronto: The Champlain Society, 1962.

Graham, G. S., ed. "The Indian Menace and the Retention of the Western Posts." *Canadian Historical Review,* 15 (1934): 46–48.

Gray, Hugh. *Letters from Canada, Written During a Residence There in the Years 1806, 1807, and 1808; . . .* London: Longman, Hurst, Rees, & Orme, 1809 (facsimile ed. reprinted by Coles Publishing Co., Toronto, 1971).

[Great Britain]. *British and Foreign State Papers.* Vols. 1–7 (1812–20). London: James Ridgway & Sons, 1834–41.

————. "Report on American Manuscripts (formerly) in the Royal Institution of Great Britain (now in P.R.O.)." 4 vols. *Historical Manuscripts Commission,* 59. London: His Majesty's Stationary Office, 1904–09).

————. "Report on the Manuscripts of Earl Bathurst, Preserved at Cirencester Park." *Historical Manuscripts Commission,* 76. London: His Majesty's Stationary Office, 1923.

————. "Report on the Laing Manuscripts Preserved in the University of Edinburgh, 2. *Historical Manuscripts Commission, 27.* London: His Majesty's Stationary Office, 1925.

————. "Report on the Manuscripts of J. B. Fortescue, Esq. (formerly) Preserved at Dropmore (now in B.M.)." 10 vols. *Historical Manuscripts Commission, 30.* London: His Majesty's Stationary Office, 1892–1927.

————. "Report on the Manuscripts of Mrs. Stopford Sackville of Drayton House, Northamptonshire." 2 vols. *Historical Manuscripts Commission, 49.* London: His Majesty's Stationary Office, 1904–10.

Hamilton, Milton W., ed. "Guy Johnson's Opinions on the American Indian." *Pennsylvania Magazine of History and Biography,* 77 (1953):311–27.

Harlow, Vincent, and Madden, Frederick, eds. *British Colonial Developments 1774–1834: Select Documents.* Oxford: The Clarendon Press, 1953.

Hawkins, Benjamin. "Letters of Benjamin Hawkins, 1796–1806." *Collections of the Georgia Historical Society,* 9 (1916).

Heckewelder, The Reverend John. *History, Manners, and Customs of Indian Nations Who Once Inhabited Pennsylvania and the Neighboring States.* New and rev. ed. Philadelphia, 1876. Reprint ed. New York: Arno Press & the New York Times, 1971.

Heriot, George. *Travels through the Canadas, . . . To Which is Subjoined a Comparative View of the Manners and Customs of Several of the Indian Nations of North and South America.* London: R. Phillips, 1807.

Hickerson, Harold, ed. "Journal of Charles Jean Baptiste Chaboillez 1797–1798." *Ethnohistory,* 6 (1959):265–316, 363–427.

Hill, Benson Earle. *Recollections of an Artillery Officer: Including Scenes and Adventures in Ireland, America, Flanders, and France.* 2 vols. London: Richard Bentley, 1836.

Holmes, Jack D. L., ed. *Journal of a Tour in Unsettled Parts of North America in 1796 & 1797. By Francis Baily.* Edwardsville, Ill.: Southern Illinois University Press, 1969.

Howay, F. W., ed. *The Journal of Captain James Colnett Aboard the Argonaut from April 26, 1789 to Nov. 3, 1791.* Toronto: The Champlain Society, 1940.

Hunter, John D. *Memoirs of a Captivity Among the Indians of North America, from Childhood to the Age of Nineteen: With Anecdotes Descriptive of Their Manners and Customs. . . .* London: Longman, Hurst, Rees, Orme & Brown, 1823.

Imlay, Gilbert. *A Topographical Description of the Western Territory of*

North America;... And An Accurate Statement of the Various Tribes of Indians That Inhabit the Frontier Country.... In a Series of Letters to a Friend in England. New York: Samuel Campbell, 1793.

Innis, Mary Quayle, ed., *Mrs. Simcoe's Diary.* Toronto: The Macmillan Co. of Canada, Ltd., 1965.

"Instructions and Dispatches of the British Ghent Commission." *Massachusetts Historical Society Proceedings,* 47 (1914): 138–62.

Jackman, S. W., ed., "A Young Englishman Reports on the New Nation: Edward Thornton to James Bland Burges, 1791–1793." *William & Mary Quarterly,* 3d Series, 18 (1961): 85–121.

Jackson, Donald, ed., *Black Hawk (Ma-Ka-Tai-Me-She-Kia-Kiak): An Autobiography.* Urbana, Ill.: University of Illinois Press, 1955.

———. *The Journals of Zebulon Montgomery Pike, With Letters and Related Documents.* 2 vols. Norman: University of Oklahoma Press, 1966.

James, Edwin, ed., *A Narrative of the Captivity and Adventures of John Tanner During Thirty Years' Residence Among the Indians in the Interior of North America.* Reprint ed. Minneapolis: Ross & Haines, Inc., 1956.

James, William. *A Full and Correct Account of the Military Occurrences of the Late War Between Great Britain and the United States of America.* 2 vols. London: printed for the author, 1818.

Jameson, J. Franklin, ed., "Letters of Phineas Bond, British Consul at Philadelphia, to the Foreign Office of Great Britain (1787–1794)." *Annual Report of the American Historical Association* for 1896, 1: 513–659; and for 1897, 454–568.

Jarvis, W. "Letters from W. Jarvis, Secretary for Upper Canada, and Mrs. Jarvis to the Rev. Samuel Peters, D.D. Between the years 1792 and 1813...." *Women's Canadian Historical Society of Toronto, Trans.,* 23 (1922–23): 11–63.

Jeremy, David John, ed., "Henry Wansey and his American Journal 1794." *Memoirs of the American Philosophical Society,* 82 (1970).

Jewitt, John R. *The Adventures and Sufferings of John R. Jewitt, Only Survivor of the Ship 'Boston', During a Captivity of Nearly Three Years Among the Savages of Nootka Sound: With an Account of the Manners, Mode of Living, and Religious Opinions of the Natives.* Edinburgh: Archd. Constable & Co., 1824.

Johnson, Alice M., ed. *Saskatchewan Journals and Correspondence.* London: Hudson's Bay Record Society, 1967.

Johnston, Charles M., ed. *The Valley of the Six Nations: A Collection of Documents on the Indian lands of the Grand River.* Toronto: The Champlain Society, 1964.

Johnston, Henry P., ed. *The Correspondence and Public Papers of John Jay*. 4 vols. New York & London: G. P. Putnam's Sons, 1890–93.

Jones, W. D., ed. "A British View of the War of 1812 and the Peace Negotiations." *Mississippi Valley Historical Review*, 45 (1958–59):481–88.

Kappler, Charles J., ed. *Indian Treaties, 1778–1883*. New York: AMS Press, 1972. Reprint of Kappler's *Indian Affairs: Laws and Treaties*, vol. 2 (Washington, D.C.: U.S. Government Printing Office, 1904).

Kinnaird, Lawrence J., ed. "Spain in the Mississippi Valley, 1765–1794: Translation of Materials from the Spanish Archives in the Bancroft Library. Part II: Post War Decade, 1782–1791." *Annual Report of the American Historical Association* for 1945, 3.

Klinck, Carl F., ed. *Tecumseh: Fact and Fiction in Early Records*. Englewood Cliffs, N.J.: Prentice Hall, Inc., 1961.

Klinck, Carl F., and Talman, James J., eds. *The Journal of Major John Norton 1816*. Toronto: The Champlain Society, 1970.

Knopf, Richard C., ed. *Anthony Wayne, A Name in Arms: The Wayne–Knox–Pickering–McHenry Correspondence*. Pittsburgh: University of Pittsburgh Press, 1960.

Lajeunesse, Ernest J., ed. *The Windsor Border Region: Canada's Southern-most Frontier: A Collection of Documents*. Toronto: The Champlain Society, 1960.

Lamb, Roger. *An Original and Authentic Journal of Occurrences During the Late American War, From Its Commencement to the Year 1783. By R. Lamb, Late Serjeant in the Royal Welch Fuzileers*. New York: New York Times & Arno Press, reprint ed., 1968.

Lamb, W. Kaye, ed. *Gabriel Franchère's Journal of a Voyage on the North West Coast of North America During the Years 1811, 1812, 1813 and 1814*. Toronto: The Champlain Society, 1969.

———, ed. *The Journals and Letters of Sir Alexander Mackenzie*. Cambridge: Cambridge University Press for the Hakluyt Society, 1970.

———, ed. *The Letters and Journals of Simon Fraser 1806–1808*. Toronto: The Macmillan Co. of Canada Ltd., 1960.

———, ed. *Sixteen Years in the Indian Country: The Journal of Daniel Williams Harmon, 1800–1816*. Toronto: The Macmillan Co. of Canada, Ltd., 1957.

Lambert, John. *Travels through Canada and the United States of North America in the Years 1806, 1807, and 1808. . . .* 2 vols. 2d ed. London: Cradock & Joy, 1814.

Landmann, George. *Adventures and Recollections of Colonel Landmann, Late of the Corps of Royal Engineers.* 2 vols. in 1. London: Colburn & Co., 1852.

Langton, H. H., ed. *Travels in the Interior Inhabited Parts of North America in the Years 1791 and 1792 by P. Campbell.* Toronto: The Champlain Society, 1937.

Lincoln, General Benjamin. "Journal of a Treaty held in 1793, with the Indian Tribes northwest of the Ohio by Commissioners of the United States." *Collections of the Massachusetts Historical Society,* 3d ser., 5 (1836): 109–76.

Longford, Thomas Pakenham, Earl of, ed. *Pakenham Letters, 1800 to 1815.* London: privately printed, John & Edward Bumpus, Ltd., 1914.

Lord, Norman C., ed. "The War on the Canadian Frontier, 1812–14: Letters Written by Sergt. James Commins, 8th Foot." *Journal of the Society for Army Historical Research,* 18 (1939): 199–211.

Loudon, Archibald, ed. *A Selection, of Some of the Most Interesting Narratives, of Outrages Committed by the Indians, in Their Wars With the White People. . . .* Carlisle, Pa., 1808. Reprint ed. 2 vols. in 1. New York: Arno Press, Inc., 1971.

Lowrie, Walter, and Clarke, Matthew St. Clair, eds. *American State Papers. Class II. Indian Affairs. 1789–1827.* 2 vols. Washington: Gales & Seaton, 1832–34.

McAfee, Robert Breckinridge. *History of the Late War in the Western Country.* Ann Arbor: University Microfilms, Inc., 1966 (facsimile of 1816 ed.).

McDermott, John Francis, ed. *Memoir or a Cursory Glance at My Different Travels & My Sojourn in the Creek Nation. By Louis Le Clerc de Milford.* Chicago: The Lakeside Press, R. R. Donnelly & Sons Co., 1956.

Mair, John. "Journal of John Mair, 1791," *A.H.R.,* 12 (1906–07): 77–94.

Manning, William R., ed. *Diplomatic Correspondence of the United States: Canadian Relations 1784–1860.* 1: 1784–1820. Washington: Carnegie Endowment for International Peace, 1940.

Marbois, Francois de. "Marbois on the Fur Trade, 1784." *American Historical Review,* 29 (1923–24): 725–40.

Masson, L. R., ed. *Les Bourgeois de la Compagnie du Nord-Ouest: Recits de Voyages, Lettres et Rapports inedits relatifs au Nord-Ouest Canadien.* 2 vols. Quebec: De L'Imprimerie Generale A Cote et Cie, 1889–90.

Maude, John. *Visit to the Falls of Niagara in 1800.* London: Longman, Rees, Orme, Brown & Green; and Wakefield: Richard Nichols, 1826.

Mayo, Bernard, ed. "Instructions to the British Ministers to the United States, 1791–1812." *Annual Report of the American Historical Association* for 1936, 3.

Melish, John. *Travels Through the United States of America, in the Years 1806 & 1807, and 1809, 1810, & 1811. . . .* London: George Cowie & Co., 1818.

Michigan. *Collections of the Michigan Pioneer Historical Society.* 40 vols. Lansing, Michigan, 1874–1929.

Morton, Arthur S., ed. *The Journal of Duncan McGillivray of the North West Company, at Fort George on the Saskatchewan, 1794–5.* Toronto: The Macmillan Co. of Canada, Ltd, 1929.

Nasatir, Abraham P., ed. *Before Lewis and Clark: Documents Illustrating the History of the Missouri, 1785–1804.* 2 vols. Saint Louis: Saint Louis Historical Documents Foundation, 1952.

Neilson, Colonel J.L.H., ed. "Diary of an Officer in the War of 1812–14." *Queen's Quarterly,* 2 (1895):318–28; 3 (1895):23–30.

O'Neil, Marion, ed. "The Peace River Journal, 1799–1800." *Washington Historical Quarterly* (1928), 250–70.

Parkinson, Richard. *A Tour in America, in 1798, 1799, and 1800.* 2 vols. in 1. London: J. Harding & J. Murray, 1805.

The Parliamentary Debates, From the Year 1802 to the Present Time. London: T. C. Hansard, 1812–.

The Parliamentary History of England, From the Earliest Period to the Year 1803. London: T. C. Hansard, 1806–1820.

The Parliamentary Register, 1775–1813. London: J. Debrett, 1775–1803; John Stockdale, 1800–1813.

Perrin du Lac, M. Francois. *Travels through the Two Louisianas and Among the Savage Nations of the Missouri. . . .* London: Richard Phillips, 1807.

Pinkerton, John. *Modern Geography: A Description of the Empires, Kingdoms, States, and Colonies. . . .* 3d ed. London: Longman, Hurst, Rees, Orme & Brown, 1811.

Portlock, William Henry. *A New, Complete, and Universal Collection of authentic Voyages and Travels, To All the Various Parts of the World. . . .* London: Alexander Hogg & Co., 1794.

Preston, Richard A., ed. *Kingston Before the War of 1812: A Collection of Documents.* Toronto: The Champlain Society, 1959.

Priest, William. *Travels in the United States of America: Commencing in the Year 1793 and Ending in 1797. . . .* London: J. Johnson, 1802.

[Proctor, George]. *The Lucubrations of Humphrey Ravelin, Esq., Late Major in the ** Regiment of Infantry.* 2d ed. London: G. & W. B. Whittaker, 1824.

Proposal for Forming a Society for Promoting the Civilization and Improvement of the North-American Indians, Within the British Boundary. London: J. Brettell, 1806.

Quaife, Milo Milton, ed. *Alexander Ross: Adventures of the First Settlers on the Oregon or Columbia River.* Chicago: The Lakeside Press, R. R. Donnelley & Sons Co., 1923.

————, ed. "General James Wilkinson's Narrative of the Fallen Timbrs Campaign." *Mississippi Valley Historical Review,* 16 (1929–30):81–90.

————, ed. *The Indian Captivity of O. M. Spencer.* New York: Citadel Press, 1965.

————. *The John Askin Papers.* 2 vols. Detroit: Detroit Library Commission (Burton Historical Collection, Records), 1928–31.

————. *John Long's Voyages and Travels, in the Years 1768–1788.* Chicago: The Lakeside Press, R. R. Donnelley & Sons Co., 1922.

————. *War on the Detroit: The Chronicles of Thomas Verchères de Bourcherville and the Capitulation by an Ohio Volunteer.* Chicago: The Lakeside Press, R. R. Donnelley & Sons Co., 1940.

Rich, Edwin, ed. *Cumberland and Hudson House Journals 1775–82.* 2d ser., 1779–82. London: Hudson's Bay Record Society, 1952.

————. *Moose Fort Journals, 1783–85.* London: Hudson's Bay Record Society, 1954.

Ritchie, Carson I. A., ed. "British Documents on the Louisiana Campaign, 1814–15." *Louisiana Historical Quarterly,* 44 (1961): 104–21.

Robertson, Donald S., ed. *An Englishman in America 1785. Being the Diary of Joseph Hadfield.* Toronto: The Hunter-Rose Co., Ltd., 1933.

Rollins, Philip Ashton, ed. *The Discovery of the Oregon Trail: Robert Stuart's Narratives of His Overland Trip from Astoria in 1812–13.* . . . New York and London: Charles Scribner's Sons, 1935.

Roseberry, Earl of, ed. *The Windham Papers: The Life and Correspondence of the Rt. Hon. William Windham 1750–1810.* 2 vols. London: Herbert Jenkins Ltd., 1913.

Ross, Daniel J. J., and Chappell, Bruce S., eds. "Visit to the Indian Nations: The Diary of John Hambly." *Florida Historical Quarterly,* 54 (1976):60–73.

Selkirk, Thomas Douglas, Fifth Earl of. *A Sketch of the British Fur Trade in North America: With Observations Relative to the North-West Company of Montreal.* London: James Ridgway, 1816.

Smith, G. C. Moore, ed. *The Autobiography of Sir Harry Smith, 1787–1819.* London: John Murray, 1910.

Smith, William Henry, ed. *The St. Clair Papers: The Life and Public*

Services of Arthur St. Clair, . . . With His Correspondence and Other Papers. 2 vols. Cincinnati: Robert Clarke & Co., 1882.

Smyth, John Ferdinand Dalziel. *A Tour in the United States of America: . . . With a Description of the Indian Nations. . . .* 2 vols. London: G. Robinson, 1784.

S.P.G. *Annual Reports of the Society for the Propagation of the Gospel* (1776–1819). (In the Archives Department of U.S.P.G. London).

————. *The Book of Common Prayer, . . . Formerly Collected, and Translated Into the Mohawk Language Under the Direction of the Missionaries of the Society for the Propagation of the Gospel in Foreign Parts, to the Mohawk Indians. A New Edition; To Which is Added The Gospel According to St. Mark, Translated into the Mohawk Language, By Captn. Joseph Brant, an Indian of the Mohawk Nation.* London, 1787. (In the Archives Department of the U.S.P.G.)

Spragge, George W., ed. *The John Strachan Letter Book: 1812–1834.* Toronto: Ontario Historical Society, 1946.

Squier, E. G., ed. "Observations on the Creek and Cherokee Indians. By William Bartram, 1789." *Transactions of the American Ethnological Society,* 3 (1853):1–81.

Stacey, Colonel C. P., ed. "Upper Canada at War, 1814: Captain Armstrong Reports," *Ontario History,* 48 (1956):37–42.

St. Clair, Arthur. *A Narrative of the Manner in Which the Campaign Against the Indians in the Year 1791, Was Conducted, Under the Command of Major General St. Clair, . . .* Philadelphia, 1812. Reprint ed. New York: Arno Press, Inc., 1971.

Stoddard, Major Amos. *Sketches, Historical and Descriptive of Louisiana.* Philadelphia: Mathew Carey, 1812.

Strickland, The Reverend J. E., ed. "Journal of a Tour in the United States of America by William Strickland . . . , 1794–1795," *Collections of the New York Historical Society,* 83 (1971).

"A Subaltern in America." *Blackwood's Edinburgh Magazine,* 21 (1827):243–59, 417–33, 531–49, 709–26; 22 (1827):74–83, 316–28.

Sullivan, James, et al., eds. *The Papers of Sir William Johnson.* 14 vols. Albany: The University of the State of New York, 1965.

Surtees, William. *Twenty-Five Years in the Rifle Brigade.* Edinburgh: William Blackwood, and London: T. Cadell, 1833.

Sutcliff, Robert. *Travels in some parts of North America, in the Years 1804, 1805, and 1806.* York: W. Alexander, 1811.

Thwaites, Reuben Gold, ed. *Early Western Travels 1748–1846.* 32 vols. Cleveland: Arthur H. Clark Co., 1904–07.

————. *Original Journals of the Lewis and Clark Expedition, 1804–*

1806. 7 vols. and an atlas. Reprint ed. New York: Antiquarian Press Ltd., 1959.

————, and Kellogg, Louise Phelps, eds. *The Revolution on the Upper Ohio, 1775–1777*. Reissue. Port Washington, N.Y. & London: Kennikat Press, 1970.

Truteau, Jean Baptiste. "Journal of Jean Baptiste Truteau on the Upper Missouri, 'Premiere Partie,' June 7, 1794–March 26, 1795." *American Historical Review*, 19 (1914): 299–333.

Tupper, Ferdinand Brock, ed. *Life and Correspondence of Major General Sir Isaac Brock, K.B.* 2d ed. London: Simpkin, Marshall & Co., 1847.

Turner, F. J., ed. "English Policy Toward America in 1790–1791." *American Historical Review*, 7 (1901–02): 706–35; 8 (1902–03): 78–86.

Tyrrell, J. B., ed. *David Thompson's Narrative of His Western Explorations, 1784–1812*. Toronto: The Champlain Society, 1916.

————. *Journals of Samuel Hearne and Philip Turnor Between the Years 1774 and 1792*. Toronto: The Champlain Society, 1934.

Umfreville, Edward. *The Present State of Hudson's Bay*. London: C. Stalker, 1790.

Vancouver, Captain George. *A Voyage of Discovery to the North Pacific Ocean, and Round the World: . . . in the Years 1790, 1791, 1792, 1793, 1794, and 1795. . . .* 3 vols. London: G. G. & J. Robinson & J. Edwards, 1798.

Van Der Beets, Richard, ed. *Held Captive by Indians: Selected Narratives, 1642–1836*. Knoxville: University of Tennessee Press, 1973.

Vane, Charles William, ed. *Correspondence, Despatches, and Other Papers, of Viscount Castlereagh, 2nd Marquis of Londonderry*. 12 vols. London: John Murray, 1848–53. Vols. 10 and 11.

Verner, Lieutenant Colonel Willoughby, ed. "The Diary of a Private Soldier in the Campaign of New Orleans." *Macmillan's Magazine*, 77 (1897–98): 321–33.

Wakefield, Priscilla. *Excursions in North America, Described in Letters From a Gentleman and His Young Companion, to Their Friends in England*. London: Darton & Harvey, 1806.

Wallace, W. Stewart, ed. "Captain Miles Macdonell's 'Journal of a Jaunt to Amherstburg' in 1801." *Canadian Historical Review*, 25 (1944): 166–76.

————, ed. *Documents Relating to the North West Company*. Toronto: The Champlain Society, 1934.

Weld, Isaac, Jr. *Travels Through the States of North America and the Provinces of Upper and Lower Canada . . . During the Years 1795, 1796, and 1797*. London: John Stockdale, 1799.

Wellington, Duke of, ed. *Supplementary Despatches, Correspondence, and Memoranda of Field Marshall Arthur Duke of Wellington, K.G. Edited by his son.* . . . Vol. 9 (1814–15). London: John Murray, 1862.

White, Patrick C., ed. *Lord Selkirk's Diary, 1803–04: A Journal of His Travels in British North America and the Northeastern United States.* Toronto: The Champlain Society, 1958.

Wilberforce, Robert Isaac, and Samuel, eds. *The Correspondence of William Wilberforce, Edited by His Sons.* . . . 2 vols. London: John Murray, 1840.

Williams, Glyndwer, ed. *Andrew Graham's Observations on Hudson's Bay 1767–1791.* London: Hudson's Bay Record Society, 1969.

———. *Hudson's Bay Miscellany, 1670–1870.* Winnipeg: Hudson's Bay Record Society, 1975.

Wisconsin. *Collections of the Wisconsin State Historical Society.* 31 vols. Madison, 1854–1931.

Wood, William Charles Henry, ed. *Select British Documents of the Canadian War of 1812.* 3 vols. in 4. Toronto: The Champlain Society, 1920–28.

Wood, W. Raymond, and Thiessen, Thomas D., eds. *Early Fur Trade on the Northern Plains: Canadian Traders Among the Mandan and Hidatsa Indians, 1738–1818.* Norman: University of Oklahoma Press, 1985.

Wright, Louis B., and Tinling, Marion, eds. *Quebec to Carolina in 1785–1786: Being the Travel Diary and Observations of Robert Hunter, Jr., a Young Merchant of London.* San Marino, Calif.: The Huntington Library, 1943.

SECONDARY SOURCES

Ackernecht, Erwin H. "'White Indians': Psychological and Physiological Peculiarities of White Children Abducted and Reared by North American Indians." *Bulletin of the History of Medicine,* 15 (1944): 15–36.

Anderson, Gary Clayton. *Kinsmen of Another Kind: Dakota-White Relations in the Upper Mississippi Valley, 1650–1862.* Lincoln: University of Nebraska Press, 1984.

Anson, Bert. *The Miami Indians.* Norman: University of Oklahoma Press, 1970.

Auchinleck, G. *The History of the War Between Great Britain and the United States of America During the Years 1812, 1813, & 1814.*

London & Toronto: Arms & Armour Press in association with Pendragon House, 1972.

Axtell, James. *The European and the Indian: Essays in the Ethnohistory of Colonial North America.* New York: Oxford University Press, 1981.

————. "The White Indians of Colonial America." *William & Mary Quarterly,* 3d Series, 32 (1975):55–88.

Beers, Henry P. *The French and British in the Old Northwest: A Bibliographical Guide to Archive and Manuscript Sources.* Detroit: Wayne State University Press, 1964.

Bemis, Samuel Flagg. *Jay's Treaty: A Study in Commerce and Diplomacy.* Revised ed. New Haven & London: Yale University Press, 1962.

Berkhofer, Robert F., Jr. "Barrier to Settlement: British Indian Policy in the Old North West, 1783–1794," in David M. Ellis, ed., *The Frontier in American Development: Essays in Honor of Paul Wallace Gates.* Ithaca & London: Cornell University Press, 1969, 249–76.

————. *Salvation and the Savage: An Analysis of Protestant Missions and American Indian Response, 1787–1862.* New York: Atheneum, 1972.

————. *The White Man's Indian: Images of the American Indian From Columbus to the Present.* New York: Vintage, 1979.

Bird, Harrison. *War for the West, 1790–1813.* New York: Oxford University Press, 1971.

Bishop, Charles A. *The Northern Ojibwa and the Fur Trade: An Historical and Ecological Study.* Toronto & Montreal: Holt, Rinehart & Winston of Canada, Ltd., 1974.

Bissell, Benjamin. *The American Indian in English Literature of the Eighteenth Century.* New Haven: Yale University Press, 1925.

Boyd, Thomas. *Simon Girty: The White Savage.* New York: Minton, Balch & Co., 1928.

Brebner, John Bartlet. *North Atlantic Triangle: The Interplay of Canada, the United States and Great Britain.* New Haven: Yale University Press, 1945.

Brown, Jennifer S. *Strangers in Blood: Fur Trade Company Families in Indian Country.* Vancouver: University of British Columbia Press, 1980.

Burt, A. L. "A New Approach to the Problem of the Western Posts." *Canadian Historical Association Annual Report* for 1931, 61–75.

————. *The United States, Great Britain, and British North America: From the Revolution to the Establishment of Peace after the War of 1812.* New Haven, Conn.: Yale University Press, 1940.

Butterfield, Consul Willshire, *History of the Girtys*. Cincinnati: Robert Clarke & Co., 1890.

Byrd, Cecil K. "The Northwest Indians and the British Preceding the War of 1812." *Indiana Magazine of History*, 38 (1942): 31–50.

Campbell, Marjorie Wilkins. *McGillivray, Lord of the Northwest*. Toronto: Clarke, Irwin & Co., Ltd, 1962.

———. *The North West Company*. Toronto: The Macmillan Co. of Canada, Ltd, 1957.

Calloway, Colin G. "The End of an Era: British-Indian Relations in the Great Lakes Region After the War of 1812." *Michigan Historical Review*, 2 (Fall, 1986).

———. "Foundations of Sand: The Fur Trade and British-Indian Relations, 1783–1815," forthcoming in selected papers of the Fifth North American Fur Trade Conference.

———. "The Intertribal Balance of Powers on the Great Plains, 1760–1850." *Journal of American Studies*, 16 (Apr. 1982): 25–47.

———. "Neither White Nor Red: White Renegades on the American Indian Frontier." *Western Historical Quarterly*, 17 (Jan. 1986): 43–66.

———. "Suspicion and Self-Interest: British-Indian Relations and the Peace of Paris." *The Historian*, 48 (Nov. 1985): 41–60.

Carter, Clarence E. "British Policy Towards the American Indians in the South, 1763–68." *English Historical Review*, 33 (1918): 37–56.

Caughey, John Walton. *McGillivray of the Creeks*. 2d ed. Norman: University of Oklahoma Press, 1959.

Chamberlin, J. E. *The Harrowing of Eden: White Attitudes Toward Native Americans*. New York: The Seabury Press, 1975.

Connelley, Thomas Lawrence. "Indian Warfare on the Tennessee Frontier, 1776–1794: Strategy and Tactics." *East Tennessee Historical Society Publications*, 36 (1964): 3–22.

Cox, I. J. "The Indian as a Diplomatic Factor in the History of the Old North West." *Ohio Archaeological and Historical Society Publications*, 18 (1909): 542–65.

Cruikshank, Ernest A. "The Chesapeake Crisis As It Affected Upper Canada." *Ontario Historical Society Papers and Records*, 24 (1927): 281–322.

———. "The Coming of the Loyalist Mohawks to the Bay of Quinte." *Ontario Historical Society Papers and Records*, 26 (1930): 390–430.

———. "The Employment of the Indians in the War of 1812." Annual Report of the American Historical Association for 1895: 321–35.

————. "General Hull's Invasion of Canada in 1812." *Trans R.S.C.*, 3d series, 1 (1907), section 2: 211–90.

————. "Harrison and Procter—The River Raisin." *Trans R.S.C.* 3d series, 4 (1910); section 2: 119–67.

Davidson, Gordon Charles. *The North West Company*. Berkeley: University of California Press, 1918.

Davis, Andrew McFarland. "The Employment of Indian Auxiliaries in the American War." *English Historical Review*, 2 (1887): 709–28.

Dobyns, Henry. *Their Numbers Become Thinned: Native American Population Dynamics in Eastern North America*. Nashville: University of Tennessee Press, 1984.

Douglass, Elisha P. "The Adventurer Bowles." *William & Mary Quarterly*, 3d ser., 6 (1949): 3–23.

Downes, Randolph C. *Council Fires on the Upper Ohio: A Narrative of Indian Affairs in the Upper Ohio Valley Until 1795*. Pittsburgh: University of Pittsburgh Press, 1940.

Drake, Benjamin. *Life of Tecumseh, and of His Brother the Prophet; With a Historical Sketch of the Shawanoe Indians*. Cincinnati: E. Morgan & Co., 1841. Reprint ed., New York: Arno Press, Inc. & the New York Times, 1969.

Edmunds, R. David, ed. *American Indian Leaders: Studies in Diversity*. Lincoln & London: University of Nebraska Press, 1980.

————. "The Illinois River Potawatomie in the War of 1812." *Journal of the Illinois State Historical Society*, 62 (Winter, 1968): 341–62.

————. *The Potawatomis: Keepers of the Fire*. Norman: University of Oklahoma Press, 1978.

————. *The Shawnee Prophet*. Lincoln: University of Nebraska Press, 1983.

————. *Tecumseh and the Quest for Indian Leadership*. Boston: Little, Brown & Co., 1984.

Engleman, Fred L. *The Peace of Christmas Eve*. London: Rupert Hart-Davis, 1962.

Ewers, John C. *Indian Life on the Upper Missouri*. Norman: University of Oklahoma Press, 1968.

————. *The Blackfeet: Raiders on the Northwestern Plains*. 4th printing. Norman: University of Oklahoma Press, 1971.

————, ed. *Five Indian Tribes of the Upper Missouri: Sioux, Arickaras, Assiniboines, Crees, Crows. By Edwin Thompson Denig*. 3d printing. Norman: University of Oklahoma Press, 1973.

————. "The Horse in Blackfoot Indian Culture, With Comparative Material From Other Western Tribes," *B.A.E. Bulletin* 159 (1955).

————. "The Influence of the Fur Trade upon the Indians of the Northern Plains," in Malvina Bolus, ed., *People and Pelts: Selected Papers of the Second North American Fur Trade Conference.* Winnipeg: Pegius Publishers, 1972, 1–26.

————. "Intertribal Warfare as the Precursor of Indian-White Warfare on the Northern Great Plains." *Western Historical Quarterly,* 6 (1975): 397–410.

Fisher, Robin. *Contact and Conflict: Indian-European Relations in British Columbia, 1774–1890.* Vancouver: University of British Columbia Press, 1977.

Foreman, Carolyn Thomas. *Indians Abroad: 1493–1938.* Norman: University of Oklahoma Press, 1943.

Francis, Daniel, and Morantz, Toby. *Partners in Furs: A History of the Fur Trade in Eastern James Bay 1600–1870.* Kingston & Montreal: McGill-Queens University Press, 1983.

Gates, Charles M. "The West in American Diplomacy, 1812–1815." *Mississippi Valley Historical Review* (1939–40): 499–510.

Gibb, Harley L. "Colonel Guy Johnson, Superintendent General of Indian Affairs, 1774–1782." *Papers of the Michigan Academy of Science, Arts and Letters,* 27 (1941): 595–613.

Gibson, Arrell M. *The Chickasaws.* 2d printing. Norman: University of Oklahoma Press, 1972.

————. *The Kickapoos.* 2d printing. Norman: University of Oklahoma Press, 1975.

Gilpin, Alec R. *The War of 1812 in the Old Northwest.* East Lansing: Michigan State University Press, 1958.

Graham, Elizabeth. *Medicine Man to Missionary: Missionaries as Agents of Change Among the Indians of Southern Ontario, 1784–1867.* Toronto: Peter Martin Associates, 1975.

Graymont, Barbara. *The Iroquois in the American Revolution.* Syracuse, N.Y.: Syracuse University Press, 1972.

Gunther, Erna. *Indian Life on the Northwest Coast of North America As Seen by the Early Explorers and Fur Traders During the Last Decades of the Eighteenth Century.* Chicago & London: University of Chicago Press, 1972.

————. "Vancouver and the Indians of Puget Sound." *Pacific Northwest Quarterly,* 51 (1960): 1–12.

Hadlock, Wendell, S. "War Among the Northeastern Woodland Indians." *American Anthropologist,* 49 (1947): 204–21.

Hagan, William T. *The Sac and Fox Indians.* Norman: University of Oklahoma Press, 1958.

Hamer, Philip M. "The British in Canada and the Southern Indians, 1790–1794." *East Tennessee Historical Society Publications* 2 (1930): 107–34.

Hassig, Ross. "Internal Conflict in the Creek War of 1813–1814." *Ethnohistory*, 21 (1974):251–71.

Hassrick, Royal B. *The Sioux: Life and Customs of a Warrior Society.* 3d printing. Norman: University of Oklahoma Press, 1972.

Heard, J. Norman. *White into Red: A Study of the Assimilation of White Persons Captured by Indians.* Metuchen, N.J.: The Scarecrow Press, Inc., 1973.

Hickerson, Harold. *The Chippewa and Their Neighbors: A Study in Ethnohistory.* New York, Toronto, London, etc: Holt, Rinehart & Winston, Inc., 1970.

Hodge, Frederick Webb, ed. "Handbook of American Indians North of Mexico." 2 vols. *B.A.E. Bulletin* 30 (1907–10).

Holder, Preston. "The Fur Trade as Seen from the Indian Point of View," in John Francis McDermott, ed., *The Frontier Reexamined.* Urbana, Chicago, & London: University of Illinois Press, 1967, 129–39.

———. *The Hoe and the Horse on the Plains: A Study of Cultural Development Among North American Indians.* Bison Books. Lincoln & London: University of Nebraska Press, 1974.

Horsman, Reginald. "American Indian Policy in the Old Northwest, 1783–1812." *William & Mary Quarterly*, 3d series, 18 (1961):35–53.

———. "The British Indian Department and the Abortive Treaty of Lower Sandusky, 1793." *Ohio Historical Quarterly*, 70 (1961): 189–213.

———. "The British Indian Department and the Resistance to General Anthony Wayne, 1793–1795." *Mississippi Valley Historical Review*, 49 (1962–63):269–90.

———. "British Indian Policy in the North West, 1807–1812." *Mississippi Valley Historical Review*, 45 (1958–59):51–67.

———. *The Causes of the War of 1812.* Philadelphia: University of Pennsylvania Press, 1962.

———. *Expansion and American Indian Policy, 1783–1812.* East Lansing: Michigan State University Press, 1967.

———. *The Frontier in the Formative Years 1783–1815.* New York, London, etc.: Holt, Rinehart & Winston, 1970.

———. *Matthew Elliott, British Indian Agent.* Detroit: Wayne State University Press, 1964.

———. "The Role of the Indian in the War," in Philip P. Mason, ed., *After Tippecanoe: Some Aspects of the War of 1812.* East Lansing: Michigan State University Press, 1963, 60–77.

———. *The War of 1812.* London: Eyre & Spottiswoode, 1969.

Howard, Dresden W. H. "The Battle of Fallen Timbers as told by Chief Kin-jo-i-no." *Northwest Ohio Quarterly*, 20 (1948):37–49.

Howay, F. W. "Indian Attacks upon Maritime Traders of the North-West Coast, 1785–1805." *Canadian Historical Review*, 6 (1925): 287–309.

Hubbard, J. Niles. *An Account of Sa-Go-Ye-Wat-Ha or Red Jacket and His People 1750–1830*. Reprinted. New York: Burt Franklin, 1971.

Hyde, George E. *Indians of the High Plains: From the Pre-Historic Period to the Coming of Europeans*. 3d printing. Norman: University of Oklahoma Press, 1970.

Innis, Harold A. *The Fur Trade in Canada*. Revised ed. Toronto: University of Toronto Press, 1956.

Jablow, Joseph. "The Cheyenne in Plains Indian Trade Relations, 1795–1840." *Monographs of the American Ethnological Society*, 19 (1950), 2d printing. Seattle & London: University of Washington Press, 1966.

Jacobs, Wilbur R. *Wilderness Politics and Indian Gifts: The Northern Colonial Frontier, 1748–1763*. Lincoln: University of Nebraska Press, 1966.

James, James Alton. *English Institutions and the American Indian*. Baltimore: The Johns Hopkins Press, 1894.

Jamieson, Melvill Allan. *Medals Awarded to North American Indian Chiefs, 1714–1922*. . . . London: Spink & Son, Ltd., 1936.

Jennings, Francis. *The Ambiguous Iroquois Empire: The Covenant Chain Confederation of Indian Tribes with English Colonies From Its Beginnings to the Lancaster Treaty of 1744*. New York: W. W. Norton & Co., 1984.

———, ed. *The History and Culture of Iroquois Diplomacy: An Interdisciplinary Guide to the Treaties of the Six Nations and their League*. Syracuse: Syracuse University Press, 1985.

———. *The Invasion of America: Indians, Colonialism, and the Cant of Conquest*. Chapel Hill: University of North Carolina Press, 1975.

Johnston, Charles M. "Joseph Brant, the Grand River Lands and the Northwest Crisis." *Ontario History*, 55 (1963): 267–82.

———. "William Claus and John Norton: A Struggle for Power in Old Ontario." *Ontario History*, 57 (1965): 101–8.

Josephy, Alvin M., Jr. "By Fayre and Gentle Meanes: The Hudson's Bay Company and the American Indian." *American West*, 9 (1972), pt. 5: 4–11, 61–64.

Judd, Carol M., and Arthur J. Ray, eds. *Old Trails and New Directions: Papers of the Third North American Fur Trade Conference*. Toronto: University of Toronto Press, 1980.

Kellogg, Louise P. *The British Regime in Wisconsin and the North West*. Madison: Wisconsin State Historical Society, 1935.

————. "Indian Diplomacy During the Revolution in the West."
Transactions of the Illinois State Historical Society, 36 (1929): 47–57.

————. "Wisconsin Indians During the American Revolution,"
Transactions of the Wisconsin Academy of Science, Arts and Letters,
24 (1929): 47–51.

Kelsay, Isabel Thompson. *Joseph Brant, 1743–1807: Man of Two
Worlds.* Syracuse: Syracuse University Press, 1984.

Kinard, M., and Wollon, D. "Sir Augustus J. Foster and 'the Wild
Natives of the Woods' 1805–1807." *William & Mary Quarterly*,
3d series, 9 (1952): 191–214.

Kinnaird, Lawrence. "International Rivalry in the Creek Country." *Florida Historical Quarterly*, 10 (1931): 59–79.

Leavitt, Orpha E. "British Policy on the Canadian Frontier,
1782–92." *Proceedings of the Wisconsin State Historical Society*, 63
(1915): 151–85.

Lewis, Oscar. "The Effects of White Contact Upon Blackfoot
Culture, With Special Reference to the Role of the Fur Trade."
Monographs of the American Ethnological Society, 6 (1942). 2d
printing. Seattle & London: University of Washington Press,
1966.

Lydekker, John Wolfe. *The Faithful Mohawks.* London: Cambridge University Press, 1938.

McAlister, Lyle N. "William Augustus Bowles and the State of
Muskogee." *Florida Historical Quarterly*, 40 (1962): 317–28.

McLaughlin, A. C. "The Western Posts and the British Debts."
Annual Report of the American Historical Association for 1894,
413–44.

McManus, John C. "An Economic Analysis of Indian Behaviour
in the North American Fur Trade." *Journal of Economic History*,
32 (1972): 36–53.

Mahon, John K. "Anglo-American Methods of Indian Warfare,
1676–1794." *Mississippi Valley Historical Review*, 45 (1958–
59): 254–75.

————. "British Command Decisions in the Northern Campaigns of the War of 1812." *Canadian Historical Review*, 46
(1965): 219–37.

————. "British Strategy and Southern Indians: War of 1812."
Florida Historical Quarterly, 44 (1966): 285–302.

Martin, Calvin. *Keepers of the Game: Indian-Animal Relationships
and the Fur Trade.* Berkeley, Los Angeles & London: University
of California Press, 1978.

Mason, Philip P., ed. *After Tippecanoe: Some Aspects of the War of
1812.* East Lansing: Michigan State University Press, 1963.

Meyer, Roy W. *History of the Santee Sioux: United States Indian Policy on Trial*. Lincoln: University of Nebraska Press, 1967.

———. *The Village Indians of the Upper Missouri: The Mandans, Hidatsas and Arikaras*. Lincoln & London: University of Nebraska Press, 1977.

Mishkin, Bernard. "Rank and Warfare among the Plains Indians." *Monographs of the American Ethnological Society*, 3 (1940).

Morton, W. L. "The North West Company: Pedlars Extraordinary." *Minnesota History*, 40 (Winter 1966): 157–65.

Murray, J. McE. "John Norton." *Ontario Historical Society Papers and Records* 37 (1945): 7–16.

Nasatir, Abraham P. "Anglo-Spanish Rivalry on the Upper Mississippi." *Mississippi Valley Historical Review* 16 (1929–30): 359–82, 507–28.

———. *Borderland in Retreat. From Spanish Louisiana to the Far Southwest*. Albuquerque: University of New Mexico Press, 1976.

Newcomb, W. W., Jr. "A Re-examination of the Causes of Plains Warfare." *American Anthropologist*, 52 (1950): 317–30.

Nicks, John S., and Trudy, eds. *The Western Canadian Journal of Anthropology*, 3 (1970), No. 1, "Special Issue: The Fur Trade in Canada."

Notestein, Wallace. "The Western Indians in the Revolution." *Ohio Archaeological and Historical Publications*, 16 (1907): 269–91.

O'Donnell, James H., III. *Southern Indians in the American Revolution*. Knoxville: University of Tennessee Press, 1973.

Owsley, Frank L., Jr. "British and Indian Activities in Spanish West Florida During the War of 1812." *Florida Historical Quarterly*, 46 (1967): 111–23.

———, ed. *The Creek War of 1813 and 1814. By H. S. Halbert and T. H. Ball*. University, Ala.: University of Alabama Press, 1969.

Parker, Arthur C. "Seneca Indians in the War of 1812." *The Southern Workman*, 45 (Feb. 1916): 116–22.

Parker, James A. "The Fur Trade and the Chipewyan Indians." *W.C.J.A.*, 3, no. 1 (1972): 43–57.

Pearce, Roy Harvey. *The Savages of America: A Study of the Indian and the Idea of Civilization*. Baltimore: Johns Hopkins Press, 1953.

Peckham, Howard, and Gipson, Charles, eds. *Attitudes of Colonial Powers Toward the American Indian*. Salt Lake City: University of Utah Press, 1969.

Peterson, Jacqueline, and Jennifer S. H. Brown, eds. *The New Peoples: Being and Becoming Métis in North America*. Lincoln: University of Nebraska Press, 1985.

332   SELECTED BIBLIOGRAPHY

Phillips, Paul Chrisler, with concluding chapters by J. W. Smurr. *The Fur Trade.* 2 vols. Norman: University of Oklahoma Press, 1967.

Prucha, Francis Paul. *The Great Father: The United States Government and the American Indians.* 2 vols. Lincoln: University of Nebraska Press, 1984.

Quimby, George Irving. *Indian Culture and European Trade Goods: The Archaeology of the Historic Period in the Western Great Lakes Region.* Madison: University of Wisconsin Press, 1966.

Ray, Arthur J. *Indians in the Fur Trade: Their Role as Trappers, Hunters, and Middlemen in the Lands Southwest of Hudson Bay, 1660–1870.* Toronto: University of Toronto Press, 1974.

Ray, Arthur J., and Freeman, Donald B. *"Give Us Good Measure": An Economic Analysis of Relations Between the Indians and the Hudson's Bay Company Before 1763.* Toronto: University of Toronto Press, 1983.

Reilly, Robin. *The British at the Gates: The New Orleans Campaign in the War of 1812.* London: Cassell, 1974.

Rich, Edwin Ernest. *History of the Hudson's Bay Company, 1670–1870.* 2 vols. London: Hudson's Bay Record Society, 1958–59.

———. "Trade Habits and Economic Motivation Among the Indians of North America." *Canadian Journal of Economics and Political Science,* 26 (1960): 35–43.

Ritcheson, Charles R. *Aftermath of Revolution: British Policy Toward the United States 1783–1795.* Dallas: Southern Methodist Press, 1969.

Robinson, Doane. *A History of the Dakota or Sioux Indians.* Reprint ed. Minneapolis: Ross & Haines, Inc., 1967. Originally published as *South Dakota Historical Collections,* 2 (1904).

Rotstein, Abraham. "Trade and Politics: An Institutional Approach," *W.C.J.A.,* 3 (No. 1, 1972): 1–28.

Ruby, Robert H., and Brown, John A. *The Chinook Indians: Traders of the Lower Columbia River.* Norman: University of Oklahoma Press, 1976.

Russell, Carl P. *Guns on the Early Frontiers: A History of Firearms From Colonial Times Through the Western Fur Trade.* New York: Bonanza Books, 1957.

Russell, Nelson V. *The British Regime in Michigan and the Old Northwest, 1760–1796.* Northfield, Minn.: Carleton College, 1939.

Russell, Peter E. "Redcoats in the Wilderness: British Officers and Irregular Warfare in Europe and America, 1740–1760." *William & Mary Quarterly,* 3d series, 35 (1978): 629–52.

Saum, Lewis O. *The Fur Trader and the Indian.* Seattle & London: University of Washington Press, 1973.

Secoy, Frank Raymond. "Changing Military Patterns on the Great Plains (17th Century through Early 19th Century)." *Monographs of the American Ethnological Society,* 21 (1953).

Sheehan, Bernard, W. *Seeds of Extinction: Jeffersonian Philanthropy and the American Indian.* New York: W. W. Norton & Co., 1974.

Sloan, W. A. "The Native Responses to the Extension of the European Traders into the Athabasca and Mackenzie Basin, 1770–1814." *Canadian Historical Review,* 40 (1979): 281–99.

Smith, Marian W. "American Indian Warfare." *Transactions of the New York Academy of Sciences,* 2d series, 13 (1950–51): 348–65.

———. "The War Complex of the Plains Indians." *Proceedings of the American Philosophical Society,* 78 (1938): 425–64.

Some Account of the conduct of the Religious Society of Friends Toward the Indian Tribes. . . . London: Edward Marsh, 1844.

Sosin, Jack M. "The Use of Indians in the War of the American Revolution." *C.H.R.,* 46 (1965): 101–21.

Stanley, George F. G. "The Indians in the War of 1812." *C.H.R.,* 31 (1950): 145–65.

———. "The Significance of the Six Nations Participation in the War of 1812." *Ontario History,* 55 (1963): 215–31.

———. "The Six Nations and the American Revolution." *Ontario History,* 56 (1964): 217–32.

Stevens, Wayne, E. "The Organization of the British Fur Trade, 1760–1800." *M.V.H.R.,* 3 (1916): 172–202.

Stone, William L. *Life of Joseph Brant—Thayendanegea.* 2 vols. New York: George Dearborn & Co., 1838.

———. *The Life and Times of Sa-Go-Ye-Wat-Ha or Red Jacket.* New York & London: Wiley & Putnam, 1841.

Sturtevant, William C., ed. *Handbook of North American Indians.* Vol. 15: Bruce G. Trigger, ed. *Northeast.* Washington: Smithsonian Institution, 1978.

Sugden, John. "The Southern Indians in the War of 1812: The Closing Phase." *Florida Historical Quarterly,* 60 (1982): 273–312.

———. *Tecumseh's Last Stand.* Norman: University of Oklahoma Press, 1985.

Tohill, Louis Arthur. "Robert Dickson, British Fur Trader on the Upper Mississippi." *North Dakota Historical Quarterly,* 3 (1928–29): 5–49, 83–128, 182–203.

Tucker, Glenn. *Tecumseh: Vision of Glory.* Indianapolis: Bobbs-Merrill, 1956.

Van Kirk, Sylvia. *"Many Tender Ties": Women in Fur Trade Society in Western Canada, 1670–1870.* Norman: University of Oklahoma Press, 1983.

Wallace, Anthony F. C. *The Death and Rebirth of the Seneca.* New York: Vintage Books, Random House, Inc., 1972.

Warrick, W. Sheridan. "The American Indian Policy in the Upper Old Northwest following the War of 1812." *Ethnohistory,* 3 (1956): 109–25.

Washburn, Wilcomb E. "Symbol, Utility, and Aesthetics in the Indian Fur Trade." *Minnesota History,* 40 (Winter 1966): 198–202.

White, Richard. "The Winning of the West: The Expansion of the Western Sioux in the Eighteenth and Nineteenth Centuries." *Journal of American History,* 65 (1978): 329–43.

Wilson, Bruce. "The Struggle for Wealth and Power at Fort Niagara, 1775–1783." *Ontario History,* 68 (1976): 137–54.

Wise, S. F. "The Indian Diplomacy of John Graves Simcoe." *Annual Report of the Canadian Historical Association* for 1953, 36–44.

Wolf, Eric R. *Europe and the People Without History.* Berkeley: University of California Press, 1982.

Wright, J. Leitch, Jr. *Anglo-Spanish Rivalry in North America.* Athens, Ga.: University of Georgia Press, 1971.

———. *Britain and the American Frontier, 1783–1815.* Athens, Ga.: University of Georgia Press, 1975.

———. "British Designs on the Old Southwest: Foreign Intrigue on the Florida Frontier, 1783–1803." *Florida Historical Quarterly,* 45 (1966): 265–84.

———. "A Note on the First Seminole War as Seen by the Indians, Negroes, and Their British Advisers." *Journal of Southern History,* 34 (1968): 565–75.

———. *William Augustus Bowles: Director General of the Creek Nation.* Athens, Ga.: University of Georgia Press, 1967.

Wright, Mary C. "Economic Development and Native American Women in the Early Nineteenth Century." *American Quarterly,* 33 (1981): 525–36.

Zaslow, Morris, ed. *The Defended Border: Upper Canada and the War of 1812. A Collection of Writings Giving a Comprehensive Picture of the War of 1812 in Upper Canada. . . .* Toronto: The Macmillan Co. of Canada, Ltd., 1964.

Index